NEHRU'S INDIA

Nehru's India

A HISTORY IN SEVEN MYTHS

Taylor C. Sherman

PRINCETON UNIVERSITY PRESS
PRINCETON & OXFORD

Copyright © 2022 by Taylor C. Sherman

Princeton University Press is committed to the protection of copyright and the intellectual property our authors entrust to us. Copyright promotes the progress and integrity of knowledge created by humans. By engaging with an authorized copy of this work, you are supporting creators and the global exchange of ideas. As this work is protected by copyright, any reproduction or distribution of it in any form for any purpose requires permission; permission requests should be sent to permissions@press.princeton.edu. Ingestion of any PUP IP for any AI purposes is strictly prohibited.

Published by Princeton University Press
41 William Street, Princeton, New Jersey 08540
99 Banbury Road, Oxford OX2 6JX

press.princeton.edu

GPSR Authorized Representative: Easy Access System Europe - Mustamäe tee 50, 10621 Tallinn, Estonia, gpsr.requests@easproject.com

All Rights Reserved

First paperback printing, 2025
Paperback ISBN 9780691227238

The Library of Congress has cataloged the cloth edition as follows

Names: Sherman, Taylor C., author.
Title: Nehru's India : a history in seven myths / Taylor C. Sherman.
Description: Princeton ; Oxford : Princeton University Press, [2022] | Includes bibliographical references and index.
Identifiers: LCCN 2022005960 (print) | LCCN 2022005961 (ebook) | ISBN 9780691222585 (hardback) | ISBN 9780691227221 (ebook)
Subjects: LCSH: Nehru, Jawaharlal, 1889–1964. | India—History—1947– | India—Politics and government—1947– | India—Social conditions—1947– | Statesmen—India—Biography. | BISAC: HISTORY / Asia / India & South Asia | POLITICAL SCIENCE / World / Asian
Classification: LCC DS481.N35 S4825 2022 (print) | LCC DS481.N35 (ebook) | DDC 954.04/2092—dc23/eng/20220222
LC record available at https://lccn.loc.gov/2022005960
LC ebook record available at https://lccn.loc.gov/2022005961

British Library Cataloging-in-Publication Data is available

Editorial: Ben Tate & Josh Drake
Production Editorial: Ali Parrington
Jacket/Cover Design: Chris Ferrante
Production: Danielle Amatucci
Publicity: Alyssa Sanford & Charlotte Coyne

Cover image: Everett Collection Historical / Alamy Stock Photo

This book has been composed in Miller

CONTENTS

List of Illustrations · vii
Preface · ix

CHAPTER 1	The Myth of Nehru the Architect of Independent India	1
CHAPTER 2	The Myth of India's Non-Aligned Foreign Policy	21
CHAPTER 3	The Myth of Hegemonic Secularism	53
CHAPTER 4	The Myth of Socialism	85
CHAPTER 5	The Myth of the Strong State	118
CHAPTER 6	The Myth of the Successful Democracy	145
CHAPTER 7	The Myth of High Modernism in India	177

Coda · 204
Acknowledgements · 217
List of Abbreviations · 221
Notes · 223
Bibliography · 251
Index · 277

ILLUSTRATIONS

1.1	'The Retiring P.M.', *The Times of India*, 2 May 1958, 7	8
1.2	Chacha Nehru stamp, issued 14 November 1964	11
3.1	Portraits from *India's Minorities* (Government of India, 1948)	60
3.2	Archaeological series of stamps, issued 15 August 1949	66
4.1	'It all adds up to 2 million tons', *The Times of India*, 12 November 1957 (supplement), vi	84
4.2	'You can be proud of your Raleigh in any company', *The Times of India*, 9 October 1965, 8	102
7.1	Saraswati Temple, Birla Institute of Technology and Science, Pilani	176

PREFACE

THIS BOOK ASKS readers to reconsider the history of India during the first seventeen years after independence, when Jawaharlal Nehru served as prime minister. Today, Nehru is widely regarded, for better *and* for worse, as the architect of independent India. His premiership (1947–64) is associated with a set of ideas, policies and institutions at the national and international level, especially non-alignment, secularism, socialism, the strong state, democracy and high modernism. The chapters in this book argue that these supposed tenets of the Nehruvian period, including the idea that Nehru designed and oversaw their implementation, are myths.

When I write of myths, I am not referring to extravagant tales of dragons or flying carpets. Rather, a myth is a story about the past, often with a grain of truth in it. Beyond this small kernel, however, the narrative takes on a life of its own as it is passed from one person to another. It is built not by the careful assemblage of contemporary evidence, but by repetition over time, especially by those with authority. Through this process, stories about the past are used to give meaning to the present. This is certainly the case for the myths identified in this book. The grain of truthiness at the heart of each one often takes the form of quotations from Nehru's books or speeches. With only scattered evidence from other contemporary sources to complicate the picture, political scientists, anthropologists, politicians, journalists, ordinary people, and historians too, have wrapped new layers of meaning around each small kernel of evidence. In the scholarly realm, the more the claims have been repeated, the less evidence seems to have been necessary to substantiate them. One often finds the myths casually dropped into works of high scholarly repute and the credibility of these statements is simply taken for granted. They are myths because they were, for many years, beyond question.

Each chapter of this work dismantles one myth, but the book also builds an alternative set of characterisations for the era. First, stretching as it does to the middle of the 1960s, this research reveals that the idea that India had a founding 'moment' does not do full justice to the period. The time between independence in 1947 and the inauguration of the Constitution in 1950 was certainly eventful. India not only coped with the violence and migrations of partition, but also reorganised its administrative services, military and police as part of the long process of separating itself from Pakistan. During this same period, it incorporated hundreds of princely states and amalgamated them into what would become the states of India. As part of this complex and tumultuous process, India went to war with Pakistan over the princely state of Jammu and Kashmir just two months after independence. In addition, the princely state of Hyderabad was forcibly integrated into India in September 1948 by a military invasion known as the Police Action. This large southern state was racked by both communal violence and a communist insurgency. During this same period, the leaders of the independence movement drafted a constitution, which came into force on 26 January 1950.

Even before the Constitution had come into force, India's new leaders had begun the process of trying to fulfil the huge promises that had been made to the people of India during the freedom movement. With the political reorganisation outlined above under way, the country also tried to achieve self-sufficiency in food grains and nearly suffered a devastating famine. Its state-level governments inaugurated the first of many rounds of land reforms, and its planners drew up its first five-year plan, which began in 1951. As the Constitution had pledged to create a democracy with full adult franchise, India's bureaucrats organised its first elections, which were conducted between the end of 1951 and the early part of 1952. India did indeed see a lot of activity at this time, but that does not mean that the course of the remaining twelve years of Nehru's premiership was determined by these first few.

Indeed, the drive to transform the country seems, if anything, to have gathered pace from 1952. Many of the government programmes of the initial years were reinvented several times over. Where refugee rehabilitation had taken the form of building new townships, for example, their economies had to be rescued by the government, which did so by providing incentives to private businesses in the middle years of the 1950s. Many of the first government-run industries to be founded after independence, including new steel mills, but also its first pharmaceutical factory, only started production in the second half of the 1950s. There was also new thinking about urban housing and town planning in this decade. This creativity was not limited to urban areas; renewed efforts at rural reconstruction were undertaken after the first elections. A nation-wide programme of Community Development was inaugurated in 1952, and it was then reinvented in the late 1950s. In its second incarnation, the programme shifted its focus from quick development projects like building wells to fostering village institutions, including *panchayat*s (village councils), cooperatives and schools. Land reforms continued at the state level in new iterations with official and non-official efforts to settle landless labourers throughout the 1950s. Separately, the focus of national-level programmes to increase agricultural production shifted from development for all to selective, intensive approaches at the end of the decade. The latter years of the 1950s also witnessed political change: the Communist Party gained voters and took power in Kerala after the second elections in 1957; new opposition parties were founded, including the Republican Party of India, which represented India's oppressed classes, and the right-wing Swatantra Party, which tended to appeal to its industrialists. The arrival of these new parties was just one expression of a larger set of anxieties about India's democracy which mounted in the early 1960s. India fought a brief war with China at the end of 1962, and the period between this conflict and Nehru's death in 1964 has tended to be seen as the twilight of his premiership. However, the new ideas of the late 1950s had only begun to bear fruit in the early 1960s, making this period just as interesting as any earlier one. Although Nehru was visibly slowing down, he was not the sole engine of change in the country, so one cannot assume that India uniformly slowed down with him.

The second new insight that this research reveals, therefore, was that the years between 1947 and 1964 were an age of experimentation in India. This experimental mindset is certainly in evidence in the framing of the Constitution, which included provisions, such as universal franchise and group rights, as well as promises of religious reform and social equality, which, it was hoped, would peacefully bring about radical change in India. This mentality was sustained after 1950. Political leaders and administrators used the word 'experiment' to describe nearly every aspect of their work throughout the Nehru years. They engaged the methods of midcentury social science as they experimented in fields as varied as architecture and international relations. This included gathering huge amounts of data about the country, starting each experiment with a pilot project and evaluating it using study teams. Throughout the full period under review, India's governments, in New Delhi and in the states, commenced new experiments, often building on or correcting those undertaken earlier.

Third, this work highlights the continued importance of popular mobilisation in the postcolonial period. India's nationalist leaders had won their country's freedom through the recruitment of its people to participate in mass protests as well as in projects of village uplift and individual self-reform. Much of their work had been in the realm of emotion. Nationalism had been a project of evoking sentiments: anti-British feeling, yes, but also attitudes of kinship and solidarity among India's diverse population. Partition and the creation of Pakistan as a homeland for India's Muslims had been this emotional project's greatest failure, for these events demonstrated the shortcomings of solidarity. After independence, the leaders of the Indian National Congress did not cease to call upon the people as they took hold of the levers of the government. Rather, they sought to tap into and redirect the enthusiasm of the population, for nation-building purposes. In some ways, this postcolonial nationalism was similar to the anti-colonial variety: it was centred on conjuring feelings that the leaders believed were central to national cohesion and social transformation; it relied on public spectacle and charismatic personalities; and it was concerned not just with mobilising the people, but with instilling in them discipline and the desire for personal reform as well. In other ways, postcolonial nationalism was a more complex dance than anti-colonial nationalism, for it sought to rouse in Indians the will to demand more from government, even as it sought to shape exactly what could be demanded of government.

Fourth, and connected to this preference for popular action, this research revises our understanding of how India's new leaders deployed 'the state' after independence. The chapters that follow show that the leaders of independent India did not want government to monopolise all initiative for transforming the country. They wished, instead, to inspire popular participation in nation building. This meant asking private industrialists to contribute to national production targets and to take responsibility for looking after their workers. It encompassed a non-official campaign to inspire village elites to transfer land to the landless voluntarily, entreating them to have a change of heart rather than to adhere to new land legislation. And it entailed encouraging villagers to build their own roads, wells and even schools. As part of this desire to harness and redirect popular enthusiasm, the leaders of independent India experimented with administrative structures, trying to transform the colonial bureaucracy into an administration suited to a free India. Indeed, most of the seminal government projects of the age were designed at a distance from the existing bureaucracy. In charting these experiments, some more successful than others, the chapters that follow uncover a picture of 'the state' which is radically different from that contained in much of the existing historiography.

Fifth, for all their efforts to enlist the people, this period undoubtedly marked the pinnacle of the power of India's elites. The democratisation of India's political life that would mark the final quarter of the twentieth century had yet to gather force. India's nationalist elites tended to use their unquestioned power for the education and uplift of the people. These modes of action reinforced India's existing hierarchies, even as they tried to transform them.

Finally, India in this period was confidently internationalist. Though its public proclamations of non-alignment seem at first glance to have set it apart from the world's dramas, India in fact sought to shape the international realm in its own image. It contributed to the creation of international institutions and it looked to establish norms relating to the treatment of peoples across the globe. Indians also sought to help other newly independent countries learn from the experiments they were undertaking at home, extending the elite's pedagogic profile beyond the nation-state. Thus, in the pages that follow, we witness Indians lecturing the world on everything from democracy to the bicycle industry. While political freedom of action and economic self-sufficiency were the oft-cited aims, the pursuit of these did not mean that India was closed to the circulation of global ideas. Artists and economists, architects and engineers, all travelled through the country and engaged in conversation with India's relatively small circle of elites. And in turn, these Indians brought their vision and their energy to bear on the world.

These six arguments grew from a seed of unease that lodged in my mind while researching an earlier project about secularism in independent India. Curious about the incorporation of the princely state of Hyderabad into India, I turned to Nehru's speeches and letters to understand what had happened, as many scholars do. As I then delved into various historical records across India, however, I became aware of a disconnect between Nehru's words and what I was discovering. What I found contrasted, sometimes subtly, sometimes sharply, with what Nehru said. This divide was not just between Nehru and local officials or ordinary Indians. It was also between how people in the twenty-first century spoke and wrote about Nehru's India, and how I was coming to understand it. If Indian secularism was more contested and complex than it appeared in Nehru's speeches, might the same be true of the other parts of the so-called Nehruvian consensus?

Ordinarily, to answer such a question, the historian would head straight to the archives. Over my career, my research has taken me to different collections in the UK, US and especially to India, where I have worked in official archives at the state and national level, non-official depositories, and in completely informal collections. It is now increasingly common for researchers working in the US or UK to swoop into an archive for a week or two, take thousands of photos and then jet off again. A sense of urgency hangs in the air in these reading rooms as scholars order, open and scan through hundreds of documents in a day. Each Indian archive has its own atmosphere, but fortunately (in my view) none replicates the air of merciless productivity found in some other places. Until recently, photographs were not permitted in many South Asian archives. Documents were not delivered 'on demand', as they say, but in two or three fetches per day. There was a lot of waiting. Working in smaller collections, I was often the only researcher, and I spent time speaking to the archivists or the other employees, in English, halting Hindi/Urdu or broken Telugu, getting advice on where to find good food or exchanging stories about weddings. These conversations often turned up clues that improved my research. They always led to better choices about lunch.

In larger archives, one of the most pleasant aspects of doing research was the daily chat held around the chai stall while waiting for files. Researchers shared what they were working on and exchanged advice on where to look next. These conversations almost invariably drifted to telling stories of woe and wonder about doing historical research in India. Tales of disappointment were not in short supply. For me, it was common for request slips to be returned with a note explaining the file was not there. It could be that the archive never had the file, or that it had been lost, stolen or damaged, or that someone else was reading it. In one archive where I spent significant time, I often received a file after hours of waiting, only to find that it contained but a single slip of paper with the file name and number on it. The substantive papers inside had been lost. In another archive, the index had been helpfully annotated to explain what had happened to each record: next to each entry appeared the words 'eaten by termites' or 'water damaged', etc.

Exchanging stories over a glass of chai, one will also hear tales of triumph. Once I visited the office of a local newspaper. I explained in Hindi/Urdu to the guard at the bottom of the building that I was a researcher from London and I wanted to look at old papers. Did they have any? No, came the answer. I requested to speak to someone inside, and I was shown in. Once in the building, the conversation was repeated: I was here to look at old papers, could I do that? No. I asked to speak to someone upstairs and was shown rather unexpectedly into the boss's office. Lo and behold, they did have an informal archive! I was even treated to an air-conditioned room and allowed to snap photos as I looked through the papers. This is what it is like researching the history of Nehru's India: you never know what you are going to get. Often, you don't even know what is out there to begin with.

In recent years, things have started to change. The National Archives of India has begun a massive digitisation project, making some material available via an online portal. This has altered the researcher's experience: rather than carefully scanning through indexes for anything that might suit our project and ordering files in order, we now have to guess at search terms, grapple with key words in metadata, and cope with search results presented to us out of chronological order and without related files. Other digitisation projects have also appeared, especially of debates in the Lok Sabha and of state assemblies. Private companies have digitised India's English-language newspapers and made them available to subscribers. Photography is now permitted in some smaller archives. Researchers have become even more creative in unearthing new sources outside of official archives. Their work in the offices of political parties, NGOs, newspapers, art galleries and architects among others has enriched the field immensely. Unfortunately, many of these finds are not made public, ensuring the work of future historians will be yet more complicated, as they struggle to access, track down and verify sources used by others.

Still, disasters large and small, man-made and natural, plague the written record of India's past. Official papers on what happened at various levels of government are patchy and uneven at best, and at worst non-existent. Many ministries stopped transferring their old files to official depositories decades ago, or sent batches of records only haphazardly. In some cases, files have been transferred but not indexed or catalogued. Collections have been divided and reshuffled first with the partition of the subcontinent in 1947 and then with the reorganisation of India's states several times over. As I write, the storage facilities of the National Archives of India look set to be demolished as part of the Central Vista Redevelopment Project. Scholars have no clear idea how materials will be preserved, and no guarantee they will continue to have access to the records of India's past. The bread and butter of the historian's work is to track the progress of official decision-making through consecutive files at a national repository, but runs of evidence on the working of governments in postcolonial India are still extremely hard to come by.

In the search for alternative sources, one excellent collection turned out to be right under my nose at the London School of Economics. The LSE has a long connection with India. Indeed, many of the personalities in this book spent time there. Founded in 1895, the LSE had an interest in studying 'good governance', not just in the UK, but in British colonies. At one point the LSE Library had a team of fifteen people collecting and cataloguing official publications from around the globe. Although heavily weighted towards public administration, the collection offers a surprisingly detailed and candid view of what governments were doing in early postcolonial India, and not just in New Delhi, but in the states as well. Sadly, the comprehensive collecting pattern tapered off in the 1960s. These publications, combined with digitised sources, a smattering of archives in the UK and materials gathered during nearly two decades of research in India comprise my makeshift archive. This project of assembling sources about Nehru's India was complex and time-consuming, and my archive—as most other historians would admit of theirs—owes a lot to chance.

This book also builds upon the impressive research of other historians who, in the past two decades, have begun to locate and interrogate the incomplete and scattered records of the postcolonial period. Beginning with the study of partition, these researchers, many of them friends and colleagues of mine, have rewritten the history of the transition to independence. They have explored the drafting and operation of the Constitution, the workings of the Planning Commission, the organisation of India's first elections, and the reorganisation of the bureaucracy. They have taken the history of women's rights, Dalit activism and citizenship in new directions. Drawing at least partly on archives from the US, this generation of historians has given us greater insight into some of the most prominent aspects of postcolonial development, including food production and Community Development. These intrepid scholars have shed light on India's borderlands, its relations with its neighbours, and its role in the United Nations. While some of these researchers come tantalisingly close to casting doubt on one myth or another, they tend to shy away from challenging them head on. Read together, this recent scholarship—cited throughout the pages that follow—provides a set of inferences that form the foundation upon which I built the arguments of the book.

Telling a different story means not only drawing on new sources, but also bringing in different characters. Although many of the most famous people, issues and events from the period are unavoidable, it is inevitable that some familiar figures will be left out of these pages. There are two reasons for this. Firstly, this book is not a comprehensive survey of all that happened, but a set of arguments about how we should understand certain aspects of this period in Indian history. It is necessarily partial, though not in the sense of being partisan. Secondly, the focus of the book is the set of abstract nouns associated with Nehru. For that reason, the focus is on official policies, programmes, and ideas, often but not always emanating from New Delhi. One figure who surprised me by his absence in my sources was Sardar Vallabhbhai Patel, home minister and minister for states, and at least in today's understanding, great rival to Nehru. Patel died in 1950, of course, so was not present for fourteen of the seventeen years of Nehru's premiership. Even in researching materials on the integration of the princely states, however, where Patel's voice as minister for states might be expected, he was not a colossal presence in the archives, and his influence could often be discerned only through inference. This is a mystery for future historians to puzzle out.

In addition, opposition movements, whether Gandhian, liberal, leftist, Hindu nationalist or caste-based, are not the centre of attention in the pages that follow. Equally, popular movements are not the heart of this research. No doubt this work would have been much richer had I been able to include every one of these movements, but it also would have been much longer. Indeed, a book incorporating all these elements would be so large as to be unwieldy. However, an understanding of opposition—whether in the form of political parties or popular movements—requires a clear view of what these groups opposed. It is hoped that by providing that view, this research will be of some use to those investigating people, movements and ideas that, though far removed from the corridors of power, have nonetheless been integral to India's history.

In each of the chapters that follow, I tease out the origins and development of one of the myths surrounding Nehru and his premiership. Each begins by briefly considering how the scraps of historical evidence available have combined with political developments in the decades after Nehru's death to make the myths so enduring. Subsequent sections then reveal new contemporary evidence to tell a different story about Nehru's India. These chapters are not organised chronologically, so it is not strictly necessary to read them in order. That being said, I would suggest reading chapter 1, 'The Myth of Nehru the Architect of Independent India', first. This chapter is not a deep dive into the life of India's first prime minister. Instead, for those who would otherwise be tempted to try to understand India through the words of Jawaharlal Nehru, this chapter explains why he is not the leading presence in the other chapters. In so doing, it sets the stage for the material that follows. Many of the myths are intertwined with one another, and the arguments outlined above echo through the early decades after independence, tying the chapters together. I expect that historians who specialise in this period will find much that is recognisable. Indeed, reading their research and engaging in conversations with them has shaped my own ideas. For those who know the era only through the myths, I hope there is much that is surprising.

Nearly six decades after his death, Nehru's name is often invoked by people from across India's political spectrum. Indeed, a virtual war over

Nehru and his legacy seems to have been waged for much of the past three decades. On the one hand, the Congress Party lauds him as the architect of independent India. On the other, opposition parties blame Nehru for what they regard as the mistakes of his era. For every opinion voiced about Nehru the opposite has almost certainly been asserted. Whether they praise or disparage him, the aim of these parties is to justify their deeds today and to gain power tomorrow, not to illuminate the past. Theirs is not a history war; it is a war of myths. I have never envisioned this research project as part of those battles. Rather, by dragging these stories from the shining heights of myth back down to the muddy domain of history, my aim is to stimulate reasoned debate and further research in a field where polemics too often seem to dominate.

NEHRU'S INDIA

CHAPTER ONE

The Myth of Nehru the Architect of Independent India

IN 1984, THE Films Division of India (FDI) released the film *Nehru*.[1] Avoiding interviews or reconstructions, the sole voice on the film, with a few brief exceptions, is that of Jawaharlal Nehru. Narrated by Saeed Jaffrey doing his best impression of the Cambridge-educated Kashmiri, and occasionally drawing on archived recordings of the man himself, almost the entire script is composed of extracts from Nehru's books and speeches. Directed by Shyam Benegal with the Russian director Yuri Aldolkhin, the film's three parts cover the span of Nehru's life. Quickly recounting his early childhood in Allahabad and then his education in the UK, touching briefly on his marriage to Kamala and the birth of their daughter, Indira, the majority of the film focuses on the freedom struggle. The script draws heavily from *The Discovery of India*, a volume that is part autobiography and part amateur history of the country. The viewer is introduced to the violence and exploitation of British rule, and then to Mohandas Karamchand Gandhi, the leader of India's independence movement. The narrative charts the mass movements that the Indian National Congress launched between 1919 and 1942, with Indians boycotting British goods, taxes, and employment in the colonial administration. It details the price Indians, including Nehru, paid for their civil disobedience, as their protests were met with violence and long periods of imprisonment. The film narrates the negotiations that Gandhi and the Indian National Congress undertook with the British from the 1930s for the devolution of power and eventually for independence. It chronicles the rise of the Muslim League, and Nehru's disagreements with the League's leader, Muhammad

Ali Jinnah, over the two-nation theory and the creation of Pakistan, which divided British India as the imperial power departed in August 1947.

Nehru's image is used sparsely in the first two parts where the story of the national movement is told. Throughout, Nehru's own words are played as scenes of India's varied landscape, its many peoples and the major historical events are displayed before the viewer. Such a presentation elevates Nehru, as one expects of this genre, but it also isolates him. Although Gandhi's image features prominently, the viewer hears the Mahatma speak but once. Other nationalist figures come and go, from Nehru's father Motilal to Muhammad Ali Jinnah, but again they are hardly given voice in the film. Instead, their ideas are delivered to the viewer through Nehru's words. In this way, Nehru is left as the sole narrator to tell the story of India's freedom struggle. In the final part of the film, titled 'Freedom', Nehru dominates the imagery while selections from his speeches are used to summarise his thoughts on secularism, socialism, non-alignment and the other ideas with which he is so strongly associated. Although they can be spotted in the archive footage used, none of the other prominent Indians of his day are mentioned by name. In this way, Nehru becomes almost the lone protagonist of independent India's story.

The film might be thought of as part of the trend of lionising, but also simplifying, Nehru for popular consumption. Although unique in many ways, the FDI's *Nehru* is evocative of a larger pattern in the way we think about Jawaharlal Nehru and in the way both scholars and ordinary people view the first two decades after independence in India. Nehru is often understood to be the 'architect' of independent India.[2] Real-world architects work in complex teams, building structures through elaborate negotiations with clients, regulators and neighbours. Their final product is mediated by constraints inherent in building materials, labour relations and consumer tastes. Used as a metaphor in historical writing, however, the term 'architect' is meant to describe an individual who has a vision for a complete edifice, set out in a blueprint and then realised through that individual's sheer ingenuity and drive.

Thus, when people today write and speak about Nehru or about India in the period after the inauguration of the Constitution in 1950, we often find an untroubled substitution of Nehru for India. Benegal's film achieves this through the layered presentation of sound and image. In written works, it is common to find the name of the first prime minister and the country used interchangeably: scholars and pundits write of Nehru's/India's policy on Korea or India's/Nehru's approach to modernisation, and there is no apparent discomfort as they slip between the two.

The impression conjured by the FDI's film is one of a tireless and dedicated, if isolated, leader. In the documentary, the sense of Nehru's isolation is achieved by excluding other perspectives, and by giving him the last, or the only, word on the conflicts of his time. In so doing, the film mirrors the story told by his biographers, among whom there is near consensus that Nehru governed India virtually alone at this time, inaccessible and unchallenged.[3] Scholars have tended to understand Nehru's isolation as a product, in part, of the fact that many of his contemporaries from the nationalist movement, including Gandhi, Vallabhbhai Patel and Sarojini Naidu, had passed away in the first few years after independence. Others, such as Bhimrao Ramji Ambedkar or C. Rajagopalachari, moved out of Nehru's orbit and away from the centre of power. Bereft of peers, Nehru was left as the sole titan on the stage of Indian politics. He is also said to have been sequestered by those around him. At the office, his personal secretary, A. O. Mathai, filled his section of the South Block with mediocre public servants, and amassed great power himself, filtering and sifting information before it landed on Nehru's desk.[4] At home, his daughter, Indira Gandhi, estranged from her husband and living with her children at Teen Murti Bhavan by the late 1940s, was said to act as a gatekeeper, restricting access to a man who, before her arrival, had been more receptive to visitors. His own cool personality was also said to be to blame for his relative solitude. He regularly lamented that Indians had seen their standards fall, that there were too few who, like him, had the drive for the tasks ahead.

At the same time, scholars agree that after around 1950 Nehru enjoyed an unchallenged position as leader. This was down to the paucity of plausible rivals, but also to his electoral success. He carried the Congress Party to power at the centre and in most of the states in three consecutive general elections between 1951 and 1962. Nehru, scholars assume, took a detailed leadership role in the projects at the heart of the nation-building endeavour. His workload was tremendous: on an average day, he received some two thousand letters, and spent four to five hours each night dictating responses.[5] Benegal's film is just one example of the archetypal image we have of the solitary and dedicated life of the great man who ruled India.

Over the years the perception of Nehru's singularity has only grown. It has developed to the point where, on the seventieth anniversary of the departure of the British, the BBC could air an assertion that Nehru had allowed a personality cult to be built up around himself, without finding it necessary to go to any length to prove it, and without, it seems, stirring any controversy.[6] Why has this picture of Nehru dominating the landscape persisted? Of the many reasons one can uncover, I would like to highlight three here, and come to a fourth later in the chapter. Firstly, Nehru's own personal stature, magnetism and longevity go some way to helping us understand why his reputation as the architect of India has only grown, even as people's assessment of his work has turned sour.[7] He was not only India's first prime minister; he served for seventeen years, longer than any other leader to follow him. To many he was genuinely charming, urbane and empathetic. He was an attractive man. And it is easy to attribute power to the attractive. To others, particularly since the 1980s, he has been vilified as representing all that was wrong with independent India's early years. But a nemesis without significant power is no villain at all, and so even those who deride his decisions invest the man with great influence.

Secondly, however, there are also important dispositional and methodological forces behind the rise of the Nehru myth. The way most people prefer to think about the past tends to favour a focus on individuals. Many (not all, but many) scholars, publishers, readers and podcast producers continue to prefer to understand the past through the lives of exemplary individuals. These tales offer the prospect of a more compelling narrative than the messy and contradictory histories one ends up telling when exploring the everyday negotiations of collectives, the functioning of institutions or the iteration of structures.

Thirdly, and perhaps most crucially for the professional historian, for over thirty years, the clearest, most coherent source of material on postcolonial India has been the Second Series of the *Selected Works* of Jawaharlal Nehru, published by the Jawaharlal Nehru Memorial Fund. The series began under the stewardship of Sarvepalli Gopal, historian and son of the second president of India, who, with the eminent biographer B. R. Nanda, had also consulted on the FDI's production of the film, *Nehru*. Indeed, the first volume was published in the same year that the film was released. The series now stands at eighty-five volumes. Even as it was still being compiled, the collection was digitised for online consumption. The *Selected Works* provide access to Nehru's letters and speeches. These are curated from his private papers; they are not the full records of the files that crossed his desk as prime minister. As such, they give us only minimal exposure to the debate, dialogue and ordinary back-and-forth of quotidian decision-making that is the essence of governance in India. In other words, the *Selected Works* present us with a universe with a celestial body at its centre that produces such heat, light and energy that it is hard to make out anything else around it.

An Origin Story

In trying to uncover how this image of Nehru has come about, one must ask, did Nehru indeed propagate a kind of personality cult, albeit a soft one? Personality cults are produced by elevating a single man above others, often imbuing his leadership with a mystical air. This is achieved both through strict regulation over the reproduction of imagery, and the ruthless demand for loyalty from officials and ordinary people alike.[8] Every image of Stalin that appeared in Russian newspapers, for example, was first approved by Stalin's secretariat.[9] These images, in turn, served as symbols of political obedience. Images of Chairman Mao, famously on Mao badges, were essential parts of the public performance of individuals professing their loyalty to the supreme leader of the People's Republic of China.[10] In these authoritarian contexts, images were used to secure one's position in an environment of pervasive fear. The consequences for those who failed to send the right signals to the right people were potentially lethal.[11]

If there was one person's image that dominated political life in the 1950s and 1960s, it was not Nehru's, but Gandhi's. True, Nehru's portraits were not in short supply, but he seemed to prefer that impulses of iconisation be directed towards Gandhi. The murder of the Mahatma in January 1948, undoubtedly a personal tragedy for Nehru, also provided an opportunity to begin to unite and heal a traumatised nation around a man who, for many, had already been transformed into a symbol.[12] From 1950, Gandhi's death anniversary coincided with Republic Day celebrations, allowing leaders, including Nehru, to connect him repeatedly with the national project as it developed after independence.[13] Gandhi's image adorned rupee notes and postage stamps. When local governments, despite Nehru's objections, renamed roadways, Mahatma Gandhi Marg was, for many, the first choice. After his assassination, Gandhi's name, his face and his ideas all provided important symbols around which citizens could be rallied, and policies justified. Although there were important debates about Gandhi's ideas and his legacy in this period, his death helped to stabilise his image in a way that could be put to political use.

As for Nehru, his biographers have detailed his ambivalence and introspection about his own power.[14] There is little evidence that he sought to maintain much control over the ways in which he was portrayed. He professed to be 'allergic' to having things named after himself, and pleaded with the public to stop making such requests.[15] His image and his name may have been used during election campaigns, but ordinary citizens and individual government servants did not use them to prove their fidelity, let alone to save themselves from liquidation. While touring Kanpur for his final election campaign in 1961, he told a crowd, 'I like your love but I don't want yes-men.' He scolded businessmen for donating to more than one party, telling them to keep their money if they did not have 'faith in the ideals and aims of the Congress'.[16] In fact, Nehru is known to have enjoyed a joke at his own expense. Inaugurating the satirical magazine *Shankar's Weekly* in 1948, Nehru told the cartoonist, '[W]e are apt to grow pompous and self-centred, and it is good to have the veil of our conceit torn occasionally. And so I gladly pay my tribute to Shankar and I hope that he will long continue to enlighten us and amuse us and pull us down a peg or two.'[17] To conflate the use of Nehru's name and his political charisma in democratic contests with the cults of personality developed by dictators would be to misunderstand the function of secular iconography in both types of regime.

If Nehru did not put special effort into his own myth-making, when and how did it arise? We find that the myth of Nehru's indisputable and indispensable leadership in India was propagated by Congress, at least in part, to keep an exhausted prime minister in his job. To understand this claim, we might look at one episode in which the prime minister made his weariness visible to the nation. In the hot weather of 1958, Nehru asked his party for permission to retire, if only temporarily, from his post as prime minister. At the time, the sixty-eight-year-old Nehru was at the height of his popularity and influence. He had established institutions that he hoped had launched the country towards a democratic and more prosperous future. By 1956, central and state governments had launched their second, more expansive and ambitious, five-year plans. Nehru had also seen the Congress Party through to success in the second general election in the following year. Even though the party had won a smaller share of the vote, and had lost Kerala to the communists, Nehru's personal stature was undiminished. Just before the election, in the first poll of its kind in independent India, the Indian Institute of Public Opinion had surveyed people with the question, 'What is your Opinion of Nehru?', and a full 74 per cent had answered, 'very good', with another 11 per cent answering 'good'. Though only 33 per cent of Hindu Mahasabha voters had a 'very good' opinion of the prime minister, a full 60 per cent of Jana Sangh voters did so, and 72 per cent of Communist Party voters felt likewise.[18]

Along with these accomplishments came further burdens. In February 1958, Maulana Abul Kalam Azad, a close friend who was only a year older than the prime minister, had passed away. Shortly thereafter the finance minister T. T. Krishnamachari had been forced to resign as a result of one of the first big political scandals of the era.[19] Nehru had temporarily taken on the finance portfolio on his departure, adding it to his work as prime minister, chairman of the Planning Commission and minister for external affairs.

Addressing his party in April 1958, Nehru confessed to feeling 'tired and stale'. In a meeting of the Congress Parliamentary Party, he told Congress MPs that he wished to 'seek a period of calm and quiet'. He regretted that he had no time to read or to really think through the problems faced by India or by the world.[20] At around the same time, he had begun to collect his correspondence from the freedom struggle, publishing letters written to him by his father, by Gandhi, by Sarojini Naidu and a host of others, in a volume he called *A Bunch of Old Letters*. Introducing the collection, the prime minister wrote that '[n]early all of them belong to a period which now seems remote'.[21] It was but one expression of his nostalgia for a time when the stakes were higher and the motives purer.

When he told the Party of his wish to retire, or at least take a sabbatical of perhaps half a year, they listened to his speech in 'stunned silence', cheering only when one member interrupted him to shout, 'No, Sir, you must continue.'[22] Around the country, the reaction was similar. The editorial board of *The Times of India* greeted the news with disbelief, saying the Party and the country were filled with a 'sense of bewilderment' as to why the prime minister might wish to retire. Even the opposition parties fretted at what a future without Nehru might bring: the Communist mayor of Bombay, S. S. Mirajkar, appealed to Nehru 'in the name of the working classes', urging him to remain in office out of fear that without him the social progress envisaged in the five-year plans would be subjected to 'sabotage'.[23]

Nehru had requested that Congress MPs consider his words carefully before arriving at a decision, but within minutes, they had drafted a letter declaring, 'It is universally felt that the nation needs Mr Nehru's continued leadership.'[24] Two days later, in a resolution adopted by acclamation, the Congress Parliamentary Party categorically refused to contemplate relieving Nehru of his duties for any length of time whatsoever. U. N. Dhebar, the Congress president, declared that at this 'crucial hour', the country 'will not be able to spare Mr Nehru'.[25]

Nehru dismissed their resolution, saying he had not been fishing for a vote of confidence, but rather was searching for a way out of his own mental impasse. He also offered a fuller explanation for his request in a longer speech in which he detailed his disappointment that Congress

FIGURE 1.1. 'The Retiring P.M.', *The Times of India*, 2 May 1958, 7. Published with permission of ProQuest LLC. Further reproduction is prohibited without permission.

members were absorbed more by jobbery and factionalism than by the pursuit of ideals. He decried 'the deterioration of our standards' and the creeping entry of 'coarseness' and 'vulgarity' in the public life of the country. He was disturbed by majoritarianism among Congress members and the wider public. And the tense international situation had further burdened his mind.[26] The Congress Parliamentary Party responded by treating Nehru to a series of speeches declaiming his indispensable position as leader of the nation.[27] He was persuaded to withdraw his request for a lengthy leave of absence.

In the way that sometimes only satirists can do, R. K. Laxman captured the prime minister's position in a cartoon run nationally on 2 May 1958, as Nehru and his party contemplated his future (Fig. 1.1). Nehru was depicted as a giant, laid out on his back, viewing with fatigue his tiny fellow Congressmen as they squabbled on his chest.[28] This was neither the first time nor the last that Nehru would be portrayed as somehow greater than his peers by the cartoonists of the day. Given what we know about the episode to which it refers, we can see that the cartoon hardly captured

Nehru's state of mind. Instead, it was feeding the legend of the Great Man, who, if only he could be freed from petty problems, would stand tall again.

Nehru asked his party to let him step down, even temporarily, and there was no unseemly jockeying for position, no scramble to the top of the pile. The Congress Party simply refused to countenance life without Nehru. Was this, perhaps, the origin of the myth of Nehru as the unparalleled leader of independent India? Certainly, we need not point to a single origin to understand the significance of this episode: Nehru is revealed as a man of great energy, but one who could also become exhausted. He was the matchless leader of India, but not always in his own mind. Indeed, a wider reading of his letters uncovers regular bouts of self-doubt beyond this episode.[29] Unwilling to dictate to his party, even on the matter of his own retirement, he is revealed as a man who knew how to move forward only by consensus, and by building up and then bowing to institutions.

Propagating the Myth

The image of Nehru as the titan of postcolonial India was not the creation of Jawaharlal the aspiring supreme leader. Rather, the myth of Nehru as indispensable was orchestrated by his party to persuade a weary senior citizen to stay at his desk. But why has this image persisted for more than half a century? Why has Nehru not been exposed, not as a fraud, but as a mortal? The answer lies in the work of both the Congress Party and opposition parties after Nehru's death.

When Nehru's heart finally gave out on 27 May 1964, his doubts were eclipsed as the world eulogised him. His death was announced in the Lok Sabha with the same words he had used to inform the nation of Gandhi's death: 'the light is out'. Indians around the world began to grieve: Indian women in South Africa reportedly wept at the news, and Indian residents of London gathered at a vigil at India House.[30] In the ink that was spilled over his death, he was often lionised as the sole leader of independent India. Jayaprakash Narayan, sometime member of the socialist opposition and friend of the late prime minister, lamented, 'The captain of the ship is no more. The leader has left the people desolate and forlorn.'[31] *The Economic Weekly* portrayed Nehru as a man who had chosen 'to die in harness', unwilling to 'lay down his burden' because of his 'complete and utter commitment to the tasks that still remained unaccomplished'. Here we have a picture of Nehru yoked to the country, displaying his 'ceaseless striving, restless energy, audacious daring' as he pulled it in the direction of his dreams.[32] Reporting in a special edition on the day after his death, *The New York Times* claimed, 'When he was alive, he had authority to decide on his own and prevail upon his party to accept his decisions.'[33] Describing his funeral the following day, *The Times of India* correspondent claimed to have detected, 'beneath the measured words of official and personal condolences the accents of a deep and genuine grief' among the world's leaders. The tributes of leading international figures, according to the paper, seemed to confirm 'Mr Nehru's standing as a global figure' who had a 'unique and precious ability to weave a web of magical sympathies stretching to many countries and continents'.[34] Nehru was remembered for his personal sacrifices, especially the time he spent in jail during the freedom struggle. He was lauded for his love of children and his desire to educate Indians. His illimitable energy and charisma were praised. The president of India, Sarvepalli Radhakrishnan, told the nation in a radio address, 'As a fighter for freedom he was illustrious, as a maker of modern India his services were unparalleled [...]. It will be difficult to reconcile ourselves to the image of an India without Nehru's active and all-pervasive leadership.'[35] The rituals of mourning seem to demand hyperbole. Nehru certainly received at the very least his fair share.

In the weeks and months after his death, we begin to see a proliferation of Nehru iconography. At condolence meetings in New Delhi at the end of May, national leaders led 'thousands' in taking 'a pledge to follow Mr Nehru's ideals', a vow that had been unthinkable while he was alive.[36] Within days of his death, the Municipal Corporation of Delhi had resolved to rename the capital's Circular Road 'Jawaharlal Nehru Marg', and to place a statue of him at the roundabout facing the Turkman Gate.[37] By mid-June the General Post Office had issued a fifteen-paisa commemorative stamp in memory of the first prime minister, and a second stamp was issued on his birthday, 14 November, in the same year (Fig. 1.2).[38] India's first commemorative coin was emblazoned with his face. The Children's Book Trust, founded by K. Shankar Pillai of *Shankar's Weekly*, and funded by the Ministry of Education, published *Nehru for Children*, a volume that begins, simply, 'Jawaharlal Nehru was one of the greatest men the world has known.'[39]

A month after his death, an appeal for the Jawaharlal Nehru Memorial Fund was launched.[40] One of its early activities was to organise an exhibition in his honour at Teen Murti Bhavan in New Delhi, which opened on 14 November 1964.[41] The Fund has published commemorative volumes, celebrating him as a 'colossus among men'.[42] It oversaw the publication of his *Selected Works* and, more recently, their digitisation.[43]

FIGURE 1.2. Chacha Nehru stamp, issued 14 November 1964. Author's collection.

That after his death the production of Nehru memorabilia expanded tells us more about the post-Nehru Congress Party than it does about Nehru himself. While pundits had predicted the party would succumb to skirmishes after Nehru's demise, Congress decided, in a seemingly orderly manner, to elevate Lal Bahadur Shastri to leader and prime minister. Shastri, however, had been virtually unknown to the wider public before he had begun to take on some of the prime minister's work in the last months of Nehru's life. Indeed, two opinion polls, in 1957 and again five years later, had asked the question, 'After Nehru, who?', and Shastri's name had not even appeared on the rather long list of contenders.[44] Perhaps the big players in the Congress Party found this rather unassuming man to be rather uninspiring: they looked once more to Nehru for inspiration, as they had done while he was alive. Thus, on the first anniversary of Nehru's death, Sarvepalli Radhakrishnan urged the nation to adhere to the ideals and objectives which Nehru had set for them. The president told All India Radio listeners, 'The best way to honour [Nehru's] memory is to get on with the work which he left unfinished, his work for peace, justice and freedom at home and abroad.'[45]

The Congress Party used Nehru's image to help legitimate its rule before his death, and it continued to do so after it. To understand this through but one example, we can return to the film *Nehru*. Nehru's words, his opinions, and his actions dominate the film. Thus he simultaneously addresses and represents the nation. But before this relationship between the first prime minister and the nation can be explored, the film begins with a ninety-second preface. It opens with the camera focused on a portrait of Nehru, chin on fist, looking into the distance. The camera pans to show us that the photograph is on a wall in a room where Nehru's daughter, Indira Gandhi, sits alone, addressing the camera. In 1984, she is India's prime minister, but her remarks are made in an intimate register: she refers to Nehru as 'my father', and as she speaks her eyes glow warmly with affection. Though she mentions his concern for solving the problems of India and of the world, there is no mention of the Congress Party or of the many political divisions of the day. There is only Indira and her father. The film works its magic in part by connecting the people of India to Nehru, and Nehru to Indira. The Congress Party more broadly continues to rely on Nehru's charisma and his achievements to make their claims to legitimacy in India. Each year on the anniversary of his birth on 14 November, and his death on 27 May, the Congress Party, formerly in press releases, now in tweets, lauds him as the 'architect of modern India'.[46]

Perhaps paradoxically, opposition parties have also contributed to the myth. As the Bharatiya Janata Party (BJP) has emerged as an alternative to the Congress Party, Nehru's stature has been raised, not to lend him more esteem, but to personify the alleged mistakes of Congress in one man.[47] Since the 1980s, successive Indian governments, both Congress-led and BJP-led, have made economic decisions that they characterise as 'opening up' the economy. As they have done so, they have explained their decisions with reference to the mistaken policies of the first prime minister.[48] Thus, even as they claim he was wrong, they posthumously imbue Nehru with extraordinary influence.

Towards Some Hints about Nehru's Style of Rule

The idea that Nehru towered over India, sculpting it to his will, is simply a myth. I write this not to demean him, but to humanise him. How can we be certain? Let us begin with an explanation that stands outside of the man himself. Look for a moment at the size of the country: its population stood at more than 360 million people in 1951, and more than 438 million a decade later. It measured more than 3.2 million square kilometres, with a federal system comprising, in 1947, nine provinces, hundreds of princely states and a gaggle of centrally administered territories, from Delhi to the Andaman and Nicobar Islands. Although the number of separate administrative units had been streamlined somewhat by 1964, extra layers of government in the form of panchayats and related institutions had also been added. Under the complex federal system that had emerged historically during the colonial period, the British had devolved power to Indians at the lowest levels of governance first, designing the system to allow the imperial masters to retain what they thought was control at the apex of a complex power structure. Under the pressures of an independence movement which had not only opposed the colonial government but also been elected to run significant parts of it, minor insubordination had become a habit of governance by 1947.[49] The country faced complex economic and social issues, and its governments devised a proliferation of agencies to address the problems they identified. Nehru's energy may have been boundless, but he was limited by what could be done with two hands and twenty-four hours in a day. Like all great men, his greatness was not only reliant upon, but was produced by, a web of human interactions, objects and institutions.[50]

Nehru's influence was not only restricted by India's geography and demography, or the constraints of the way humans experience space and time. His conception of his own power was that it was modest. Although he spoke and wrote extensively, he preferred not to turn his ideas into ideology.[51] In 1958, Sampurnanand, the Congress chief minister from Uttar Pradesh, called on Nehru to set down his philosophy in more concrete form, as a way of inspiring the masses again after the Congress Party's share of the vote had fallen in the second election. Nehru's reply came in the form of an essay called *The Basic Approach*, in which he explained how exasperated he was with people who, whether through religion or ideology, believed they had all the answers to the world's problems. He derided those who held to their principles without acknowledging that 'others might have some share of the truth also'. Such a dogmatic approach, he declared, was 'wholly unscientific, unreasonable and uncivilised whether it is applied in the realm of religion or economic theory or anything else'.[52] Far from producing a 'Little Red Book' containing ready answers to all questions, Nehru believed that the promulgation of such a credo would be damaging. Indeed, when someone had approached him the year before with the idea of publishing a book with extracts of his speeches under the title 'Nehru's Wisdom', he demurred at such a 'pompous' title.[53]

Nehru's biographers have been divided as to how he understood his position. Some have seen him as a man who was incapable of delegating work, with a 'Viceregal understanding' of his own role as prime minister.[54] Others have seen him as a delegator,[55] and a consensus builder.[56] Widening the scope to look beyond the man himself, one sees that Nehru had neither the desire nor the ability to work unchallenged. When he answered the question, 'after Nehru, who?', he felt it would be best to have a group take charge.[57] Indeed, his plea for temporary retirement was in part an admission that the work was too much for one person. To Nehru, governing as the representative of the people was not just a question of elections: 'In the ultimate analysis, it is a manner of thinking, a manner of action, a manner of behaviour to your neighbour and to your adversary.'[58] The primary norm in this democratic mode of being was respect for the person, even if one disagreed with his or her ideas. Opponents were to be won over by rational argument, rather than trampled underfoot. Indeed, Nehru maintained regular correspondence with members of the opposition such as Jayaprakash Narayan, and relished the way that such exchanges improved his own ideas. Taking into account the fact that he was a man enmeshed in networks of people and institutions, his preference for working with others, and his modest conception of leadership, one can say that he saw his own role as having four facets: patron, mediator, educator and symbol.

His attitude towards democratic government helps explain Nehru's penchant for institutions. Of course, he inherited institutions within which the role of prime minister was central. The most obvious of these was the cabinet. Nehru worked hard to ensure that important issues were sent to cabinet for consultation. He also fostered the status of the Lok Sabha as the central deliberative body of government. As prime minister, he attended regular question-and-answer sessions, and took debates seriously.[59] His belief in the importance of institutions extended beyond the nation-state: as chapter 2 will describe, Indian representatives helped shape many of the early UN agencies.

Far from designing and overseeing everything, however, Nehru's role in many of India's new institutions might be encapsulated in the idea of the patron. One of the ways in which he shaped postcolonial India was through supporting projects that were proposed by energetic people around him. From S. K. Dey's Community Projects Administration (see chapter 4) to Durgabai Deshmukh's Central Social Welfare Board (chapter 5), brilliant men and women who earned the prime minister's respect and esteem were given the encouragement and support necessary to build institutions and pursue their own experiments in postcolonial India. He held the most prominent office in the land and so he was invited to observe, to inaugurate, to advise and to remove obstacles as these visionaries built their institutions. But he did so as patron, not potentate. Ruling through others did not always have benign outcomes, however. Nehru's penchant for ruling through others is also witnessed in the decision to remove Sheikh Abdullah as prime minister of Jammu and Kashmir and replace him with the more amenable Bakshi Ghulam Mohammad in 1953. At a mundane level, those who benefited from his patronage were sometimes accused of extravagance or corruption, and their projects wound down after a short time.

Given the large number of people for whom he acted as patron, it should not be surprising that Nehru expended a good deal of effort in acting as a mediator between people in various parts of his government and his party. He sometimes expressed frustration at the amount of time he spent settling feuds between different cabinet members, public officials or

Congress workers. Writing to his sister in 1953, he lamented that 'the best part of my time is taken up in reconciling people or in soothing them when they ruffle with each other'. Allowing himself to fantasise momentarily of alternatives to the arduous work of reconciliation, he pondered tongue-in-cheek, 'I do not know if in other countries people are continually faced with these difficulties of individuals behaving too individualistically. In the Soviet [Union], I suppose, when this happens somebody is liquidated.'[60] It was the difficult work of ruling in concert, of finding consensus, and of consoling bruised egos that occupied much of his time. These were not the concerns of a man happy to dictate to others. These were the concerns of an arbitrator, striving to help others cooperate harmoniously.

Nehru may have faced few challengers for the position of leader of Congress or of the nation, but he faced daily challenges to his leadership. Most often, these came in the form of members of his own government or his own party acting in defiance of stated policies or the norms of democratic fair play. These were, as noted above, habits of governance inherited from the colonial period. Nehru struggled with this quotidian insubordination. Writing to B. C. Roy in 1951, he insisted that he did not have 'the makings of a dictator'.[61] Rather, he stepped into other circles of responsibility rarely, often with some hesitation, and without unwavering commitment. When he did so, he intervened by trying to persuade his interlocutor, rather than by pulling rank and issuing orders. And if his wishes were defied, he most often simply let the issue drop. Nehru did offer to resign a few times over issues within the Congress Party, but he seems to have had little in his armoury between resigning his office and resigning himself to the everyday defiance of members of his party and his administration who would not be persuaded by his efforts.

Asserting his authority over others without negotiation was something Nehru did rarely and without much success, but he did relish his role as an educator.[62] This is evident in his fortnightly letters to chief ministers. As he declared his intention to write to them regularly in his first such letter, dated 15 October 1947, he told chief ministers that the aim of his missives was to 'to keep in close touch with each other, so that we can put forth concerted efforts' to confront India's problems. At the same time, he urged chief ministers to 'put across to the public the true basis of our policy', an act of cascading communication which he regarded as 'a matter of great importance'.[63] With ordinary Indians, he was happy to take on the role of professor. Discussing the rallies held for the first general election in 1951–52, Nehru explained, 'I speak to these people and I try to tell them in some detail of how I feel and what I want them to do [. . .]. The effort to explain in simple language our problems and our difficulties and to reach the minds of these simple folk is both exhausting and exhilarating.'[64] The combination of hierarchy and benevolence suited India's first prime minister, at a time when similar attitudes were pervasive among India's elites.

Finally, Nehru understood that he was a symbol of the Congress Party, and that on the international stage he was a symbol of India.[65] Notwithstanding India's parliamentary system, whereby prime ministers are not directly elected, the Congress Party campaigned for each of the country's first three general elections on the back of Nehru's charisma and his achievements. His personal attention helped to soothe the pain of Muslims in Hyderabad after the invasion of the state in 1948. His word helped to anchor Jammu and Kashmir to India, a relationship symbolised by the tunnel the government opened in 1956, which connected Srinagar to the rest of the country. Quite exceptionally, he allowed it to be named Jawahar Tunnel. There is a difference between, on the one hand, allowing one's name, likeness and ideas to be used as symbols, and on the other developing a personality cult around carefully crafted imagery to maintain absolute power. It is certainly the case, however, that in making Nehru the centre of their electoral campaigns in the 1950s and 1960s, the Congress Party prepared the ground for the propagation of the myth of Nehru as the architect of independent India.

From Nehru to Nehruvian

Because Nehru's personal stature has been inflated, the ideals believed to define the first two decades after independence are strongly identified with the first prime minister. Thus the neologism 'Nehruvian' has made it into the reference work *Key Concepts in Modern Indian Studies*. Srirupa Roy, the author of the entry, has crafted a definition that contains all the caveats and qualifiers one expects of rigorous scholarship. She is careful to assert that 'the notion of a singular immutable Nehruvian ideology is [. . .] largely ahistorical'. Nonetheless, her definition includes 'secularism', 'a centrally planned "command" or *dirigiste* economy with an emphasis on heavy industrial growth', 'state-led social and cultural modernization', 'developmentalism', 'a demonstrable fascination with scientific and technological accomplishments and artefacts' and 'a non-aligned foreign policy'.[66] The definition comes close to pinning all of the myths of Nehru's India which this book seeks to critically explore. Each of these ideas became a 'tenet' of the Nehruvian consensus in its own way, and their path to achieving the status of myth is charted here in the chapters that follow.

For now, it is important to record that in the more measured of the assessments that appeared in the weeks and months after Nehru's death, there is one surprising absence: there was no consensus as to the ideals he stood for, nor on the extent to which he had been able to transform the nation according to his own blueprint. This was in no small part down to the fact that while he was prime minister, Nehru avoided jingoistic slogans and aphoristic definitions, saying that such things 'come in the way of clear thinking'.[67] It should surprise us, therefore, that he is so strongly associated with a series of abstract nouns—non-alignment, secularism, socialism, modernisation, democracy—which are said to amount to the Nehruvian consensus.

Each of the features of what came to be known as the Nehruvian consensus was ill-defined, if not disputed, at the time of his death. Take foreign policy. In eulogising him, many stressed Nehru's earnest desire for peace and his abhorrence of nuclear weapons. But non-alignment was often not the central feature of the way his foreign policy was understood at the time of his death. Some even implied that non-alignment was no more than rhetoric. When Harold Wilson, the leader of the opposition Labour party in the UK, was approached for a comment on Nehru's death, his highest praise included the assertion that Nehru's India was on the Anglo-American side in the Cold War: 'He adopted a neutralist posture [. . .] but when the chips were down we could see where his loyalties lay[.]'[68] V. B. Karnik, trade-unionist and founding member of the anti-communist Indian Committee for Cultural Freedom, drew the opposite conclusion in his postmortem on Nehru's foreign policy: 'Nehru's non-alignment [. . .] was not non-aligned in the real sense [. . .]. It was more non-aligned against the West and less non-aligned in the case of Russia and other Communist powers.'[69]

The case of secularism was no clearer. *The New York Times* declared that 'Mr Nehru, although of Hindu heritage, considered himself an agnostic'.[70] But on the first anniversary of his death, Sarvepalli Radhakrishnan, the president of the Republic of India, remembered Nehru as a 'deeply spiritual man though he did not uphold any particular form of religion'. Radhakrishnan noted that Nehru 'deeply distrusted all absolute philosophies and dogmas' but he went on to claim that the man had 'worked for the spread of [. . .] a liberal, spiritual religion among the people of India'.[71] Whereas there was room for more than one opinion on his personal faith, many agreed that Nehru's secularism had not taken firm root in the rest of the country. As the president mourned Nehru on All India Radio on the day of his death, he conceded that Indians had been unable to live up to

Nehru's ideal of non-communal politics.[72] Many others wrote of the 'gulf between principles and practice' in India's secularism.[73] This is a mirror image of the late twentieth-century version of Nehru, who was widely considered to be personally atheistic, but successful in securing hegemony for his version of secularism in the country.[74] By the twenty-first century, the consensus would have shifted yet again.

On socialism, views were equally diverse. Upon reporting his death *The Wall Street Journal* may have deemed Nehru to have been a 'doctrinaire socialist',[75] but closer to home the verdict was more ambiguous. In his first address to the nation on the death of their leader, the word socialism did not pass Sarvepalli Radhakrishnan's lips. Instead the president extolled Nehru's 'steadfast loyalty to certain fundamental principles of liberalism'.[76] A postmortem review of Nehru's ideas in a special number of *The Economic Weekly* included a chorus of voices which concluded that the socialism Nehru pursued was 'curbed',[77] or perhaps most damningly, nothing more than 'a rather weak and hollow reed in which one can blow almost any kind of music'.[78] Many agreed, however, that capitalism and capitalists not only remained in India, even as it pursued a socialistic pattern of society, but were in a stronger position than they had been at independence.[79]

The verdict on democracy and the state was also surprisingly mixed. Nehru was universally praised for not just adhering to parliamentary procedure, but for elevating India's Lok Sabha by taking its role in debating policy seriously. At the same time, most people acknowledged that democratic governance went beyond elections and parliamentary procedures; it was also about the functioning of the bureaucracy, and the establishment of institutions that served the will of the people. On this plane of democratic governance, Nehru's contemporaries were split as to his achievements. Sarvepalli Radhakrishnan argued that Nehru 'used the existing social and political institutions and breathed into them a new spirit, a new vitality'.[80] In his biography of Nehru, which is otherwise full of praise for him, the Communist Party leader Hiren Mukerjee noted that the prime minister had done little to curb corruption at the highest levels.[81] Rajni Kothari, writing outside the genre of eulogy, praised Nehru and his governments for overseeing 'the maturing of the nation's institutional growth', from the party system and parliament, down to village-level institutions.[82] Others, however, were not so generous. An unsigned assessment in the same special number of *The Economic Weekly* in which Kothari extolled Nehru's institutional achievements claimed that during the Nehru years, 'the administration underwent practically no change [. . .] and became, if anything more rigid and impervious to the [...] aspirations of the people'.[83]

When it comes to modernisation, in the twenty-first century Nehru is strongly associated with an authoritarian high modernism that took the form of steel plants and mammoth concrete dams, and his vision for India's future is most often contrasted with that of Gandhi, who imagined a future of village republics. At the time of his death, however, those who knew Nehru best, including his daughter, resisted calls for memorials to him to be built in 'iron and concrete'.[84] Some commentators observed a split between Gandhi's ideas and Nehru's.[85] Radhakrishnan, by contrast, emphasised the ways in which Nehru 'was trying to put into practice all the great ideals which Mahatmaji taught us'.[86] There are only scattered hints of the so-called Nehru–Gandhi divide that dominates the thinking of scholars today about what visions for India's future were articulated in the first decades after independence.[87]

If there was no agreement on what Nehru stood for or what he had achieved, what are we to make of the idea of the Nehruvian consensus? This notion owes a great deal to Rajni Kothari, India's foremost political scientist for decades after independence. Kothari, having taken his BSc at the London School of Economics, had founded the Centre of Developing Studies in 1963. The Centre became the place to study Indian politics, and Kothari's influence on the nation's intellectual elite and its understanding of India was profound. Writing in *The Economic Weekly* just weeks after the first prime minister's death, Kothari argued that Nehru's greatest gift to India was 'the development of a national consensus'. At this point, however, Kothari argued that the consensus that Nehru brought about was not in the realm of ideas, but rather in the sphere of political conduct. Leading by example, Nehru had brought about a 'pragmatic orientation' of politics, channelling it away from theatrics driven by transcendental nationalism, and towards the management of people and institutions guided by self-interest. This practical politics fostered a culture of accommodation and flexibility and was marked by the ability 'to hold the temper of political struggle low'.[88] Kothari was describing a way of managing conflicting ideas, not a state of unanimity about the ideas themselves. By the end of the 1960s, however, as new national problems and new political competition had opened up a new sense of uncertainty in the country, Kothari had added the idea of an 'ideological consensus' to his analysis of the Nehru years.[89] With each new crisis, the sense that the past was a more coherent and harmonious place has grown.[90]

Within two decades of his death, the nuanced and contradictory reviews of the Nehru years had been largely forgotten. Let us circle back to the film *Nehru*. The third part of the film is called simply, 'Freedom', and it tells the story of India between 1947 and 1964 in less than an hour. The film covers Nehru's opinions on peace and war, the treatment of minorities, foreign policy, parliamentary democracy, development and modernisation. By playing Nehru's words over pictures of dams flowing and scientific laboratories being opened, the film abolishes the often yawning gap between intention and implementation. By flipping rapidly between scenes of Nehru greeting cheering fans, inspecting nuclear plants, and meeting international leaders, it overcomes the limits which constrained the real Nehru from achieving everything he hoped.

The craftiest trick of the film, however, is reserved for the finale. It ends with the words from Nehru's last will and testament, in which he expressed his wish that the major portion of his ashes be taken high in an aeroplane and scattered 'over the fields where the peasants of India toil so that they might mingle with the dust and soil of India and become an indistinguishable part of India'. While we listen to his last wish, we watch his daughter and his sister carrying it out. His request was a humble acknowledgement of his own relative insignificance. But the effect of the film is the opposite: India becomes indistinguishable from Nehru.

Nehru as the architect of independent India was never more than a myth. With this in mind, the remaining chapters re-examine one by one the tenets of Nehruvianism: non-alignment, secularism, socialism, the strong state, democracy and modernism. They not only reassess each of these aspects of postcolonial Indian life, but also bring to light how these abstract nouns have become myths about the Nehru era, and explore why these have been so enduring in the years since Nehru's death. Readers more familiar with the period will find that the man himself is not prominent in the rest of the book. Nehru was aware, at least in outline, of most of the issues that will be discussed here, and yes, he often had opinions on these matters. But in the chapters that follow, I have chosen not to fetishise Nehru's own words. Moving attention away from the myth of Nehru the architect has often meant choosing to avoid quoting the man himself, and privileging other people, institutions and structures instead. I would like to think that he would not mind being, to use his own phrase, pulled down a peg or two in this way.

CHAPTER TWO

The Myth of India's Non-Aligned Foreign Policy

IN JANUARY 1957, THE city of Bombay played host to a Festival of Soviet Films. From around 1950, Soviet film festivals had become a feature of metropolitan Indian life. For each festival, an organising committee, comprised of 'prominent representatives of the Indian industry', previewed available Soviet films and chose six to screen to audiences over a week or two.[1] In 1957, six representatives of the Soviet film industry arrived in Bombay to participate in the Festival. They included Igor Rachuk, assistant head of the cinema department of the Soviet Ministry of Culture and a noted cinematographer, as well as the young actress Olga Zabotkina.[2] The six were treated to a reception at Bombay's Regal Theatre, where they were garlanded by three of the biggest Indian film actresses of the day, Durga Khote, Nargis and Kamini Kaushal.[3] At the end of the festival, P. M. Lad, secretary of the Ministry of Information and Broadcasting, presented the six visitors with 'souvenirs' and told them he hoped there would be 'many more such occasions for strengthening the cultural links between the two countries'.[4] Two of the Soviet films screened during the festival, *Othello* and *Twelfth Night*, were dubbed into English, but the others, including one with the very Soviet title *Pedagogical Poem (Road to Life)*, were shown with English subtitles only. That same week, without any official fanfare, MGM's *Bhowani Junction*, starring Ava Gardner and Stewart Granger entered its fifth week at Bombay's Metro Theatre, while Warner Bros' *Dial M for Murder*, featuring Grace Kelly and Ray Milland, hit its sixth week at the Excelsior theatre.[5]

The contrast between the assiduousness with which Indian officials courted the Soviet film delegation and the popularity of American films provides a window into the dynamics of the Cold War in India, and helps us come to grips with the reality of India's non-aligned approach to the superpowers. While half a dozen Soviet films might feature in special festivals, American studios sent roughly two hundred films to India each year between 1947 and 1964.[6] This was at a time when Indian studios were themselves producing only around three hundred films each year.[7] While their share of the Indian market was itself tiny, at around 3 per cent of Indian audiences, American films dwarfed Soviet ones in India.[8] Not just in film, but in nearly every aspect of India's economic, cultural and political life, countries from the western bloc had a greater presence in India than did those of the Soviet bloc, as this chapter will detail. Because their country had been carved from the British Empire, Indians inherited a system that was already enmeshed in the Anglo-American economic and cultural world. When the Government of India courted the Soviets, whether to screen films or deliver fighter jets, they were not balancing the scales of influence, at least not in any real material sense. Rather, they were conjuring the idea that India was not beholden to the western bloc, that it was non-aligned.

This myth, like most of the others discussed here, is built upon the foundation of Nehru as the architect of independent India. While the best historians acknowledge that Nehru worked with ambassadors and envoys, it is in the field of international affairs that one most frequently finds the effortless substitution of Nehru for India in the scholarship.[9] Like the other supposed tenets of the Nehruvian era, India's non-alignment was never defined or elaborated into a credo. Nehru, acting as both prime minister and minister for external affairs, declared early in the Cold War that India would 'avoid these foreign entanglements of joining one bloc or the other',[10] but did not develop this into a coherent doctrine.

In the absence of a fully worked out ideology, non-alignment became shorthand for the policy of not being drawn into either of the two power blocs that attempted to dominate the international landscape during the Cold War.[11] On the one hand, after the Second World War, the United States systematically persuaded groups of states to form collective security arrangements with the aim of fighting communism. Meanwhile, the communist states of eastern Europe were corralled into the Warsaw Pact. As the states of Africa and Asia slowly gained their freedom from European imperial powers, they became battlegrounds of the Cold War.[12] Non-alignment has been described as an idea that helped India in these circumstances to 'retain the ability'—recently gained by achieving independence—'to make relatively autonomous decisions' in international affairs.[13] For its advocates, non-alignment was also an attempt to develop a collective vision for an alternative world order. Insofar as it took any real shape, this 'active neutrality'[14] coalesced relatively late in our period, as Nehru, Gamal Abdel Nasser and Josip Broz Tito met to establish the Non-Aligned Movement in 1961. India's foreign policy, nonetheless, has long been tidily encapsulated in the term 'non-alignment'.

India's foreign policy was both more complex and more expansive than non-alignment, however. This has been ignored by non-specialists for a number of reasons. Firstly, because Cold War neutrality was a posture adopted towards both the Soviet Union and the United States, western scholars and lay people outside India have been able conveniently to sum up the role of a country that was, in their understanding of the 1950s and 1960s, a marginal player, by resort to the simple idea of non-alignment. This tendency has only been reinforced by the sources available to scholars. For the Indian perspective, scholars long had to conduct their research without access to files from the Ministry of External Affairs. In the absence of any detailed understanding of India's priorities and approaches, scholars have been left to work primarily with public pronouncements. No country's foreign policy can be understood simply by looking at what its leaders said in public; and yet for a long time Nehru's words were the basis of much scholarship in this field.

A second aspect of the problem of sources is that, without full access to files from India's Ministry of External Affairs, historians long had to rely on material from the US archives. It is almost impossible to exaggerate the prevalence of Cold War paranoia in American thinking about the world in the 1950s and 1960s. Fear drove US officials to imagine the effects of neutralism among newly independent states in catastrophic terms. Relying on US records, historians have tended to transpose the obsessions of American policymakers onto the minds of Indians. In so doing, they have inflated the importance of the Cold War in Indian foreign policy. They have also mistaken the rhetoric of non-alignment for reality.

The concept of non-alignment simply cannot contain, like a tidy box, all of India's ideas about and interactions with the world. To develop a more wholistic understanding of Indian foreign policy, it is important to bear in mind that it was conceived and implemented by dozens of men and women posted across six continents. As minister for external affairs, Nehru chose the country's first ambassadors on the basis of their eminent status in the national movement, as well as that of their wit, charm and intellectual abilities. Acting as patron, he regarded these freedom fighters, lawyers, writers and philosophers as confidants and interlocutors, not as his subordinates. They reciprocated his patronage by taking their own initiatives, often without cabling home for instructions. Joining these public figures was a host of career civil servants in the newly formed Indian Foreign Service. Historians have characterised these professional diplomats as more realist and professional than Nehru's comrades, at whose freewheeling diplomacy they are said to have bristled. Back in New Delhi, the prime minister appeared to value the frequent disagreements he had with his civil servants, and the Indian Foreign Service gradually evolved to become more independent of him.[15]

This made India's foreign policy somewhat messy and sometimes disorganised, but it was not completely devoid of coherence. Indeed, early independent India's approach to the world as a whole can best be understood as post-imperial.[16] This descriptor has a number of dimensions. In the most basic sense, India's foreign policy was post-imperial because India itself was emerging from an imperial form: its borders were ill-defined, its responsibilities were spread across far-flung spaces, and it was still in the process of becoming a nation. The international system and its constituent parts are in a constant state of becoming, and the period between the 1940s and the 1960s witnessed a 'process of struggle between entrenched formations and new forces'.[17] As part of this struggle, India grappled with its post-imperial problems by working to usher in a new international order, as Raphaëlle Khan has shown.[18] In addition, Indian foreign policy was post-imperial in a second, normative, sense: India sought to bring about the end of imperialism and its attendant cultural and economic systems. To this end, India articulated a set of norms and then worked to try to get them universally adopted. Derived from the country's experience of colonialism, these norms included racial justice, adherence to the will of peoples and the pursuit of international peace. The means to these ends included cooperation, friendship and transparency.

Having just emerged from the anti-colonial movement, India's foreign policy was also unusually concerned with people. The lessons of the struggle for independence had been that solidarity between people could be nurtured and then deployed in revolutionary ways, but also that the interests of minorities had to be protected. On the international level, this translated into support for independence movements, but with a distinction between peoples who could themselves become independent nations, and those who had to be protected as minorities within a larger nation. Attention to people meant concern for identifying the will of populations, but also courting the people's favour, to secure their loyalty. It also entailed pinning down populations, through passport and visa regimes, restrictions on movement and repression of those who did not display the 'right' loyalties.

India was born into a world where the borders between empire, the international and the nation-state were remarkably uncertain; where peoples and governments sought clarity, but rarely on the same terms. It is for this reason that India's approach to overseas Indians, Kashmir, Arunachal Pradesh and Nagaland are included in this chapter. I am not taking a position on the righteousness of India's claim to any disputed territory. Rather, because they existed in the fuzzy margins of an India disentangling itself from an empire, these issues and territories reveal the dynamics at play in the formation of both the national and the international.

Beginning with India's relations with the superpowers, the first section of this chapter uncovers the depth of India's entanglement with the Anglo-American world. Non-alignment was at most an ambition, which gave India some tactical advantages in limited circumstances. But if non-alignment was not the central principle, how are we to characterise India's foreign policy? Exploring the rhetoric of freedom-fighters turned emissaries, the second section outlines the principles that underpinned their admittedly uncoordinated action on the international level. The second half of the chapter traces how India's post-imperial internationalism operated through different spheres of policy, from the global level through to its relations with overseas Indians, and its struggles with its neighbours.

India and the Superpowers

By virtue of the fact that it was born out of the British Empire, and the British had become closer to the Americans in the first half of the twentieth century, India arrived on the international stage already embedded in the Anglo-American system. From military ties to trade and aid, India had already existing relationships with Britain, the US and western Europe, which only deepened in the ensuing period. Nehru's regular public proclamations of non-alignment and his willingness to criticise them irked the Americans, but many of India's first envoys to the US and the UK worked generally to strengthen Indian ties with both countries.[19] This meant building upon existing relationships and personal connections.

India did not join any of the large military alliances of the Cold War era, but its armed forces remained tied to the west, especially to Britain. This was particularly true with regard to the top brass of the Indian military. The Indian army got its first Indian commander-in-chief, K. M. Cariappa, in 1949, and the highest-ranking officer in the Indian air force was replaced by an Indian in 1950, but in the Indian navy, the highest post was held by British men until Vice-Admiral Ram Dass Katari became the first Indian chief of the naval staff in 1958. The navy bought all its larger ships from the British, often at preferential rates, all the way through the Nehru years.[20] While the rest of the military was not as dependent upon the British, nearly all of India's military cooperation faced westward. Certainly, the Soviets presented India with two transport aircraft in 1955, and India bought a handful more, along with ten Soviet helicopters in 1960. But in the fifteen years after independence, India bought 214 combat aircraft from the French and fifty-five from the US, as well as 262 from the British, with another 230 manufactured in India under licence from the UK. By the time of the Sino-Indian war in 1962, all of India's tanks were manufactured by either the British or the French. The rest of its defence procurement, from guns to clothing, was licensed for production in the UK, France, the US or Sweden. In 1962, India made its first substantial purchase from the Soviets of equipment that could be used directly for war when it agreed to buy just twelve MiG-21 aircraft. The first of the MiGs were only delivered in the early part of 1964.[21]

The material entanglement of India with the Anglo-American system is equally evident when it comes to trade, where the US and the UK continued to be India's largest partners throughout the Nehru era. Britain's trading relationship with the subcontinent dated to the seventeenth century, and the two had extensive links. After independence, India remained tied to the imperial trading system by the 'sterling balances'—the £1.3 billion debt Britain had accrued to India during the Second World War. Sterling's convertibility remained limited, meaning, in effect, that to use its money, India had to trade with Britain and the Commonwealth until 1956, when the balances were finally wound down.[22] These and other historical private business ties ensured that Britain remained India's second largest trading partner.

Independent India's largest trading partner, however, was the United States. Links between the US and India had expanded rapidly in the first half of the twentieth century. During the First World War, as shipping from Britain had been disrupted, the US surpassed the UK to become the top importer to India, supplying consumer goods to India's tiny but growing middle classes. The developing relationship was not completely one-sided, as the US relied on Indian exports of manganese for its steel production, and later of monazite, which was essential for atomic energy.[23] Still, by 1951 46.5 per cent of all imports to India came from the US, while

Britain provided 20 per cent. In other words, two-thirds of all foreign goods entering India came from these two countries alone.[24] While their relative share of imports varied, the two remained the top importers to India through the Nehru years.[25] The UK was India's top export partner, meanwhile, receiving roughly 26.5 per cent of exports, and the US was second, with 16.3 per cent of the market.

After the US and UK came the Federal Republic of Germany. India and West Germany seemed to find each other at just the right time. After the war, India was trying to industrialise, and West Germany's post-war recovery plan focused on exports of capital goods. In 1957, for example, fully 88 per cent of capital goods required for iron and steel works to be built under the second five-year plan were purchased from the Federal Republic.[26] Regarding exports, the picture is not markedly different: India was the second largest exporter to West Germany in the 1950s.[27]

Whilst antagonism to the presence of British businesses in India had been one of the cornerstones of the Indian independence movement, postcolonial India was cautiously receptive to foreign direct investment. Early proposals to expropriate large parts of the industrial landscape were quickly dropped, and plans for nationalisation were limited, as will be discussed in chapter 4. Anti-business sentiment was channelled into more aggressive legislation against management agencies, the businesses at the heart of the imperial relationship.[28] For the rest, India was more welcoming than is often acknowledged. Although the Lok Sabha had passed legislation limiting foreign ownership to 49 per cent of any joint venture, in practice this requirement was sometimes quietly circumvented.[29] British firms continued to prosper in India. In 1957, UK firms accounted for 80 per cent of foreign investment in the country, mostly in older industries such as jute, tea, banking and managing agencies.[30] India also opened, cautiously, to the US. It signed the American Investment Guarantee Agreement, permitting firms to repatriate profits to the US rather than requiring them to reinvest in India.[31]

Building on existing relationships, the value of foreign investment in India more than doubled in the first decade after independence, reaching £425 million in 1958.[32] German companies initiated a number of partnerships with Indian firms in the 1950s. In 1954, for example, Tata and Mercedes-Benz began making lorries in a joint venture at Jamshedpur; around the same time, Bosch reached an arrangement with 49 per cent ownership of Motor Industries Co. Ltd of Bangalore.[33] During the Second World War, American firms had engaged in joint ventures in businesses ranging from automobiles to electrical equipment. After independence,

American companies producing in India made everything from pharmaceuticals to Coca-Cola, which opened its first bottling plant in Delhi in October 1950, and one in Bombay six months later.[34]

By contrast, the Soviet Union's trade and business links with India at independence were negligible. Trade between the two countries seems to have begun during the food crisis that gripped the new nation in the five years after independence. In 1949, the Soviets agreed to a barter deal by which they supplied wheat in exchange for Indian jute, tea and castor oil.[35] As bilateral relations began to expand gingerly, India and the Soviet Union signed three five-year trade agreements between 1953 and 1964.[36] By the time of Nehru's death, however, the Soviet Union still provided less than 10 per cent of India's imports, with an even smaller percentage of India's exports going to the USSR.[37] Recent historiography has shown that the Soviets were more enmeshed in the Anglo-American economic system than had previously been recognised.[38] In other words, India was born into the Anglo-American economic system, and there was no real alternative to it.

Trade and business partnerships were not the only aspect of economic relations. Aid too was important. Some scholars of India's Cold War assume that Pakistan received American aid and bought American weapons, while India tilted towards the Soviets.[39] Others have argued that the superpowers competed in India, virtually on equal terms.[40] The numbers simply do not bear either argument out. Western aid dwarfed Soviet bloc aid to India throughout the Nehru era. During the first three plans, India's number one donor was the United States. In addition, India drew on loans from the Commonwealth's Colombo Plan and from the International Bank of Reconstruction and Development. India's donors also included smaller western powers, from Italy to Japan.[41] These were not minor players: all the way through the third plan (1961–66), India received more aid from West Germany than from the Soviet Union.[42] No communist equivalent of West Germany, Japan or Italy emerged to take part in the contest over aid-giving. To focus once more on the superpowers alone, by 1965, the United States had given a total of $6.3 billion in aid to India, while the Soviet Union had provided the equivalent of just over $1 billion.[43] Pakistan, as it turns out, received from the US just under half of what India received in the same period.[44]

Aid was not simply about flows of money; it was about experts and advice. Here, too, the western specialists had a head start. Indian private firms had been drawing on American expertise for decades. For example, from the early twentieth century, Tata Iron and Steel Company (TISCO) had employed managers from the US in its foundries in Jamshedpur.[45] During the Second World War, American experts had followed in the wake of the more than one hundred thousand American troops that were stationed on the subcontinent. By the end of the conflict, American individuals and firms had been hired to consult on everything from rural development to urban planning. Some of their contributions are assessed in chapter 7.

Whereas the capitalist bloc had people on the ground before India had even obtained independence, the communists were late to the game. Although there were some tentative moves towards greater contact in the early 1950s, it was not until after the death of Stalin that any substantive links between India and the Soviet Union were established. Even these were primarily diplomatic and cultural spectacles. Thus, during 1955, Nehru and Khrushchev swapped visits, and the two countries exchanged a dozen or more delegations, ranging from statisticians to volleyball players.[46] The Soviet football team undertook a lengthy tour of India in early 1955. In its six-week tour, it defeated Indian teams in every one of the nineteen games they played, scoring one hundred goals, and conceding only four.[47] When the Indian squad toured Russia later in the year, journalists reported that they had 'won the hearts' of the spectators, even as they had lost their games.[48]

While the Soviets taught the Indians a lesson on the pitch, the interactions had a different dynamic in the economic sphere. Indian planners were certainly interested in understanding how communist economies operated. Indian delegations travelled to the Soviet Union and Soviet bloc countries to study their approach to agriculture in 1954, and in the early 1960s, delegations went to look into Soviet education and textile production. On the whole, however, Indians tended to conclude that communist methods were not suited to Indian conditions.[49]

Does all of this add up to an alignment in the Cold War? Let us look at the situation in reverse. Arms sales, military advisors, aid—when a developing country accepted these things from the Soviet Union, American policymakers were quick to assert that the country had 'turned' to the Soviets. If we apply the same standard in reverse, it is difficult not to conclude that India was aligned with the western bloc through the first two decades of the Cold War. Indeed, histories of other neutral countries, such as Sweden, have come to similar conclusions.[50] The US remained anxious about India's rhetoric of non-alignment, and unhappy with its willingness to question American policies and engage with other partners. The Americans were in fact unwilling to countenance any posture short of full-throated allegiance, and India refused to make such a public declaration of its intentions. However, this cannot be allowed to obscure the military, economic and cultural ties between India and the capitalist bloc, which were not only deep and complex, but continued to grow during this period.

If India was born into the American-dominated system, what purpose did its repeated proclamations of non-alignment serve? They created the impression, especially among the American foreign policy establishment, that India was always on the verge of defecting to the Soviet side.[51] India's diplomats used this to work the superpower competition to their country's advantage.[52] A mere hint that India might be interested in purchasing arms from the Soviets was enough to send the British or Americans running to offer discounts on their own.[53] When the West Germans agreed to build a steel mill at Rourkela, the Soviets came tumbling after, promising to get the Bhilai steel mill up and running before the German-sponsored furnaces at Rourkela started firing.[54] Claims of non-alignment also helped to manoeuvre India into a situation where it was not overly dependent upon a single country for any of its needs. The rhetoric of non-alignment also made India's overtures of friendship or offers to broker peace in the international sphere genuine and unconditional. For a domestic audience, the language of non-alignment provided reassurance that India was not submitting to a new imperial relationship.

Non-alignment had multiple dimensions: it involved not only reserving the right to make independent judgements on world affairs, but also creating capacity for India to act independently of the great powers.[55] While the country certainly asserted its right to have its own view on the conflicts of the day, its strategic freedom of action was curtailed by its deep entanglement with the Anglo-American bloc. However, non-alignment is not all there was to Indian foreign policy. Unable to disentangle itself from the Anglo-American bloc, India focused its efforts on transforming the wider international field.

India's Post-Imperial Internationalism in Theory

Rather than defining their entire foreign policy around the Cold War, Indian leaders and diplomats articulated a set of aims, standards of conduct and working practices for international society. These were primarily concerned with winding up imperialism and its legacies, and so can be called India's post-imperial internationalism.[56] Just as the mid-century universalisms espoused by the US or the USSR equated western-derived norms with global values, India's foreign policy leaders developed an internationalism that was equally rooted in self-interest and the ideals of the Indian national movement. Indeed, India's assertion of the right to define universal norms was part of its post-imperial claim to equality.

India's representatives abroad were a mix of civil servants and eminent figures of the freedom movement. While the former tended to be pragmatic, the latter, having come up together through the fight against British rule, shared a reasonably consistent set of ambitions and norms. While all of these emissaries acted as 'India' when posted abroad, they rarely produced a unified foreign policy. This section discusses the shared goals, approaches and ethics that tended to underpin the actions of India's freedom-fighters turned diplomats across the world. The following sections, which examine the post-imperial problems India faced on the international plane, peel back the layers to show that reasonably consistent objectives and principles did not always produce coherent policy.

The goals of India's foreign policy in this period revolved around unwinding imperialism and its legacies. As one Congress spokesman put it in 1951, 'imperialism is the breeding ground of many of the evils the world is suffering from and [. . .] only the destruction of the imperialistic ideology can create a brave new world.'[57] This objective comprised not only self-determination for colonised people, but opposition to racialism in all forms. To this end, India used international fora to speak on behalf of colonised peoples, to demand their concerns be heard, and to lobby for their independence. In so doing, India helped transform the UN from an organisation that seemed destined to preserve the imperial status quo into a force for decolonisation.[58] At the same time, India insisted that not every people could form a nation-state. Freedom, therefore, would have to include protection for minorities, in part through the international recognition of their human rights. Elevating the fight to ensure the security of minorities to the international plane helped India make the case to protect non-Muslims in Pakistan and overseas Indians across the world, as well as Tibetans in China, as we will see below.

A second major foreign policy aim of India's was the pursuit of international peace. Non-alignment, as a critique of the Cold War system of security, was a means to this broader aim.[59] Peace was a *sine qua non* in the struggle for true independence, as M. C. Setalvad, soon to be India's first attorney-general, told an India-America Conference in December 1949: 'Apart from the rejection of war on moral and utilitarian grounds, a long period of peace and stability is essential to India for [. . .] economic development.'[60] When a dispute did not involve India, its diplomats nonetheless poked their noses in, offering their services for conciliation, and proposing alternative solutions. The most common metaphor heard at this time was that India wished to act as a bridge: a bridge between the two sides in the Cold War or between the warring parties in Korea.[61] And yet, India had a modest conception of peace: the emphasis was on creating stability for people rather than on settling disputes altogether.[62]

The means were as important as the ends. At the heart of Indian internationalism was a recognition that the world was in a state of flux, that there were complex uncertainties and deep inequalities that had to be resolved. Problems were often too large to be solved by a single country, especially for those countries with limited resources.[63] International collaboration was essential, and the basis of such cooperation could only be friendly relations between states and between peoples. Friendship has a long history in international affairs, dating at least to ancient Greek treaties of *philia*,[64] but Indian representatives tried to add new depth and breadth to the term. Friendship was both a manner of working and a working objective. The roots of this ideal were struck in India's anti-colonial campaigns. The idea of *ahimsa* had been central to the goal of *swaraj* (self-rule). *Ahimsa* is often translated as 'non-violence', but if it is understood instead as 'neighbourliness', as Ajay Skaria glosses the term, this gives us insight into the normative content of the notion.[65] *Ahimsa* meant working as equals, even with adversaries, on the basis of friendship. No matter what their differences of opinion, appropriate conduct meant treating adversaries as friends.[66]

Cultivating friendship and securing peace applied to peoples as much as to countries. Scholars of Indian foreign policy have not paid sufficient attention to what Nehru often called the 'human dimension' of problems and their solutions. The chairman of the Indian delegation to the first session of the UN General Assembly, Sir Ramaswami Mudaliar, explained: 'Wars are but the outward result of something far deeper, a malady [. . .] that spreads out of economic maladjustment and of [. . .] social injustice.'[67] To replace this maladjustment with friendship between peoples, Indian representatives tended to attach importance to public parades and speeches, as well as to exchanges of students, sports teams and experts. Equally, India's approach to its many border conflicts tended to be characterised by relative patience on the larger questions of borders, coupled with assiduous attention to people. This included securing their loyalty through the provision of roads, schools, healthcare and other developmental projects. Creating certainty around people also meant protecting minorities, evolving a passport regime and enforcing it, as well as policing political expression and imprisoning dissenters. Securing people and providing security for people often complicated Indian foreign policy, as the sections below will detail.

If friendship was to be secured, the international order had to be based on transparent rules, applicable to all. As Asaf Ali, India's first ambassador to the US explained, 'real justice depends on universally accepted axioms and sanctions.'[68] These rules were best elaborated through international organisations such as the United Nations.[69] International law also included the idea of reciprocity. As much as India tried to set the rules of the game, if another state refused to adhere to them or altered the playing field, India adapted accordingly. Thus, the use of force was not out of the question.[70] India's policymakers met and matched forces with their rivals in Pakistan and China, sometimes successfully, sometimes woefully, but always on the basis that the rules of international order allowed India to respond to force with force.

It helps to think of India's foreign policy as being drawn in imperfect, unstable, overlapping circles. Doing so underlines the extent to which India itself is an entity always in the process of formation and re-creation; this was particularly so in the decades after independence. The widest circle embraced the whole world, and especially the institutions designed to rebuild the international order after the Second World War. The next circle might be called the Indo-sphere: it encompassed those parts of the contemporary and former British Empire where large numbers of overseas Indians resided. In this circle, the concern to fulfil the country's moral obligations to the children of India dovetailed with its wider pursuit of racial justice. The next circle could be drawn around India's neighbours, including China, where securing people was as important as defining borders. The final circle contained India and Pakistan. Together and separately, India and Pakistan had not only to create and define their respective territories, citizens and economies, but to work to make their separateness a lived reality. The following sections sketch India's foreign policy in each of these spheres, focusing on the dynamic interplay between the practical challenges it faced and India's vision of international order.

The Theory in Action

THE INTERNATIONAL SPHERE

Working on the largest possible international canvas was attractive to many of independent India's elites, firstly because India's problems, from colonial occupation to the treatment of Indian workers around the world, were issues which required international solutions. India's post-imperial foreign policy had begun to take shape between the wars, when the country had secured membership of the League of Nations. There, Indian representatives contributed to work on the abolition of slavery, human trafficking and the opium trade, and used the International Labour Organisation to raise concerns relevant to Indians worldwide. The relationship was not one-sided: research conducted in India informed the League's emerging health and sanitation policies,[71] while India sought the League's advice for its economic planning.[72] As the Second World War drew to a close and the shape of the post-war international order became the subject of international dialogue, India set out to shape the conversation. It had a vision of 'One World', and sought to mould the new United Nations Organization to this end. At San Francisco, India had an official delegation appointed by the British and led by experienced civil servants, as well as a non-official, Congress-led delegation, headed by Nehru's sister Vijaya Lakshmi Pandit. Pandit called for the end of imperialism, and made the case that racialism was a violation of human rights.[73] India also sent a delegation to Bretton Woods, where it pressed for the charter of the IBRD to mention less-developed countries, and for staff from all regions to be represented in the World Bank.[74]

India seemed to seek a leadership role on as many UN bodies as possible. Hansa Mehta helped draft the Universal Declaration on Human Rights, and when she departed Kamaladevi Chattopadhyay took her place. Ramaswami Mudaliar, whom we met above at the first session of the UN General Assembly, and Palamadai S. Lokanathan were respectively the first president of the Economic and Social Council (ECOSOC), and the first executive secretary of the Economic and Social Commission for Asia and the Far East. Rajkumari Amrit Kaur represented India as a founding member of the World Health Organisation, and the physicist Homi J. Bhabha presided over the first UN conference on peaceful uses of atomic energy. Indians also populated the rank and file of the UN's operations. Indian experts occupied eighty-four out of 136 places in the UN Technical Administration by 1952. These men and women advised governments from Lebanon to the Philippines on everything from cooperatives and malaria control to training civil servants and radio operators.[75] India has also been the largest single contributor of soldiers to UN peacekeeping missions. Indians did not only take orders, but shaped how these missions were commanded. Indar Jit Rikhye, as chief of staff to the commander of the UN Emergency Force (UNEF I) streamlined the force's command structure in a way that became standard practice.[76] Indian representatives were a constant fixture in the architecture of international life, not only as beneficiaries and foot soldiers, but as chairpersons and experts.

India's engagement with the wider Asian and African world was rooted in the global fight against racism and imperialism. Whilst concerned with the treatment of Indians in other colonies, a main aim of Indian foreign policy was to cultivate respect for and equality with other nations as they stepped into freedom. India brought this aim of fostering a global spirit of friendship to the Bandung Conference. It is now clear that Bandung was not a precursor to the Non-Aligned Movement. Indeed, the twenty-nine states that came to Indonesia in 1955 were split on Cold War questions, and public debate at the conference became polarised along Cold War lines at several points.[77] Instead, what they could agree on was a unified platform of anti-racism and anti-colonialism, and a set of norms for the conduct of international relations.[78] Anti-racism dovetailed perfectly with India's conception of friendship based on equality, while the articulation of rules of conduct was in line with India's desire for transparency and reciprocity in international affairs.

Cultivating friendship was not just a matter of large international conferences like the one at Bandung, but also a question of the activities of Indian emissaries. The most prominent example was Apa Pant. Born in the princely state of Aundh, near Pune, the second son of the raja, Pant studied at the University of Bombay and then at Oxford. Appointed as India's first representative in East Africa, Pant worked to encourage friendship between Indians and Africans in Kenya. Along with his wife Dr Nalini Devi, and his first secretary, A. R. Rehman, Pant used his office, his home and his family to promote this cause: he hosted social gatherings, and he urged Asians to fund-raise for African causes, including education. As he left his post for a role in Sikkim, Pant explained that his work as India's high commissioner for East and Central Africa had involved 'easing the birth pangs of this new nation that is struggling to be born', so that the people of what would eventually become Kenya 'will march forward together, in co-operation and as equals, to establish a new and happy pattern of human relationship'.[79]

THE INDO-SPHERE

India's internationalism called on the nations of the world to cooperate to tackle the legacies of imperialism, including the presence of Indians across the British Empire. South Asians had migrated to every corner of the Empire, taking on different roles in each colony, from indentured labourers to traders and administrators. By the time the British had left the subcontinent, there were an estimated three million overseas Indians residing from Trinidad to Fiji.[80] While Indian pronouncements about these overseas Indians seemed to adhere to the international norm of non-interference in the affairs of other states,[81] beyond the rhetoric the country remained committed to securing their rights and safeguarding their welfare.[82]

India took responsibility for overseas Indians in former British colonies in part because it did not wish to repatriate them to the subcontinent. Urging people of Indian origin to remain abroad was not a new policy in 1947. During an earlier phase of the anti-colonial movement, Indian nationalists had sought to unite Indians across the globe by calling for the repatriation of Indian indentured labourers. After a report in the early 1930s found that returnees had had trouble reintegrating into Indian society, however, nationalists switched to assisting overseas Indians in their campaigns for greater rights in their adopted homes.[83] Independent India stayed this course. Overwhelmed by the arrival of partition refugees, the Government of India was keen to avoid taking on more people who would require rehabilitation. India's official policy, articulated by Nehru as he toured those places where overseas Indians resided, was that 'Indian settlers abroad should identify themselves, as far as possible, with the interests of the nationals of the country of their adoption and really become part and parcel of its national life'.[84] However, Nehru's pronouncements concealed more than they revealed.

India's approach to the treatment of Indians in South Africa quickly transformed into a broader stance against apartheid. When South Africa began, after the Second World War, to institute ever more discriminatory laws against the nearly three hundred thousand Asians who resided there as well as against Black South Africans, India stood against these laws. It took this issue to the UN, where Vijaya Lakshmi Pandit secured a resolution in the 1946 General Assembly against South Africa's discriminatory legislation. In the debates surrounding this first resolution, the outlines of India's early policy were made clear. Madame Pandit declared that India had a 'moral obligation' to Indians who had migrated overseas.[85] At the same time, she made her case on universal lines: 'We believe that peace and freedom are indivisible and the denial of freedom anywhere must lead to conflict and war.'[86] Moving from the particulars of overseas Indians to the principle of non-discrimination enabled India to unite an issue of urgent domestic importance with a post-imperial international principle.

A similar process was at play in relations with neighbouring countries, especially Burma and Ceylon, where newly independent governments took measures to marginalise people of Indian origin and exclude them from citizenship. The Government of India did not dispute the right of its neighbours to define their citizens or control immigration, but it argued that measures to do so should be based on bilateral agreement with India.[87] India elevated its approach beyond the narrowly pragmatic by articulating the principles that should guide any such agreement: first, the will of the people concerned, that is, overseas Indians, ought to be paramount; second, any rules ought to apply to all non-nationals, and should not discriminate against Indians. The Government of India declared that it was only seeking 'equitable and just criteria' for the determination of citizenship for Indians abroad.[88]

Nehru had limited success in his personal endeavours to influence the terms by which Burma and Ceylon defined citizenship. The best that could be managed was an agreement in 1954 with his counterpart in Ceylon, John Kotelawala. Behind the pact, the two reached an informal understanding that each country would consider claims by Ceylon Indians for citizenship and endeavour to approve half of them.[89] Beyond the bilateral talks between the leaders, however, there was a great deal of activity on the ground.

In many cases, the Government of India was pushed to take action by its citizens at home, who, ignoring international norms, argued that 'if Indians are ill-treated because they are Indians, then we must protect them because they are Indians'.[90] At the same time, India's representatives in Ceylon and the ambassador to Burma did not simply repeat the official line and sit on their hands. V. V. Giri, Congressman, trade-unionist and future president of India, was high commissioner for India in Ceylon until 1951. In this role, he attended the annual sessions of the Ceylon Indian Congress (CIC), where, along with other Indian visitors, they hoisted the tricolour and sang 'Vande Mataram'.[91] As late as 1959, the president of India, Rajendra Prasad, visited Ceylon and addressed a gathering of Indians there. Prasad told his audience, 'I request you to do this—nay, as President of India, I order you to do your best to help the country you live in. It is in this way you will help yourselves and your motherland best.'[92] All of this can be understood as the international side of postcolonial nationalism: the feelings of kinship that were cultivated during the anti-colonial campaigns could not be simply forgotten. Indian citizens demanded that their government act on behalf of their kin abroad, while officials sought to redirect those emotional ties to further their international goals.

During the 1950s the Government of India's representatives seemed to expand their support for Indians in Burma and Ceylon, even as the official line, articulated by Nehru, did not change. Indian representatives took up the case when it came to questions of nationality, democratic representation and property. During this period, the governments of Burma and Ceylon took practical measures to encourage Indians to leave, including introducing costly residence permits.[93] Indians were barred from working in certain professions.[94] Interestingly, Indian sweepers, employed in the tens of thousands in each country, were neither forced out nor nationalised.[95] Indian representatives met regularly with resident Indians to discuss these measures. Although the two neighbours' citizenship laws were restrictive, they did not bar Indians entirely. Therefore, the Government of India helped and encouraged Indians to apply for citizenship of Burma and Ceylon. Large numbers of Indians applied for Ceylonese citizenship. When, in spite of the Nehru–Kotelawala Pact, their applications were stalled or rejected in huge quantities, the Government of India took up the matter with its counterpart across the Palk Strait.[96] On the Burmese side, more than a decade after independence, around twelve thousand Biharis, who had moved to Burma to cultivate land at the end of the nineteenth century, had applied neither for Burmese citizenship nor for residence permits. This was not surprising, because the permits cost Rs.50 and had to be renewed regularly. In 1959, India's ambassador to Burma, Lalji Mehrotra, personally visited the Zeyawaddy area of Taungoo District, promised a house-to-house census, and took up the matter with the Government of Burma to ensure that these Bihari migrants were not prosecuted for not having the proper paperwork to live in Burma.[97]

Relations between India and overseas Indians were not limited to questions of nationality. When the Government of Ceylon tried various means of disqualifying Indians from voting, the Ceylon Indian Congress launched a *satyagraha* (non-violent protest) in 1952, to 'secure removal of all discriminatory legislation against the Indian community in Ceylon'. At the same time, the CIC opened its membership to 'all communities irrespective of caste, creed or race'.[98] This deliberately echoed the language of non-discrimination, articulated most prominently by Vijaya Lakshmi Pandit at the UN, in order to garner support from the Government of India. In this case, the Government of Ceylon asked the Government of India to persuade the CIC to halt the satyagraha, but New Delhi replied that the movement ought to be 'treated with sympathy and understanding'.[99]

Finally, under keen pressure from their relations in India, the Government of India represented the interests of overseas Indians when their property rights were curtailed. When the governments of Burma or Ceylon periodically placed restrictions on remittances sent to India, the Government of India almost always took up the cause, noting the detrimental effects such restrictions had on the families of overseas Indians back in India.[100] In the first few months of 1964, after Burma nationalised all privately owned shops, warehouses and brokers in the country without compensation, Indian diplomats were compelled to act. When the Government of Burma restricted the cash and jewellery that people could remove from the country, the Indian embassy in Rangoon took possession of their cash and jewellery, promising to negotiate compensation with the government in Rangoon.[101]

India's approach to the question of overseas Indians was overwhelmingly concerned with providing security for people, and certainty for India about people. In this case the will of the people, overseas Indians, was stressed. Where Indians did not wish to stay abroad, India helped them come home, but this had to be the choice of the people concerned; India would not let them be bullied into leaving a country against their will. Thus, although it worked hard to help Indians remain in Burma, when Indians wished to leave because of the land reforms or the civil war, India helped to bring around twenty thousand of them home.[102] Similarly, after the Nehru–Kotelawala Pact in 1954, India repatriated around twenty-five thousand Indians from Ceylon.[103] And after Nehru's death, his successor as prime minister, Lal Bahadur Shastri, negotiated to bring tens of thousands of Ceylon Indians back to India.[104] At the same time, creating certainty around people also entailed restricting movement, introducing passports and policing borders where few such measures had existed before.[105]

NEIGHBOURS: CHINA

Further from its own borders it was easier to act on the principles of post-imperial internationalism and produce a reasonably coherent policy. India's relationship with China, however, was a perfect storm of post-imperial problems: both countries inherited indistinct imperial borders and the people of these spaces had not yet been fully integrated into either nation. India's troubles with China had three dimensions: bilateral recognition, disputes over borders and the question of minorities. Although it was possible for Nehru and India's diplomats to devise a principled approach to each one, the end result was incoherence and conflict.

India's ultimately troubled relations with China also had their origin in the imperial period. One characteristic of the 'empire-light' form of rule maintained by the British and Qing empires in the Himalayan region was ill-defined borders.[106] The blurry edges where the Qing Empire had met the British one in the high mountains had also been characterised by overlapping and layered imperial sovereignties, including British recognition of Chinese suzerainty over Tibet, with simultaneous trade privileges for British subjects there, and Tibetan (but not Chinese) recognition that the area south of the McMahon Line was part of India. Both states claimed the tract south of the McMahon Line now known in India as Arunachal Pradesh. Both viewed the Aksai Chin plateau to the west, wedged between Ladakh, Tibet and Xinjiang, as their own.

In addition to the relationships they inherited from the British, Indians also had prior connections with Tibetans in the same region, primarily through Buddhism. As will be discussed in chapter 3, India's governing elites laid claim to Buddhism, celebrating the Buddha as a son of India, and they stressed the ways in which Buddhism provided a shared Asian history and culture. They consciously equated Buddhist tolerance and nonviolence with their own approach to the mid-twentieth century world.[107]

India's early policy towards the People's Republic of China (PRC) was an example of the substantive form friendship-as-international-diplomacy could take. When the Chinese Communist Party emerged victorious from the civil war in 1949, it was immediately pulled into the politics of the Cold War, as China's seat at the UN was occupied by the Guomindang government, by then confined to Taiwan. Indian diplomats worked to bring the PRC fully into the international fold for three reasons. Firstly, to avoid the UN succumbing to the same fate as the League of Nations, it was essential, in India's view, that the PRC be brought into the new machinery for international peace. Secondly, India shared a long and indistinct border with China, and a China fully integrated into the post-war international system would be a more reliable partner at the negotiating table. Thirdly, the idea of ensuring China's amicable entry into international society was simply a recognition of China as a great power and its emergence on the world scene as a fact.[108] With all of this in mind, India became one of the first countries to recognise the Communist victory in China and to send diplomatic representatives to the PRC. In addition, India argued that the PRC ought to be allowed to take up its seat on the Security Council, replacing Taiwan in the seat for China. Indeed, the US and the Soviet Union each separately approached India holding out the prospect of an Indian seat on the Security Council, but twice India refused to countenance any such offer until the PRC had been brought onto it.[109] Endeavouring throughout the 1950s to bring China into contact with other states, it was Nehru who secured an invitation for Zhou Enlai, China's premier and foreign minister, to come to the Bandung Conference.[110] All of this was in line with India's understanding of friendship and reciprocity in international politics.

With no representation at the United Nations, and the United States refusing to recognise the PRC, India also offered to act as an interlocutor between China and the western world during the Korean War, which had begun in June 1950. Both the Americans and the Chinese used Indian representatives to convey their intentions to one another. Throughout 1950, B. N. Rau, recently released from his role as constitutional advisor to the Constituent Assembly to take up a post as India's representative at the UN Security Council, gathered small and medium powers together to study the Korean conflict and put forward proposals for its resolution. Meanwhile, V. K. Krishna Menon worked to find an agreed way to repatriate prisoners of war on each side.[111] Krishna Menon sometimes irked the other members of India's UN delegation, who did not all work together in concert.[112]

Weaving China into a world shaped by India's internationalist norms had a bilateral element as well. In 1954, Zhou Enlai met Nehru in Delhi. While they did not resolve the border issue, the two agreed the 'Five Principles of Peaceful Coexistence', known by the Sanskrit term *panchsheel*. These were: mutual respect for sovereignty and territorial integrity; non-aggression; non-interference in other countries' internal affairs; equal and mutual benefit; peaceful coexistence.[113] The mention of sovereignty and territorial integrity concealed more than it revealed, however. The agreement appeared to surrender all Indian claims to privileges in Tibet, but in return, India hoped China would recognise its pre-eminent position in Nepal, Sikkim and Bhutan. In other words, while panchsheel seemed to lay out a vision for an international order of nation-states, Nehru's interpretation of what was achieved at the meeting was more in line with imperial notions of layered sovereignty.[114] Zhou Enlai had put off the border issues, saying they could look at them again in future when the PRC would not have to rely on maps drawn up by the Guomindang, and Nehru seemed willing to leave the contentious issue of the border aside. He interpreted the agreement as China's acceptance of the status quo.[115]

This fledgling relationship, founded on a public elaboration of minimum norms of conduct, and a fudge over borders, changed in the late 1950s. Part of the reason it changed was that there were layers of Indian foreign policy that operated below the level of international institutions and bilateral summits. These layers concerned the peoples of the borderlands, especially Tibetans and those who lived in the Indian states that would become Arunachal Pradesh and Nagaland.

India's approach to Tibet and Tibetans was not unified. Nehru did not direct the policy single-handedly; he was pushed by his own officials and by the actions of Tibetans. When the PRC first moved into Tibet in 1950, declaring it part of China, the Government of India did not formally object.[116] However, the contacts between India and Tibet below the surface were pushing in the opposite direction. Harishwal Dayal, India's political officer in Sikkim, threatened to resign if the Government of India did not encourage Tibetans to resist the Chinese communists.[117] Throughout the early and middle years of the 1950s, Tibetan rebels and exiles received quiet encouragement.[118] B. N. Mullik, director of India's Intelligence Bureau, and Apa Pant, formerly friend to East Africans and now India's political officer in Sikkim, met regularly with Tibetan exiles in Kalimpong, in the northern reaches of West Bengal. Mullik, after consulting Nehru, agreed to allow Tibetan exiles to continue their opposition to the Chinese occupation while in India, albeit primarily non-violently. India's Intelligence Bureau, welcoming the information they gathered from these exiles, provided them with funds and equipment. Apa Pant, comparing his work with what he had done in Kenya, promised the exiles that if they built up a peaceful independence movement, he would urge the government in Delhi to assist them.[119]

Tibet's main exiles pressed their Indian contacts for assistance of all kinds, from publicising the plight of Tibet in the press, to aiding refugees and funnelling funding for Tibetan rebels through India.[120] For their part, Indian representatives communicating directly with Tibetans often pushed the boundaries of what the Government of India's official position would allow. This tension was on display when the Dalai Lama travelled to India in late 1956 and met with Nehru. The Tibetan leader was prepared to seek asylum in India at that point, but the prime minister advised him to return to Tibet, telling him there was nothing India could do at that moment. Nehru's move surprised Tibetan exiles who had been in regular contact with Pant and Mullik who, they had believed, had been encouraging the Dalai Lama to make just such a request.[121]

Tensions between its different principles and within the Government of India's multiple policies towards China and Tibet became obvious when the Chinese cracked down on the Tibetan uprising against the communist occupation. The Dalai Lama and tens of thousands of refugees fled on foot to India in April 1959, which put the Government of India in a bind. Everyone in India seemed to have an opinion on what it ought to do. Though the options before India were rather starkly opposed, each one could be justified with reference to one of the principles of post-imperial internationalism. The Jana Sangh greeted the arrival of the Dalai Lama with chants of 'Hindi-Tibeti Bhai Bhai', substituting Tibet in a chant that usually celebrated India–China brotherhood in the form 'Hindi-Chini Bhai Bhai'.[122] Non-official Tibet conferences were held in Calcutta and Madras, in which the case was made for India to recognise Tibet's right to self-determination. Jayaprakash Narayan made this appeal: 'A united world opinion must be created *against Chinese aggression and for Tibetan independence*.'[123] On another side of India's political polygon was the Communist Party of India (CPI) which, notwithstanding contemporary allegations to the contrary, tended to support the Government of India's position on the border dispute.[124] The CPI argued that the rebellion in Tibet had been 'organised by a handful of serf-owners and bigoted lamas' and had 'nothing to do with the interests of the Tibetan people'. The CPI called on 'all national and patriotic forces to rise to the occasion and defend India–China friendship'.[125] A third position straddled these two: Asoka Mehta, leader of the Praja Socialist Party in the Lok Sabha, recognised China's position in Tibet, but called on the Government of India not to 'purchase' the friendship of China 'by sacrificing the legitimate and rightful claim for preserving the distinctive cultural way of life of the People of Tibet' within China.[126] Self-determination, international friendship, protection of minorities—all were consistent with Indian principles, but not with one another in this case. At this point, the official Indian position was that it would provide assistance included settling refugees in camps across India, but this support did not extend to recognising the Tibetan government in exile.[127] A layered approach focused on people as much as territory in this instance complicated matters for India, raising tensions with China.

Meanwhile, India faced parallel, if not identical circumstances in its north-eastern territories. In India's North East Frontier Agency (NEFA), the focus on people took the form of what Bérénice Guyot-Réchard has called 'state-shadowing', whereby China and India competed to secure the loyalty of the diverse and highly mobile populations of the eastern Himalayas.[128] They had not paid much attention to NEFA, but as the communists took firmer control of Tibet and Kham in the 1950s, the Government of India sought to establish its claim to the territory south of the McMahon Line by persuading the people of NEFA that India would be a more hospitable home for them than China. After a few initial mis-steps, Delhi extended its developmentalist approach to this disputed land: it opened a medical department and schools, it initiated agricultural reform and cultural revival, and it built a lot of roads.[129] India was as much concerned with security and restricting movement as it was with development. Frontier officials introduced a permit system to try to limit movement in these sensitive areas. Indian officials in the region also tried to prevent anyone from emigrating from China to India, even as they watched the PRC try to entice inhabitants of NEFA to migrate north.[130]

Nearby, in what would become Nagaland, relations with the Government of India set off from a different footing. Administered as a frontier tract by the British, and regarded as 'backward', the region of north-east India the Nagas inhabited had not been paid much attention in Congress's anti-colonial movement. Led by Angami Zapu Phizo and the Naga National Council, some Nagas declared their own independence on 14 August 1947. They subsequently boycotted Indian taxes, government jobs and the first general election. Nehru and Phizo did not have any personal rapport and did not see the future of the area in the same terms, leaving Nehru without an intermediary for whom he could act as a patron. Though the army and the Assam Rifles were despatched to shut down the movement in 1953, this only pushed it underground. Parallels on the level of principle between the Nagas and the Tibetans were noted by India's communists in the Lok Sabha.[131] On the material level, while Indians helped the Tibetans, MPs fretted about the possibility that the Chinese may have been assisting the Nagas.[132] These similarities may have helped push the Government of India towards a settlement with a group styling itself the Naga People's Convention. The Convention met first in 1957, negotiating between different Naga groups and even trying to bring in those who had gone underground, and then presenting demands to the Government of India. By the middle of 1959, as Tibetan refugees were arriving en masse in north India, the Government of India agreed to form India's sixteenth state, Nagaland. Explaining this decision to the Lok Sabha, Nehru presented it as but an extension of existing policy: 'Our policy has always been to give the fullest autonomy and opportunity of self-development to the Naga people, without interfering in any way in their internal affairs or way of life.'[133] The words echoed what the Government of India was asking for Tibet.[134]

India concentrated on people and its many borders remained indistinct, while the PRC was working rapidly to consolidate its territory by drawing definitive frontiers. China settled its borders with Nepal in March 1960, and with Burma later the same year. The Chinese began negotiations with Pakistan over their disputed territories in 1961.[135] In 1960, Zhou Enlai visited Nehru and made an offer to settle their overlapping claims to territory with a land swap: tracts in the east would go to

India, while in the west, the Aksai Chin would go to China. His offer was essentially a formal acknowledgement of the existing facts on the ground, but Nehru could not accept it.[136] He was reluctant to bargain away territory when he felt right was on India's side. Moreover, the Supreme Court had ruled that revisions to India's territory had to be made by amending the Constitution, which in turn would have to go through the Lok Sabha, and the public uproar at the situation seemed to rule out the possibility of concessions.[137]

Over the course of the next two years, India and China inched towards confrontation. Under the advice of V. K. Krishna Menon and B. N. Mullik, India adopted the 'forward posts' policy, stationing Indian troops on land claimed by China. Competition for the loyalty of people in the eastern region escalated.[138] By October 1962, India found itself in a short, sharp war against the Chinese for which its military was unprepared. Indian troops suffered immediate losses, but just as things looked desperate, China announced a unilateral ceasefire and withdrew its troops. When Indian officials returned to NEFA after the war, however, they were welcomed back. Guyot-Réchard argues that this was because India's relative vulnerability had made officials more responsive to the needs of locals, who in turn appreciated India's flexibility as compared to China's rigidity.[139] Equally, the Naga People's Convention had called on all Nagas to 'form a united front to fight the Chinese invaders'.[140] India's work on winning over the population of the north-east seemed to have secured it a place in the territory, however tenuously and temporarily, even as it lost the war.

The war with China helps us to see how India's consistent principles could produce incoherent, and ultimately disastrous, foreign policy. At the highest level, Nehru sought to engage with Zhou Enlai, and agree a set of norms that might form part of the basis for the relationship between the two countries. Through the 1950s, however, Indian foreign policy operated on multiple registers, as representatives below Nehru encouraged Tibetans in their fight against the PRC. As the Tibetan issue escalated in the late 1950s, the contradiction between the two registers and the tensions between the different principles produced a crisis for Indian foreign policy.

NEIGHBOURS: PAKISTAN, PARTITION AND THE CONFLICT OVER JAMMU AND KASHMIR

The most pressing post-imperial issues facing India sprung from its relationship with Pakistan. The long threads of partition show us something of the texture of independent India as it emerged as a state. No area of scholarship has expanded as rapidly, or changed its interpretations as thoroughly, as the field of partition studies. It is now widely agreed that partition was a long and intricate process, which had profound implications for the shape and conduct of each state involved.[141] Sketching out India's policies towards Pakistan and Jammu and Kashmir, we see the surprising importance of friendship, and the tangled situation that could result from India's focus on people and principles.

Drawing borders was an essential part of the creation of India, but this task was not completed until long after independence. After the Indian National Congress and the Muslim League agreed in early June 1947 on the plan to partition the subcontinent, the British appointed a Boundary Commission, chaired by Sir Cyril Radcliffe. With limited time and a circumscribed understanding of the situation on the ground, Sir Cyril's boundaries were inevitably abstract.[142] After the lines were drawn on maps, therefore, it took more than a decade to make the borders between India and Pakistan a lived reality. While local officers had to find a modus vivendi with their counterparts on the other side of the border,[143] a formal Boundary Disputes Tribunal was formed, which worked through the 1950s. Indeed, disputes on the Punjab side were not finally resolved until April 1960.[144]

Control of territory per se did not seem to be India's main concern in the aftermath of partition; instead, it was anxious to control as far as possible the movement of people. The migrations associated with partition were complex, fitful and prolonged, creating uncertainty for governments and citizens. Many people crossed the borders multiple times, in search of safety or in pursuit of a livelihood.[145] Several were displaced more than once, either by physical violence or by the commands of indifferent bureaucracies.[146]

In this state of uncertainty, the new governments of India and Pakistan cooperated in a process of state-making. A Partition Council was established, and at bilateral summits over the course of five years, bureaucrats and diplomats worked through the practicalities of partition in what Pallavi Raghavan characterises as a 'highly constructive' manner.[147] The various diplomats and bureaucrats involved in making partition a reality often marvelled at the amicability of the relationships they formed. This was yet another surprising facet of friendship-as-international-diplomacy.

Representatives of the two states engaged in a process of border-making through the organisation, categorisation and policing of bodies. They arranged a transfer of population in Punjab in the first months after partition.[148] After this, the two governments worked to pin down people on all sides of the new borders in a series of inter-dominion conferences beginning in the autumn of 1947. Through these conferences, the two sides set up joint mechanisms whereby representatives from India would recover Hindu and Sikh women abducted and taken to Pakistan during the violence and restore them to their families in India. Reciprocal arrangements were made for Pakistan to do likewise.[149] They agreed, jointly, to discourage people from leaving and to encourage them to return to their homes. They agreed too to guarantee equality of rights to minorities, and set up provincial and district-level minority boards to enforce respect of these rights.[150] By the middle of 1948, both India and Pakistan had introduced a permit system to try to regulate who could cross the border, and then, in October 1952, they introduced passports.[151] All of these moves were calculated to create certainty on two planes. On one level, the agreements were designed to make minorities—Muslims in India, Hindus and Sikhs in Pakistan—feel confident enough to remain in place. On another, citizenship laws, the policing of movement, and the recovery of abducted women were designed to create certainties for governments about who their citizens were.

While the status of Kashmir was an even more tangled issue than partition, we can still see some of the main characteristics of India's post-imperial policies in operation with regard to this disputed land. Kashmir, too, was a problem arising out of Britain's imperial system. While Britain had directly ruled parts of India, it had signed treaties with more than five hundred princely states, which epitomised the layered nature of imperial sovereignty. These agreements gave Britain paramount power over foreign affairs, defence and communications, but left domestic issues within the states in the hands of the princes and princesses who ruled them. At partition, Britain, India and Pakistan pushed, prodded and persuaded each state to join either Pakistan or India by signing an instrument of accession. Maharaja Hari Singh, the ruler of the state of Jammu and Kashmir, was one of the princes who held out.[152]

India's approach to the question posed by the existence of the princely states was to accept the legal accession of the princes where convenient, and where not, to focus on the will of the people. Adherence, as far as possible, to an international order based on law helps to explain why, as irregular militiamen from Pakistan poured into Kashmir's Poonch region in the autumn of 1947, the Government of India insisted that Hari Singh sign an instrument of accession before they would send troops to assist him. It also helps to explain India's appeal to the United Nations the following year. On the one hand, India believed in the rules-based international order that the UN represented, and it expected—wrongly it transpired—the great powers to uphold India's position in Kashmir because it had been secured via the instrument of accession. At the same time, Indian troops were facing a winter in the mountains, worried about having to fight the *lashkars* from the frontier, who would be better acclimatised to the terrain, and with news that Pakistani regular troops had quietly joined them.[153] Bringing the matter to the UN allowed India to seek a pragmatic time-out while appealing for an idealist solution.

A solution in conformity with India's post-imperial ideals required the assent of the people of Kashmir to join the Indian Union. Focusing on popular consensus was not only a continuation of Congress's earlier support for the popular movements which had pushed for reforms in princely states before 1947, but also helped bolster India's case for absorbing Junagarh in September 1947 and invading Hyderabad in September 1948. In each of these states, India justified the action it took by claiming that the majority Hindu population of each state *wished* to join the union. In Jammu and Kashmir, the quest to gauge the will of the people went through many iterations. Initially, India was intent on consulting the people directly via plebiscite. Recent research has shown that India's commitment to a plebiscite was unilateral at first: Mountbatten, as governor-general of India, wrote to the Maharaja shortly after accession informing him of the need to take the question of accession 'to the people' as soon as conditions in the state permitted.[154] As the United Nations took up the issue, the plebiscite only gained salience in Indian policy towards Kashmir. However, the prospect of creating conditions conducive to an impartial and unimpeded plebiscite across all of Jammu and Kashmir quickly faded. In particular, India's insistence that Pakistan withdraw not only its armed forces but all of its nationals from the territory before a referendum was anathema to Pakistan. After Pakistan signed a defence pact with the United States in 1954, India's official line became that this pact made a plebiscite unworkable by altering the strategic balance in the region.[155]

By this time, however, alternative means of conjuring and displaying popular consent in Jammu and Kashmir were already becoming available. At the recommendation of Sheikh Abdullah's National Conference, and after elections, a Constituent Assembly for Jammu and Kashmir convened for the first time on 31 October 1951. Elections to the Assembly had been marred by malpractice, as opposition candidates were arbitrarily disqualified from standing.[156] But flawed though it was, and established in violation of UN directives, Kashmir's Constituent Assembly not only drew up a constitution for Jammu and Kashmir, but broadened the basis for the claim that the accession of the state to India had been achieved with popular consent.

India's efforts to curate and exhibit the will of the people went beyond constitutional methods. There was, to begin with, the search for a reliable individual to act as interlocutor and agent. We know that Nehru preferred to act as patron, sponsoring others in projects that shared his ideals or objectives in some way. Sheikh Abdullah seemed a natural choice at first. He shared not only Nehru's secularism, but also his developmentalist ambitions. His party, the National Conference, also claimed to represent the majority of Kashmir's population, especially the Muslims of the Kashmir Valley. So long as the Sheikh's project was to bring Kashmir closer to India, Nehru and the Government of India would be his patrons. However, when, from India's perspective, Sheikh Abdullah seemed to shift towards laying more emphasis on the possibility of Kashmiri independence, Nehru had to find a new Kashmiri leader to sponsor. In August 1953, the Sheikh was detained without trial and Bakshi Ghulam Mohammad took his place as prime minister in Kashmir. Relying heavily on one person however, meant accepting that individual warts and all, making it difficult to get rid of Bakshi as evidence of electoral malpractice and corruption mounted in the state.[157]

Bakshi's period also witnessed a strengthening of the administrative ties between the governments in Delhi and Srinagar. Jammu and Kashmir had secured a 'special status' in India via Article 370 of the Constitution. While recognising the special position of Kashmir, the Government of India also worked to integrate the territory into the Indian Union in as many administrative areas as possible. In effecting this transition, Bakshi was more amenable than Sheikh Abdullah. Whereas the Sheikh had resisted fiscal and administrative integration, Bakshi's government did not demur when the Indian president ordered the expansion of New Delhi's jurisdiction to Kashmir in the fields of audit, customs and finance.[158] While government jobs had been reserved for state residents under the Maharaja, in 1958 the Indian Administrative Service and the Indian Police Service were both extended to Kashmir.[159] The following year, The National Conference requested that the state be brought under the jurisdiction of the centre's Election Commission,[160] and the Supreme Court's jurisdiction was extended at around the same time. By the end of the period, Gulzarilal Nanda, Union home minister, admitted that Kashmir's special status as reflected in Article 370 of the Constitution, had been 'completely emptied of its contents'.[161] Rajendra Prasad, who as president of India issued many of the orders that brought the territory closer to India, had noted the dubious constitutionality of these measures at the time.[162]

A final feature of India's approach to Kashmir in this period was the endeavour to secure the consent of Kashmiris through a combination of development and dampening of dissent. This was a policy pursued as enthusiastically by the state as by the central government. Kashmiri opinion was to be gauged and broadcast by Article 370 of the Constitution combined with the Kashmiri Assembly. Any attempt to challenge this arrangement had to be quashed. From one side, in 1952, the Praja Parishad, the main political party in Jammu, where Muslims were not a majority of the population, launched a campaign demanding the abrogation of Article 370 and the full integration of the state into the Indian Union.[163] Nehru dispatched the chief of the Intelligence Bureau, B. N. Mullik, to persuade the Praja Parishad to withdraw their agitation.[164] At the same time, the military presence in the state provided Ladakhis with employment, and military recruitment infused their identity with a new sense of being the sentinels of independent India.[165] From the other side, Sheikh Abdullah, with Bakshi in charge of internal security, worked on the Kashmir valley. They formed a 'Peace Brigade' which was dispatched to harass those in Kashmir with divergent political views. When Bakshi took over, he deployed the Brigade, the local police and home guard units against the supporters of the Sheikh, subjecting them to imprisonment and torture, or hounding them into exile. Wherever the Peace Brigade was deployed, it claimed that the people subjected to its force held 'pro-Pakistani' sentiments.[166] All of this underscores the extent to which India's borders were forged by establishing new types of relationships with people as much as through the demarcation of geographical space.

Development was the flip side of creating certainty around populations. Fiscal aid from the Government of India expanded nearly 600 per cent between the first and the third plans, making Kashmiris the highest per capita recipients of central aid. Again, it was Bakshi's administration that oversaw Jammu and Kashmir's integration into Delhi's developmental regimes. While Sheikh Abdullah had pursued self-sufficiency for the state, as soon as he was in jail, Bakshi and the Government of India worked together to broaden connections between Jammu and Kashmir and the rest of India. The state was brought into the National Extension and Community Development programmes. Hundreds of miles of new roads were built, including a new tunnel at Banihal, linking the Valley of Kashmir to the rest of India. The Jawahar Tunnel, reported as 8,115 feet (approximately 2.5 kilometres) in length, was opened in December 1956, with Vice President Radhakrishnan and Bakshi Ghulam Mohammed in attendance. Bakshi declared, 'No one can doubt the fact of Kashmir's accession to India. But the barrier of Banihal continued to stand between us and India [...] and used to isolate us physically from one another. Now, this barrier is also removed.'[167] The tunnel allowed Indian tourists and traders to travel to Kashmir all year round, movement that would be encouraged in 1959 by the abolition of the system of travel permits that had been introduced in 1947.[168] Of course, the tunnel also facilitated the movement of intelligence agents, as well as military personnel and equipment.

As with China, the situation in Jammu and Kashmir underscores the fact that India's attempts to mop up the post-imperial crises it faced by developing a post-imperial internationalism did not produce a coherent set of policies. In this disputed territory, India appealed to international institutions and adhered to at least nominally constitutional methods of accession. It also recognised that the will of the people was something that could not only be measured, but could be cultivated. And this was a game best played out over the long term. The Government of India thus attempted to cultivate Kashmiri goodwill towards India, through working with Bakshi on development. At the same time, the impulse to control populations called for securitisation, co-optation and coercion. Taken in isolation, each strand made sense in its own way, but together they could work at cross purposes.

Conclusion

The fabric of myth is woven with a few strands of truth. There can be no doubt that India did not wish to pledge allegiance to either side in the Cold War, and it loudly proclaimed its opposition to the division of the world into competing military blocs. Because of this, it is fair to say that India was a rather marginal player in the Cold War. The reverse is equally true: the Cold War was relatively marginal in India's foreign policy. If Indian foreign policy was a six-yard sari, non-alignment might be likened to the intricate *zari* work on the borders and the *palloo*: it required expertise to imagine, it was laboriously produced, and it drew the eye, but the rest of the garment was woven with different thread. Even loud claims of non-alignment could not unpick the many strands by which India had been woven into the Anglo-American system over more than three centuries.

As India emerged from the British Empire, it did not easily or swiftly become a nation-state, territorialised within clear borders. Instead, the country's foreign policy was dominated by the problems it inherited from the imperial relationship. To cope with them, India articulated a vision for a new post-imperial international system, in which warring blocs of states could have no reasonable part. That vision included the fight for decolonisation and racial justice. It promised the pursuit of these aims through friendship, institution-building and elaborating norms, rules and laws. In a world of emerging and competing states, it focused attention to a surprising degree on creating certainty around people. This focus on people had idealistic elements, including helping to draft the Universal Declaration of Human Rights, trying to secure rights for minorities and promising refuge to the people of Tibet. But it also involved pinning people down, ending their habits of movement and policing their loyalties through violence, intimidation and imprisonment.

India's internationalism was not limited to foreign policy. In each of the chapters that follow, we will see that India sought not isolation and autarky, but exchange, cooperation and international leadership as it set out to unwind the domestic legacies of imperialism.

CHAPTER THREE

The Myth of Hegemonic Secularism

IN THE WEEK before the monsoon arrived in 1956, Indian officials gathered in the stifling heat across the country to celebrate the life of the Buddha. The occasion was the 2,500th anniversary of the birth of Prince Siddhartha, which was also said to be the day he achieved parinirvana, abandoning his body on earth, some eighty years after he had been born. Preparations for Buddha Jayanti, as the week of events was known, had been under way for months. The Maha Bodhi society, which sought to promote the revival of Buddhism in India, took a lead role in festivities in some sites, especially at Bodh Gaya, Bihar, where the Buddha was said to have first achieved enlightenment under the bodhi tree. However, this was also an officially sponsored celebration. In the run-up to the day, the Archaeological Survey of India had undertaken works at most of the major Buddhist sites, from the caves at Ajanta to Bodh Gaya.[1] The Government of India sponsored exhibitions, commemorative publications, special stamps and a documentary. Prisoners in Uttar Pradesh were even treated to a 'jail holiday' with a 'special meal at Government expense'.[2]

The main event in 1956 fell on 24 May. Across India, as well as in neighbouring Burma and Nepal, the occasion was marked by unveiling statues and images of the Buddha, by planting trees, and singing hymns.[3] In Bhopal, where the emperor Ashoka had commissioned a great stupa at Sanchi some twenty-two centuries previously, the Union defence minister, Dr K. N. Katju, presided over a procession of Buddhist relics recently returned from the Victoria and Albert Museum in London.[4] In Bodh Gaya, the occasion was marked with a procession, which wound its way through what was then a 'tiny township'. The parade included 'people from

India, Pakistan, Ceylon, Burma, Thailand, Cambodia, Viet Nam, Tibet, Nepal and France'.[5] Indeed, Buddha Jayanti was not only a religious event; the Government of India turned it into an opportunity for international diplomacy.

The festivities celebrated the life and ideas of the Buddha and also proclaimed his relevance for modern times. Nehru, finding in the Buddha an approach to leadership akin to his own, praised him for having urged his followers to accept his teachings only after they had been tested by practical experience. The prime minister called this the Buddha's 'scientific way of life'.[6] President Rajendra Prasad noted that for ordinary people the Buddha's teachings were 'essentially practical'. His 'principle of avoiding extremes and preferring the golden mean is a valuable contribution to world thought,' Prasad told the nation in a radio address.[7] Providing a visual display of the modernity of Buddhism, Calcutta's Buddha Jayanti procession featured 'nearly 40 decorated lorries carrying the images of Lord Buddha and a replica of the Bodh Gaya Temple',[8] while in the city of Madras, specially chartered aircraft dropped flowers and leaflets on the metropolis.[9]

Senior figures in the Indian administration not only echoed the theme of the modern relevance of Buddhist thought, but also linked it to their government's policies. President Prasad, in his broadcast to the nation, noted that the teachings of the Buddha had resonance in the international climate of the mid-1950s. He warned, 'Following the path of peaceful coexisting as preached by the Buddha appears to be the only alternative to destructive wars and subsequent misery.'[10] At Sanchi, Dr Katju declared that India was 'implementing the teachings of the Buddha in the national as well as international sphere'. To prove his point, he noted that India was engaged in peaceful negotiations with Portugal over the return of the territories of Goa, Daman and Diu.[11] Five years later, the Indian army would annex the Portuguese territories by force, but in 1956 that was a distant prospect.

Rather than eschewing religion altogether, Indian secularism was conceived as a mechanism for including members of all religions in the national project.[12] The sight of India's most prominent statesmen organising elaborate religious celebrations should not be surprising, therefore. Under the aegis of Congress, minority demands were to be recognised so long as they were folded into Indian nationalism and did not stand aside from it. It was precisely the question of the inclusiveness of Congress, however, that had been the focus of contention between the Muslim League and the Congress Party before independence. When the

Muslim League raised the demand for Pakistan in 1940, Congress leaders framed it as the antithesis of secularism, as nationalism's 'other'.[13] In nationalist lore, therefore, the partition of British India was a betrayal of the national movement. Partition was attended by widespread enmity and fear: though no definitive tally was taken, up to 1.5 million people were slaughtered, and some ten to twelve million crossed the yet-to-be-defined borders as they fled for safety in the months around August 1947.[14] As the smoke cleared, Congress leaders began to understand the violence as a period of 'insanity' from which the nation had to recover.

Postcolonial Indian secularism, therefore, was burdened with multiple responsibilities.[15] Firstly, it was a route to secure a sense of belonging for religious minorities. While it included all religions, the major work to be done was with Muslims who remained in India after the traumas of partition.[16] As part of this endeavour, Hindu nationalism would have to be kept at bay. Although Hindu nationalists had gained prominence in the run-up to partition, the new Congress leaders of the Government of India tried to sideline them. After Gandhi's assassination on 30 January 1948, members of the Rashtriya Swayamsevak Sangh were arrested, and the Hindu Mahasabha declared it would not take part in politics. In short, though raging before partition, the flames of Hindu chauvinism were quickly doused after independence, at least according to the old nationalist narrative. Secondly, the reform of Hinduism was seen as an essential element of secularism.[17] To this end, a prominent Dalit, Bhimrao Ramji Ambedkar, was put in charge of both writing the Constitution and overseeing reform of Hindu personal law. Within a short time after independence, so the myth goes, India had a secular state, and was on course to establish a sense of security and belonging for the two groups who had raised the loudest objections to Congress's nationalism: Muslims and Dalits.

As with so many of the myths that have arisen about this period after independence, the myth of India's secularism owes a great deal to Jawaharlal Nehru. Although Nehru had dabbled in theosophy as a teenager, he had lost touch with it after a short time. By the 1930s, he was writing openly that he believed organised religion, full of 'dogma and bigotry', was a cloak for 'the preservation of vested interests'.[18] Nehru's personal pain at the slaughter that accompanied the partition of the subcontinent is well documented.[19] In the aftermath of the violence of partition and the integration of the princely states, he pleaded that 'we should forget old matters', no matter how painful. His aim was 'to unite the hearts of the people' and move forward in the common endeavour of building the nation.[20] He repeatedly appealed to Indians to focus on what they had in common. To this end, he was a great propagator of the idea that the palimpsest of India's different faiths made up the country's unique 'composite culture'.[21] For decades, scholars, taking for granted the notion of Nehru's dominance over the period, cast his wish for India as one of the hegemonic organising ideas of the state.[22] Even those who decry the shortcomings of the secularism of the era place Nehru at its centre.[23]

This belief that Nehru's conception of secularism was spread through the sinews of administration more broadly seemed only to have been reinforced by the events of the last decades of the twentieth century. Since the 1980s, Hindu nationalism has emerged as a major force in Indian politics, prompting what has been widely understood as a crisis of Indian secularism.[24] A Hindu nationalist political party, the Bharatiya Janata Party (BJP), has risen to prominence. Its underlying ideology, Hindutva, maintains that India's character is essentially Hindu; that India's Muslims are outside the fold of the nation; and that conversion, to Christianity, Islam, Sikhism or Buddhism, is a threat to Hindus and therefore to the nation. The BJP first gained a foothold in the states, and then took power in New Delhi at the head of a coalition after elections in 1998. Under Narendra Modi's leadership, the party returned to power with a majority in the Lok Sabha in 2014. Simultaneously, and not unconnected to the BJP's ascent to political power, the country has witnessed a rise in communal violence, from the demolition of the Babri Masjid in Ayodhya in 1992 to the massacre of Muslims in Gujarat in 2002. Inter-caste violence, too, has seemed to take on a new vehemence, and multifarious forms of exclusion suffered by Dalits and converts have attracted increasing attention. Thoughtful people of all kinds have fretted about these trends. In so doing, they have often contrasted the tumult and division of recent decades with a more peaceful and secular period which, they presume, had followed independence.[25]

The idea that the first decades after independence in India were characterised by resilient and widespread secularism has been significantly revised in recent decades, however. Firstly, scholars of partition have found that there were members of the Congress Party in Bengal and Punjab who were partial to Hindu nationalism and who demanded the partition of the subcontinent.[26] Further research has shown that Congress's inclusiveness was conceived in narrow terms: in order to be represented, minorities had to drop the right to be recognised as having separate political interests.[27] Scholars have also uncovered the extent to which the leadership of Congress articulated a vision of the nation that was rhetorically inclusive, but in practical terms served the interests of male, Hindu, high-caste elites.[28] These findings have destabilised the idea that the pre-1947 Indian National Congress was essentially a secular party. This then has opened up the possibility of exploring whether and to what extent the postcolonial Indian governments which Congress ran conformed to its own claims about secularism.

While the logic behind raising the slogan of secularism in the aftermath of partition is apparent, exactly what Indian secularism required of politicians and public servants was anything but clear in the decades after 1947.[29] Depending upon the context, secularism could require politicians to not espouse any religion, or to celebrate many religions; it could call for the employment of public servants who treated people from different communities equally, or for administrators to be appointed on the basis of quotas defined by religious affiliation; it could bring forth calls for governments to protect the rights of minority religious communities, or for governments to punish members of different faiths in equal numbers after a disturbance; it could require the retention of separate personal laws, or the drafting of a uniform civil code.[30] In addition to this daunting array of contextual meanings for secularism, scholars have revealed the gaps that frequently opened between the high ideals of secularism and the messy reality of how Muslims and Dalits were treated after 1947.[31]

Although there certainly was a breach between secular ideals and reality in post-partition India, to focus on this is to assume that if only Indians had lived up to the rhetoric of the day, Nehruvian secularism would have met with easy success. Doing so ignores the infinite quotidian negotiations required to bring about meaningful secular practices in endless specific contexts, from appointments to government jobs to decisions about how to deal with an outbreak of violence. Indian secularism required officials to square the circle between protecting faiths and maintaining a principled distance from the faithful. This was neither simple nor straightforward.

India's official secularists were most adept at doing this in monumental mode, staking a claim to secularism through the exaltation of people and sacred sites. In this celebratory secularism, senior figures underscored what was universal in each creed. Simultaneously, they were careful to claim what was Indian in each religion. The simplest means of establishing the Indianness of a religion was to focus on ancient monuments: a creed could be claimed for India due to the mere fact of the presence of sacred sites in India. Secularism as commemoration drew a line between honouring India's faiths in abstract, monumental terms (which was to be encouraged) and showing favour to the people who were the adherents of any particular religion (which was to be avoided). Using the tools of pageantry developed during the nationalist movement, this secularism was an attempt to elicit a certain kind of a sentiment in the wider population.

Buddha Jayanti was a near perfect occasion to observe this kind of secularism. For one, as the Maha Bodhi society spearheaded the revival of Buddhism in South Asia from the late nineteenth century, its members had tended to stress Buddhism's universal humanist rationality, distancing the religion from diverse local rituals. This project was aided by the archaeological excavation and restoration of Buddhist sites in India, from Nagarjunakonda and Amaravati in the south, through Sanchi in Bhopal, and up to the university at Nalanda in Bihar. These restored sites acted as canvases upon which a new universalist version of the faith could be projected without the uneasy presence of regular worshippers at these locations. The Maha Bodhi society tried to attract Buddhist pilgrims from across Asia. These pilgrims may have shared little in terms of language, texts or ritual, but could all agree on the sanctity of the sites and the importance of the act of pilgrimage.[32] Thus, in 1956 we find the Government of India had invited Buddhists from across Asia to visit pilgrimage sites, and we find President Prasad declaring that the Buddha's ideas were an important addition to *world* thought.[33]

Crucially, though India did have practising Buddhists, their numbers were tiny: they constituted less than 1 per cent of the total population of India, and they were concentrated largely in remote hill regions. This made it easy to focus on Buddhist sites without the risk of appearing to favour the adherents of Buddhism, or worse, one of any number of competing Buddhist sects. Buddha Jayanti, therefore, helps us understand the central feature of the secularism of the age: the gulf between the iconic and the everyday.

To deem something iconic is to recognise its singularity. The iconic is beyond doubt, beyond dispute, beyond politics. In early postcolonial India, the Constitution, the law, internationally recognised sacred monuments and some nationally acclaimed personalities managed to achieve this monumental status. Each could be celebrated for what was both universal and Indian in them. Each was used, in the mode of postcolonial nationalism, to attempt to bring forth feelings of affinity between the followers of India's different religions. Below and around these iconic texts, objects and people was ordinary life, where there were no ready formulas that would produce justice out of the tough negotiations over material belonging. The abstract idea of secularism could never solve real problems without significant feats of interpretation by politicians, government servants and the people concerned. In contrast to the iconic, the everyday is a world of contrasting claims, the relative value of which can rarely be measured on the same set of scales. It is full of complex problems that do not admit tidy solutions.

The following pages demonstrate that, in the quotidian negotiations that took place in the two decades after partition, politicians and government officials tended to default to majoritarian solutions when confronted by these complex problems. In trying to resolve conflicting claims that arose regularly in the decades after independence, those in charge regularly chose the paths that would spark the least resistance among non-Muslims, and among powerful caste Hindus. This chapter explores the gulf between the monumental and the mundane in the treatment of the two most prominent groups with a stake in secularism: Muslims and Dalits.

Muslim Belonging

In 1948, the Ministry of Information and Broadcasting put together a slim volume for domestic and international circulation, entitled *India's Minorities*. As a piece of propaganda, the pamphlet conforms to all we might expect of Indian secularism in this period. Its opening paragraph proclaims, 'India has had minorities within her territory for many centuries. Tolerance being the essence of Indian culture, and cultural synthesis the spirit of her history, India never presented the spectacle of religious or racial warfare that has marked the history of Europe.' The body of the publication outlines the 'minority problem', and the various rights and activities of minority groups. It also addresses the treatment of Muslim refugees of partition in India. It is replete with quotations from prominent Congress members, mostly Hindu, such as Sardar Patel, or Acharya Kripalani. The latter is quoted as saying, 'As regards minorities in the Indian Union, Muslims or others, I assure them that they have nothing to fear.'[34] What makes the publication of interest for the student of the iconic is the images which are published alongside the text (Fig. 3.1). In the opening pages, the reader is greeted with eight images of prominent Indians: Rajkumari Amrit Kaur, Maulana Abul Kalam Azad, Sardar Baldev Singh, Asaf Ali, Akbar Hydari, Syud Hussain, M. R. Masani and Zakir Husain. Each of the subjects is listed by name and designation: for example, 'H.E. Mr. M. R. Masani, Ambassador in Brazil'. Beyond their pictures, these illustrious figures are not discussed in the volume. A person familiar with the coding by which South Asian names reveal the bearer's religion can tell instantly that the list includes a Sikh and a Parsi, Sunni and Shia Muslims. The only woman, Rajkumari Amrit Kaur, was well known to be a Christian.

Within the official secularism as articulated by the Ministry of Information, these extraordinary individuals served a number of purposes.

FIGURE 3.1. Portraits from *India's Minorities* (Government of India, Ministry of Information and Broadcasting, 1948). The captions which accompanied each portrait in the publication read (clockwise from top left): The Hon'ble Rajkumari Amrit Kaur, Minister of Health; The Hon'ble Abul Kalam Azad, Minister of Education; H.E. Mr. M. R. Masani, Ambassador in Brazil; The Hon'ble Sardar Baldev Singh, Minister for Defence.

First, they were icons: the success and prestige of each was indisputable. They were meant to stand as proof that minorities could and did succeed in India. Their accomplishments could be referenced as a means of conjuring feelings of pride and fellowship in every Indian. These figures were also to be read as exemplars of 'good minorities', who displayed all the loyalty and sacrifice of a nationalist, without deviating so far as to make separate demands on behalf of their communities. It is not coincidental that all but two of the figures pictured were members of the Indian National Congress at the time of publication. One of the exceptions was Baldev Singh, who had been a member of the Panthic Party, but was at the time cooperating with Congress in the role of defence minister. By 1952, Singh had joined the ruling party, winning election to the Lok Sabha on a Congress ticket. The other non-Congressman, Akbar Hydari, was more a civil servant than a political man. By their working through Congress, these men's loyalty could not be called into question. For the Government of India this was an important way of distinguishing itself from Pakistan, as well as from South Africa, Ceylon and a number of other countries with populations of overseas Indians subject to discriminatory legislation.

Variations on this theme are evident in the lives of individual Muslims who excelled outside of government, including the painter M. F. Husain, the sarod player Ali Akbar Khan, the cricket captain Ghulam Ahmad and the film goddess Nargis. These Muslims may not have been Congress members, but during the Nehru years they tended to maintain their distance from politics. Successful and esteemed Muslims seemed to give the lie to allegations from the other side of the new borders that Muslims in India were not faring well. What made these individuals anything but ordinary, however, was their talent and their ability to represent India. Nargis's fame, for example, reached new heights with the 1957 film *Mother India*. Produced and directed by Mehboob Khan, the film was a box office hit, running for over a year in Bombay's Liberty Theatre.[35] Nargis plays Radha, who suffers through endless misfortunes, but always retains her dignity and self-respect. Embodying not one woman, but the whole of India, Nargis was named best actress at the Filmfare Awards for 1958,[36] the year in which the president of India also recognised her achievements with the award of the civilian honour of the Padma Shri.[37] In their unrivalled achievements, such figures represented not their own community, but all of India.

This iconic status, of necessity rare, was out of reach for the average Indian. Instead, ordinary Muslims were hounded by suspicion and by their structural inability to live up to the example set by these iconic figures. To be fair, this was not unanimous. A small group of senior figures, from Jawaharlal Nehru to Sarojini Naidu, sought to reassure Muslims that they belonged in India, meeting them and sharing their pain. One can find accounts of everyday civility and friendship between Muslims and their neighbours of other faiths in postcolonial India. But the overwhelming finding of recent research has been that much of the official machinery that grew up to administer partition and the integration of the princely states did not adopt the same approach.

We begin with the matter of simply determining who was Indian. The system of permits, passports and citizenship that emerged in the years after 1947 was ostensibly applied by a neutral bureaucracy and designed merely to determine who had a right to live in India. In practice, this bureaucracy worked to exclude Muslims. Without the means to travel long distances, few South Asians had had the need to possess a passport before 1947. Around a year after partition, India began to restrict movement across the new borders. The move had been proposed after thousands of Muslims who had crossed to Pakistan began returning to India. In May 1948, it was reported that up to two thousand Muslims were returning to India each day. Police correspondence as well as newspaper reports were full of allegations that these Muslims were Pakistani spies, or intent on causing trouble in India.[38] A permit system was therefore introduced in July 1948, to deal with what was conceived of as the problem of the 'influx' of Muslims into India. Under the new rules, Muslims and non-Muslims had to apply for a permit to enter India. Pakistan introduced an almost identical system in October the same year. Although everyone had to apply to enter, there were different categories of permit for non-Muslims and Muslims. The former could apply to enter India and for 'permanent resettlement', taking advantage of official rehabilitation schemes if necessary. Muslims applied for 'permanent return', and most found that official permission for permanent return was extremely difficult to obtain. Many Muslims, therefore, were forced to travel from Pakistan to India on temporary permits, even if they intended to remain in India.[39] Visiting sick relatives, or completing business transactions on the other side of the border became increasingly difficult.[40]

At the same time, the Constitution was being drafted. Though ostensibly framed in a neutral manner, the rules opened up routes to citizenship for non-Muslims while restricting them for Muslims. Article 5 of the Constitution established *jus soli* citizenship rules: anyone born in India, that is, could claim citizenship. However, this simple principle was expanded for certain categories of persons. First, it was extended to include 'refugees', a widely recognised euphemism for non-Muslims who had left Pakistan for India. Second, persons of Indian origin living outside India, could obtain citizenship, even if they had never been domiciled in India, so long as they did not take another nationality. This was designed to encompass overseas Indians in Burma, Malaya, Ceylon, South Africa and so on.[41] As the constitutional definition of citizenship expanded in one direction, however, it contracted in another. With Article 7 of the Constitution, Muslim 'migrants', that is, those who had departed for Pakistan and wished to return, were granted citizenship, but under restrictive conditions: for instance, these individuals were required to obtain a permit for permanent return—a permit that was not readily forthcoming.[42]

Even though rules for citizenship were laid down in the Constitution, India's citizenship regime was not fully determined until the Citizenship Act of 1955.[43] In the years between 1947 and 1955, therefore, citizenship was often decided by court cases, and by officials on the ground based on their own sense of who belonged in India, often excluding Muslims. Overseas Indians who were Muslim could be regarded with suspicion when they applied for citizenship. For example, Indian diplomatic representatives in East Africa used the category of the 'constructive evacuee' to avoid processing citizenship applications from Muslims. The constructive evacuee was a person who had never been to Pakistan, but who was deemed to have shown loyalty to Pakistan, and therefore could not be granted citizenship. The Commission worked on the sweeping and inaccurate assumption that most Muslims in East Africa had been loyal to the Muslim League.[44]

While one category of Muslim struggled to get in, the government of Hyderabad sought to kick others out. At independence, most princely states had joined either India or Pakistan, but Hyderabad, like Jammu and Kashmir, had not. In September 1948, as it worried about a deteriorating communal situation and a communist uprising in the state, the Government of India sent the Indian army into Hyderabad in what it called the Police Action. When he arrived in the territory, the military governor, J. N. Chaudhuri, regarded almost all Muslims there as suspect, especially those deemed to be 'foreign'. Working on the majoritarian assumption that all but a handful of Muslims could not be trusted, the military government tried to deport anyone of Arab and Afghan origin from Hyderabad State to their so-called home countries, even if they had been resident in India for generations. Although these efforts were frustrated on several fronts, they demonstrate the ways in which, below an official citizenship regime which was superficially non-discriminatory, officials tried to close off routes to citizenship for Muslims.[45]

Muslims who remained in India, but who had family connections to Pakistan were often regarded with suspicion, especially if they were government servants. The partition of the subcontinent naturally included the division of the Raj's government services. Those in the most senior ranks of the imperial bureaucracy, the Indian Civil Service (ICS), were given the choice to opt for either India or Pakistan. Many, though by no means all, Muslim ICS officers opted for Pakistan, leaving the highest echelons of the ICS with considerably fewer Muslims. However, the services were not rendered completely homogeneous by the choices of individual Muslims. Rather, over several years, a cascade of small-scale decisions, and the occasional major reform, edged out many more Muslims who had remained in the Indian police and bureaucracy.

Even before the violence of partition had begun, for example, Vallabhbhai Patel, the home member in the Interim Government formed in 1946 as the British prepared to depart, ordered the chief commissioner of Delhi to remove Muslims from the ranks of the Delhi police. After the violence surrounding partition had begun, allegations that police forces had become 'infected' with communal bias were common. In Punjab and parts of Uttar Pradesh, Muslim police were stripped of their weapons on the basis that they had become 'communal', after which many quit their posts. In Hyderabad, after the Police Action of 1948, the military government sought to reduce the number of Muslims in the service of the state from 85 to 50 per cent in six months, shifting as many as ten thousand men out of work in a very short period of time. Apart from these more dramatic moves, Muslims could be pushed out of the service by false allegations of corruption.[46] Even though the Constitution, by the time it came into force in January 1950, prohibited discrimination in the field of hiring for government service, many states retained informal policies against hiring new Muslim recruits.[47] Central and state governments soon became anxious to ensure that every employee's entire family lived in India. In November 1948, for example, Uttar Pradesh called on its state employees to bring back any family members who had migrated to Pakistan. Hyderabad made a similar demand in January 1950. Government servants who were unable to obey the orders were told they could not remain in post.[48] As a whole, the reorganisation of the civil services brought about an Indian bureaucracy that seemed to be underwritten by doubts about whether Muslims could loyally serve India.

While this reorganisation was taking place, the Ministry of Information and Broadcasting published *India's Minorities*, in which it was stated, 'No one can deny that in the Indian Union Muslims are more than a protected minority. They are a valued community.' As proof of this point, the publication named prominent Muslims such as Brigadier Usman, who 'gladly gave his life for the honour of India in the Kashmir struggle'.[49] It mentioned by name Muslims who served in senior positions in state ministries or in the police. There were in addition, the pamphlet noted, 'as many as seven Muslims holding diplomatic posts abroad, as against thirty-five non-Muslims from all other communities put together', again naming them. It continued, bitterly, triumphantly, 'Incidentally, there is not a single non-Muslim holding a diplomatic post abroad on behalf of Pakistan.'[50] While it is easy to write off the publication as an example of hypocrisy, it is better understood as evidence of the ease with which India shone a celebratory light on exemplary Muslims whose iconic status rendered them capable of representing India. This was an important part of how India represented itself in the international sphere. Living as they did in the shadow cast by these colossal public figures, however, the conditions of ordinary Muslim men and women were not visible to many.

SPACE AND BELONGING

The Government of India was also adept at celebrating the Muslim presence in India in monumental terms. To mark the second year of independence, for example, India issued a new set of stamps on 15 August 1949 (Fig. 3.2). Each of the sixteen stamps presents an image of a monument from over two thousand years of Indian history. The earliest is of the East Gate to the stupa at the Buddhist complex at Sanchi in Madhya Pradesh, from the first century BCE. The latest is from the seventeenth century, the Gol Gumbaz of Bijapur, the mausoleum of Muhammed Adil Shah, completed in 1656 CE. In between are images taken from every corner of the country, from the caves at Ajanta in what was then Hyderabad State and is today Maharashtra, and the Konarak Temple in Orissa (Odisha), to the Vijaya Stambha at Chittorgarh in Rajasthan, and an image of Shiva from a Chola temple in Thiruvalangadu in today's Tamil Nadu. With the notable omission of Christianity, the collection includes a major monument from each of India's religions, including the Sikh Golden Temple at Amritsar in Punjab, and the Jain Shatrunjaya Temple at Palitana in today's Gujarat. It is not hard to see that the stamps were a statement of the new India's approach to religion. Belief systems not only existed side by side, as the individual monuments did, but they formed a meaningful collective, as the separate stamps formed a collection.

This official secularism was also reflected in the Constitution. Article 25 protects the right to 'profess, practise and propagate religion'. The subsequent article protects the right to establish religious institutions, manage their affairs and control their charitable properties. Article 30 gives religious and linguistic minorities the right to establish and run educational institutions. If the new issue of stamps was a statement of India's

FIGURE 3.2. Archaeological series of stamps, issued 15 August 1949. Author's collection.

official secularism, it is also a point of departure to contrast the preservation and celebration of the monumental against the struggles over more mundane spaces.

Official funds were spent on the preservation of the most iconic monuments associated with Muslim history in India, from the Taj Mahal to Tipu Sultan's palace,[51] but the rest faced a precarious future. As the princely states were absorbed and zamindari abolished, at least on paper, the sources of money that India's Muslim institutions had relied upon dwindled. In the case of Hyderabad, after the Government of India took over the administration of the state, the new rulers debated how to define the obligations of a secular state in the new India. Some in the government of Hyderabad argued that it was inappropriate for the state to fund any religious institutions; some held that state funding should be allotted to different communities according to their relative size in the population. Both arguments resulted in reducing funding to Muslim institutions in Hyderabad and in India more broadly. Funding for institutions within Hyderabad was reduced by as much as 95 per cent. Nehru and Azad occasionally were moved to intervene to preserve funding for institutions of international importance when they received notice that a grant was in danger, but the government of Hyderabad often ignored their appeals, without repercussions.[52]

Every institution, with its unique history and its own vision of its future, had to make its way in the challenging environment of the 1950s. Jamia Millia Islamia in Delhi, founded to take part in the Congress project, continued on this same path. It focused on developing Basic Education, social reform, refugee rehabilitation, and on repairing Hindu–Muslim relations after partition. The vision, elaborated by its first vice chancellor Zakir Husain and those who succeeded him, was to contribute to the shared culture of the nation through service, downplaying the importance of religion for individuals and communities.[53] In contrast, Aligarh Muslim University (AMU) found it harder to navigate the post-partition environment. Questions of loyalty swirled around AMU because many of its members had supported the call for Pakistan. AMU had to prove its loyalty by severing ties with Pakistan. A new vice chancellor, in the form of Jamia's Zakir Husain, was brought in to bring stability to AMU in 1948. However, members of the university remained polarised over whether and to what extent their Muslim identity ought to have a place in everything from the name of the university to the content of their education.[54]

Institutions such as schools and universities were easier to maintain because they were in constant use. Sacred sites, by contrast, came under sustained pressure after 1947. Partition and the incorporation of Hyderabad witnessed violence not just against people, but against mosques, graveyards, madrassas and historic sites. In West Bengal, many graveyards were gradually swallowed by encroaching structures.[55] In and around Delhi, it was reported that over one hundred mosques had been damaged, destroyed or converted into temples in the violence surrounding partition. A common tactic was to instal an idol in a mosque and declare it had been converted into a temple. Although the princely state of Alwar did order the destruction of Muslim sacred sites after independence, many acts of destruction across India were undertaken by private individuals.[56] A survey of the entire country was not undertaken, but in Hyderabad, the Jamiatul Ulama reckoned that 227 mosques had been demolished in the ten months after the invasion of September 1948. Nonetheless, there were several cases in which low-level officials declined to discipline non-Muslims who broke the law. In Hyderabad, for example, after an old mosque at Shorapur was destroyed in the period surrounding the Police Action, the local officer refused to sanction the reconstruction of the mosque on the grounds that to do so would cause a riot.[57]

In the better-known case of the disputed Babri Masjid in Ayodhya, Uttar Pradesh, idols were placed in the mosque in December 1949, but the local district magistrate declined to remove them, in spite of being requested to do so by Nehru and G. B. Pant, then chief minister of the state. The manner in which the courts placed the dispute on ice at the time seems to be indicative of the wider trend of defaulting to solutions that would not inflame Hindu chauvinists. The idols were left in place and the gates to the mosque were locked: no one could pray inside any longer. Hindus continued to pray outside.[58]

When space under contestation was not sacred, it was even harder for Muslims to hold their ground. Many Muslims who had been ousted from their houses during the partition violence found that their properties had been occupied by non-Muslims, and it was difficult to reclaim them. Although official policy was that illegal occupations of property would not be recognised, government servants, from ordinary constables to custodians of evacuee property, tended to default to solutions that deprived Muslims of their property. For example, Muslims in Delhi who wished to return to their homes in mixed neighbourhoods were deterred from doing so by the threat of violence, while the custodian of evacuee property recognised the 'right' of non-Muslim refugees who occupied Muslims' properties during the violence of September 1947 to remain in place.[59] On the other side of the country, police in Calcutta who attempted to oust non-Muslims who illegally occupied Muslim property were met with resistance, not only from the illegal occupiers but from their sympathetic neighbours. Officials variously left disputed sites to occupiers, sealed them off altogether or left them in ruins. The eventual 'solution' found for many of these battles was to default to the majoritarian wishes of the more assertive non-Muslim communities.[60]

Where was Nehru in all of this? Firstly, it is important to understand that as prime minister he was not regularly looped into information concerning what was happening on the ground. Instead, individual cases had to be brought to his desk for exceptional attention. Often, Muslim groups approached Maulana Azad, not in his official capacity as education minister, but as the most prominent Muslim in the Union government. Azad then often brought the issue to the attention of Nehru, who sometimes wrote to the chief minister concerned, who in turn would request a reply from the local officer in charge. However, by the time a reply came to Nehru, the situation had often been 'settled', not to the satisfaction of the parties concerned, but to the point where it was easy for officials on the ground to argue, as did the local officer in Shorapur, that to reopen the issue would risk inciting violence. A missive from the prime minister could sometimes remove bureaucratic obstructions, but Nehru's word alone could not rebuild a mosque or restore a family to their home. He had to work through local channels.

Instead of providing material relief, therefore, Nehru became a symbol of his own version of Indian secularism. In Hyderabad, where Muslims, their property and their sacred sites had all been targeted in violence after the Police Action, local officers were often complicit in the violence, and the state government refused to acknowledge the full extent of what had happened to Muslims. When Nehru visited the state to campaign for the first general election at the end of 1951, he publicly recognised the suffering of the Muslims in the state. He then urged them to journey forward with him. In so doing, Nehru was lauded by one Urdu-language newspaper as 'not just giving hope and consolation' to ordinary Muslims, but 'also showing the way forward' to all Indians.[61] When Nehru visited again the following year, it was reported that he 'gave solace to the aggrieved and assured them that the government will try fully to remove their sorrows'.[62] In 1953, he again promised, 'I will work for Hyderabad until my last breath.'[63] Each time, he vowed to get local rehabilitation efforts working for the displaced Muslims of the state. However, he had to return to the state repeatedly to make the same promise, for the local government dragged its feet.[64] Nehru, as a symbol of Indian secularism, could offer solace and hope. As a patron who had to work through state and local governments, his power was limited.

REPRESENTATION

Given the fragile and contested nature of the Muslim presence in India after the creation of Pakistan and the integration of the princely states, there was a host of questions to be answered about the ways in which

Muslims might participate in public life, in political parties and in legislatures. Indeed, the issue of representation had been central to Muslim political participation since the early twentieth century.

With the inauguration of the Constitution, Muslims lost their separate electorates and reserved seats in state and national legislatures. Many Muslims, like Dalits and other minorities, had long felt that separate electorates and reserved seats were a way of guarding against majoritarian democracy. The Muslim League had pushed for, and won, separate electorates almost from its inception. Congress eventually came to view separate electorates for Muslims as the midwife for the demand for a separate state for Muslims. During the drafting of the Constitution, therefore, the Minorities Sub-Committee of the Constituent Assembly, decided that separate electorates would have no place in the new India.[65]

Although there were few areas of national life that were as polarised as the question of Muslim belonging, there seems to have been a consensus through the mid-1950s that Muslims should not form a separate political party. The Muslim League collapsed in its heartland, north India, after many of its leaders left for Pakistan, and the loss of separate electorates seemed to deprive the party of one of its *raisons d'être*.[66] Other parties formed by and for Muslims were largely shunned. The All-India Jamaat-e-Islami called for a boycott of independent India's major institutions, including elections, the judiciary, the banking system, the army and western-style universities. Muslims, for the most part, seemed to have responded by boycotting the Jamaat.[67] Likewise, the Majlis-i Ittehadul Muslimeen (MIM) in Hyderabad was spurned in the aftermath of the Police Action. After the first general election, when the Hyderabad branch of the Jamiatul Ulama briefly tried to turn itself into a political party giving voice to Muslims, its efforts were discouraged by other Muslims in the state, who felt that organising in this way would just create a 'substitute for the Muslim League or the Ittehadul Muslimeen'.[68] Muslim Conventions were held periodically during this period, but they tended to urge Muslims to abandon the idea of organising themselves in any sustained way.[69] In the first decade after partition and the integration of the princely states, Muslims who organised to bring attention to Muslim problems had their presence in India challenged, as they were likened to the Muslim League and told to go to Pakistan.[70]

The Congress Party, as it had done prior to partition, claimed to speak on behalf of all Indians, including Muslims. In the run-up to the first general election, Nehru, as president of the All-India Congress, urged state Congress parties to live up to this claim by nominating candidates from minority communities 'in adequate numbers' for Congress tickets. He warned, 'If we fail to discharge this responsibility, critics will be entitled to say that joint electorates have failed[.]' Writing from a position of strength, the president of Congress pressed local Congress bodies to make an extra effort to find 'good Muslim candidates', even taking the risk of losing a seat or two.[71] Nehru was not able to assign Congress tickets personally; he could only ask Pradesh Congress Committees (PCCs) to do so. Here again, he acted as patron, urging local parties to live up to his ideals. His circular was the opening bid in negotiations between the All-India Congress Committee and these state committees, during which some PCCs could and did try to water down the directives from the centre. Overall, the results were rather disappointing for Congress Muslims, as fewer entered state and national assemblies in 1952.[72]

By the late 1950s and early 1960s the predominant disposition against forming Muslim political parties began to wane among some groups of Muslims. After a decade in the wilderness, the Indian Union Muslim League began to win seats in elections in Tamil Nadu and Kerala.[73] In Hyderabad city, the MIM was revived by Abdul Wahid Owaisi in the late 1950s. Owaisi was careful to emphasise the party's loyalty to the Constitution, and to distance the party from 'communalism'. He positioned it as giving Muslims a voice to claim their 'share of rights' in India. The revival of the MIM was greeted with much consternation across India, with Urdu papers in Hyderabad and Maulana Azad condemning the move. Owaisi was arrested under the Preventive Detention Act in March 1958 and held for ten months. This earned him empathy and esteem: the MIM won a majority in the Hyderabad municipal elections in 1960.[74]

There seems to have been a rapid shift in the early 1960s. This was, in part, induced by Hindu–Muslim riots in Jabalpur and unrest over language in Assam. In the first years of the 1960s, India's political parties began rethinking several aspects of their democracy via a National Integration Conference (see chapter 6). Muslims who had accepted Congress's strategy became willing to express their dissatisfaction that their loyalty had not translated into a more secure sense of belonging in India. Nehru privately acknowledged there was a 'feeling that nationalist Muslims have been let down'.[75] Dr Syed Mahmud, Congress's most senior Muslim after the death of Maulana Azad in 1958, who had served as minister for external affairs and then as a member of the Rajya Sabha, addressed a Muslim Convention in 1962 and urged Muslims to form a deputation to study the 'backwardness of Muslims in each state' in order to 'chalk out a programme for the uplift of Muslims'. He called for the community to pursue 'unity and integration'.[76] The Convention agreed to form a Majlis-i Mashawarat to address Muslim concerns over education, language and personal law.[77]

By the early 1960s, the consensus that any separate political activity by Muslims was ipso facto anti-national was breaking down. Some Muslims made tentative attempts to re-link separate Muslim political organisation with Indian secularism. These moves were not without controversy: within the Muslim community voices were raised against these new more assertive positions. Though by no means speaking with a unified voice, many in these organisations expressed a shared sense of physical insecurity and isolation. Some considered the community to be subject to what Dr Syed Mahmud called 'manifold injustices and prejudices'.[78] These new self-styled leaders were not content with the notion that they could be fully represented only by the Congress Party without some action on their own part. The celebration of iconic individuals and the preservation of majestic Muslim sites had not spread a feeling of secularism through the multiple tiers of government. Muslims, who were at the heart of Indian secularism, had decided the bargain initially struck was not enough.

Secularism and Untouchability

As Indian secularism took shape in the 1940s, it acquired meaning as a term that could encompass reform of Hinduism and justify special protections for Dalits.[79] This surprising formulation had a long history. Internal critique had been an important part of Hinduism and had helped spur its revival during the British period. Throughout the nineteenth century, reform of Hindu practices, from the abolition of *sati* (widow burning) to changes in the laws for marriage, divorce and inheritance had been the subject of intense debate.[80] Some of those who opposed legislative changes under the Raj had argued that a foreign government had no authority to try to change indigenous practices. With the departure of the British, and the election of overwhelmingly Hindu legislatures, this argument lost its force.[81] Therefore, the Constitution committed the government to reforming Hinduism, especially to abolishing the practice of untouchability in the Hindu community, and to working towards the uplift of Dalits.

The gulf between the iconic and the everyday was evident in governments' approach to the abolition of untouchability. Here, the politics of monumentalism did not centre upon historic preservation, for Dalit sacred sites were rarely recognised as worthy of such attention. Nor was there much official celebration of outstanding individuals. Today, Bhimrao

Ramji Ambedkar is recognised as a serious political thinker, and lionised as the man who, as chairman of the drafting committee, had piloted India's Constitution through to its inauguration on 26 January 1950, but this reputation has been erected in more recent decades.[82] In the years surrounding independence, the Congress Party had shown extreme reluctance to acknowledge Dalit demands and accept Dalit participation in politics.[83] The ruling party had put up what was called at the time 'violent Congress opposition' to the Dalit leader's election to the Constituent Assembly in 1946.[84] In spite of these efforts, Ambedkar reached the Constituent Assembly. His elevation to the cabinet as law member came, apparently, at the request of Gandhi.[85] After helping frame the Constitution, he remained critical of the government, even though he was a member until October 1951. He resigned with a series of speeches criticising the government and Nehru personally, for being 'utterly indifferent to the welfare and progress of the Scheduled Castes and Backward Classes'.[86]

In leaving the cabinet and speaking on behalf of the Scheduled Castes, Ambedkar had violated the unwritten terms of recognition under Indian secularism as policed by Congress: minority representatives could find a place in the national project, but they could not separate themselves from the nation by representing only their own community interest. Moreover, minorities had to verify their 'loyalty' by refraining from criticising Congress or the government.[87]

After his departure, Ambedkar proved irksome to India's leaders. He had been as enthusiastic as other statesmen about the association of the Indian government with Buddhism. He had advocated for the government to mark the Buddha Jayanti as an official holiday, and he had been involved in the adoption of the Buddhist symbols of the chakra and the lion capital of Ashoka as India's official insignia. While government officials were speechifying on the Buddha Jayanti festivities on 24 May 1956, Ambedkar announced he would convert to Buddhism during the second round of the celebrations in October. When the conversion ceremony was conducted, he brought hundreds of thousands of his followers with him.[88] Far from being welcomed, this would have complicated the official commemorations. Indian officials enthusiastically embraced Buddhism precisely because doing so did not show favour to any particular political constituency, due to the fact the faith had so few followers in India.

Upon his death on 6 December 1956, official tributes to Ambedkar were muted. Announcing the news in the Lok Sabha, Nehru managed to praise Ambedkar's revolt against the practices of untouchability, even as he returned time and again to the 'virulence' of his views, and the fact that he 'was not a person of soft speech'.[89] Only a handful of MPs spoke to the adjournment motion that followed. President Prasad did not address the nation over the radio; his message of condolence was a mere three sentences long.[90] A small collection of cabinet ministers, including Nehru, G. B. Pant and Jagjivan Ram, paid respects at Ambedkar's residence in Delhi before his remains were flown to the city of Bombay. None, however, attended his funeral the following day, nor did Bombay's chief minister, Y. B. Chavan, who departed for Delhi to attend a meeting of the National Development Council.[91] Official indifference meant little to the crowd who attended Ambedkar's cremation, which was said to have been the largest of its kind to date.[92]

Ambedkar statues may be a common site in the country in the twenty-first century, but the first one did not go up in India until five years after Ambedkar's death. In September 1961, the Municipal Corporation of Bombay replaced a statue of the Prince of Wales with one of Ambedkar, made by the sculptor B. V. Wagh.[93] Indeed, in the 1950s and early 1960s, commemoration of Ambedkar's achievements and his contribution to the life of the nation was the work of non-official organisations. The Maha Bodhi society, the same organisation that had taken the lead in promoting Buddha Jayanti, began marking Ambedkar Jayanti on 14 April, in commemoration of 'the role he played in the revival of Buddhism'.[94] The day was only added to the calendar of official holidays in the twenty-first century, however.

If the iconic was not to be found in great monuments or great men, it was located instead in great documents: the Constitution, and certain laws. In the final months of the Raj, it did not seem likely that Dalits' demands would be recognised in the new India. However, Dalit groups organised a satyagraha to have their voices heard, both within Congress, and in the Interim Government.[95] Ostensibly at the urging of Gandhi, Nehru responded by appointing Ambedkar to chair the drafting committee of the Constitution.

With Ambedkar in place, India's founding document appeared to fulfil many of the demands Dalits had been making since the 1920s.[96] The Constitution abolished untouchability (Article 17) and declared that no citizen shall be restricted from accessing shops, hotels, wells, tanks, roads or other facilities on the ground of caste (Article 15). It also directed the state to protect the 'weaker sections' of Indian society, especially Scheduled Castes and Scheduled Tribes (known by the abbreviations SCs and STs), from 'social injustice and forms of exploitation' (Article 46). The same article enjoined the state to promote the economic and educational interests of these groups. A Commissioner for SCs and STs was established to oversee progress in all these areas. A further article opened temples to all Hindus. Scheduled Castes and Tribes were granted reserved seats in legislative bodies, but not separate electorates, at the centre (Article 330) and in the states (Article 332); they were allotted reservations in government jobs (Article 335). Knowing the reputation these provisions had for fostering Muslim separatism before 1947, and overly optimistic that rapid change would be made in independent India, it was decided that provisions for reservations would expire after ten years (Article 334). While granting privileges to SCs and STs, groups that had been identified by the imperial power as 'criminal tribes' were excluded from the special provisions.[97] As Rochana Bajpai has argued, reservations for Scheduled Castes and Scheduled Tribes were a means of circumscribing claims to group rights in the Constitution.[98] Indeed, the more expansive reservation policies in southern states like Mysore and Madras were curtailed by the new Constitutional arrangements.[99]

As the members of the Constituent Assembly discussed the draft article abolishing untouchability, there was impatience on the part of Dalit members, and a call for more patience among some of the caste Hindus. Dr Mono Mohan Das, an SC member of the Assembly from West Bengal declared that it was a 'great and memorable day for us the untouchables'. The day, he said, would 'go down in history as the day of deliverance, as the day of resurrection' for India's Scheduled Castes.[100] Shibban Lal Saxena, perhaps giving voice to a larger body of caste Hindus, warned of the 'revolutionary character' of the article opening access to shops, hotels, wells and tanks. He suggested that, in order to give 'the necessary time to Hindu Society to adjust itself', the article ought to be made a directive principle, moving it to the unenforceable section of the Constitution.[101] When the Assembly passed the final draft of the Constitution the following year, members congratulated themselves on their 'great achievement' in abolishing untouchability. According to B. M. Gupta, the provision was a 'triumphant constitutional fulfilment' of the one mission that was 'dearest' to Gandhi's heart: his crusade against the practice of untouchability.[102] The Constitution was a symbol around which Indians could be rallied in the mode of postcolonial nationalism, stirring their collective sense of pride and accomplishment, without requiring much else.

The inauguration of the Constitution was a day for hyperbole and encomium, but even before that day many Dalits were finding that everyday life in independent India was nothing to celebrate. Until recently historians had assumed that the traumas of partition had a levelling and homogenising effect on the internal dynamics of the Hindu and Muslim populations. It turns out, however, that the violence and uncertainty of partition served to reinscribe caste hierarchies in India. Wealthier families could afford to flee, and were sometimes ousted from their property earlier in the cycle of violence. Dalits, who performed essential menial labour, were some of the last to be evacuated from West Punjab.[103] In East Bengal, where there was no official evacuation regime, wealthier, upper-caste Hindus had more resources to deploy to help them move if and when they wanted. Dalits who remained behind became the focus of anti-Hindu violence and ended up moving to West Bengal in a later wave of migrations.[104]

Secondly, the regimes of rehabilitation offered differentiated relief depending upon one's status. Thus, some Dalits who fled West Punjab were resettled in the Karol Bagh neighbourhood of Delhi, but they were settled in separate colonies, composed of mud huts with tarpaulin covers, rather than in pakka houses.[105] Some new colonies, such as the Harijan Colony on Plassia Road in Indore, were built without proper toilets.[106] In the west, there was a great tussle for land, in part because landowners had left behind six million acres of land, but only 4.5 million acres was available in India. Although some of those in charge of relief, including Rajendra Prasad, and Rameshwari Nehru, the honorary head of the Women's Section of the Union Ministry of Rehabilitation, pushed the government of Punjab to allocate land to Dalits, it often did so only reluctantly, and after allotting land to higher-caste landowners first.[107] In West Bengal, where governments were reluctant to do anything to rehabilitate refugees, those with social and cultural ties to government officials were better able to mobilise to demand rehabilitation locally.[108] Meanwhile, the West Bengal government's plans for Dalit refugees involved forcing them out of the state altogether and into remote regions with few facilities.[109]

In areas undisturbed by partition, ordinary life was no better. Despite the provisions of the Constitution, the commissioner for Scheduled Castes and Scheduled Tribes, L. M. Shrikant, reported annually that Dalits were still denied entry to shops, restaurants and hotels, and that they were refused access to wells, tanks and bathing ghats.[110] In some areas, Dalits were passed up for regular work, while in others, 'semi-slavish' conditions characterised the position of agricultural labourers.[111] Forced labour (outlawed by Article 23 of the Constitution) was still a common practice.[112] In terms of reservations for government jobs, upper-caste members of the services showed what Shrikant described with generosity as 'apathy' towards fulfilling the quotas.[113] Almost everywhere the working procedures and conditions of those who collected night soil, were at best 'not satisfactory' and at worst, 'inhuman'.[114]

Dalit members of the Lok Sabha pushed for more to be done to recognise the continuing injustices their communities faced, and to enforce the Constitution. In April 1953, Mini Mata, representing the reserved constituency of Bilaspur-Durg-Raipur, in what was then Madhya Pradesh, moved a resolution calling for the Lok Sabha to pass new legislation to protect Dalits. Speaking in Hindi, she noted that the Constitution had abolished untouchability, but the articles doing so had 'not come into operation in practical form'.[115] It was necessary, she argued, to draft all-India legislation making the practice of untouchability a cognisable offence, for without this, village officers 'do not take the least care' in enforcing the provisions of the Constitution. As she made her case, she was careful to note that 'us Harijans are not all against Congress', but rather, '[w]e understand the Congress government as the cow of plenty'; in other words, Congress rule was a necessary vehicle for the deliverance of Dalit demands.[116] Her resolution promised that a law providing for the punishment of the practice of untouchability would 'enable Scheduled Castes to enjoy effectively the same rights in social, civil and religious matters as are enjoyed by others'.[117] The resolution was framed in a way that did not separate Dalits from the nation at large, and Mini Mata was careful not to criticise Congress. In other words, her proposal conformed to the unwritten rules of the way Congress policed Indian secularism. The ensuing debate was marked by high emotion, with some Dalit MPs expressing anger at the government's failures, and the deputy minister for home affairs, B. N. Datar, censoring those who had criticised the Congress government, calling their statements 'most unparliamentary'.[118] He went on to promise that the government would bring legislation along the lines requested. However, he was sure to note that 'untouchability has to be removed by private effort and I think also by legislation only to a small extent'.[119] Mini Mata's resolution was passed, 'unanimously and amidst applause'.[120]

True to its word, the government introduced the Untouchability (Offences) Bill in the Lok Sabha in 1954. The legislation prescribed punishment for a range of acts, including preventing someone from entering a place of worship, shop, hotel or restaurant, excluding them from certain professions, preventing them from accessing any place, or building a residence, or refusing to admit them to hospitals or educational institutions. Crucially, as it would transpire, the legislation required that this discrimination had to be 'on the ground of untouchability'. It placed the burden on the accused to prove that they had not acted on the grounds of untouchability. Dr Katju, who would preside over the Buddha Jayanti ceremonies at Sanchi in 1956 as defence minister, introduced the bill in 1954 as he was then the minister for home affairs and states. His speech is an astonishing piece of the parliamentary record. Dr Katju was certain that the bill would be passed, and that it 'will receive wide acclaim'. And yet, he was equally certain the act 'will not succeed'.[121] What was really required, he explained, was 'a good deal of propaganda and persuasive education', to turn public opinion against the practices of untouchability.[122] It would be even more effective if what Katju called a 'personality'—a saint and a reformer, a new Gandhi, perhaps—could take up the issue. There were many MPs from across the spectrum who shared Katju's sentiment. They both applauded the legislation and were certain it would fail. Ram Das, who held the reserved seat for Hoshiyarpur-Rachit, in Punjab, exemplified this perspective, as he declared, 'There can be no doubt [. . .] that the law cannot remove this social evil[.]' He noted that there was widespread apprehension that 'it cannot be implemented' because, in his opinion, 'those who implement it are those who have an interest in not removing untouchability'. He, too, called for education, propaganda and even 'missionaries' to do the hard work of changing people's hearts and habits.[123] Reader, they passed the bill.

What explains the odd approach to this piece of legislation? In one sense, it speaks to the widespread scepticism about the competence of the state in postcolonial India (discussed in more detail in chapter 5). It is also exemplary of the divide between the iconic and the everyday. It was relatively easy to pass resolutions and laws. Doing so invariably earned acclaim and applause. But implementation required descending from the heights of righteousness to the messy process of building a new social order. Abolishing practices of untouchability meant breaking old habits of thought and everyday life; it meant upending hierarchies and discarding quotidian privileges. This process was neither simple nor swift, not least because it was agreed that change had to be brought about by persuasion.[124] The invitation to saints and missionaries was an appeal to find an other-worldly solution to these very earthly problems.

As a declaration of goodwill, the act can be understood as part of Indian secularism. As an instrument for transforming the everyday lives of Dalits, the Untouchability (Offences) Act of 1955 was largely a failure. The wording of the legislation, combined with subsequent interpretations by higher courts, tended 'towards a restrictive interpretation of the Act'.[125] Conviction rates, though nearing three-quarters of all cases in the first year, dropped to between 30 and 40 per cent in subsequent years. Dalits in many areas lost faith in the act, and stopped bringing cases.[126]

Not long after the Act came into force, the country witnessed large-scale violence against Dalits in Mudukulathur, in the district of

Ramanathapuram, in today's Tamil Nadu, which highlighted the everyday difficulties Dalits faced across the country. There, the Maravars were one of the dominant castes. Though a former 'criminal tribe', the Maravars considered themselves above Dalits in the pecking order. As Dalits had begun to assert themselves, some Maravars had sought to put them back in their place. R. S. Arumugam, the MP holding the reserved seat in the area in 1957, in a powerful speech, explained the daily humiliations his community suffered:

> At Ponthampalli village in Muthukulathur [sic] Taluk, a Harijan clerk, Shri Rajamanickam, was beaten with his chappals [sandals] by Maravars for having walked with chappals in their street. [...] In Chitrankudi village, a Harijan lady teacher, Miss Lily was beaten by Maravars for having used umbrella in a Caste Hindu street. [...] In Maranthai village, in a tank where cattle used to be washed, four Harijans wanted to take a bath. For this, they were driven away from that village. Cattle can be bathed, but Harijans should not take a bath![127]

Dalit women were not allowed to wear blouses with their saris, and men were not permitted to wear long dhotis. In their own houses they were prevented from using anything but mud pots.[128] Dalit children were often excluded from school.[129]

These individual acts of aggression grew into widespread violence against Dalits during the general election of 1957, and then a by-election shortly after. The local strongman, U. Muthuramalinga Thevar, who had won a seat in both the Lok Sabha and the Madras Legislative Assembly, expected Dalits to vote for him and for his preferred candidate when he resigned his seat in the state assembly. When they defied him, his followers, primarily from among the Maravars, kidnapped Dalits, poured kerosene in their wells and robbed and destroyed their property over several weeks. Immanuel Sekaran was one of the young Dalit leaders in the area. Immanuel had joined the Quit India Movement, and then the Indian army in 1945. He had returned to Ramanathapuram with the goal of pursuing equality for Dalits.[130] After a confrontation with Muthuramalinga Thevar at a peace conference called by the local collector, Immanuel was murdered on 11 September 1957. Collective violence escalated with Maravars attacking Dalits, and then Dalits retaliating. Figures from the Government of Madras recorded that over more than a week, some 2730 Dalit dwellings were burned while nearly one hundred Maravar houses were destroyed by fire. Seventeen Dalits were killed in the fighting, as were eight Maravars, the latter primarily by police called to the area to calm the disturbances.[131]

The most haunting incident occurred at the village of Veerambal, where Dalit villagers took refuge in St Paul's church. A group of Maravars in pursuit set fire to the church's windows and doors, and fired into the building, which contained some four hundred people. Arumugam was joined in the Lok Sabha by fellow SC MP B. S. Murthy in recalling past national tragedies as he recounted this one: 'The tragedy of the "Black hole of Calcutta" and the ghastly scenes of Jallianwalla Bagh [sic] in Amritsar pale into insignificance as we see the lonely church and its helpless inhabitants[.]'[132]

Although some tried to claim the events were anomalous, Sri Balmiki, MP from Bulundshahr, noted with an air of despair that there was 'no special issue' behind what had happened at Ramanathapuram: it was ordinary anti-Dalit prejudice.[133] The *Times of India*'s editorial board agreed, writing that the 'riots are a symptom of the malaise that affects our caste-ridden and stagnant society in many parts of the country'.[134] The official response had multiple elements. At a local level, it took more than eighteen months, but Muthuramalinga Thevar was tried, albeit acquitted, for abetment to murder. A handful of his followers were convicted.[135] He was re-elected to the Lok Sabha at the third general election, but died in 1963. Though the 1955 Act had quickly become a dead letter in most places, by 1964 Madras was lauded as the one state that enforced it.[136] It is unclear if the events in Ramanathapuram were connected to this, or if it stems from the longer history of lower-caste activism in the state.

The second element of the official response to the violence was to promise that these problems would all go away as India developed. In the words of M. Bhaktavatsalam, home minister in the Madras Government, 'only the educational and economic development of the area can produce a lasting solution of the problem'. The local government immediately sanctioned more National Extension Scheme Blocks, housing facilities, irrigation and drinking water provision, as well as the extension of electricity to the area, with the expectation that the government in Delhi would help with funds.[137]

At the centre, there was an abstract appeal to hearts and souls. It was Violet Alva, newly appointed deputy home minister, who addressed the Lok Sabha on behalf of the government, telling the house, 'No amount of crores of rupees are going to solve this problem.' What was required was the 'actual practice of the pure heart, a belief deep down in your soul'.[138] Although it is tempting to dismiss this response as vacuous, it is not without content. Above all, it is an appeal to Gandhian means of social change, where the powerful see the error of their ways and reform themselves.

Indian secularism in this period, focused as it was on the celebration of exceptional individuals and reverence for great monuments, was in part about evoking this feeling among Indians, especially among the powerful. Alva's appeal was also in line with Delhi's approach to social problems of an unfathomable scale: official policies tended to stress the need for people to help themselves. Chapter 4 covers in more detail the ways in which this kind of self-help was central to Indian socialism.

Meanwhile, Dalits were organising themselves in new ways in the late 1950s and 1960s. Shortly before his death, Ambedkar began preparing to found a new political party. Though formally established after his passing, the Republican Party of India (RPI) became his last attempt to organise and advocate for Dalits and Other Backward Classes in national politics. The RPI achieved some success aligning with Muslims in Uttar Pradesh, and with the coalition of groups demanding Bombay state be split into Maharashtra and Gujarat.[139] Shortly after Nehru's death, the RPI leader Dadasaheb Gaikwad organised a major protest in Delhi, on 1 October 1964. Before the march, the RPI published its Charter of Demands.

To read the Charter is to understand the enduring appeal of the iconic, even among those who suffered at the level of the mundane. The party called for, inter alia, the proper implementation of the reservation policy for government jobs and education; for stronger legislation against the practices of untouchability; for the Minimum Wages Act to be enforced; and for land to go to the tiller.[140] The RPI's first demand, however, was for a portrait of Ambedkar to be installed in the central hall of the parliament building, in recognition of his role as 'Father of the Indian Constitution'.[141] The demand for a representative to be included in the national iconography was met reasonably swiftly, as the second of B. V. Wagh's statues of Ambedkar was erected outside Parliament House in 1967. Inaugurating the statue, President Radhakrishnan evoked secularism as a feeling: 'We should not only preach equality but practise it. Whether you are a Hindu, Muslim, Sikh or Christian, the question is whether you are friendly to your neighbour and treat him as a brother.'[142]

Conclusion

A myth often has a basis in truth. Nehru's version of secularism, whereby people of all faiths shared equally in the national project and felt an equal sense of belonging, was not the foundation upon which India's interreligious life was built. India's celebratory secularism might be likened to the facade of a building, rather than its foundation. A foundation is largely unseen and yet keeps an edifice steady. A facade, by contrast, does not offer much stability. I do not mean to imply that this secularism was duplicitous or disingenuous. Architecturally speaking, a facade is important because it is the most visible part. It can lend coherence to a complex structure. It makes a statement, and thereby tries to direct the mood. But behind the facade, all manner of incongruous formations may be hidden. In India's case, some of what lay beyond the celebrations did match the facade. But this public exterior also obscured an often sharp distrust of Muslims and a long-standing unwillingness by dominant castes to relinquish their privileges. While India's leaders celebrated iconic individuals, buildings and texts which represented Muslims and Dalits, quotidian decisions by unseen government officials tended to marginalise Muslims and reinforce existing caste hierarchies. This does not mean that the ideal vision of an inclusive secularism was meaningless, but just that it was limited in crucial ways.

By the end of the Nehru era, many of those claiming to speak on behalf of Muslims and Dalits were anything but satisfied with their position in India and with India's official secularism. Focused as it was on monumental spaces, revered personalities and iconic pieces of legislation, this secularism had left India's least advantaged communities beleaguered and frustrated in their everyday lives. Indeed, in the late 1950s and early 1960s a series of riots sparked a new sense of worry. Conflict had occurred not just on religious lines, but on caste and linguistic lines as well. To meet the rising alarm about these tensions, the Government of India formed a National Integration Council, appointed an Emotional Integration Committee, to look into the role of education in fostering or quelling 'disruptive tendencies' in the country and held a National Integration Conference. One hundred and thirty Union ministers, chief ministers, party leaders, vice chancellors of universities, scientists, industrialists and 'leading personalities' attended the conference in the autumn of 1961. They discussed requiring children to say a prayer for national unity, or read the Constitution each day at school; they contemplated asking adults to pledge their 'faith in the universal principal of civilised society, namely that every dispute [...] should be settled by peaceful means'.[143] The bulk of their discussions focused on three things: education, economic development and elections. Education, it was widely agreed, was 'the most powerful instrument for bringing about national integration', for it could shape young people's attitudes.[144] Equally, 'the development of the more backward areas' of the country was stressed. Eminent economist V.K.R.V. Rao led the discussion on development for national integration, and he called for a special fund to be established for this purpose.¹⁴⁵ Elections were blamed for promoting narrow-mindedness and arousing internecine strife. Therefore a 'code of conduct' for political parties was proposed. The different fields of life in postcolonial India were interlocking: it is impossible to separate secularism from the other goals of the state at the time. It is to those goals most associated with socialism that we now turn, while chapter 6 then returns to the connection between caste and democracy.

FIGURE 4.1. 'It all adds up to 2 million tons', *The Times of India*, 12 November 1957 (supplement), vi. Published with permission of ProQuest LLC. Further reproduction is prohibited without permission.

CHAPTER FOUR

The Myth of Socialism

TODAY, AS WE move further from a world in which socialism is a working reality anywhere, our understanding of this term has tended towards caricature. As the various socialisms that were developed across the twentieth century have been forgotten, the Soviet system has come to stand in for socialism everywhere. It is often assumed, therefore, that India's socialism was modelled on that of the Soviet Union.[1] Even scholars who do not associate India with Soviet-style socialism share with this first group a number of assumptions: that India's rulers sought to bring as much of the economy under state control as possible; that planning was the chief mechanism through which they achieved this aim; that private industry was thereby constricted; that socialism was primarily concerned with cities and the development of heavy industry like iron and steel; and that India's governments barely spared a thought for the countryside in the Nehru years.[2]

The image displayed opposite (Fig. 4.1) is of an advertisement that appeared in November 1957 in a special supplement of *The Times of India* on India's iron and steel industry. The special section reported on the fact that the second five-year plan had set the target of vastly increasing the production of iron and steel. By this point, India had struck agreements with the Germans, the Soviets and the British to build state-owned steel plants across the country. The first two plants—at Rourkela in Orissa (Odisha), and Bhilai in what was then Madhya Pradesh and is now Chhattisgarh—did not begin production until the first months of 1959.[3] Scholars have long referenced these steel plants as a way of exemplifying the command economy. And yet, in the advert shown in Figure 4.1, a private firm, the Tata Iron and Steel Company (TISCO) describes its expansion programme, due to be completed in 1958, promising that its expanded plants will double its capacity. Once completed, TISCO would be able to produce two million tons of ingot steel: as the advert says, 'one-third of the national target of six million tons by the end of the Second Plan'.[4] This is unexpected, since the myth of India's socialism includes the assumption that private industry was either sidelined or restricted in these years. And yet, as this chapter will show, this advert is a reasonable exemplar of the connection between socialism and private enterprise in the early decades after independence, albeit in surprising ways.

The myth of India's socialism is entwined with the myth of Nehru as the architect of postcolonial India. As we have seen in other chapters, the shadow cast by Nehru and his published works is long. Writing his autobiography while in prison in 1944, Nehru had confessed that studying Marx and Lenin had 'produced a powerful effect' on his earlier self.[5] Skipping through his life, one can easily find material to define him as a socialist. For a start, he helped found the Congress Socialist Party in 1934. Then, in the early years of his premiership, India established a Planning Commission and drafted five-year plans as a way of organising the efforts the country would make towards economic development. Shortly thereafter, Nehru as president of the Indian National Congress steered the ruling party to commit itself to pursuing a 'socialistic pattern of society', in 1955. During his time as prime minister, Nehru refused to define 'socialism'; and the use of the word without a clear definition has created a gap that has been filled with the assumption that Indian socialism can be equated with Soviet-style planning.[6] This lazy understanding is also entangled with the myth of the strong state: it has been assumed that India deployed the strong administrative apparatus that it inherited from the British Raj to pursue economic development along socialist lines.

As in the cases of the other myths discussed in this book, an overly simplistic understanding of Indian socialism has been forged through a combination of history and politics. The Swatantra Party laid the groundwork for a caricature of Indian socialism as having 'totalitarian' ambitions. Founded in the late 1950s, the conservative thinkers of the Swatantra Party favoured big business and free trade, and also emphasised the importance of voluntary efforts by individuals in the pursuit of economic development. They drew on the debating tactics of Friedrich von Hayek and Milton Friedman to paint a picture of Indian socialism as aiming at an economy fully controlled by the state,[7] usurping private property and suppressing individual liberty.[8] This narrative has been sustained through the 'opening' of India from the 1980s, during which the economy has been liberalised. As they have told their story, India's reformers have contrasted their work with what they have derided as India's socialism.⁹ The triumph of the west in the Cold War, and the shift towards neo-liberal economics worldwide, at least temporarily discredited models of economic growth that allotted a significant role to the state. The state-controlled economy failed the communist world, the argument ran, so it must have been the cause of India's failure to take off economically in the Nehru years.

Until very recently, historians had been unable to counter, or even add nuance to, this narrative, because they have had only limited access to the relevant sources. Apart from Nehru's works, historians have long had access to the five-year plans, which were published and disseminated widely at the time. However, the quotidian departmental records, not just of the Planning Commission but of other ministries at the centre and in the states, have not been opened in any systematic manner. In the absence of a more complete picture, the blazing furnaces of steel plants have been left to stand for India's official socialism.[10] Scholars who have attempted to understand Indian socialism beyond the plans have either focused on opposition parties,[11] or concluded that India was not very socialist at all.[12]

India had socialism in the Nehru years, but it was more expansive and decentralised than has been recognised. India's socialists encompassed a wide and diverse array of Congress and opposition personalities, all of whom had been shaped by the experience of colonialism and the national movement.[13] Indian nationalism had been forged during the devastating famines of the late nineteenth century, burning the image of starving Indians and indifferent imperialists into the minds of India's leaders. A parallel narrative of deindustrialisation had also been developed by India's nationalists, who had spotted the ways in which imperial policies had benefited British industries while depleting Indian ones.[14] Having based the demand for freedom on the fact that the colonial power had drained India of its wealth, it was widely agreed that independent India had to produce more: more food to feed the population, and more goods to sell to begin to provide for the basic needs of all Indians. Therefore, it is often tricky to differentiate between socialism and development more broadly, because the two shared similar goals in terms of production.

What distinguished postcolonial socialism from general development was that evoking socialism was a way of summoning contributions from everyone and promising that the fruits of India's development efforts would be shared by all. This did not necessarily imply a large amount of public investment. While the country did have some wealthy individuals, the fiscal context for the period of Nehru's rule was one of austerity, and of a recurring balance of payments crisis. Every need, every wish, every plan, every programme, had to contend with the ubiquitous sense that there was not enough money for any of it. If India was to have socialism, it would be a socialism of scarcity.

This austerity socialism did not seem to daunt the country's new leaders. During three decades of mass civil disobedience in the service of the anti-colonial movement, India's nationalists had discovered the power of collective effort to achieve their political goals. The country's new leaders, fresh from these victories, had no desire to 'demobilise' their followers;[15] instead they sought to channel the power of the people towards development. This was not all directed by or through the state, but was rather another aspect of India's postcolonial nationalism.

Building upon Gandhi's constructive programme, socialism in India aimed at the 'all-round development of the individual', as the Uttar Pradesh Congress leader Sampurnanand put it.[16] Purposeful occupation was understood to be character-building. This focus on individual growth was also part of an Indian critique of Stalinism. Discussing Soviet communism in 1958, Nehru noted that he had 'the greatest admiration for many of the achievements of the Soviet Union', but that communist countries had been wrong to coerce individuals in the pursuit of larger aims and to exterminate those who did not comply. He argued that 'real social progress will come only when opportunity is given to the individual to develop'.[17]

Official socialism, elaborated by governments and enacted in state programmes, would therefore be a socialism of self-help. Socialism-as-participation was meant to draw in everyone, from private corporations to ordinary villagers. This was a complicated form of mobilisation, for it involved top-down efforts to rouse the people to demand the kind of development the government was willing to provide for them. The context of fiscal austerity and the enthusiasm for self-reliance help explain a further characteristic of Indian socialism: it did not pose a threat to private property. Instead, India's elites were asked to make themselves part of the plan.

This links to two more aspects of India's socialistic development that this chapter will highlight. First, the end goal was to reduce inequality, but not produce 'dead equality'. As Rajkumari Amrit Kaur explained, 'Manifold diversity is a part of the fullness of social life provided man realises that the fruits of such diversity are for the use of others.'[18] Social hierarchies were not to be abolished, but mobilised for developmentalist ends. Companies were expected to implement the social welfare policies enacted in laws, and were encouraged to go further by providing housing, education and basic welfare to their workers. In villages, elites were asked to treat landless labourers as part of their family, and to mobilise resources for the good of the entire community. Because those with more capital, whether financial or social, started from a higher base and had more to mobilise, this self-help socialism reified and even exacerbated existing inequalities. The final pattern in Indian socialism that emerges, therefore, is that during India's socialist years, the gaps between India's richest and poorest widened.

To understand the nature of Indian socialism, this chapter begins with an overview of planning and its ambitions. It then turns to the role of private enterprise in Indian socialism, presenting the township of Faridabad as a case study. The following section outlines the limited extent of nationalisation, and then the expectations and hopes India's leaders had for its business sector. In the second half of the chapter, socialism in the countryside is investigated. Two practical manifestations of the slogan 'land to the tiller' are explored: land reform and the Bhoodan (land-gifts) movement. The chapter concludes with a discussion of the ways in which Community Development programmes were part of India's self-help socialism.

Socialism and Economic Planning

While Indian socialism was wider than economic planning, it helps to begin with planning, because that is where other scholars tend to begin.[19] Planning per se was not socialist. Rather, the relationship between planning and the state existed on a spectrum: at one extreme stood the Soviet Union where the plans set out the economic objectives of a state that tried to take complete responsibility for allocating most resources, setting prices on all domestic goods, mobilising labour, and reordering property rights.[20] At the opposite end of the spectrum, there was no inherent antipathy between planning and capitalism: after the experience of the Depression it was widely agreed that the state could help private industry by shielding businesses from competition, helping in the supply of inputs, or correcting market failures.[21] Planning was also not the monopoly of socialist countries: Pakistan's first five-year plan began in 1955, yet the country is hardly known as a paragon of socialism.

India, like the Soviet Union, drew up formal five-year plans, but that did not mean that India's model was the Soviet one. First of all, India was not starting from scratch. Independent India had inherited a government that had put together a system of protections for private industry, in the form of tariffs, enacted after the Government of India had devolved power over this sphere to Indians in 1919.[22] Secondly, India began thinking about planning during the Second World War, and its first plan, for 1951-56, was drafted before the Soviet Union opened relations with decolonising countries. The man said to be the primary author of the second plan, P. C. Mahalanobis, may have invited Soviet experts to consult during the drafting, but he invited around four hundred specialists from all over the world to advise the Planning Commission on the plan, and did not appear to have any special devotion to Soviet opinions.[23] Indeed, the Soviets recognised that they could not offer India much of a model in the largest sector of its economy, namely agriculture.[24] Meanwhile, the model for Indian industry was 'import substitution industrialisation'. This was the formula endorsed by the US and prescribed by the newly emerging field of 'development economics' for every late-industrialising country at the time.[25] Still, import substitution industrialisation was not a total formula for the economy; it was a prescription for the narrow field of heavy industry.

Even in the sphere of large-scale industrial development, however, the planning apparatus did not allow the Indian government to command economic activity. The centre of planning activities was the Planning Commission. Those who first sketched the outlines of this institution in the late 1940s included K. T. Shah, Gulzarilal Nanda and Shankarrao Deo. Shah, who had been trained at the London School of Economics, was concerned with tuning the economic system to a more equitable distribution of wealth per capita,[26] and had helped form the early socialist opposition in the Indian parliament.[27] Their original vision was of a body that would not only suggest which paths to take, but also have the power to allocate resources and enforce its recommendations. When the matter was passed to the cabinet, however, Vallabhbhai Patel opposed the idea. When finalised, the Planning Commission found itself without enforcement powers, and with no resources to allocate: it was 'basically advisory'.[28]

In spite of this, the Planning Commission did fulfil three important functions. First, led by the Cambridge-educated statistician P. C. Mahalanobis, it was at the heart of postcolonial knowledge production about India's population and its economy. Mahalanobis had overseen the development of new methods of gathering data and new institutions to analyse them. When he offered his services to national planning, Nehru jumped at the opportunity to act as patron.[29] The production of statistics did not always make India's population or its economy fully legible, however, or the problems each faced more tractable. Second, at this time when India was abuzz with experimentation, the Planning Commission, employing all the tools of mid-century social science, tended to oversee pilot projects, testing out new ideas before they were introduced to the country as a whole. Finally, the Planning Commission's Programme Evaluation Organisation (PEO) studied the working of these experiments, and continued to do so as they were rolled out. Established in 1952, with D. G. Karve, a prominent economist from Bombay, at its helm, the PEO was funded by the Ford Foundation, and its initial task was to evaluate the Community Development projects. As the years passed, the PEO's ad hoc committees visited sites, wrote reports and made recommendations for improvements on virtually every aspect of India's development. Its work underscores the experimental and heuristic nature of India's planned development.

Much of the rest of India's developmental administrative machinery was characterised by rivalry. In New Delhi, individual ministries not only refused to cooperate with the Planning Commission, but also held the purse strings. As a result, separate divisions of government gathered their own data, set their own targets and allocated funds through ad hoc bargaining.[30] In the context of scarcity, the planning dynamic between the centre and the states was tense and complex. In the first two plans, the Planning Commission tried to incentivise states to raise revenues themselves and to fund their own plan projects. At the same time, the centre provided matching funds for some types of projects. Rather than raising revenues, however, states tended to run up debt to pay for projects with matching central grants. Because they were able to raise less revenue, poorer states fared worse under this system, increasing inequalities between states.[31] The predominant dynamic within government was one of suspicion and competition over scarce resources, rather than of collaboration, let alone widespread coordination towards a single purpose.

Perhaps more important than the shortcomings of the administrative apparatus was the fact that India's planners circumscribed their own ambitions. In a series of speeches after the inception of the second plan, Mahalanobis partitioned the economy into what he called two different 'spheres'. One sphere, that of large-scale industrial development, he argued, ought to be directed by the state. But for what he called the 'diffuse' sphere, he felt state intervention would be too difficult.[32] To get a sense of the scale of the sphere he set aside, according to one estimate the diffuse or unorganised sector comprised 90 per cent of employment and 84 per cent of India's gross national product in the early 1950s.[33] For this vast sector, the plans amounted to something between a government stimulus and a Christmas wish-list. To understand India's official socialism, therefore, one must look beyond the five-year plans.

Private Enterprise and Socialist Development

India's planners have been stereotyped as either holding Stalinist ambitions, or being beholden to big business. Neither characterisation is entirely accurate. Private enterprise, as this section will show, was important to India's socialist development. Industrialists were called upon to make themselves part of the plan; taxation targeted them for help with redistribution; legislation tried to require them to accept what today would be known as corporate social responsibility. Rather counter-intuitively, however, the overall effect of these measures was to increase inequality in India. To understand the place of private initiative in independent India, let us begin with the story of Faridabad.

In circumscribing planning, Mahalanobis was acknowledging how hard it was to direct already existing sectors of the economy. Where there was a clean slate, however, there was room for imagination and innovation. The partition of the subcontinent was both a crisis and an opportunity to forge new communities and new economies from scratch. To help resettle Punjabi refugees, five new townships were built: Etawah, Nilokheri, Faridabad, Rajpura and Tripuri. The central government quite literally broke new ground in these townships, meaning each could be a 'national laboratory for new approaches'.[34] Uninhibited by existing interests, these experiments offer a unique glimpse into the minds of Indian administrative entrepreneurs imagining the possibilities of a new India in the context of socialism.

Faridabad is not ordinarily associated with socialism, but without using the word, many of the characteristics of the age were nevertheless evident in this township. Its story is largely known through Sudhir Ghosh, the bureaucrat who claimed responsibility for initiating a scheme to build Faridabad. Educated at the University of Cambridge, Ghosh returned to India and joined Gandhi's entourage. After independence, he worked in the Ministry of States, and then made his way to the Ministry of Rehabilitation. According to Ghosh's version of events, he was aghast when he saw that the Government of India was due to spend Rs.40,000 per day on housing and feeding forty thousand refugees from the North-West Frontier. He proposed that instead of merely meeting their basic needs, the money ought to be given as a loan and the refugees put to work. He would 'invest this capital in such a manner that out of their work would grow a new town which would be their permanent home, with industries that would provide permanent means of livelihood for them'.[35] Here we have another example of the way in which Nehru could act as a patron for the projects of others, for Ghosh recalled that when he proposed the scheme to the prime minister, 'Mr Nehru jumped at the idea. He was always willing to support any revolutionary idea'.[36] Other like-minded nationalists, including Kamaladevi Chattopadhyay, had similar ideas at around the same time.

Ghosh and Chattopadhyay insisted that Faridabad ought to be built not by the Public Works Department, but by the refugees themselves. To bring this ideal about, refugees were organised into labour cooperatives. With some outside expertise, these cooperatives made their own bricks and did their own carpentry to build simple two-room houses, without latrines or private water taps.[37] According to Ghosh, they also laid fifty miles (eighty kilometres) of metalled road, and '[e]very bit of the stone that was required for the building of the roads was broken by the manual labour of the settlers'.[38]

The township included a hospital, health centres, schools, a polytechnic institute, and a water works system. It was even said to have a 'socialised health service that is probably unique in India'.[39] Those who fell sick or were injured were entitled to relief. The town acquired a second-hand power plant, which had been received from Germany as part of war reparations.[40] A diesel engine workshop was opened, and again, learning from German diesel engines obtained through reparations, refugees began to manufacture their own generators and engines for power tube wells.[41] Faridabad, like the other new townships, was lauded as a model of the ideal economy for the new India. In the words of one correspondent from *The Times of India*, its initial success was a testament to the 'enthusiasm generated among the people to do new and better things'.[42] The other new townships were built on the same basis: they were exemplars of what self-help could accomplish for individuals and for the nation.[43]

Even though it was built through labour cooperatives, and had socialised healthcare, private industry was to be the mainstay of the economy of the township. This set Faridabad apart from Nilokheri, a much smaller refugee township, where nearly all economic activity was organised into cooperatives.[44] Plans for Faridabad included one hundred plots to be sold off to various enterprises. As the director of the Delhi School of Economics, V.K.R.V. Rao, explained in a review of the project, 'The expectation was that industries would spring up,' because the government had provided basic facilities like water, power and communications. However, 'the expectation was not fulfilled'.[45] Instead, by the spring of 1952, unemployment in the township began to bite. By the time of the fifth anniversary of independence, it was reported that half of the able-bodied employable population was unable to find work. They were surviving by selling their gold and taking out loans.[46] The same fate befell most of the new model settlements.

Each of these townships had its own flavour, as they were the separate experiments of the administrators who founded them, but as the Government of India responded to the crisis in the model townships, we can get a taste of what it had in mind for India's future. While the Government of India handed over the running of the hospital, health centres, school and power plant to the Government of Punjab,[47] its efforts for industry remained focused on the private sector. Although the Government Press at Simla was moved to Faridabad, it came with six hundred of its own employees, and only expanded later.[48] The Government of India tried to lure private industries with a raft of 'concessions and facilities to industrialists'.[49] These giveaways included lower utility rates, loans for up to 50 per cent of machinery to be installed in any new enterprise, and the offer that the government would have new factories built to the spec required by the industrialist, with these construction projects using refugee labour.[50] Gradually, by the middle of 1954, new enterprises had agreed to move into facilities at Faridabad, including an auto-lamp factory, a drainage-pipe factory, and a British-Indian joint-venture bicycle factory.[51]

One thing not to be found in the Faridabad experiment was a strong impetus towards government control. Ghosh boasted of the transformative effects of the self-help township: '[t]he real achievement of Faridabad was not the houses, roads, hospitals and schools but what happened to the human beings as a result of doing the work they did'.[52] Indeed, Faridabad was indicative of the shift, to be discussed in chapter 5, away from the bureaucratic machinery inherited from the Raj. Ghosh, like so many senior nationalist bureaucrats at the time, found the ordinary administration, in this case, the Ministry of Rehabilitation, to be a 'stumbling block' to his plan.[53] To avoid working through the 'normal machinery of government', the Faridabad Development Board was founded. The Board, according to Ghosh, 'would be free to function as an autonomous body, something like a small-scale Tennessee Valley Authority'.[54] The Board was chaired by Rajendra Prasad until he became president of the Republic, when the prominent Congressman Hriday Nath Kunzru took over as chairman. The other members were Kamaladevi Chattopadhyay, president of the All-India Cooperative Union, and Asha Devi Aryanayakam, of the Basic Education Organisation. Though not a member of the Board, Nehru was said to have attended its meetings.[55] When the township's economy failed to thrive, the instinct of the Government of India was not to move a raft of state-run enterprises into Faridabad, but to provide more aid to private industry.

Faridabad was indicative of the era's approach to the problem of how to pursue economic development with social equality.

So what role was there for government control of the economy in Nehru's India? Nationalisation was a relatively small feature of Indian economic life in this period. Initially things looked as if they would take a different turn. Just as with the Planning Commission, early plans for nationalisation were ambitious. Thus, in January 1948, the report of the Economic Committee of the Indian National Congress called for progressive nationalisation of the Indian economy. India's businessmen had different ideas, however. Eight of the country's largest industrialists had already outlined their preferred course of industrialisation, via state protections and assistance for private enterprise, in the Bombay Plan of 1944.[56] After the 1948 report, fifty prominent industrialists convened a meeting in Bombay at which they voiced 'grave apprehensions' about the proposals, and warned that large-scale nationalisation would reverse the industrial progress so far achieved.[57] Although partially overshadowed by the assassination of Gandhi, the 1948 report did cause a storm, and the Government of India eventually adopted a much softer line. The government's Industrial Planning Statement, which was published in April 1948, reserved only three areas of economic activity for the exclusive purview of the state: defence, railways and atomic energy.[58] Eight years later, as India's planners were approaching the apex of enthusiasm for state-led industry, a public monopoly had been extended to seventeen industries which were deemed strategic, while in another twelve industries, the state committed itself to investing more, and declined to guarantee private enterprises against nationalisation. These so-called basic industries included machine tools, ferro-alloys and fertilisers.[59] These industries tended to require high capital inputs and had a long horizon of returns. In other words, the public sector's primary investments were in areas where private firms had little incentive to venture.[60] Moreover, government involvement in heavy industry benefited private industry to the extent that it ensured cheaper inputs.

To be fair, a few sectors were brought under state ownership, and the history of official thinking about state-run enterprises is discussed in more detail in chapter 5. Briefly, most states nationalised road transport in the late 1940s, for example. These moves helped to reduce competition with the railways, and also to provide better facilities to both bus passengers and drivers. In Uttar Pradesh, for instance, nationalised road transport meant the introduction of regular timetables and fixed bus stops, as well as waiting halls with refreshments and toilets for passengers. The staff of the UP State Road Transport Corporation acquired canteens, clubs, rooms for resting at night, paid holidays and a benevolent fund 'to assist low paid employees in case of dire need'.[61] Beyond road transport, India's fledgling airline industry was nationalised in 1953. Insurance firms were nationalised and the Life Insurance Corporation of India was founded in 1956. In addition, the Reserve Bank of India took increasing control over the banking sector. By the end of Nehru's rule, the Reserve Bank had the power to inspect banks' accounts and to prevent them from winding up, as well as the authority to merge weak banks with strong ones. All of this, combined with a national deposit insurance scheme, helped to stabilise the banking system, reducing the number of bank failures and increasing savings.[62] Electricity, too, was partially nationalised, but this was done in such a way as to avoid harming big business.[63]

Indeed, this limited role for state-run industry is consistent with the fact that India had a mixed economy, part socialised, part private. The working assumption among scholars, however, has been that India's governments, representing the socialist side of this equation, were generally hostile to private enterprise.[64] This is not borne out by either the statistics or the rhetoric of the time. The ambitious nationalisation proposals of the late 1940s were fleeting, and they quickly gave way to a general acceptance of the place of private industry. By the end of the third plan, public sector investment had risen from 3.3 per cent to just 8.3 per cent of GDP. Meanwhile, the state's share in total investment went from 25 to 50 per cent.[65] In other words, the government was investing more money, but it was not all going to the public sector.

Instead of calling for nationalisation, many on the left of Congress were content simply to urge entrepreneurs and business leaders to work for the common good rather than only for their own profit. This did not change, even as governments prepared for the expansion of public sector industry. Shortly after the Congress Party committed itself to pursuing a 'socialistic' pattern of society at its Avadi session in 1955, M. S. Shah, the Union minister for revenue and civil expenditure, looked to mollify the Indian Merchants Chamber, telling them that 'the field left open to the private sector was a vast one', and that Government would encourage and assist private enterprise during the second plan.[66] Similar moves were made at the state level. The Mysore chief minister Kengal Hanumanthaiya, for example, met with business leaders to assure them that 'socialisation is not the same as nationalisation', and that in Mysore, the government would rely on the private sector to meet the industrial targets of the second plan.[67]

The prime minister joined the charm offensive. Nehru inaugurated the twenty-eighth annual session of the Federation of Indian Chambers of Commerce and Industry in New Delhi, a forum he was invited to address almost every year. Acting in his favourite role as the nation's educator, Nehru addressed the idea of socialism in his 1955 speech, informing India's industrialists, 'There is no sense in getting frightened of a word.'[68] Indeed, he noted that 'whenever I use the words socialism, capitalism or communism, immediately all kinds of arguments and passions rise up in your minds [...] which confuses thinking'. Instead, he preferred to 'put aside these particular words'.[69] Planning would cover private industry, he explained, but he reassured India's most influential industrialists that for the private sector, planning would 'not be quite so precise and definite'. Indicating where initiative would lie, he appealed to large industrialists to make themselves 'part of the plan', to coordinate their efforts with the government's, and above all to 'think of what is good for the people as a whole'.[70] In the corporate sector, postcolonial nationalism took the form of this kind of self-help socialism. When TISCO took out the advert that opens this chapter, therefore, the firm was declaring to the country and to the government that it had made itself part of the plan.

Companies were not just left to their own devices. They were expected to contribute to the socialistic society by paying their taxes to allow for redistribution, and by looking after the welfare of their employees. Increasing government revenues through taxation was certainly on the radar of India's new leaders. It was widely known that during the Second World War, private individuals and companies had amassed huge profits through government contracts and by playing the system of controls. It was equally well understood that they had hidden their money, either to avoid admitting how it had been acquired, or to evade taxes on it.[71] To bring this money out of the shadows, the Interim Government established an Income-Tax Investigation Commission. As the Commission began its work, the government also set about recouping some of this lost revenue through a 'disclosure drive'. It promised that any person who came forward to confess 'the fact of his past frauds and their full extent' would be given lenient treatment. Those who made such a disclosure and offered 'every possible facility to the income-tax officer in the investigation of the frauds' would be spared criminal prosecution.[72] Unfortunately, as *The Times of India* reported three years later, there was 'no evidence' that the drive 'had excited any co-operative response from the tax evaders'.[73]

In the absence of willing cooperation, the Commission also undertook dramatic raids on businesses and private residences, carrying away cartloads of materials, through which it would then sift to make its case.[74] This work helped to unearth the many ingenious ways in which enterprises evaded taxes. The practice of under-reporting income was widespread: the Commission found that in the average case, actual income was more than 600 per cent of what was originally reported to the tax authorities.[75] Companies tended to hide their income by 'making the field of inquiry so wide that investigation might become difficult and exhausting', and so wearing down investigators.[76] To this end, companies tended to open a large number of subsidiaries, only for a short time, and then close them again; they shifted money between these companies in opaque ways. To uncover the true extent of a company's liability, the Commission had to go through 'a maze of false account books [...] spurious sales, under-invoicings [*sic*], fictitious entries, and a hundred and one other practices and devices'.[77]

By the end of 1953, the Commission had uncovered Rs.46 crore of concealed income.[78] By 1957, however, all income tax arrears, including those owed via the Commission process, amounted to no less than Rs.200 crore.[79] For perspective, this is about half of what the Centre expected to spend on social services, including housing, education, health and welfare of the backward classes, during the whole of the second five-year plan, which had begun the year before.[80] Actual recovery of tax due was extremely slow. Even after a business owner confessed to fraud and began to negotiate a settlement with the Commission, 'the admission begins with a small figure which is gradually and grudgingly increased, as the Commission goes on confronting the assessee with incontrovertible evidence', so that the final amount due was only reached after protracted negotiations, and tended to represent a fraction of the true income involved.[81] When the final amount was agreed, people were then permitted to pay in instalments, eroding the value of the settlement through inflation.

Unsurprisingly, the government still wished to increase the revenue at its disposal.[82] It brought in an expert, Nicholas Kaldor, to advise on how the tax base might be expanded. Kaldor had been trained at the London School of Economics and then went on to a career at Cambridge, where he garnered fame for his work on redistribution. He spent two and a half months in India in 1955, after which he recommended that the central government move from reliance on high income taxes to more moderate taxes, levied on a broader base. On the basis of these recommendations, between 1956 and 1958 the Government of India, spurred by the then-finance minister T. T. Krishnamachari, introduced a barrage of new revenue streams, including an excess dividends tax, a bonus tax, a wealth tax, a capital gains tax, an expenditure tax and a gift tax.

India's middle and upper classes howled at the 'crushing' new burden, not least because the Government of India simply ignored Kaldor's recommendation that the top rate of income tax ought to be lowered to 45 per cent as these new taxes were introduced.[83] Instead, the top rate of tax hovered around 80 per cent. And the taxes did not garner as much as had been hoped: the wealth tax, for example, was projected to bring in Rs.15 crore, but in 1957-58 raised only Rs.9 crore.[84] New taxes spawned new forms of tax evasion, moreover. In 1961, as yet another Income Tax Bill was debated in the Lok Sabha, Banarsi Prasad Jhunjhunwala, representing Bhagalpur, lamented in Hindi that 'no matter how many laws we make, we cannot remove the habit in our country's citizens of stealing taxes and being dishonest'.[85]

While paying taxes was a patriotic duty few seemed inclined to fulfil, another avenue by which private companies were to be 'part of the plan' was corporate welfare. Indian statute books were filled with legislation to improve workers' lives. This body of legislation covered factories, mines, plantations, transport and commercial establishments. These laws set rules for wages, safety, welfare and social security (including maternity and workers' compensation). Special acts provided for the protection of children, relief from indebtedness and shelter from the predation of contractors.[86] Some of these laws had their origin in the interwar years; some were amended after 1947; many new ones were passed. By the count of the Ministry of Labour and Employment, by 1961 there were thirty laws at the centre and another eighty-two in various states (and this number did not include acts related to industrial disputes). The overall thrust of this body of legislation was that the burden of improving the lives of Indians ought to fall on the private sector.

Some patriotic businessmen of the period did bear in mind Nehru's appeal that they should work for 'what is good for the people as a whole'. Benefits at the TISCO corporate town of Jamshedpur,[87] in what was then Bihar and is today Jharkhand, are almost legendary: housing, healthcare, education for children, maternity benefits, paid leave, workers' compensation, retirement and provident funds. However, a closer look reveals that these benefits accrued primarily to higher-ranking employees. For example, throughout its history, TISCO has only provided company housing to around one-third of its employees. This accommodation went to skilled workers and middle-level management. For the rest, there were the *bustees* (informal settlements), where conditions were so poor that workers went on strike in 1958.[88] Overall, the effect of government legislation and corporate welfare was to produce a more differentiated workforce with a bafflingly complex array of privileges.[89] The net result was increased inequality.

The leather tanning industry is one example of a private industry which benefited from government aid, but without its increased wealth passing to its poorest workers. The tanning process requires extensive use of lime, chromium and other harsh chemicals to treat the raw hides. Labourers, usually Dalits, often stand in vats of chemicals as they work, exposing them to severe skin and lung irritations. Back in 1946, an enquiry found that working conditions were 'most deplorable in almost all the tanneries', whether in Calcutta, Madras or Kanpur: employees were given protective boots and gloves in only a tiny proportion of tanneries; bathing and washing facilities were 'totally absent' except in two large tanneries. The provisions of the Factory Act were 'flagrantly violated in all the smaller tanneries'. Hours of work were not regulated, and children were employed 'in a fairly large number'. Women received maternity benefit at only one large tannery in Madras; in Kanpur this obligation was evaded by ensuring that female workers were not entered on the registers of the tannery. The enquiry report called for 'stringent and rigorous enforcement of the provisions of the Factories Act in all the tanneries', as well as 'housing, education, medical aid, and similar welfare activities' to be undertaken 'on a large scale'.[90]

Over the next twenty years, the tanning industry expanded with government assistance. By the late 1960s, India was the world's third-largest exporter of leather. Exporting more than Rs.28 crore-worth of cured hides and skins each year, the industry was an important source of foreign exchange for the country.[91] Government restricted exports of raw hides and skins, ensuring that most had to come through the tanneries before export. When access to South African wattle bark was lost as India cut off trade relations over apartheid and the treatment of overseas Indians there, the Government of Madras sanctioned both the harvesting of wattle bark from government forests and new schemes for wattle trees to be planted, ensuring tanneries had access to this primary input.[92] Technical training was expanded, but it tended to go to those who already had some education, rather than to the men and women who handled the hides.[93] The Uttar Pradesh Government provided loans to small-scale footwear manufacturers, and organised a quality marking scheme to help improve standards.[94] Improved education, better access to inputs, help with quality control and marketing: all of these helped to increase profits for those selling the finished product. Meanwhile, for the Dalits who did the hardest jobs in the tanneries things had barely improved: many still worked without protective equipment, in workplaces without latrines or washing facilities.

While there were seemingly innumerable examples of businesses that ignored the request to 'think of what is good for the people as a whole', a business willing to play by the rules could also do well in independent India. Take the bicycle industry. Cycles had been imported, largely from British firms, since the late nineteenth century, slowly gaining a place in Indian life. After independence, with protection in the form of a 60 per cent import duty,[95] and restrictions on foreign ownership, Indian bicycle factories expanded from nine factories in 1951 to eighty-eight a decade later, with production expanding nearly tenfold.[96] Although all-in-one production facilities were encouraged through licensing, by the middle of the 1950s the decentralised production of cycle parts had expanded too.[97] In Punjab, the industry was helped not only by incentives in Faridabad, but by a government finishing and testing centre in Ludhiana.[98] In addition to the furnaces of the iron and steel plant, therefore, the advert below for Sen-Raleigh cycles (Fig. 4.2) helps represent the transformative effects of industry on Indian society in this period.

According to the legend about is foundation, Sudhir Kumar Sen, the company's creator, had won a cycle race while a student at the University of Calcutta, and thereafter had 'decided to devote his future to making India bicycle-conscious'.[99] Through personal contacts, he had negotiated a deal with the Nottingham-based company Raleigh to produce bicycles in India. Foundations for the joint venture's factory in Kanyapur, near Asansol in West Bengal, were laid in 1951. Production began the following year, with a capacity of one hundred thousand cycles per year, and quickly doubled.[100]

The venture conformed to the ideals of private industry in socialist India: it was nationalist, not nationalised. For one, from its inception it had 'absorbed a large number of refugees', doing its patriotic duty by providing work to those who had come from East Bengal.[101] As the township at Kanyapur grew, the company built housing in a 'workers colony' that was reported to have tree-lined streets and 'ample playing facilities' for children, as well as electricity and sanitation for all homes.[102] While Sen-Raleigh Industries was not state owned, the West Bengal government had provided direct assistance in the form of training for refugee workers, and the promise of assistance in 'securing its requirements', as the factory was built.[103]

Figure 4.2 presents us with the image of a couple, each prosperous enough to own a bicycle, and with leisure time to spare.[104] Like radios and

FIGURE 4.2. 'You can be proud of your Raleigh in any company', *The Times of India*, 9 October 1965, 8. Published with permission of ProQuest LLC. Further reproduction is prohibited without permission.

trips to the cinema, owning a cycle had become a marker of the gentle rise of India's middle classes.[105] Directly addressing the reader, and implying that the couple are courting, the advert promises to make 'you feel proud'. It is a message of empowerment, even if the scale of this empowerment might have differed for men and for women.[106] The advert includes a pun implying that the Raleigh is the bit of the company's name to take pride in, while the fact that the cycles are made by Sen-Raleigh is noted in smaller print. Rather than representing all Indians, however, the couple provides us with an illustration of the increasing spread of India's inequality in this period. Wealth accrued to the middle classes, represented by small business owners, middle-management in larger-firms, government servants and English speakers.

By the end of the Nehru era, the bicycle industry had been drawn into India's internationalism: the United Nations Industrial Development Organization studied the country's industry and recommended that other developing countries could start their own bicycle industries 'based on the Indian experience'. Their recommendations included government assistance to private industry in the form of protective tariffs, importing raw materials, training of workers and managers and providing testing labs.[107] Meanwhile, Sen-Raleigh Industries had begun exporting cycles, particularly to Africa and the Middle East.[108]

A full picture of Indian socialism must be taken with a lens that can capture more than the five-year plans. Doing so reveals that governments in the Nehru era were pro-business, albeit selectively so. While this stance can be clearly distinguished from the free market advocated by neo-liberals, which would see as little government involvement with business as possible, governments in Nehru's India were nevertheless keenly aware of the significance of the private sector in the mixed economy. TISCO was as essential to this process as was government-owned Hindustan Steel. Indeed, in the two decades following the Second World War, the corporate private sector witnessed 'a clear and significant increase in the concentration of economic power', according to a report published in the mid-1960s. The four largest groups, including Tata, increased their share of private share-capital in the economy.[109] Private small and medium businesses also did well: bicycles, sewing machines, electrical fans, machine tools and electrical motors saw production increase by between one hundred and one thousand per cent in the years before the third plan.[110]

What gave this model a socialist flavour was that governments provided support for private industry with import and export controls, by securing inputs and finance, by providing access to technical training, by assisting with quality control and marketing and by attempting to contain strikes. In turn, they urged these businesses to provide corporate welfare for their employees and to pay an increasing array of taxes. Business, for its part, seems to have honoured India's tax code and labour laws only selectively. Moreover, the system, reliant on the goodwill of the wealthy, seems to have increased existing inequalities and even created new ones, albeit at a pace that was slower than that witnessed in more recent decades, as neo-liberal expansion has been accompanied by the rapid widening of wealth gaps.

Village India: Socialism as Participation

Focusing on industry as the potential heart of India's socialism, scholars had until relatively recently assumed that the needs of the countryside were subordinated to the imperatives of industrial development.[111] This is far from the case. In the first two decades after independence, India's governments had one urgent priority for rural life: increasing production. After the deprivation of the war and the devastation of the Bengal famine, the overriding economic aim in the years after independence was to grow more food. The period can best be understood as a time of experimentation to this end.[112]

The first attempt to increase production was an extension of wartime efforts. A national campaign to grow more food had been launched in 1943, as the imperial government became aware of impending food shortages, but it had come too late to ease the pain of the great Bengal famine. At independence, India faced a different, albeit related, set of constraints: it had not only lost access to food produced on the Pakistan side of the borders, but also was looking to preserve foreign exchange to use for importing inputs for industrialisation. In 1949, therefore, the Government of India launched a campaign to make India self-sufficient in foodgrains by 1951. To achieve this end, governments called on all Indians to 'Grow More Food', as the campaign was known. Nehru took to the airwaves to enlist recruits in the 'crusade for food production', telling them that it was 'a war in which every citizen can be a soldier and can serve his or her country'.[113] Styled exactly as the anti-colonial campaigns had been, the Grow More Food campaign included public pledges, and themed days and weeks such as Compost Week. At the same time, governments made fertilisers, improved seeds and implements widely available to farmers for purchase.

Instead of growing more food, however, the country came perilously close to famine in 1950 and 1951. This was at least partly down to the fact that the summer monsoons failed in both years. A cyclone hit the states of Madras and Orissa in 1950, and the same year the Kosi river flooded, devastating Bihar and eastern Uttar Pradesh. The wartime system of procuring food from surplus areas to distribute to deficit regions, always based on guesswork and hard-nosed bargaining rather than genuine estimates of production, failed to ensure food went to the hungry. In Kishtwar District in Jammu, a team of journalists discovered that livestock had perished, and people had been forced to survive on herbs and grass.[114] In Bhagalpur, Bihar, it was reported that citizens in the most precarious economic position were only managing to eat 'one full meal in two or three days'.[115]

Meanwhile, the statistics devised to estimate how much food was produced and how much was required were dismissed as utterly unreliable. Only with the help of massive imports of food aid, and the return of the monsoon, did the situation ease after 1952.[116]

Conducting a postmortem on the movement, the Grow More Food Enquiry Committee noted that when the campaign was launched, 'it was not realised that all aspects of village life are inter-related and improvements could not be split up into a number of detached programmes operating independently'.[117] Instead, a broad reordering of rural life seemed to call for the restructuring of rural institutions: property rights, panchayats (village councils), cooperatives and schools. While not conforming to essentialised understandings of rural socialism as collectivisation, many parts of these rural reforms were framed in socialist terms.

'Land to the tiller' was the slogan raised most often, and with increasing fervour through the 1950s, to call for the transformation of rural life. Widely associated with socialism around the globe, it was the basis of numerous attempts to reorder property relations in the countryside. These were partly a matter for land reform legislation, but, as will be shown below, redistribution was also the object of a mass movement. It would be a mistake to regard land reform as a one-off effort that was mostly completed in the first years of the 1950s.[118] The agenda for land reform was too expansive and too decentralised to complete quickly. Moreover, each new law produced unintended consequences and gave rise to calls for corrections. Land reform, therefore, was a near constant preoccupation of governments during the first three plans. Indeed, as late as 1961, the Planning Commission's panel on land reforms, presided over by the then-Union planning minister, Gulzarilal Nanda, pleaded with states to 'complete all land reforms' within the period of the third plan, that is, by 1966.[119] In this long process, lawmakers took aim at four broad areas of reform: the elimination of intermediaries, placing a limit on the size of large holdings, providing security to tenants and, finally, rehabilitating landless agricultural labourers. As land reform was a state subject, the Planning Commission acted primarily as surveyor and supervisor, appointing a near constant stream of committees of experts to review existing legislation, outline the successes and failures of various measures, and make recommendations for changes.[120] Because of the decentralised and heuristic nature of the project, tracking the details of land reform via state legislation can fill volumes.[121] Here, a schematic overview of reforms tracks their relation to socialism and reveals their effects upon inequality in the countryside.

In the early years after independence, Indian states did abolish most titled intermediaries, including zamindars and jagirdars, who had collected taxes and maintained order at a local level for hundreds of years. Most states also introduced a ceiling on land ownership, decreeing that land above the cap ought to be made available to those who tilled it, in most cases, for purchase. Both of these measures, however, increased the number of landless labourers. Large landholders were permitted to 'resume' land for personal cultivation, and as they did so, they evicted tenants. Even the most radical reform, enacted under Sheikh Abdullah on the Indian side of the disputed state of Jammu and Kashmir, suffered a similar fate. Enacted in 1949, the Big Landed Estates Abolition Act set a ceiling for personal cultivation. Above the limit, land was handed to tenants without compensation to landlords. While 450,000 acres were redistributed under the law, there was also widespread evasion. With advanced warning of the changes to come, landlords circumvented the ceiling by partitioning their land among their relatives, or even entering their relations in local records as tillers, to make them eligible for redistributed land.[122] Across India, landlords adopted similar strategies to bring their holdings nominally under the cap without sacrificing their wealth.[123] As they did so, they evicted tens of thousands of tenants, swelling the ranks of landless labour.

Many states did pass laws aimed at conferring rights upon tenants to either purchase land or to remain as tenants without fear of eviction. Tenancies tended to be oral contracts, however, and it was difficult for tenants to prove their rights. In the parts of Assam that were included in the Permanent Settlement by which rates of land tax had been fixed in the late eighteenth century, officials did 'not have accurate statistics on the size of holdings' to implement land ceiling legislation, while for the cultivators themselves, '[n]o adequate record of rights' existed.[124] In Punjab, as in most states, the laws were administered by the lowest revenue officials, known as patwaris. These officers were known to accept 'gifts' to change their records in favour of landed elites. They were said to have recorded tenants as 'dead, deserted or ejected even though they were still tilling the land'.[125] A minority of tenants with well-founded rights had them secured, while sharecroppers, contract farmers and those with annual tenancies could lose even this tenuous access to land.[126]

Legislative land reform widened the wealth gaps in the countryside. While more households became owner-cultivators, the absolute number of landless agricultural labourers rose in this period. Differences between states were marked: the percentage of the rural population eking out an existence as agricultural labourers rose in Uttar Pradesh, Assam and Madras, but fell in Kerala, Madhya Pradesh, Punjab and Rajasthan.[127] As more men searched for work on farms, women lost access to work altogether. Many were unable to even find enough casual labour to be counted as labourers.[128] Real wages fell and did not recover.[129] As the disappointments of one wave of reform after another became known, the cry of 'land to the tiller' was raised with increasing frequency in the 1950s, not just by the Communist Party, but by Congress[130] and even the new opposition Swatantra Party,[131] which was known for opposing state interference in the industrial sector.

Legislation was not the only means by which land was transferred from the rich to the poor. It was also part of a mass movement conceived by an anti-communist messiah. In 1944, the people of Telangana, then a region of the princely state of Hyderabad, had taken up arms against the landed elites, demanding land to the tiller, and the transformation of social life. The Nizam's regime had sought to suppress the uprising with force. After the Government of India invaded the state in September 1948 and removed the Nizam's government, it ramped up efforts to quell the insurgency through military operations and large-scale imprisonment. In April 1951, Acharya Vinoba Bhave walked, quite literally, into the conflict, and launched a plan to end it with love and the voluntary redistribution of land.

Born in Kolaba District, in today's Maharashtra, accounts of Vinoba's life have an air of hagiography about them. He is said to have taken an oath of celibacy at the age of ten and learned some eighteen foreign and Indian languages during his long life. He studied in Benares (Varanasi) for a time, and then joined Gandhi's ashram.[132] Although he spent time in jail during the Second World War, he was not a member of the Congress Party. From Gandhi's death until he marched into Telangana, he had lived a life of relative seclusion on his ashram.

In April 1951, Vinoba attended a meeting nearby and, having heard of the unrest in the Telangana districts, decided to walk through the area to get a sense of the situation, and 'to spread his message of love, trust and peace'.[133] When he arrived in the village of Pochampalli, several Dalit families attended his public meeting and urged him to find a way to give them land. Initially, according to lore, Vinoba was speechless, and he muttered something about approaching the government for assistance, 'but then a sudden thought crossed his mind'. He decided to ask the others in attendance to donate land to the landless. At this, Sri Ramachandra Reddy, a local landholder, offered up one hundred acres, half of his holdings. 'That evening Vinoba reflected deep into the night and the unmistakable call from the inner sanctuary of his heart came distinctly commanding him to dedicate himself to this new kind of Yajna [sacrifice].[134] The Bhoodan mission was born.

Vinoba dedicated himself to turning this single act of sacrifice into a movement. He began walking through India on his mission. On a quotidian level, his schedule was modelled on that of Gandhi. He woke at 3 a.m. and began the day with ninety minutes of prayers. By 5 a.m. he had started walking so that he and his entourage could reach their destination by noon. He was preceded by volunteers who announced his arrival to the villagers.[135] After a small meal, and some spinning, he held a meeting every afternoon, where he heard grievances, tried to settle disputes and collected donations of land. Every day at 5 p.m. he held a prayer meeting, which began with readings from 'all the sacred scriptures of all the major religions of India', including the *Bhagavad Gita*.[136] This was followed by a sermon from the Acharya, 'in the nature of a heart-to-heart talk with the audience' on any number of subjects, from the virtues of sobriety and spinning to the utility of cooperative farming.[137] Whilst he received spontaneous donations of land, he also made demands of landlords. Telling them that they should treat him as if he were an extra son, the Acharya insisted that each give him his rightful share of their property for him to redistribute to the landless. Vinoba tended to use the Gandhian neologism *Sarvodaya*, meaning uplift for all, to describe his project. He stressed that there was no conflict between Marx and Sarvodaya, and he emphasised that Sarvodaya was ready to 'absorb everything that is good in other ideologies and isms'.[138] While not everyone felt the same way, the compatibility between socialism and Gandhian Sarvodaya was stressed by many.[139]

Nehru, spotting an opportunity to act as patron, wrote to Vinoba asking him 'to remain there as long as he conveniently can'.[140] Having overseen a lengthy and unsuccessful military campaign against the communists in Telangana, Nehru now began to speculate that, 'a psychological and friendly approach often yields greater results than coercion'.[141] The prime minister was quick, too, to bring states on board as patrons. Upon hearing of Vinoba's mission, Nehru wrote to the Government of Hyderabad to request them to assist the Acharya in any way possible.[142] Hyderabad, and then most states, passed laws and established committees to help administer the redistribution of land. Official publications broadcast Vinoba's story to help it reach a larger audience. The Planning Commission began to include Bhoodan in its surveys of land reforms.[143] As the planners drew up schemes to settle seven hundred thousand families of agricultural labourers during the third five-year plan, they eyed Bhoodan land for this purpose.[144]

Bhoodan exemplified both postcolonial nationalism and the way that Indian socialism addressed inequality. Firstly, India's land problem needed a solution that could both overcome the opposition of landlords and circumvent the need to provide them with compensation. To do this, Bhoodan mobilised new sentiments among those at the top of existing social hierarchies for redistributive ends. While moral pressure was exerted on landlords in the brief periods during which Vinoba camped in their villages, redistribution ultimately relied on their goodwill. Secondly, the role of government was essentially auxiliary, supporting and encouraging private initiative. Drawing on the experience of Gandhi, it was widely believed that a messianic figure such as Vinoba might just provide the moral inspiration required to transform rural India. As we saw in chapter 3, when it came to changing the most ingrained forms of inequality, such as untouchability, India's legislators argued that this kind of moral pressure was the only way to bring about real change.

Bhoodan is representative of Indian socialism in less flattering ways as well, because it exemplifies just how difficult it was to turn the simple idea of voluntary redistribution into prosperity for all. At the Bhoodan settlement at Bhupnagar, Gaya District, Bihar we get a full picture of how Bhoodan operated on the ground. Bhupnagar did not begin with natural advantages, for it was 'located amidst jungle', some five kilometres (three miles) from the nearest settlement. This was typical of Bhoodan donations, as landlords tended to 'sacrifice' their least productive lands. Because of its features and its location, Bhoodan workers found it difficult to recruit people to colonise the donated lands. Twenty-one Scheduled Caste families were eventually persuaded to settle in the new colony around 1957. While each family was given between three and five acres of land, the settlers tended not to make use of the wells dug, or to use improved seeds, manures or better implements, making it challenging to eke out a viable existence. The PEO blamed agricultural extension workers for these failures, claiming they did not visit the colony due to its remote setting. Overall, families still resorted to wage labour to make ends meet eight years after colonisation had begun. In other words, their economic position seems hardly to have budged. Indeed, in the first decade of its existence, fourteen families left Bhupnagar. Some fled because their previous employers, to whom they were still indebted, threatened and intimidated them until they returned to their former village. Others departed because there were not enough opportunities for waged employment in or near the colony to support a family. Some were simply unwilling to live a life of 'privation' in the depths of the forest.[145] Although the call of land to the tiller was simple, it turned out that, in order to prosper, the tiller needed much more than just land.

SELF-HELP SOCIALISM AND COMMUNITY DEVELOPMENT

If entirely new communities found it difficult to escape existing social hierarchies, most village dwellers did not even have the option of trying. For most of India, village reform, or Community Development, as it was called, was the prescription. In the late 1940s, the idea of remaking communities through collective self-help was somehow in the air: we have already encountered urban experiments on this front in the form of refugee townships. Community Development drew on ideas of village reconstruction that had been circulating globally for decades. In India, these included Tagore's Sriniketan and Gandhi's ashrams, first in South Africa and then at Sabarmati in what was then Bombay Province and is today Gujarat.[146] The early years of the Community Development programme were supported by funding from the Ford Foundation and from the United States' government. Scholars have tended to debate whether Community Development was revolutionary, as its practitioners claimed, or conservative, as some later scholars have charged.[147] Both of these perspectives have failed to see that Community Development was the primary manifestation of government-initiated Indian socialism in the countryside. Rather than collectivising private property, government sought to inspire, spur and complement private initiative. Instead of challenging existing power structures, it sought to mobilise them for new purposes. Rather than redistributing wealth directly, it aimed at channelling nationalist energies to encourage rural dwellers to work together for the benefit of their village and of the nation. This kind of mobilisation, repeated across several sectors including social welfare[148] and youth work,[149] was a complex dance: government officials mobilised Indians to demand those improvements which the officers were willing to help them request.

While historians with access to US archives have credited Americans with the inception of the programme,[150] on the Indian side, it was S. K. Dey who steered Community Development through the Nehru years. Born in a village in Sylhet, in what would become Bangladesh, Surendra Kumar Dey, according to his own dramatic account of his life, grew up with twenty members of his family living off just six acres of land. He went on to train as an engineer in the US, first at Purdue University and then at the University of Michigan. For sixteen years he worked as a manager for a company selling medical equipment, but at independence, he quit his job to serve the nation by rehabilitating partition refugees at a new township he named Mazdoor Manzil, in Nilokheri. Though the two refugee townships of Nilokheri and Faridabad were similar, Dey used the language of socialism more often than Sudhir Ghosh did, to say nothing of the Americans. He repeatedly described Nilokheri as 'an ideal socialist island'.[151]

It was Dey who was chosen to oversee Community Development as it moved, with the aid of money from the US, from being a pilot project to a nation-wide one. He was exactly the energetic kind of individual that tended to thrive under Nehru. Sceptical of the existing administrative machinery, Dey did not oversee a ministry for the first four years of this programme. Instead, he was installed at the helm of what was called the Community Projects Administration. As with the other experiments of the time, to be discussed in chapter 5, this was done because the administrative machinery inherited from the Raj was seen as being 'accustomed to rule by the sword' and would take time to be remoulded 'to serve a free people'.[152] Only in 1956 did the administration of Community Development become a ministry in the Union government.

Dey argued that Community Development, Sarvodaya and the socialist pattern were 'expressions of the same concept'.[153] Participation was the central force through which this socialism was to be achieved. In a pamphlet, *Road to Welfare State*, his Ministry for Community Development laid out both a diagnosis and a cure for mid-century rural India. Colonialism had left the economy 'static for generations',[154] while the Second World War had 'knocked the bottom out of the Indian economy', leaving 'universal distress in its wake'.[155] Building a 'new and better way of life' for Indians was a tremendous task, given that India had a population of 362 million spread across an entire subcontinent.[156] On top of all this, government, whether at the centre or in the states, lacked finance and trained personnel. 'Our country is poor,' the Ministry of Community Development stated bluntly and frequently.[157]

India may have been poor, but its people were regarded as a potential resource. Ignoring the many different ways rural dwellers scraped together a livelihood, the Ministry estimated that in non-irrigated areas, farmers had, 'about six months to spare in the year'. In a statement typical of the way in which landless labourers were framed as lazy rather than on the margins of survival, officials estimated that those without land had 'roughly eight months in the year to idle away'. Community Development was conceived of as a way of mobilising this 'idle time' to build roads, schools, irrigation and drainage, and 'the thousand other necessities of life' all with 'limited government finance'.[158] While the people were often seen as a resource, they were simultaneously a burden. In order to be mobilised for nation-building, Indians had to be made to 'develop a proper outlook'.[159]

National transformation through self-help seemed feasible because of the successes of the anti-colonial movement. When Indians had banded together to force the British to quit their country, that had only been the first phase of India's revolution, according to the Ministry of Community Development. Invoking the nationalist slogan 'inquilab zindabad' (long live the revolution), the Ministry declared, 'The battle continues.' National reconstruction, the 'second phase' of the revolution, would be 'arduous and long' and would have to be waged through both industrialisation and Community Development.[160] The people would have the central role to play: 'They have to gird their loins and get down to the ground with the axe and the shovel and start multi-purpose development on their own individually, collectively and in groups.'[161] The aim was the foundation of 'the Welfare State envisioned in the Constitution'.[162] Government agencies were to be mere 'complements to the people'.[163]

Community Development was not one programme begun in 1952 and rolled out over time. Rather, it was reinvented more than once in pursuit of the aim of rousing what was repeatedly referred to as the enthusiasm of the people. It initially focused on mobilising people and capital for one-off tasks such as building roads and wells. Although villagers did seem to join the first round of projects readily in many areas, their passion quickly waned. To try to build a more sustained form of enthusiasm, Community Development later evolved to be concerned with building village institutions: panchayats, cooperatives and schools.

Attention shifted first to centre on democratic participation. In the mid-1950s, Balwantray Mehta, Congressman from the former princely state of Bhavnagar, in what would become Gujarat, was commissioned to look into ways to 'discover or create' the interest required to sustain Community Development. He developed a scheme in which the village panchayat, elected by universal franchise, would be given responsibility for making decisions about development. The idea was that 'local discretion' would give rise to 'local initiative'. Mehta conceived of Panchayati Raj as a three-tier system of decentralisation, in which a panchayat would have 'the sole authority' over development projects in its area. While the idea of creating panchayats was seized upon by Dey and others, the kind of radical decentralisation whereby panchayats would be given 'the power to make mistakes and to learn by making mistakes', as Mehta recommended, was never really contemplated.[164] District officers were reluctant to give up their powers; while Dey himself worried that village panchayats lacked an 'integrated picture of the development of the whole of India', to the point where allowing them to really make decisions over development would mean 'national planning will become a farce, if not a total fiasco'.[165]

Panchayats proved to be a laboratory for experiments in local democracy such as election by public show of hands, or by unanimous vote,[166] but when it came to socialist local development, they did not fulfil expectations. Local elites tended to dominate in these councils. Even where reservations provided for positions on the council for Scheduled Castes, these members tended to be treated as subordinate.[167] Meanwhile, panchayat members from dominant castes did not, in Dey's evaluation, 'look at these resources as a trust and themselves as joint trustees for the entire community'. As a result, Dey lamented in 1964, the economic assistance coming from the government 'continued to flow, on a preferential basis to the people who are more powerful, who least need economic assistance from government'.[168] This was typical of India's socialism. Rather than challenge existing hierarchies, it attempted to co-opt them, and awaken in elites a sense of trusteeship and responsibility towards their fellow countrymen. Instead, the elites simply co-opted the new institutions and worked them for their own benefit.

Shortly after panchayats were reinvented, cooperatives were added to the list of 'basic institutions' every village ought to have. Cooperatives were envisioned as institutions that would enable universal participation in the village economy. Even this simple premise, however, was rife with contradictions. Dey, whose Ministry for Community Development was given a Department of Cooperation in 1959, explicitly connected cooperatives with the 'reduction of inequality between citizens' and with socialism: 'Cooperation by its very definition means mutual aid between members of a cooperative society on the basis of equality.' And yet, the cooperative was also likened to the joint family, which Dey described rather unsparingly as the 'co-existence of the genius and the moron, the artist and the buffoon'. Regarding the cooperative as a joint family also meant 'aid by the strong to the weak so that the latter can rise to the level of the strong as equal members of the community'.[169] In other words, this was an attempt not to level existing inequalities, but to change the affective foundation of village hierarchies, and repurpose them for developmentalist ends.

For all the talk of them functioning as a joint family, different cooperatives tended to serve different sections of the rural population. Credit cooperatives tended to be colonised by the very rural moneylenders they were meant to replace. Instructed to lend on business terms, they excluded the neediest.[170] Governments did try to organise the most marginal members of rural society into farming cooperatives, particularly for those who were settled on 'waste' land. For example, in Pilibhit District in Uttar Pradesh, the government earmarked more than 14,600 acres of uncultivated land to be reclaimed by some 1,100 settler families over the course of the second and the third five-year plans. These colonisers were a mixed group, with a majority of Other Backward Classes, and then smaller numbers of Scheduled Castes and educated unemployed. The Uttar Pradesh Government built roads and bridges, while the Colony Administration built houses and allocated them to settlers. Although the families were required to join the local joint farming cooperative, this did not meet their needs. For one, keeping accounts of inputs, profits and so on necessitated the employment of a full-time accountant, but settlers did not have the funds to employ one. More importantly, farming cooperatively required produce to be brought to market and sold rather than consumed by the tillers, with profits returning to farmers only after sale. For the most marginal, however, the point when crops were ripe was the point at which their resources were exhausted. Quite understandably, these farmers needed direct and immediate access to their produce, which participation in a cooperative did not allow.[171]

The third 'basic institution' essential for every village was to be the school.[172] At independence, India's new leaders had acknowledged that the country needed education, writing into Article 45 of the Constitution an obligation for governments to provide free and compulsory education for children up to the age of fourteen by 1960. Nonetheless, universal education did not become a priority of the Union government until more than a decade after independence. Individual states, however, not only pursued policies closer to the Constitutional directive, but also pushed the centre to do more.[173]

In this sphere, the centre followed the example set by the state of Madras. Before 1947, this southern state had had one of the most progressive and extensive education programmes in British India.[174] After independence, it restarted some programmes that had been discontinued due to the war, including a mid-day meal scheme, relaunched in 1956, which fed 1.3 million children.[175] Madras was also at the forefront of an innovative scheme to urge people to build their own educational institutions: the

School Improvement Conference. At these conferences, communities were mobilised to start or improve a local school. Beginning with a pilot project in February 1958 at Kadambathur in Dangleput District, within three years 133 such conferences had been conducted. They amassed contributions amounting to Rs.4 crore, including everything from construction and electrification of buildings to provision of books, musical instruments and first aid materials.[176]

The centre realised that this model fitted in perfectly with India's socialism of scarcity. As the Union government began to think seriously about fulfilling its constitutional obligation on education, a National Seminar on Compulsory Education in 1961 estimated that just finding buildings for schools would cost Rs.330 crore. The Seminar called the problem 'colossal', and proceeded to decide 'unanimously' that 'the time had now come to place the responsibility of providing school buildings squarely on the village community itself'.[177] The Seminar recommended that the country adopt the self-help model developed in Madras to expand education, and so did the third plan.[178] As the school completed the trio of village institutions, it was imagined as essential to 'accelerating social revolution in the villages', because '[s]tudents of all castes and creeds meet here together, play together and read together'.[179]

When Indians were handed responsibility for building their own educational institutions, this burden did not fall evenly on the population, however. Communities with more experience of education would have had concrete ideas about how the local school ought to function. Those with resources, whether land, buildings or equipment, would have been able to deploy these to build and supply their school to a higher standard. Those who understood how the bureaucracy worked or had connections to politicians would have been able to tap into programmes of government assistance.[180] India's most marginalised populations, the poorest and most remote communities, did not lack the 'urge' to educate their children, but they may have lacked the means to turn it into reality. Even within a relatively prosperous village, it was not inevitable that community efforts would level inequalities. In many cases, Dalits were excluded from schools altogether. Where they were not, they often had to sit separately in classrooms, or even outside them,[181] and it was alleged that they were made to eat their free mid-day meals separately from the other children.[182]

Dey seemed genuinely surprised and dismayed at these developments. At a meeting of development experts at the end of 1964, he lamented that in the Ministry of Community Development they had been unable to provide either safeguards or incentives to ensure that Panchayati Raj would function for the benefit of all members of the village: 'We have appointed many committees and many study groups [. . .] but no satisfactory answer has yet been forthcoming.' He appealed to the experts assembled to use their brainpower to find a way to ensure that the strong sections which run the institutions 'attend to the more urgent needs of the weaker sections'.[183] India's official socialism was premised on the haves extending benevolence towards the have-nots. Instead, the privileged monopolised social institutions and the resources that came with them.

Meanwhile, just as panchayats and cooperatives were being introduced to reinvigorate Community Development in October 1959, another nationwide push to grow more food was being initiated. This one, however, departed from the model of mass participation. The 'package' programme was designed to provide all inputs—seeds, fertilisers, insecticides and irrigation, plus the credit—simultaneously for intensive use in selected districts.[184] This shift was credited at the time to the Ford Foundation, which recommended it in 1959, but it also drew inspiration from experiments in India. In Madras, the government had adopted a 'selective and intensive' approach to the Grow More Food scheme, aiming for coordinated, integrated changes in the methods of agricultural production, but on a limited scale, between 1949/50 and 1951/2.[185] During the first decade after independence, governments in India had held competitions for 'Krishi Pandits' (master farmers), which tended to be won by wealthy farmers who had been able to afford their own version of a package programme.[186] When the Intensive Agricultural Area Programmes were launched with pilot programmes in several districts 1960, they targeted already better-off agriculturalists, who were well placed to take advantage of these schemes.

At first glance there seems to have been a tension at the heart of rural development, a conflict between providing inputs to those who could most readily use them to increase production and encouraging universal participation. During the 1950s and 1960s, governments in India at the state and national level pursued both, throwing everything they had at increasing production, without seeking consistency between the different experiments. Collective self-help was the hallmark of Indian socialism in the countryside. It was both a democratic programme, and a way of channelling postcolonial nationalism for new purposes. At the same time, it was not designed to produce equality in India's villages: fresh from the altruism of the national movement, Dey and the community developers expected elites to exercise their power for the good of the village as a whole. This self-help socialism was a paternalistic attempt to redirect existing hierarchies to new ends.

Conclusion

For every myth cooked up, the recipe calls for an ounce of truth. In this case, it is true that India had planning, and that the plans called for state control of some industry, especially the 'commanding heights' of the economy. But this was a relatively small part of what was considered socialism in independent India. Planning for state-run industry was like a painstakingly crafted icing on a cake that otherwise lacked a recipe. Instead of dictating and carefully measuring all that was to go in, India's governments called on all Indians to become bakers, and to mix in whatever ingredients they could contribute. This was not a deviation from 'pure' socialism; this *was* Indian socialism. Indeed, as historians have learned more about postcolonial socialism, whether in Asia or in Africa, they have found that other socialisms too tended to be decentralised and 'deviant' in their own exciting ways.[187]

Socialism as Community Development in village India relied on mass participation, albeit on highly unequal terms. There was a corollary for the cities. Nehru and Mahalanobis, as well as leaders at the state level, accepted not only that private property and private enterprise would continue to exist, but that they had to be encouraged. Industrialists were invited to make themselves part of the plan. They could do this by producing the goods India needed most, but also by providing for their employees through corporate welfare schemes. State-run enterprise was part of the picture; and the next chapter explores this in more detail.

Indian socialism aimed not to demolish existing hierarchies, but to invest them with new emotional foundations and then redeploy them for benevolent, developmentalist ends. Many exemplary individuals rose to the challenge and helped to hold back the forces of inequality that seem to press ineluctably on a developing economy. But the very nature of self-help was that those who already had capital would deploy it and see it increased.

Self-help was chosen because of the fiscal austerity of the time, because it drew on habits mastered in the anti-colonial campaigns and because work was understood as an essential part of character-building for individuals. One further reason that self-help was chosen to be the mechanism through which development and socialism were pursued was that India's new political leaders were sceptical of the administrative machinery that they had inherited from the Raj. This scepticism about the 'state' in India is the subject of the next chapter.

CHAPTER FIVE

The Myth of the Strong State

OPENING A CHAPTER with a vignette, as readers and writers know, is a way of using a smaller episode to illustrate a larger point. Chapter 1 began with a discussion of the film *Nehru* because it is an example of the wider trend of understanding India's first prime minister as an isolated figure who singlehandedly shaped India's postcolonial life. I have refrained from using a vignette here, however, because the starting point of the chapter is to disaggregate the state. Until the late twentieth century, scholars commonly thought of the state (any state) as a unified entity. We imagined this thing as having a character and sometimes even a will. In many ways many of us still do this. Indeed, political responsibility seems more meaningful if we adhere to this conceit. History writing, too, is a simpler task. However, what we speak of as the state is really a complex set of institutions and people. This set is not fixed or bounded. It does not have a single or homogeneous character. The different segments do not communicate seamlessly; coordination is an ideal never realised. Much of this is accidental, but some of it is intentional: an independent judiciary is designed to be a check on the powers of the legislature and the executive, even as each of these three 'branches' of government are composed of people and institutions which are regarded as part of the state. That we nonetheless speak of 'The State' is a tribute to the power of narrative in shaping our understanding of the world. When one takes a single event and weaves it into a story of an interlocking whole, the effect is to conjure the state as unitary, separate from society, and with the potential to act upon the people and the economy in a rational and coordinated manner.[1]

Even though this understanding of the state has grown in popularity in the scholarship on India, one of the biggest canards that still finds its way into discussions of postcolonial India is the idea that India had a strong state. The story goes that independent India inherited the administrative machinery of the Raj, and that because of the turmoil the government faced in the aftermath of independence, partition and the integration of the princely states, as well as the imperatives of socialist nation-building, the leaders of new India did little to reform the bureaucracy or the police which they had inherited.[2] Most of those who propound the myth of the strong state do not disaggregate the thing they purport to describe. Instead, India's 'strong state' is often shorthand for three characteristics: a unitary state with a tendency towards the centralisation of power; an effective state that monopolised development and modernisation; and an authoritarian state that was maintained at a distance from society and was therefore able to clamp down on dissent and ensure political stability.[3]

As we have seen in other chapters, the notion of India's strong state is closely linked with the myth of Nehru as the architect of independent India, for he is said to have been committed to 'statist' change.[4] It is certainly easier to imagine a unitary and centralising state if it can be personified in one man wielding extraordinary control from his residence at Teen Murti Bhavan. When contrasted with the messy compromises that India's coalition governments often have had to make, one-man rule certainly does seem efficient and effective. The strong state is also linked to the myth of India's socialism. Without a nuanced understanding of the local character of Indian socialism, it has been easy to assume that socialism leads inexorably to the creation of a unitary state, monopolising economic activity, and perhaps even flirting with authoritarianism. Finally, scholars of the broader project of nation-building after independence have also tended to argue that nationalism with all of its popular initiative was wound down after independence, as the state monopolised nation-building activity.[5]

While tied to the other myths, the legend of the strong state has its own origins in the successful myth-making of both the imperial government and the national movement about the character of the colonial state. Under the Raj, the governing centre set itself up as moral exemplar, arbiter between quarrelling parties, pace-setter for reform and guarantor of the peace and stability of the time.[6] As the British devolved power to the provinces with the Government of India Acts of 1919 and 1935, the focus on the federal government as the crucible of power intensified. In part this was because the British convinced themselves that the responsibilities they retained at the centre would be enough to hold India to empire.[7] By the end of its days, the British Raj had come to maintain its authority with a mix of carefully choreographed pomp and bursts of overwhelming force.

This veneer of authority was draped over the thin steel frame of the Indian Civil Service, to conjure the effect of a leviathan imperial state. But like the Great and Powerful Oz, when one pulls back the curtain to examine the levers of power and those that pulled them, one often finds diminutive men unable to achieve very much.[8] Nonetheless, the idea that the colonial state had overwhelming strength was useful to the anti-colonial movement. Nationalist leaders could criticise the excesses of the police (so much power), and the imperial authority's half-baked reforms (so much wasted potential) and win the argument either way.

Once again, the sources available to historians have only reinforced the idea of the strong, centralised state. As with the other myths, the dominance of Nehru and his *Selected Works* in the scholarship for this period cannot be understated. If one's main subject is the leader, and one's sources are his letters, it would take extraordinary imagination not to place him at the centre of the narrative one constructs about power. Nehru had a more realistic understanding of his own position, however: 'Even though [...] I may be the head of the administration, the head is so far removed from the other parts of the body, that I can hardly see the tail!'[9] The prime minister made this observation not as a casual aside, but at the inauguration of the Indian Institute for Public Administration, an institution established for the scientific study of the bureaucracy.[10] Somehow, Nehru's understanding of the limitations of his own powers has not stopped historians from ignoring their subject's views on the question.

In the case of the strong centralised state, a few other figures have played a role in creating the myth. One was Abul Kalam Azad, who as president of the Congress Party in the mid-1940s, had led the Congress delegation to the Cabinet Mission, the team sent by the British to negotiate with the Muslim League and Congress to finalise the terms of the transfer of power. From his position as Congress president and also as the Party's most prominent Muslim member, Azad had worked to devise a constitutional scheme for a united India. Because the other players in the drama of the Cabinet Mission, the Interim Government, and the decision to partition British India all passed away without offering their own account of these tumultuous years, Azad's autobiography is one of the only accounts of partition by a senior figure intimately involved in the negotiations. In it, he claims that Lord Mountbatten convinced Patel, Nehru and Gandhi of the merits of dividing the subcontinent. He did so on the basis that 'if the Muslim League were not there, then we could make a plan for a strong central government' which would help secure India's unity.[11] Later historians have picked up on this assertion as they have re-evaluated the history of partition.¹² The idea that, however reluctantly, Nehru, Patel and eventually Gandhi too agreed to partition in order to have a strong central government in free India has echoed through the scholarship ever since. What India's first leaders got was certainly more unitary in character than any arrangements for a free, undivided India would have been; but that is not the whole story.¹³

Another key figure in the making of the myth was B. R. Ambedkar. Often lauded as the author of the Constitution, Ambedkar, as chairman of the drafting committee, is said to have argued over every proposition, while the other members of the committee were often absent. Ambedkar, it must be noted, also credited the civil servants who worked with him, especially S. N. Mukherjee, and B. N. Rau.¹⁴ He was sceptical that politicians working in the states would implement the provisions of the Constitution that he held dear, such as the abolition of untouchability. It is said, therefore, that he preferred codifying as much as possible to ensure 'centralized control' in his constitutional structure.¹⁵ Although not everyone in the Constituent Assembly agreed, scholars argue, Ambedkar won the day.¹⁶ But desiring control and successfully establishing it are two rather different things. Moreover, as the state is not a unitary entity, one must be careful about assuming the imprint of a single individual, or even a small cadre of them, across all of its varied institutions, rules, laws and structures. Finally, one must be wary of assuming that India's 'founding moment' set everything in stone.¹⁷ Constitutional scholars note that, far from being static, the character of a constitution emerges and changes as it is 'worked' by politicians, administrators and ordinary citizens.¹⁸

Still, the sense that newly independent India had had a strong state was only heightened during the era of instability that stretched from the 1980s to the early 2000s. Encompassing the assassination of two prime ministers, and multiple regional insurgencies, there was a widespread perception that India was suffering a 'crisis of governability' in this period. Its state was said to be 'omnipresent but feeble', with central and state governments beset by interminable power struggles.¹⁹ This was coupled with academic analysis and anecdotal stories of a local state that had undergone 'radical privatisation, informalisation and now mafianisation', while public respect for official authority had waned.²⁰ This was also the period in which new political parties dominated by Dalits and Other Backward Classes began to come to power in state governments, spawning a discourse among the elite, however unjustified, of a coarsening of politics. In the face of such widespread change, nostalgia for an earlier time in which India had had an administrative apparatus that was stable and predictable flourished.

To begin to dissect this myth, we must ask the question, 'What is a strong state?' Undoubtedly, perception of strength depends on which functions or institutions of the state one is examining. Democrats tend to stress the importance of free and fair elections, and the peaceful transfer of power. Parliamentarians and politicians would probably argue that strength lies in passing legislation. Those concerned with the bureaucracy might focus on the integrity of low-level public servants and their ability to implement laws or executive orders. Lawyers and judges would almost certainly take a different view, insisting instead that a strong state is one in which the judiciary is able to overturn laws and executive actions that contravene the Constitution. Indeed, the more one looks into the state, the harder it is to discern as a unified institution.[21]

This chapter begins by demonstrating that Indians were not impressed by the administrative apparatus that they had inherited from the British. The next two sections explore socialist programmes, including social welfare and state-run enterprises. They find that India's new leaders sought to distance their most favoured projects from the administrative apparatus of the Raj. These experiments in postcolonial state-building often did not reify a state imposed above Indian society, but rather imagined a state that was intimately connected to the Indian people. Moreover, the experimental character of these projects ensured that the administrative apparatus became more complex and varied over time.

The second half of the chapter explores the disciplinary aims of postcolonial leaders as well as the function of emergency powers in postcolonial India. These sections underscore the fact that the shortcomings of India's postcolonial police and bureaucracy were reasonably well understood at the time. In contrast with their socialist programme, the disciplinary projects of postcolonial leaders required that the existing police and bureaucracy be deployed, no matter how flawed. Building on the inadequacies of the British period, however, the postcolonial disciplinary state was anything but united, coherent or effective.

On India's Inheritance

Given the pervasiveness today of the idea of the strong state inherited from the Raj, it is striking how difficult it is to find anyone who praised India's administrators, or its administrative system, in the two decades after independence.[22] Instead, the members of the administration, from village officials to those in the top echelons were almost universally criticised, even by those who came from among their ranks. These critics called for a transformation in everything from working methods to attitudes to bring about the democratic, welfare state at which India was aiming.

It was quite common for politicians to lambast the administration. Their messages to graduating classes at various universities were similar over the years. Zakir Husain, newly elected vice president, addressing the Indian Institute for Public Administration in 1962, described what the Indian administration had inherited from the British: this inheritance included, a 'forbidding touch-me-not attitude', as well as a 'stand-offish sense of superiority', and a 'lack of initiative' to boot.[23] At the village level, one civil servant-turned-Gandhian social worker lamented that 'complaints of harassment, petty exactions, failure to render service to the people are somewhat common'.[24]

With this inheritance, it is unsurprising, then, that throughout the Nehru years there were frequent calls to develop a new type of civil servant for the new India. The first holder of India's most senior civil service post, that of cabinet secretary, Sir Narayanan Raghavan Pillai, described this new civil servant as one who 'should, it is clear, possess the traditional service virtues—efficiency, integrity, and loyalty'. But, he continued, India's public servants must rid themselves of the key virtue of the imperial civil service, 'neutralism'.[25] Famously, British civil servants were meant to be politically neutral. In its first year of publication, *The Indian Journal of Public Administration*, the main publication of the Indian Institute of Public Administration, republished an article by Clement Attlee, Britain's prime minister from 1945 to 1951, which explained what civil service neutrality meant in practice: 'The civil servant', according to Attlee, 'is prepared to put up every possible objection to [a minister's] policy, not from a desire to thwart him, but because it is his duty to see that the Minister understands all the difficulties and dangers of the course which he wishes to adopt.'[26] It was this feature of the bureaucracy that leading politicians and senior administrators believed ought to be discarded, even if bureaucrats were still expected to stay out of political activities.

In place of neutrality, Indians called for a radical change in the working methods of civil servants. The idea was to cultivate administrators who displayed 'a measure of spontaneity and initiative', in the words of Narhar Vishnu Gadgil, a senior Congressman from Maharashtra, member of the Congress Working Committee and member of the Executive Council of the Indian Institute of Public Administration.[27] Cold neutrality ought to be replaced with 'a sense of deep devotion and duty', for public servants should be willing to put their 'heart and soul' into their work, according to the senior Congressman from Uttar Pradesh, Govind Ballabh Pant.[28]

These new administrators could be drawn from the cadre of freedom fighters, especially Congress members, recently victorious in the anti-colonial struggle and looking for avenues in which they might continue their work for the nation. Equally, technical experts with great enthusiasm for their subject and love of country were welcome.

This was part of a larger transformation of notions of loyalty in the services across South Asia during the transition to independence. As discussed in chapter 3, religious affiliation and political loyalty came to be associated during the partition violence. In this tumultuous period, the cry arose that members of the services had become infected with communal bias. Historians have shown that there were instances of communal hatred in the police and bureaucracy, as well as examples of altruistic behaviour towards other communities. But many of those in government in India responded to the sweeping allegations, rather than to the complex reality. In so doing, they disarmed, transferred, retired and hounded out Muslim members of the services. Between 1946 and 1949, governments from Uttar Pradesh to Madras replaced Muslims (and Anglo-Indians) in the ranks of the administration with Hindus and Sikhs.[29] Community came to be substituted for secular displays of loyalty. The same steps were used to cleanse the ranks of government of anyone who might be loyal to a number of political groups which were deemed dangerous. Membership of the Communist Party, the Rashtriya Swayamsevak Sangh, the Muslim League National Guards and the Khaksars was banned for all government servants after the assassination of Gandhi. It was in this context of a new conception of loyal service that senior figures like N. R. Pillai called for civil servants to work with passion, rather than dispassion. All of this transformed the police and bureaucracy into services where the safest position was not a neutral one, but one that was aligned with the political party in government.[30]

Experiments in Radical Postcolonial State-Building

Although India's elected leaders and top administrators called for a new breed of public servant, they were not willing to wait for him (the state was gendered male, as we shall see) to appear. Instead, those who led India's early experiments in a new type of government almost invariably set up institutions *at a distance* from the existing bureaucracy. The seminal initiatives of the period, the Planning Commission, the Damodar Valley Corporation, the Faridabad Development Board, Community Development, the Industrial Finance Corporation and the Central Social Welfare Board, to name a few, were all initially established so as to be either governed by independent boards or run as independent corporations. The Planning Commission, famously, was neither mentioned in the Constitution nor established by statute; it had no legal status. This was no accident. These novel administrative set-ups were prized for their flexibility, which was contrasted with the rigidity of the ordinary administration.[31]

One example of India's experiments with a new style of administration conceived in the years after independence was the Central Social Welfare Board (CSWB). The CSWB appears to have been the brainchild of Durgabai Deshmukh. Born in Rajahmundry, Durgabai had been a child bride who had refused to consummate her marriage, an act that later propelled her into welfare work. Later she was a founding member of the Andhra Mahila Sabha. After an unsuccessful bid for a seat in the Lok Sabha in the first general election, she was invited to join the Planning Commission in 1952. There she met and married Chintaman Dwarkanath Deshmukh, who as finance minister in Nehru's government had been known as India's second most eligible widower, after the prime minister himself, of course.[32] Durgabai had earned Nehru's esteem before her marriage, but her position as wife of the finance minister doubly secured her place in a charmed circle of people who were given licence to conduct their own institutional experiments in the policy field of their choice. Durgabai's field was social welfare, especially women's welfare.

Social welfare was a new sphere of concern for the Indian state. The colonial state's approach to what were called the 'weaker sections' of society had hovered between Malthusian indifference and neglect, under the assumption that this area fell under the remit of the charitable sector. By contrast, India's new leaders set out to build a welfare state. Crucially, however, this did not mean just adding welfare to the duties of the existing state.

The CSWB, founded in 1953, was one of the institutions at the forefront of this effort. Like the Planning Commission, it was neither a statutory body, nor a society, nor a joint-stock company; it was established only by a resolution of the Government of India. It was not a legal person: it could not own property, could not sue or be sued. It was placed under only the 'minimum necessary' oversight, to allow a 'wide measure of freedom to act with decisive promptitude'.[33] The idea was to give the Board the power to implement its own decisions 'without passing through the usual criss-cross ways of government procedure'.[34] Not only did the Board have an unusual legal status, but its composition was distinctive, too. It had twelve members, including five non-officials, all of whom were women volunteers.[35] Below the Central Board, State Social Welfare Boards were established in 1954 with a similar composition, including non-official, non-salaried women. These women likely drew on their experience as social workers, aligned with but not directly part of official programmes for relief and rehabilitation efforts during the Bengal famine and in the aftermath of partition.[36] Here, postcolonial nationalism took the form of redirecting the energies of nationalist workers: already experienced in this field, their enthusiasm could now tapped to experiment with a new form of administration.

Although the initial aim was only to coordinate the work of charity organisations, the CSWB soon learned that charities rarely stretched outside of urban areas. To reach the population in the countryside, the Board set up its own rural welfare scheme, primarily aimed at improving the welfare of women and children in villages. This involved establishing Project Implementation Committees at district level, which, again, were a combination of officials and local female voluntary social workers. These district-level committees oversaw the work of village welfare, which was done by salaried women: *gram sevika*s (village workers), *dai*s (indigenous midwives), allopathic midwives and craft instructors. At least initially, they mostly paid salaries only to women doing actual welfare work. As far as possible, the oversight, planning and coordination, that is, the administration, was to be done by volunteers. Their efforts and expenditure were to be matched by the villagers themselves, who were expected to contribute to their own uplift.

In substance, the idea of these welfare projects was to 'tempt and encourage' women to take 'the next step' on a very long walk towards female emancipation.[37] Where village women practised purdah, they were encouraged to give up the practice. If they did not have the habit of gathering except in relatives' houses, the gram sevika would organise *bhajans* (devotional songs) and festival celebrations, when the women of a village could gather together for the first time. If they did not regularly access medical facilities for themselves or their children, they were steered towards very basic care, especially for maternity services. Where women were not earning any money for the family, they were asked to 'think that there is more in one's life than just cooking and bearing children', and then given the opportunity to make a supplementary income by producing crafts or simple goods like matches.[38] If they were keen to earn an income, the CSWB helped them form cooperatives. These steps were hardly a radical break from existing local practices. They were thus in line with the socialism of the age, which insisted that social progress could only be made with the consensus of the powerful. Indeed, perhaps the women who found the CSWB programmes most transformative were the ones who were employed to deliver the welfare, rather than the beneficiaries of the scheme.[39]

In the conception of those who ran the CSWB, the state and its functions were gendered. Social work was understood as feminine, and the state bureaucracy was gendered masculine, and the feminine was valued. Voluntary social workers were introduced to provide a 'human touch' instead of the 'impersonal' logic of government bureaucracy.[40] Social workers were expected to display 'flexibility', in contrast to the state's 'rigidity'.[41] The CSWB was, in other words, a radical experiment in establishing a decolonised administration.

While the constitution, composition and conduct of the CSWB may have been unique, the Board reflected wider trends of the time. Firstly, it was a product of the feeling that the state did not have the resources to take on wider responsibilities. As discussed in chapter 4, when enormous social challenges arose, the planners tended to unload responsibility for them onto the wider population. Thus, the first five-year plan called on 'local communities [to] accept responsibility for solving their own problems'.[42] At its inception, the CSWB was only meant to be a body coordinating community efforts. This reflected the larger trend, as well as Durgabai's own scepticism about the possibility of change through legislation. She warned of the danger that legislation would 'remain merely words on the Statute book' without concerted efforts in communities.[43]

Secondly, the CSWB was a manifestation of widespread concern about creating an overly powerful state. None other than the president of the Republic, Rajendra Prasad, warned of the 'danger of the State encroaching upon and monopolising' welfare services, even as he inaugurated the first conference of the very state bodies that were put in charge of social welfare.[44] These first two trends dovetailed with the widespread scepticism of the existing civil service noted above. The CSWB was thus an experiment in calling forth a new type of administrator—the self-sacrificing volunteer—to replace the self-serving bureaucrat. This was a parallel effort to those that called for a new type of public servant; it was a demand for Indians to commit to public service more broadly. The same arguments were repeated across many different experiments in development and socialism in the late 1940s and 1950s, including the Damodar Valley Corporation,[45] and, as we saw in chapter 4, the building of Faridabad.

If the first decade after independence was marked by this experimental approach to administration, the second decade witnessed reversal and retreat, at least for the CSWB. In 1959, the Programme Evaluation Organisation (PEO) of the Planning Commission audited the CSWB's main village social welfare scheme, and its findings were damning. The PEO recorded not only that some of the projects funded by the welfare boards were 'in a very bad state', but also that the CSWB seemed to have no idea of their condition.[46] When the PEO visited Bihar in April 1958, in spite of the fact that the state board had received a grant from the Central Board, 'not a single village level worker, Chief Organiser, Accountant or Jeep Driver' had been paid for six months. Three months later, the PEO returned to find nothing had changed.[47] In many cases, the volunteers did not exhibit the altruism expected of them: instead, Project Implementation Committees were beset by 'jealousies and rivalries' among the women, which made 'smooth working very difficult'.[48] Far from approaching their work with a human touch, the women at each level of the structure behaved like 'bosses' over their subordinates, treating them like 'servants'.[49] And they failed to coordinate with those working in Community Development in the same spaces.[50] These findings dovetailed with existing calls for more oversight and official coordination: the previous year, state-level officials involved in social welfare had already recorded that they 'strongly felt' that 'a Ministry of Social Welfare in the Union government' ought to be established.[51] Shortly thereafter, the CSWB's welfare extension projects were absorbed by the Ministry of Community Development and Cooperation, while the Central Social Welfare Board was made a statutory body in 1962, integrating it into the central system of bureaucratic oversight.

Again, the CSWB was emblematic of a wider trend. Faridabad's independent Development Board was disbanded, also under the cloud of allegations of financial misconduct. And, in the words of Sudhir Ghosh, the outside-the-box civil servant who had overseen the experimental project, '[a] genuine bureaucrat was imported from Bombay to "clean up" Faridabad'.[52] As they became incorporated into formal ministries, these new institutions did not assume a uniform type; they added more diversity to the forms of administration. They also added a new element of coordination with other ministries, or, as was more often the case, competition with them.

As for Durgabai, like other beneficiaries of Nehru's patronage, she took India's experience to the wider developing world. In 1964, she delivered two lectures at the Asian Institute for Economic Development and Planning in Bangkok. She made the case that '[s]ocial progress is [...] as urgent as economic growth', and argued that social programmes ought to be seen as 'creating the capacity to create wealth'. By this time she was calling for greater state involvement in social welfare work, to help avoid wasting money and to develop uniform standards of service.[53]

More Postcolonial State-Building: Public Enterprises

Ironically perhaps, social welfare is not strongly associated with India's socialism. Instead, when scholars think of Indian socialism, they tend to refer to state-led industrialisation. Here, too, there was scepticism about using the levers of the existing administration to manage India's industrial development. Shortly after its own work began, the Planning Commission appointed A. D. Gorwala to inquire into the most efficient way of running state enterprises. Gorwala, who had had a career in the Indian Civil Service in the provinces of Bombay and Sindh before independence, was known for his faultless integrity and his careful scrutiny of the issues put before him. He studied the subject of how to ensure the success of any state-run enterprise and concluded that public enterprises ought to be run by an 'autonomous authority'.[54] According to Gorwala, this could best be achieved by creating joint-stock companies or statutory corporations.

Gorwala's recommendations combined global trends with local proclivities. Across the senior echelons of government in New Delhi, experts could be found quoting Franklin Delano Roosevelt, whose New Deal favoured autonomous bodies like the Tennessee Valley Authority. Roosevelt had lauded such organisations for being 'clothed with the power of Government, but possessed of the flexibility of private enterprise'.[55] Gorwala's recommendations also echo those of E.F.M. Durbin, who, a few years earlier, had warned Britain's newly elected Labour party against running nationalised industries from Whitehall.[56] Back in India, this inclination dovetailed with scorn for the existing bureaucracy to make the autonomous body run on 'business principles' the preferred method of managing state-run industries.

As he explained the difference between the government officer from the 'days of the British government' and the administrator in the age of 'democracy and the establishment of the welfare state', R. G. Saraiya, president of the All India Cooperative Union and chairman of the Bombay State Road Transport Corporation, produced a variation on the themes heard in discussion over the Central Social Welfare Board. The bureaucrat inherited from the Raj had had to only 'carry out well-chalked out instructions', and often maintained a 'high-handed' attitude to the people. By contrast, the new administrator of a state-run enterprise had to have 'quickness of decision and flexibility of operations'. Moreover, he ought to 'cultivate the habit of taking risks', and possess the 'moral courage' to resist political pressures. To run the enterprise like a 'good businessman', he ought not to 'insist on his pound of flesh' in every contract, but rather should 'earn the goodwill of his customers'.[57] All of this was meant to mark a contrast from the administrators of the Raj. There was just one problem: it was widely believed at the time that there were simply not enough civil servants of the 'right type' to take on this work. To meet this challenge Gorwala recommended a highly centralised form of government oversight. He suggested that the Government of India establish a single Policy Board for all state enterprises.[58]

However, India ended up with a huge variety of state-owned enterprises, each managed by their own unique structures. Why did this decentralised, heterogeneous system emerge? Firstly, independent India had inherited some state-owned bodies, like the railways, which were run departmentally, and the Damodar Valley Corporation, which was designed to function as an autonomous corporation. Secondly, while the Planning Commission was poring over the theory of how to run industrial units or infrastructure projects, these very things were being established by the Union and in the states without conforming to any grand plan. By 1959, India had over fifty entities which were regarded as state-run. Their management arrangements took a baffling array of forms: banks, statutory corporations, control boards, commodity boards, boards with commercial functions, limited companies, cooperatives and companies run on an operating-contract system. While not particularly numerous given the size of the country, these ran the gamut from finance to fertilisers, from hotels to antibiotics.[59]

The 1950s, in other words, was a decade of experimentation with the management of public enterprises. As with other forms of administrative experimentation, this tendency seems to have been reined in towards the end of the decade. On the one hand, the Ford Foundation expert Paul Appleby had recommended consolidating state-run companies into groups.[60] On the other, the Mundhra scandal erupted in 1958 and seems to have provoked a call to put these independent public bodies under more public scrutiny. In this complicated affair, the state-owned Life Insurance Corporation had bypassed its own investment committee and bowed to pressure from government to purchase shares to the value of Rs.124 lakh in six troubled companies owned by Haridas Mundhra.[61] Mundhra, in turn, was bleeding the companies and manipulating their share prices, in part by producing forged share certificates. When the purchase did not work to stabilise the share prices, the scandal came to light. The finance minister, T. T. Krishnamachari, resigned over the allegation that he had pressed the Life Insurance Corporation into buying the shares in order to try to stabilise the markets.[62] While two separate enquiries looked into the Mundhra affair, the Lok Sabha's Estimates Committee, chaired by Balwantray Mehta, took up the broader task of calling for state-run enterprises to be brought under greater parliamentary scrutiny.

In 1960, as MPs took stock of the public undertakings established since independence, a rather mixed picture emerged. To be sure, there were some successes: Chittaranjan Locomotives, for example, was commended for having 'more encouraging' achievements than most.[63] Others were not without their crises, small and large. Hindustan Antibiotics and its factory at Pimpri, near Pune, for example, were lauded by those involved in the project for being a model of a state-run enterprise. Conceived in the early 1950s, as penicillin use was spreading rapidly around the world, the effort to begin manufacturing antibiotics at Pimpri received technical and financial assistance from UNICEF and the World Health Organisation as well as the UN Technical Assistance Administration. After four years, the first antibiotics produced by the factory went on sale in September 1955.[64] By 1959, Pimpri's annual profit was more than Rs.1 crore.[65] It used the money not only to expand operations, but to pay bonuses to workers, who also benefited from on-site housing, schools, a hospital and training facilities.[66] The factory was credited with spawning subsidiary industries, including the production of glass vials, and factories for tableting of penicillin.[67] And yet, the enterprise could not escape scandal. On 18 November 1959, the MP Vishwambhar Dayalu Tripathi died after being injected with penicillin from the factory. Although fatal adverse reactions to penicillin were a known side effect of the drug, some of Tripathi's colleagues in the Lok Sabha alleged that the factory had not followed the proper quality control measures for the batch that killed Tripathi.[68] To restore public confidence in the firm's products, the government had to promise to commission a probe by eminent scientists to ensure the factory's methods were sound.[69] Tests from six laboratories around the world eventually confirmed that the batch 'fully conformed' to international safety standards.[70] But the fears created by the death of the MP combined with the other scandals to produce a discourse in the early 1960s that many state-owned businesses were not being run well.

Given how much investment had been poured into these ventures, this picture was hardly satisfactory. Intriguingly, however, a significant part of the blame was placed on the notion that the enterprises were not being given 'the autonomy they need'.[71] Far from being run by deft, business-minded administrators, these enterprises were in fact governed by over-worked civil servants. In all there were seventeen government employees who were each directors on the boards of at least four different state-run enterprises. One MP lamented that 'there is one government officer who is a director of 9 corporations and out of these 9 corporations he is Chairman of two'.[72] In an environment where there was a pervasive sense that India lacked administrative talent, a handful of senior civil servants seem to have monopolised control of state-owned autonomous enterprises. But, as another MP put it, 'I wonder whether it would at all be possible for them to do justice either to the corporations or to their official duties.'[73] In other words, the diagnosis was that these entities were too state-like.

If at the Union level, the desire to move away from the existing administration gave rise to an assortment of forms, in the states there was no universal drive for state-run industry and infrastructure. Take the case of electricity production. In the east of the country, in 1946 the Government of India established the Damodar Valley Corporation (DVC), a multi-purpose river valley scheme designed to be run as an autonomous corporation (and considered in more detail in chapter 7). The governments of West Bengal and Bihar, concerned about the ballooning costs of the scheme, successfully lobbied to scale down the number of dams from eight to four. While they secured an agreement that the DVC would supply power to Calcutta, Patna and Gaya, the two states refused to allow the DVC to expand its power-generating capacity, arguing that there was no demand for more power in the Valley. By 1958, it was clear that demand was rising and that the DVC could not produce the power necessary to meet it. Rather than strengthening the DVC, the Government of West Bengal refused to pay for any more power production within the scheme. Instead, it entered the now profitable field of power production. Around the same time, the governments of West Bengal and Bihar took over all the DVC's transmission lines and power stations outside the Valley.[74] While the Government of West Bengal elbowed its way into electricity production, a different pattern emerged in the state of Bombay (later Maharashtra and Gujarat). There, profitable power production was concentrated in the hands of private companies: Tata Power generated electricity to be sold in the city of Bombay, while Killick Nixon serviced the capital's suburbs as well as the cities of Surat and Ahmedabad in the future state of Gujarat. In the late 1950s and early 1960s, as other states expanded electrification in nationalised electricity bodies, Bombay's Electricity Board chose not to nationalise these companies. Rural electrification, in turn, was not so much pioneered by the state's Electricity Board as spurred by sugar cooperatives, which helped shoulder the costs of getting individual farmers onto the grid.[75]

This seems to have been something of a pattern in Bombay. In this western state, the government did nationalise road transport in the 1940s, but there appears to have been, if not a policy, then a broader tendency to eschew state control of industry and infrastructure. In chapter 4, we witnessed politicians running to industry to reassure them and bring them onside after the announcement of the second five-year plan. The Government of Bombay State was at the heart of efforts to lure private businesses into making themselves part of the plan. The central government would take the lead on heavy industry, certainly, but the rest would be left to private enterprise; and this was regarded as an opportunity. Accordingly, the Department of Industries in Bombay published a brochure, advertising to private entrepreneurs 'the possibilities of setting up various industries in the different regions of the state' during the second plan period.[76] The Department provided essential information such as the location, capital, employment potential and licensing requirements of different industries, from bauxite mining and the production of aluminium to cold storage and refrigerated transport services for fruits and vegetables. However, the self-restrained state was not a blanket policy in Bombay, as we will see in the following section, for the new governors of the territory tried to use the coercive powers of the administration to quash what they regarded as the ills of alcohol consumption.

There is no doubt that state-building was a priority in the early postcolonial period, but that does not mean that the makers of independent India set out to build a leviathan. Given its rickety inheritance, this could hardly have been the case. Although the approach of those in power differed over time and by sector, in the 1940s and 1950s, there were multiple, uncoordinated moves away from the structures, institutions and personnel inherited from the British, even in the areas closely associated with socialism like welfare and industry. State-led initiatives were not ruled out, but India's new governors, whether politicians or bureaucrats, did not universally, enthusiastically embrace 'the state' bequeathed to them by the Raj. Away from New Delhi, India's federal system allowed for yet more variety, the extent of which is impossible to detail in its entirety here. India's experiments in state-building took a baffling array of forms, many of which were a far cry from the centralising, unitary state that is often imagined for this period.

Incompetence, Exceptionalism and the Disciplinary State

In spite of their desire to reform the structures they had inherited, there were arenas in which politicians and administrators agreed that the existing administrative machinery, however flawed, had to continue to be used. Many of these fell within the broad range of institutions, laws and regulations aimed at disciplining various segments of the population. Still, the police, courts, jails and low-level bureaucracy required to deal with these problems were recognised as weak and disjointed even as they were put to work at these new tasks.

Let us return briefly to industry, for we do find central initiatives aimed at disciplining private industry. The new Government of India inherited a system of licensing and controls, which had been cobbled together largely during the Second World War. On paper, it looked like state control. Under this regime, however, prices of essential goods were set by boards which were packed with producers, who quickly co-opted the system.[77] After the war, there was a widespread sense that, as one MP put it, 'industrialists as a rule mis-behave[, . . .] that they make illegitimate profits [. . . and] that they do not treat the labour fairly'.[78] As for the planners, they worried that owners funnelled capital *out* of industry and into moneylending and trade, bleeding enterprises, and damaging the larger project of industrialisation.[79] Accordingly, independent India's politicians and planners wanted to redirect the energies of businessmen into areas that would both assist in the development of the nation and not take advantage of ordinary Indians. They wanted private enterprise, as Gulzarilal Nanda, minister for planning, told the Lok Sabha in 1951, 'to become national in spirit'.[80]

To this end, the Industrial Development (Regulation) Bill, had been put forward in 1949. Under the initial proposals, the central government would have been able to direct firms' investment decisions, and to step in and manage firms or revoke licences when firms acted so as to reduce the value of the venture. However, big business put pressure on their personal contacts in the Government of India to see that the bill was revised, and they undertook an investment strike to underscore their influence in the economy. Their manoeuvres spooked the government and, in the end, the Industrial Development (Regulation) Act of 1951, was gutted of its more ambitious powers. The final version required larger enterprises to acquire an array of permissions, licences and permits, but contained few levers by which the government could actually shape investment decisions.[81]

Even as they passed the act, many MPs, Congress members no less, expressed doubts about whether 'the state' could succeed at the tasks they were assigning it. After all, since the war they had had plenty of experience of controls over essential commodities, and the administration had been found to be 'far from satisfactory'.[82] Banarsi Prasad Jhunjhunwala, a Congress MP from Bihar, treated his peers in the Lok Sabha to a disquisition on his experience of the bureaucrats overseeing sugar controls in his state and in neighbouring Uttar Pradesh. 'Those who were at the helm of affairs', he claimed, 'were simply acting on mere technicalities trying only to justify their existence, without understanding what they were doing.'[83]

The much-diminished act was nonetheless central to the 'permit-and-licence raj' which has often been exhibit A in the case to prove India's socialism had state-control of the economy at its heart, a case made most prominently at the time by the Swatantra Party.[84] Under the act, a licence was required to establish a new industrial unit, to increase production or to change location. When this was combined with the system of controls, the result was the creation of a vast bureaucracy. For every item under control—that is, where production was only by permission obtained through a licence or a permit—there had to be a control officer, assistants, inspectors and so on.[85] Businesses had to submit mountains of forms to remain in compliance. A single mill in Bombay, for example, had to fill out some 577 forms each year.[86]

And yet, there is little indication that licensing was used successfully to bend industry to the will of the government. Firms applied for multiple, overlapping licences to increase their chances of success, making it impossible to gauge how much investment was planned.[87] Although one of the stated aims during the period was to correct for the concentration of industry in particular areas, a great number of licences went to already industrialised states.[88] In 1966, the Planning Commission appointed the young economics professor R. K. Hazari to enquire into the working of licensing. Hazari was not impressed by the mushrooming bureaucracy that handled licensing. As they navigated a maze of departments, Hazari explained, applications went through multiple agencies where they were considered and reconsidered 'without improving the feasibility of the projects concerned'.[89] Indeed, those in the licensing authority and correlated departments worked 'without clear and definite criteria' by which to judge each application.[90] With so many applications sloshing around the system, and so many different offices that had to review them, *'Even the authorities concerned are not fully aware of the total investment and foreign exchange commitments of licences issued or those under implementation at any particular period of time.*'[91] Overall, the success of licensing in channelling investment appeared to Hazari to be 'extremely doubtful'.[92] These failings, he stressed, were 'obvious and admitted' among those working within the system.[93]

From the perspective of business, obtaining a licence to start a new undertaking did not guarantee that all the other requirements would be lined up for the licence holder. Many projects were held up at the point of obtaining foreign exchange, for which permission had to be obtained from a different authority. The *Economic and Political Weekly*, where Hazari would take up the post of editor the following year, wryly summed up licensing thus: 'A licence is only a permit which entitles the holder to apply for numerous other sanctions and permissions.'[94] Within this tangled bureaucratic complex, corruption reigned.[95] Instead of a 'scientific' approach to the allocation of licences, industrialists pestered state officials they knew, who, in turn, put pressure on their connections in New Delhi to obtain licences for their contacts.[96] The system drew in India's democracy, where elections were expensive, as chapter 6 will detail. The prevailing conclusion by the end of the period was that '[i]ndustrial licensing [. . .] has failed to fulfil its principal purpose'.[97]

Businesses seemed to use the regulations when they suited them and ignore them when they did not. Take the handloom industry in western India. As Douglas Haynes has shown, small firms based in smaller urban centres benefited from official controls over cotton and yarn: the centrally issued Cotton Textiles (Control) Order of August 1948, for example, required composite mills to sell most of their yarn to handloom and powerloom firms; spinning mills had to provide all their yarn to this sector.[98] And they were protected by further regulations preventing larger mills from producing similar products. When the government sought to further protect the smallest handloom producers by limiting to four the number of looms a firm could own, however, businesses simply evaded the measure. They formally divided their assets among family members, or underreported the number of looms they had.[99] The 'permit-and-licence raj' was an annoyance to business, absolutely; but the primary inconvenience lay in all the efforts required to evade government control, rather than in submitting to it.

There were countless other areas in which different levels of government were employed to interfere in the lives of Indian citizens, dictating which animals they could slaughter, which professions they could pursue and which food and drink they could trade in. Let us zoom in on one such project: the prohibition of alcohol in the province of Bombay. Temperance had been part of social reform movements in India since the nineteenth century, ensuring that legal prohibition was an inheritance from the national movement.[100] Gandhi and other advocates of temperance had held that alcohol was a scourge for India's poor communities, draining their limited finances and enervating the population. Bombay and Madras had set out on this endeavour even before independence, introducing at least partial prohibition after Congress assumed power in 1937. Prohibition, like other social ambitions of the postcolonial state, was included in the Directive Principles of the Indian Constitution. Article 47 urged 'the state' to 'endeavour to bring about prohibition' of alcohol consumption as part of the larger aim of improving the health and standards of living of Indians.

When Congress resumed office after the war, it again took up the project of prohibition. The Bombay Prohibition Act of 1949 outlawed the production, distribution, possession and consumption of alcoholic beverages from 5 April 1950. Certain classes of people could obtain an exemption, including members of the army, foreigners and those medically proven to be 'addicts'. The act also empowered police to conduct searches without a warrant and detain without trial those suspected of contravening the provisions of the act.[101] Simultaneously, a Prohibition Board was established to coordinate education on the subject. It focused on non-literary forms of propaganda, especially bhajans, kirtans (call and response songs) and dramas, 'so as to appeal to the masses'.[102] The government founded 'sanskar kendras' (culture centres), where people could partake in wholesome alcohol-free recreation. In true nationalist style, the law was inaugurated with a 'Prohibition Week', which included a public holiday, posters, processions, public meetings and radio talks. The culmination of festivities was marked by the unfurling of the national flag at midnight on 5 April by Bombay's excise minister.[103]

If one were to believe the celebratory materials produced by officials, prohibition was an unqualified success which transformed the lives of India's poorer classes. On 26 January 1956, for example, the Bombay Government released *The People's Raj, Republic Day Number*, a magazine celebrating the government's work in everything from irrigation to education. On the subject of prohibition, the publication boasted,

> Prohibition has in effect raised the standard of living of the poorer classes and they now lead happier and healthier lives. They eat better food and wear more clothes. More and more of their children go to schools and the women folk are happier. They can now go out for shopping and purchase articles which, prior to prohibition, were

unthinkable for them. Resort by the poorer classes to cinemas, hotels and other places of public amusement is also more frequent.[104]

All this was made possible by 'the most obvious and outstanding effect' of the legislation, which was the 'release' of Rs.35 crore into the 'hands of the people' by the act, ensuring their money was spent on trips to the cinema rather than on booze.[105]

As with prohibition around the world, the reality was both more mixed and more murky. Illicit alcohol production flourished in many rural areas, and it nearly blanketed Bombay city. According to an early report by a member of the Bombay State Prohibition Board, Professor J. C. Darivala, in Bombay City there was 'hardly any area over half a square mile where illicit distillation and retail sales [were] not carried on and fairly well-known in the locality'. Professor Darivala worried that the failure of the law was having 'adverse effects on the very prestige of the Government'. Within the Bombay State Prohibition Board, a debate simmered about what to do. Professor Darivala recommended loosening the laws, allowing the production and consumption of 'low potency drink [...] at a moderate price' in order to undercut the bootleggers.[106] Others pushed in the opposite direction. One member of the Board suggested that 'public flogging' ought to be used to counter the ever-increasing number of prohibition-related offences in the state.[107]

The entire state witnessed scenarios that seem to have been pulled straight from a Bollywood film. Smugglers dropped booze in the shallow, muddy waters along the coast to be picked up by those next along in the supply chain.[108] Smaller quantities were hidden in suitcases and fishing baskets or stored in hidden compartments. One passenger arriving at Victoria Terminus on a train from Kalyan was found to have a 'specially devised contrivance which looked like a book' used to store a quarter pint of illicit liquor.[109] Bootlegging and smuggling could be lucrative ventures: a taxi driver might earn between five and eight rupees per day plying his ordinary trade, but he could pocket fifty rupees for every trip he made transporting illegal liquor.[110]

Smugglers and consumers took advantage of every nook, cranny and loophole. Temples, churches, shrines and graveyards became places to cache contraband. One man was busted on his weekly visits as a 'devotee' to Pooja Mandap at Kamatipura. Every Monday he received '"teerth" (holy water)' from the *pujari* (priest) at the mandap, but when he emerged, he 'smelt of liquor'. The police arrested the 'devotee', but the 'pujari' somehow disappeared without a trace.[111]

After the Supreme Court declared that the law could not restrict medicinal products, plenty of room was left for the use and abuse of tinctures, often Ayurvedic herbs or homeopathic remedies in an alcohol suspension. The production of many of these tinctures increased exponentially in the period.[112] Some had alcohol content as high as 88 per cent.[113] Restaurants in the city of Bombay were reported to be selling tinctures at 'between eight and twelve annas a peg'. Mixers were sold separately, of course. One popular drink was the Ayurvedic remedy Tincture Gulanch, which had hitherto been used for malarial fever. It was said to be popular in restaurants, for it had 'a pale buff colour' and resembled 'brandy in appearance and taste'.[114]

Although cultural and educational programmes were included in the prohibition programme, the police seemed to have borne the brunt of the burden of bringing prohibition into practical effect. The inheritance of the police in Bombay, however, was not widely regarded with enthusiasm. In a discussion in the Bombay Legislative Assembly in 1950 on a bill to consolidate the state's police authorities, which gave rise to a broader discussion on the colonial inheritance, the opposition MLA (Member of the Legislative Assembly) Peter Alvares lamented that 'this police force has a tradition which works disadvantageously for the people'.[115] His fellow MLA R. A. Khedgikar noted that during the Raj, the police had been used 'to suppress the legitimate aspirations of the people', and though three years had passed since independence, 'there has not been any change in the mentality of the Police Force'.[116] Even the chief minister, Morarji Desai, conceded, 'I cannot deny that there may be members in the police force who may not have forgotten the past habits and traditions', though he claimed that 'a large majority' of police were 'trying to behave according to the requirements of the times'. Desai simply urged that 'patience is required'.[117] In the meantime, members of the government would work with what they had.

On the face of it, the police seemed engaged in a heroic game of cat and mouse sparked by the new law. They conducted 'raids' on villages, and posh city hotels. They not only nabbed country toddy tappers, but also caught wealthy urban Parsis with 'choice foreign liquor' and 'fashionable looking' wine glasses.[118] Police 'in mufti' (indigenous disguise) pursued suspects in high-speed car chases, producing a 'thrilling spectacle' watched by hundreds.[119] There were tragic cases of villagers attacking police with stones and receiving bullets in return.[120]

One noteworthy sanction made available to enforce prohibition was the posting of punitive police. A colonial-era measure, the stationing of punitive police was a collective punishment aimed at villages or urban neighbourhoods where the authorities were certain that illegal activities had occurred, but where they could not prove a crime against individuals in a court of law. Police were posted to the 'guilty' area, and a punitive tax was levied on residents to pay for them. Bombay's Legislative Assembly reaffirmed this holdover from the British period in February 1951.[121] To take just one example of the practice, in January 1958, punitive police were posted in the villages of Jiav, Gabheni and Bamroli in the Chorasi *taluka* (sub-district) of Surat. The villages were said to be 'notorious for Prohibition offences'. Note the importance of reputation rather than evidence in the decision to post the force. Police had raided the villages, and seized thousands of maunds of wash and liquor, 'but they could not trace the offenders'. In the face of the apparent inadequacies of the police, the villagers were burdened with a collective sanction, in this case a force of six policemen stationed in the area for a year with the promise that the 'cost will be recovered from the people of the villages'.[122]

In spite of the spectacular display of police activity, senior police, members of the Prohibition Board and members of the public all became aware early in the life of the law that at least some of the police were in on the racket. In June 1951, a senior, unnamed Congressman revealed in a press interview that most illicit distillers, smugglers and owners of bars were 'known' to the ordinary police. In exchange for monthly payments ranging from 'Rs300 to Rs500 the illicit traders and manufacturers are not only left alone, but assured of protection from surprise raids by the special Prohibition Police'.[123] Shortly thereafter, top police officers in the state told the prohibition minister, M. L. Patil, that 'it could not be denied that some at least from the rank and file of the force were not above temptation'.[124] At the very end of the Nehru era, the Planning Commission called for an inquiry into the working of prohibition. Led by Tek Chand, a former justice of the High Court of Punjab, the resulting report noted widespread 'connivance' between police and criminals:

> As a result of mutual agreement between the bootlegger and the police, all types of cases are put in court as a proof of police vigilance and activity. The offences can be preselected [...] but the accused are men of straw. They are consenting scape-goats and stooges who are produced as accused person at the bidding of their employer [...] all the expenses [...] are borne by the boss, who pays the fines and looks after the family if the accused is awarded a jail sentence.[125]

This revelation gives new meaning to those Bollywood-style police scenes mentioned above. One cannot help but wonder how many of them were staged melodrama, produced for the consumption of the upper ranks of the police, politicians and the public, bearing more resemblance to street theatre than to a police procedural.

Within the first year of its operation, it seems that plenty of people understood that the Prohibition Act was unenforceable. It took nearly fourteen years, and the division of Bombay State into Maharashtra and Gujarat, for Congress to come round to what Vasantrao Naik called, a 'more reasonable and rational view' on alcohol consumption.[126] Naik, who took office as chief minister of Maharashtra on 5 December 1963, announced that from 1 April 1964, the government would make beverages of less than 3.5 per cent alcohol content, as well as toddy of similar strength, available without a permit. This was accompanied by a 'liberalisation' of the permit regime, so that anyone over forty years of age could obtain a permit for stronger booze with a 'straightforward declaration that they need alcoholic drinks for maintaining their health'.[127] In announcing the new policy, Naik admitted that 'the law could not reach every culprit'. Where the law had failed, it was hoped that the market might succeed, for the aim of the more liberal regime was to make it 'unprofitable for these anti-social elements to indulge in their evil practices'.[128]

Prohibition is a conspicuous but not atypical example of the disciplinary state in postcolonial India. India's politicians had made promises to the people about the transformation of India's social, political and economic life. Many of them had a background in social reform, and they recognised that social change would have to come through education and economic transformation. But they had also been newly elected to state power. Unsurprisingly, they sought to use the law, police and bureaucracy to further their social ambitions. The weaknesses of these mechanisms were either obvious before, or became apparent soon after, such policies came into force.

THE STATE OF EXCEPTION AND THE CONSTITUTION

Whether it was the sugar trade or the sex trade, the histories of disciplinary action in these fields rarely reveal a picture of an administration that could act efficiently, effectively and with integrity using ordinary legal proceedings. Independent India inherited systems which had been adapted by the British in order to work around their defects. Police investigated cases indifferently at best. Courts struggled to sort fact from fiction or guilty from innocent. Jails not only failed to reform convicts, but often provided spaces in which pernicious ideas could spread. All were overwhelmed in times of large-scale unrest. To compensate for these multiple inadequacies, colonial administrators had relied on collective punishments, pre-emptive detention, the use of force and exceptional executive powers. All of these measures were initially understood as 'emergency' powers to be used, sparingly, in times of crisis, but they became increasingly normalised through the seemingly constant crises of the independence movement. By 1947, then, the police, administration and legislators had become habituated to the practice of finding ways to work around existing laws and institutions.[129]

Punitive police were one of the hallmarks of the colonial system, but that so-called extraordinary penalty remained as common after 1947 as it had been under the Raj. It was used or sanctioned for use to punish communal unrest in West Bengal and caste violence in Gujarat;[130] the murder of a Congressman in Rajasthan, and of an opposition MLA in Uttar Pradesh;[131] to combat agrarian unrest in Rajasthan, and cutting of canals in Punjab;[132] against dacoits in Madhya Bharat, and those fighting for independence in Nagaland.[133] Almost invariably, those in authority blamed the people for imposition of the measure, claiming they would not cooperate with the police. However, the origins of collective penalties lie in the failure of colonial police.[134] In postcolonial India, the same failures remained, and so too did the same circumventions.

With this background, the provisions of the Constitution appear in a new light. It is common to note that the Indian Constitution, with its 395 articles and eight schedules, was at the time one of the longest ever written. Its length derives partly from the fact that its framers understood that their nation and their administration were evolving. The most prominent recognition of this fact was the inclusion of Part 21, which was entitled 'Temporary and Transitional Provisions'. In this section, the Union gave itself special powers, for a limited period of five years, to make laws in areas that were on the list of those over which the states had legislative power (Article 369); Article 370, by which Kashmir was incorporated into the Union under special conditions was located in Part 21; Article 371 gave the governors of some states special powers in certain regions. Temporary provisions were not limited to Part 21, however. Reservations for Scheduled Castes and Scheduled Tribes were slated to expire after ten years (Article 334); the use of English as the language of government was meant to last for only fifteen years (Article 343). While Article 22 laid out conditions for preventive detention, it anticipated that the Lok Sabha would pass a law on the practice, and that law was also intended to be a temporary measure lasting only thirteen months.[135]

Exceptional measures for exceptional times was the theme that also ran through the provisions in the Constitution relating to an emergency. Power to declare an emergency under the Indian Constitution rests with the executive. It is the president, according to Article 356, who decides that a state cannot govern itself, and imposes presidential rule. In other countries, by contrast, it is states, rather, that invite the federal government in to assist them.[136] After the declaration of an emergency, the Union executive can make laws for the states, with those laws expiring six months after the end of the emergency. The emergency provisions of the Indian Constitution are perhaps most striking when it comes to fundamental rights: Articles 358 and 359 allow the resident to suspend all but two of the fundamental rights granted under Part 3 of the document. Any order suspending fundamental rights has to be put before parliament and approved,[137] but this is not much of a safeguard, given that the president is usually an appointee of the ruling party, and the executive is not separate from the legislature in India's parliamentary system. Those who see the state as a unitary machine commonly assume that these punitive and emergency measures were the features that imbued the state with its strength. It is more accurate, however, to view them as just one of many ways in which the rulers of independent India tried to overcome the flawed legacy of colonialism.

Conclusion

There is, perhaps, a grain of truth to the claim that India inherited a strong state from the Raj, but it is just one grain in a sackful. The truth of the statement lies in the fact of inheritance rather than in the quality of the bequest. We have seen how the disciplinary apparatus of the police and bureaucracy actually worked in the postcolonial period. The ordinary powers they had did not automatically invest these organisations or the individuals that peopled them with the ability to 'get things done' in the different spheres of government activity. One must not rule out the possibility that there were fields of action in which the government did intervene relatively successfully; nor can one discount the possibility that there were effective administrators who did a decent job in difficult circumstances. If the larger story of the state is of a disjointed set of institutions and people that rarely acted in concert, however, the larger story of India's disciplinary desires was one of inadequacy, and, where it was deemed necessary, emergency powers as compensation for weakness.

India's new leaders knew this. That is why they treated the Raj's administrators who now worked for them to endless speechifying about developing a newfound 'sense of deep devotion and duty' to serve 'their masters, the people'.[138] It is also why they often tried to shift the projects they considered to be most important away from existing official institutions and administrators. As they made these moves, they created an administration that was yet more varied than the already irregular one they had taken over from the British. Although many of these initiatives came from the centre, they often shared an impulse towards decentralisation. Top-town decentralisation was one of the most striking paradoxes that emerged from these efforts.

Here is the pattern: Indian statesmen and stateswomen recognised that India was a union in the making. To meet the differential needs of the nation-to-be, asymmetric privileges were granted and basic rights were curtailed on an exceptional basis. While meant to be transitional, these measures became entrenched, as each attracted a constituency that argued for its extension. In the case of 'law and order' measures, the constituency was the police and the home ministers. In the case of reservations, the SCs and STs who benefited from the measures insisted on their extension. As the next chapter shows, this was part of a larger conversation about the shortcomings of Indian democracy, which took place after the second general election.

CHAPTER SIX

The Myth of the Successful Democracy

EVERY TIME AN election occurs in India, we read of the incredible feats the Election Commission undertakes to enable every adult in the country to vote. For the first general election in 1951–52, election officials traversed the high Himalaya, ferrying election materials across rivers using rope suspended over the rapids in the Spiti river in today's Himachal Pradesh. In the mountainous districts of Mohindergarh and Kohistan, '[c]amels, mules, ponies and porters' were used to transport polling materials. On the other side of the country, in Assam, 'polling parties and porters had to march on foot for days together through virgin and trackless forests to reach their polling stations'.[1] Detailing the extent of their efforts, Sukumar Sen, the first chief election commissioner of independent India, recorded that his Commission had overseen the establishment of 132,560 polling stations, including 16,088 temporary structures at which Indians would vote. The smallest polling station served just nine citizens.[2] The message conveyed was clear: democracy in India was not easy, but it was successful, particularly in the Nehru years.

This story of the success of India's democracy begins with the introduction of universal adult franchise. Agreed as the Constitution was drafted, and when India had an electorate of some 176 million, many of whom could not read or write, the decision to introduce universal franchise in the first elections was seen as an 'act of faith—faith in the common man of India and in his practical common sense', in the words of Sukumar Sen.[3] It was a gamble that seemed to have paid off: Indians voted without great misunderstandings or significant misconduct. And they elected Nehru and his Congress Party in three consecutive elections, providing stability for India's central government. The extended version of the tale of India's successful voting apparatus is often centred on the technical challenges involved in drawing up electoral rolls and printing them in dozens of languages, appointing election officials and ensuring they perform their job with integrity, devising a system of voting by symbols to cater to India's largely illiterate electorate, procuring ballot boxes and keeping them secure and, finally, counting votes. India's achievements in the administration of elections should not be discounted: it took, and continues to take, imagination, perseverance and a lot of resources to enable people to vote every five years in the country's general elections.[4] While historians have debated whether the strength of India's Constitution and its legislatures ought to be credited to its inheritance from the British or to the national movement, to institutions or to ordinary people, they argue, in essence, about why—not whether—early Indian democracy was successful.[5]

This narrative of the stability of the early years of India's parliamentary democracy has only been given greater credence by the sense of disequilibrium pervading the decades that have followed. The 1960s and 1970s witnessed the decline of the Congress Party, and the suspension of democracy during the Emergency of 1975–77. A narrative emerged that, while her father had been the architect of Indian democracy, Indira had undermined its foundations, not just with the Emergency but with her ruthless approach to the Congress Party and to electioneering.[6] From the 1980s, the rise of the Dalits and Other Backward Classes as political forces upended the patrician order of Indian democracy and created a sense of flux more broadly.[7] Since the 1990s, the ascent of the Hindu-nationalist Bharatiya Janata Party to hold power in government, coupled since 2015 with the assault on the free press, universities, courts and other institutions, has further bolstered the sense that the healthy years of India's democracy may just be behind it.[8] Indeed, international organisations have recently downgraded India's democratic status, and political scientists have begun to suggest that today's frequent invocation of India as a democracy is more myth than reality.[9] These developments have fostered a sense that throughout the Nehru years, 'democratic politics appeared to work reasonably well, and according to standard expectations'.[10]

So far as there is dissent, it is voiced by those who take a more expansive view of democracy, including in their definitions the advancement of economic equality, social justice and the successful exercise of rights by marginalised citizens.[11] These scholars recognise that elections are events, while democracy is a state of being. Democracy as a political system is made possible by everyday attitudes and modes of working which are given special precedence during elections but are not limited to them. Whereas the Election Commission (EC) is rightly credited with safely administering India's elections, democracy is dependent upon the working of a wider range of institutions, including at a minimum, the Constitution, the legislatures, political parties and the press.[12]

India's elites in the middle decades of the twentieth century were keenly aware that democracy entailed far more than elections. India's founders were practitioners as much as thinkers and their definitions of a successful democracy were often nebulous and evolving. They built their democracy with a mix of high aims and wary realism. The lofty ideals included persuading others 'by the force of logic and not the force of arms' and accepting that '[w]e can have changes of governments without breaking heads', as India's first vice president, Sarvepalli Radhakrishnan, put it.[13] In addition, there was near consensus that political democracy required social and economic change. Bhimrao Ramji Ambedkar pioneered efforts to build mechanisms for social change into the Constitution, as part of the recognition that political democracy and economic democracy were inseparable. By the late 1950s, Radhakrishnan was describing political democracy as both dependent upon rapid economic development and 'a method by which we attempt to raise the living standards of the people'. He urged Indians 'to crowd the sweat and tears of centuries into a generation' to 'reduce inequalities' and 'shake up social relations'.[14] In this conception, democracy and development existed in a dynamic relationship, mutually dependent upon and reinforcing one another.

The same was true of social democracy, which was understood as a matter of conduct in everyday life. Radhakrishnan, referring perhaps to John Dewey, called democracy a 'habit of mind' that entailed an awareness of how one's view was situated with respect to the demands of others.[15] Ambedkar concurred: 'Democracy is not merely a form of Government. It is primarily a mode of associated living, of conjoint communicated experience. It is essentially an attitude of respect and reverence toward fellow men[.]'[16] It was widely agreed that this habit of mind had to be cultivated in the population and that elections were the means to educate Indians to become democrats. The process of electing representatives and participating in public debates was expected to inculcate in the Indian public democratic sensibilities. This was not just a lesson in how to vote: the experience of democracy was expected to release Indians from parochial influences, especially caste, and make them a unified nation.[17] Whereas British imperialists had insisted that social and economic modernisation was a prerequisite for democracy, India's democratic thinkers insisted that the three facets of political, economic and social democracy could be developed simultaneously, in a dynamic relationship with one another.

Even while these soaring hopes were voiced, these same founders expressed scepticism about the actual working of India's democratic institutions. These misgivings derived not from the theory of democracy, but from experience. India's founders knew that their ambitions existed alongside competing ideas of democracy as majority rule or the pure pursuit of power. These alternative expressions of democracy were found less often in speeches than in everyday practice. During the years of provincial autonomy under the 1935 Government of India Act, Indians, Congress members included, gained a reputation for majoritarianism, factionalism and double-dealing in their provincial legislatures.[18] Radhakrishnan, addressing the Andhra Mahasabha back in 1938, had worried that recent events in organisations large and small across the country, 'make one suspect whether we have developed the democratic frame of mind which expresses itself in what we may call political good manners'.[19] It is with this background in mind that Ambedkar told the Constituent Assembly that India's people would have to learn 'constitutional morality' for, as he famously put it 'Democracy in India is only a top-dressing on an Indian soil, which is essentially undemocratic'.[20] Part of Ambedkar's motivation for codifying so much of India's Constitution was a distrust of the ways in which the country's elected politicians might work the legislatures. Rajendra Prasad, India's first president, had also favoured a long constitution, to avoid interpretation causing confusion. Ambedkar met with no objections when he told the Constituent Assembly that the 'purity' and 'fairness' of India's elections could only be safeguarded by removing responsibility for them 'from the hands of the executive authority and to hand it over to some independent authority', by which he meant the Electoral Commission.[21] Democracy as a state of being was something that had to be constantly guarded from distortion, protected from the very politicians who were elected to serve the system.

India's democracy was thus established with a mix of idealism and wariness. It was the functioning of the system over the first three elections that would determine which would prevail. The following pages explore the dynamic relationship between elections and democracy more broadly, with elections as the focal point. One might easily focus elsewhere, but this chapter puts under the microscope the widespread scholarly assumption that elections themselves worked well. Although India successfully held elections, the conduct of those elections brought increasing disquiet among those who hoped democracy would transform Indians, rather than the other way around. First, while democracy was supposed to create bonds that transcended caste, it in fact revitalised caste during the first three elections. Second, the insidious influence of money spread from fighting elections to the working of government. And finally, India failed in one of the first major tests of whether democracy could be sustained through a transfer of government from one political party to another, in Kerala. By the time of the third election, therefore, Indians were engaged in a series of conversations about how to broaden, deepen and clean up their democracy.

THE IDEAL, PUBLICLY REALISED?

Make no mistake, the administration of India's first general election was a well documented, internationally recognised success. This monumental undertaking began with the preparation of electoral roles, which in the context of the draft constitution and the upheavals of partition took nearly thirty months.[22] It involved the mobilisation of vast resources, including two million steel ballot boxes made from 8,200 tonnes of steel. And it required the training and deployment of civil servants on a large scale, with some fifty-six thousand presiding officers assisted by more than a quarter of a million staff.[23] When the election came off without violence or malpractice, India's voters were praised. *The Manchester Guardian* commended the people of India for voting with 'intelligence and discernment'.[24] The chief election commissioner declared that the elections had proven that, despite his lack of literary education, India's common man possessed 'enough common sense to know what is good for him'.[25]

This success allowed India to proclaim its leadership among democratising nations. Abroad, Sukumar Sen was appointed in 1953 to oversee elections in the Sudan, then still governed by the British. Upon arrival in the country, Sen found that the entire machinery for the election had to be devised 'from scratch'. He oversaw the revision of laws and the drafting of rules based on India's experience.[26] Sen insisted upon the 'Sudanification' of the administrative structures, 'partly to educate the nationals in managing this important public affair' but also to keep the British out of it.[27]

Back at home, after India had completed its second general election, New Delhi hosted the Commonwealth Parliamentary Association Conference in December 1957. Inaugurating the conference, and speaking to the cheers of the attendees from forty-nine delegations, President Rajendra Prasad noted that India did not need to boast about its democratic achievements, for 'encomiums have been showered on us'. He ventured that, while the 'younger parliaments' could hope to learn from the conference, 'I am also vain enough to think that perhaps even the older parliaments may derive some benefit by studying the work done in the younger parliaments'.[28]

By this point in India's democratic journey, however, the breezy confidence of the early years had passed. And it was Nehru who provided a more circumspect view of democracy, away from the inaugurals, at the heart of the conference. The prime minister began by noting that just because India had adopted parliamentary democracy as its form of government, 'that does not mean, of course, that parliamentary government is without any failings'.[29] Having adopted this system, he noted, 'one has to see how to tamper it, how to fit it in, so that it can answer the major questions of the age'.[30] In typical fashion, his sweeping and philosophical speech touched on economic democracy, education, communications, world order and even bureaucracy. He concluded by declaring, 'I am a person full of doubts and hesitation when I look at the problems of the world[.]' He noted that he opposed dogmatic thinking, and argued that it all came down to the development of the individual: 'If a political structure does not help the individual to develop, then it is lacking, it is bad.'[31] This was not a repudiation of democratic government; it was a typically judicious analysis of the abstract idea of parliamentary democracy. With the experience of the working of India's democratic system across multiple elections, more people came to share Nehru's ambivalent judgement. The following sections explore the dynamic interactions between elections and, respectively, social democracy, economic democracy and the transfer of power.

Caste, Reservations, and 'Associated Living'

In October 1952, Dr B. R. Ambedkar stood before an election tribunal in Bombay to argue that the results of the first general election for the constituency of Bombay City North, where he had stood for the reserved seat to the Lok Sabha, ought to be set aside. It might have been the trial of the decade, had Ambedkar not been so comprehensively sidelined by Congress in the run-up to the election. After all, Ambedkar would become known as the author of India's Constitution, and now he was alleging he had been fraudulently deprived of a seat in India's first elected national assembly. His case illustrates the nexus between caste and election campaigning that would only grow in this era.

Although not a Congressman, Ambedkar had been brought into Nehru's cabinet, but resigned from his position as law minister just before the election campaign had begun in earnest. The proximate cause was Nehru's decision not to put the Hindu Code Bill through the Lok Sabha in 1951, but Ambedkar cited a litany of reasons for his resignation, from the 'neglect of Scheduled Castes' to India's policy in Kashmir. And he pinned the blame squarely on the prime minister.[32] Indeed, his resignation speech might also be read as the opening volley in his election campaign. That contest was fought with particular zeal. Nehru, during a seventy-minute speech on Chowpatty beach, rebutted Ambedkar's allegations against him on as many points as possible.[33] Part of Congress's campaign against Ambedkar was to insinuate that he had played a 'very insignificant part in drafting the Constitution'.[34] In the end, Ambedkar lost the election by around thirteen thousand votes. Petitioning the election tribunal to overturn the result, he made allegations of 'corrupt practice' and 'undue interference', not against Congress, but against the leftist candidates and their agents, who had manipulated the system of joint electorates established by the Constitution.

To understand these claims, and what they say about the relationship between elections and social democracy, we must come to grips with two somewhat arcane aspects of Indian elections: reservations in seats with joint electorates, and the system of casting multiple ballots in constituencies with a reserved seat. Doing so helps shed light on the bigger issue of caste in the very early years of India's democracy. Although Ambedkar had originally opposed a system of joint electorates, as they were called, he eventually told the Constituent Assembly that reservation as embodied in the Constitution had a double purpose: 'It must recognize the existence of the minorities to start with. It must also be such that it will enable majorities and minorities to merge some day into one.'[35] While Ambedkar articulated the purposes of the Constitution's arrangement, they must be seen as a compromise worked out between different parties, and not the product of Ambedkar alone.

On the one hand, there was a sense, articulated by Ambedkar, that Dalits and Adivasis required special recognition in order to overcome historical discrimination. To this end, Scheduled Castes and Scheduled Tribes were allotted reserved seats in legislatures. On the other hand, there were three key features of this system that distinguished it from the colonial architecture of representation and were meant to reduce the importance of caste identities in elections. First, the mechanism for SC and ST representation in legislatures would be reserved seats, but joint electorates. As discussed in chapter 3, as the Constitution was drafted, separate electorates were uniformly ruled out, in the interests of national unity. Instead, where there was a reserved seat, the constituency was double in size and also hosted an unreserved seat. In these two-member constituencies, every voter would elect both a candidate for the reserved seat and one for the non-reserved seat. This was meant to ensure that candidates for either seat had to appeal to the public on the basis of shared interests rather than identity. Reserved seats were, therefore, coupled with extra attention elsewhere in the Constitution to the 'uplift' of the groups concerned. Together, these first two measures were intended to integrate these communities into the fold of the general electorate. Third, and in consequence, reservations were meant to last just ten years: it was expected that the working of the Constitution, the experience of self-rule and the progress of economic development would transform Indians to the point where SCs and STs would no longer suffer discrimination. These features, emerging through carefully constructed compromise, were held together by the hope that caste as a feature of Indian politics would lose its salience as the people were educated by the experience of democracy and the promises of the Constitution came to be realised.[36]

Because of the view among the Congress leadership, Nehru included, that caste was a potential source of division not unlike religion had proven to be, the Representation of the People Act 1951 made it a corrupt practice to appeal to the public 'to vote or refrain from voting' for a candidate on the basis of 'religion, race, caste, community or language'.[37] In other words, the recognition afforded was instantly circumscribed, not only by joint electorates, but by restrictions on the terms of electioneering: Scheduled Castes and Scheduled Tribes could have representation, but the terms on which their representatives gained their place in the legislatures could not be based on their identity as SCs and STs. At least in theory, they, like all candidates, were meant to appeal to the abstract interests of an electorate where every voter was equal. Providing representation in a way that was supposed to reduce the importance of caste in elections proved to be tricky, however.

Before discussing why this was so, it is worth noting that there were some in the Constituent Assembly, especially members of the Scheduled Castes, who had warned that reservations might not have the effect on caste that Ambedkar had hoped. H. J. Khandekar, leader of the Depressed Classes League, and one of the few SC members of the Assembly, though supporting reservations, warned that both premises upon which the reservations were based might prove illusory. He noted that over three decades, Gandhi had 'made every effort physically, mentally and financially' for Dalit uplift, but 'no appreciable improvement' could be discerned. He was certain that ten years would not bring much change either. And secondly, he worried that caste would not fade from politics: 'Divisions will be created amongst us,' in election campaigns, he warned.[38] Khandekar, in other words, foresaw one of the many ways in which caste differences would become central to political battles instead of being replaced by abstract material interests.

The second technical aspect of Ambedkar's case has to do with how voting was conducted. Because of the high rate of illiteracy in India, voters did not read and mark a ballot in the first elections. Instead, they were handed a blank ballot paper, marked only with a serial number, which they dropped in a box marked with a candidate's name and election symbol. In two-member constituencies, voters were given two ballots, one for the reserved seat, and one for the general seat. It is these ballots that were at the heart of Ambedkar's complaint to the tribunal. Ambedkar alleged that communist-leaning Marathi newspapers had urged 'caste Hindu voters' to put both of their ballots in the box for their preferred candidate in the unreserved seat. Doing so invalidated the second ballot, which was identifiable because every voter was given two ballots with identical serial numbers. When two were found in the same ballot box, one was discarded. Ambedkar told the court it was a 'gross perversion of the law' to encourage voters to do this, declaring, 'I cannot find worse propaganda than this[.]' In total, 74,333 votes had been 'wasted' in this manner. Ambedkar told the tribunal, 'I am not very presumptuous, but [. . .] I would certainly have got a large number had it not been for the crucial propaganda[.]'[39]

Ambedkar's argument was concerned both with the specific aspects of his case and with the working of the system he had helped to design. His allegation that the particular campaign in Bombay City North had involved a perversion of the system was also an expression of the incipient fear that the Constitution was not being worked as its framers had intended. Instead of eliminating the importance of caste in politics, the system of voting was itself being drawn into caste conflict. Instead of cultivating 'an attitude of respect and reverence toward fellow men', elections were being twisted to reinforce caste hierarchies.

Indeed, during the course of the hearing, the depth of caste Hindu prejudice became apparent. In spite of acknowledging that persuading voters to cast two ballots for one candidate was 'wrong', the tribunal refused to find that the caste Hindus involved had committed any corrupt practices, as defined by the law. It found that dropping two ballots in one box was not listed as an offence in the Representation of the People Act, and that the newspapers that urged voters to do this, 'could not be said to have in any way exercised or attempted to interfere with the free exercise of franchise by voters'.[40]

The Election Commission reported that what happened in Bombay City North was a common occurrence during the first elections. In the North Bengal constituency, 133,063 out of a total of 990,800 votes cast were 'wasted' in this way. In another constituency, in Uttar Pradesh, it had taken twenty days to count votes because such double voting was detected by painstakingly matching serial numbers.[41] Indeed, it was later widely acknowledged among members of the Lok Sabha that voters were often either encouraged to drop both ballots in one box, or they were paid 'to carry on a kind of make-believe' in the booth, and 'bring back the ballot papers' to have them cast illegally elsewhere.[42]

To try to eliminate this kind of fraud before the second general election, therefore, Sukumar Sen proposed that a system of marking ballots be introduced, but upon consultation with the main political parties, marked voting was not used for the second elections.[43] In the end, Sen got his way by agreeing to conduct a series of 'experiments' in by-elections in the aftermath of the second general election. The new system was introduced first with a 'rehearsal' before each by-election, which was accompanied by a lecture from the chief election commissioner, in which he told his audience that in the new system 'the evil of disposing of voting papers or selling them would be eliminated'.[44] Sen was said to have spared 'no effort' to have the new system in place by the time he left his post in December 1958, and it was adopted widely for the third general election.[45] By the time of the third election, two-member constituencies had also been largely abolished.[46] Although the Election Commission was able to use technical changes to halt this particular perversion of the system, there were no technocratic answers to the larger question of the way caste intersected with democracy as the new system was worked by politicians and the electorate.

Indeed, during the late 1940s and 1950s, India's social scientists were beginning to uncover the intersections between caste and politics, demolishing the presumption that caste was a 'traditional' feature of society which would disappear with the arrival of 'modern' political institutions. M. N. Srinivas, for example, documented how caste associations had mobilised to raise the ritual status of their members and transform their social position.[47] An overview of the first elections in *The Indian Journal of Political Science* noted that 'ideological and political considerations had to yield place to communal, caste, provincial, sectional, local and personal ones' during the contest. The piece concluded by emphasising the need for further 'training of the electorate'.[48] A further contribution in the journal recorded that parties selected candidates in the first elections 'to accommodate sub-communal claims and make sure that elections were won'.[49] Rajni Kothari and Rushikesh Maru demonstrated that in the first two decades after independence caste had become 'politicised', as new alliances were formed during political campaigns.[50]

In the second general election, this realisation spread beyond the academy. It was widely acknowledged that whatever restraint on appeals to caste had been in place in the first elections had been entirely discarded by the second. H. M. Patel, senior IAS officer, noted that the 'monster' of casteism had been 'given a fresh lease of life' during the second campaign. Many parties, including Congress, had chosen candidates based on their ability to mobilise the members of their caste.[51] Jayaprakash Narayan noted that while every party claimed to denounce caste, they paid 'obeisance to it in deeds'. Far from fading away, he observed, the 'caste system is feeding upon this system of parliamentary democracy'.[52]

As awareness grew of the rising importance of caste affiliation in India's electoral campaigns, its parliamentarians and political leaders experimented with different responses. Ambedkar repudiated reservations altogether. The All-India Scheduled Castes Federation, meeting with Ambedkar as president in August 1955, called for the abolition of all reserved seats, from the Lok Sabha to district boards.[53] Shortly before his death in December 1956, Ambedkar announced proposals to establish a new political party, the Republican Party of India (RPI), which was founded the following year to represent 'all backward and downtrodden people of India'.[54] Throughout his life, Ambedkar had oscillated between supporting political organisations for Dalits alone, and trying to forge larger alliances. Having tried the former for more than a decade, at the end of his life, he returned to the latter.[55] As he did, he brought many of his allies and followers with him, although there remained a constituency of SCs who favoured reservations.

Largely composed of SCs who had followed Ambedkar by converting to Buddhism, the RPI held the new line against reservations when they came to be renewed. As the Constitution had provided for reservations to last only ten years, when they were due to expire, the home minister, G. B. Pant, moved the Lok Sabha in 1959 to extend them. He told members of the House that, in spite of money spent on development and education, SCs and STs still suffered from 'backwardness'.[56] Members of the RPI organised protesters to surround the Lok Sabha, shouting 'Down with these reservations' and 'Down with political slavery'. D. A. Katti,

RPI member in the House, explained that reservations had not had the effect of providing true representation in the assemblies. He pointed to Ambedkar's electoral defeats to prove that 'the real representatives of the Scheduled Castes have not been returned' in elections. In the wider social field, since the introduction of reservations, the higher castes' attitude towards Dalits had not budged: 'The same atrocities are being committed [against] them, their share in the services not given to them; they are suffering from the same poverty.' Change had taken place in the minds of Dalits, though: 'There has been a political awakening among the Scheduled Caste people. [. . .] Of course, they are still poor and they are still oppressed by caste Hindus, but they do not consider it irreligious to aspire for power, aspire for wealth.' Accordingly, they did not need gifts from the powerful, in the form of reservations: 'We do not want such charity.'[57] Like many others during the debate, Katti called for the laws relating to education, development and the Untouchability (Offences) Act to be properly implemented. In the end, Pant warned that if the house failed to extend reservations, 'there will be grave discontent which will lead to frustration and would affect this process of emotional integration'. He reiterated his belief that without reservations, SCs would not find sufficient representation in the house. Bringing them into the Lok Sabha via reservation, 'gives the Scheduled Castes a sense of participation in the affairs of the country and that, by itself, helps the process of integration; they are not isolated from the rest.'[58] The bill passed and reservations were extended for another ten years.

The senior leadership of the Congress government, urged on by Nehru, not only stayed the course on reservations, but also doubled down on efforts to stop candidates talking about caste (or race, religion, community or language) during elections. The Government amended the Representation of the People Act and the Indian Penal Code to outlaw appeals to vote on the basis of community and to make it illegal to promote feelings of enmity between groups in an election.[59] At the Party level, Congress forbade its members from being members of caste or communal organisations at the Avadi session in 1955, and became more hesitant in their overt affiliations with caste-based organisations, at a time when Dalit and backward class associations were rising.[60] In the final years of Nehru's premiership, National Integration, which is the subject of the final section of this chapter, was put at the heart of Congress's campaign against what Nehru identified as the problem of 'looking at things in a narrow way'. He warned that India could not achieve its goals if its people remained 'in little circles of community'.[61]

There was a third space, an alternative to these two positions, occupied by disparate members of the leftist and independent opposition in the Lok Sabha, which supported reservations and the right of the oppressed to openly discuss caste and other ascriptive identities. These arguments came out in debates over amendments to the Representation of the People Act in 1961, which made it an electoral offence to promote 'feelings of enmity' on the grounds of 'religion, race, caste, community or language' during campaigning. Several MPs pointed out that the new wording would open up the possibility of endless litigation in the election tribunals, for any expression of an opinion on contentious issues might be construed as the promotion of enmity. Dr Krishnaswami, an Independent MP from Chingleput in today's Tamil Nadu, noted that during debates about social problems and social change 'there will always be heated discussions either on grounds of religion or language or other aspects', a fact that the Congress elites refused to recognise. He argued that in a country with such a variety of social groups, 'we will have to allow them a certain place in any election campaign. It would be unrealistic to think that we can totally wish away these factors.'[62] Renu Chakravartty, a Communist member from West Bengal, stated simply, 'We cannot just by saying that in the matter of elections we cannot raise these matters, remove these problems.' She argued that minorities and caste communities ought to be able to express 'legitimate grievances' related to 'social oppression'.[63] These objections notwithstanding, the new wording was inserted, and remains to this day part of the act.

In spite of Nehru's leadership and the legal changes the Union government introduced, the ground on which candidates campaigned clearly shifted over the first three elections. Political parties, including Congress pradesh (state) committees, chose candidates based on their caste affiliation, and indirect appeals to caste were common during quotidian electioneering by all parties. While Congress eschewed new formal connections with some Dalit or backward caste associations, other parties, such as the Swatantra Party, jumped at the opportunity to expand their appeal by tapping into these networks.[64] Meanwhile, the law prohibiting appeals to caste, religion or language or promotion of enmity between communities does not seem to have been used to combat the practice. For the third elections, the Representation of the People Act had also made it more difficult to file election petitions, and the number declined by over a quarter.[65]

In these developments, we can discern some of the antecedents of the democratic deepening India has experienced since the 1980s.[66] Trying to explain the increase in Dalit political participation and the rise of parties like the Bahujan Samaj Party, scholars have credited the importance of reservations in creating a Dalit middle class, and also cited the changing fortunes of the Congress Party in the 1970s. However, the increase in direct and indirect mobilisation of community sentiment in the 1950s and 1960s is a part of the story that deserves more attention. It is a development that disturbed the Congress elites, and Nehru in particular, for it took their democracy in a direction diametrically opposed to the one that they had intended. We will return to their dismay, and the steps they took to try to alleviate it, at the end of the chapter.

Economic Democracy and the Price of Elections

When it came to economic democracy, India's senior politicians soon noticed that a similarly pernicious dynamic came into play. Just as elections were being commandeered to serve caste interests, they were also being worked in such a way as to harness democracy to money and its corrupting influences. This feeling has peaked at various points, including in the first half of the 1970s. By 1973, the storm had begun brewing that would eventually lead Indira Gandhi to declare an Emergency two years later. While the Emergency had several sources, including an economic crisis, mass hunger and large-scale protests, one of these was the favour Mrs Gandhi was said to have shown to corrupt politicians. In August 1973, *The Times of India* ran a story by Ajit Bhattacharjea with the headline, 'Ministers on the Make: a History of Corruption and Cover Up'. Bhattacharjea demanded to know why Dr Harekrushna Mahtab, former Union cabinet minister, Bombay governor and Orissa chief minister, had gone unpunished when a report earlier in the year had found he had committed 'serious improprieties' and amassed wealth 'much beyond his ostensible sources of income'. And how, Bhattacharjea asked, had Keshav Dev Malaviya been appointed chairman of the Heavy Industries Corporation in 1968, when five years earlier he had been forced to resign from his position as minister for mines and fuel in the Union cabinet for accepting donations in exchange for help with an import licence?[67] Both men had been associated with Mohammed Serajuddin and his two nephews in one of the first election-expenses scandals in independent India, which dated to the 1950s.

To understand the Serajuddin affair, and the dynamics by which India's economic inequalities were fed into the democratic system, let us go back to the first elections, where election expenses seemed to create a great deal of work for the Election Commission and significant consternation among MPs. In these first elections, candidates for the Lok Sabha were permitted to spend up to Rs.25,000, unless they were contesting a seat in a double-member constituency, where the ceiling was Rs.35,000. Returns were meant to be filed by candidates as well as by their agents. Receipts and records were meant to be kept and every last pai accounted for. The system was so intricate and demanding that more than a quarter of candidates for the Lok Sabha in the first general election were disqualified for errors related to expenses. Indeed, the Election Commission was forced to 'take a lenient view' in those cases where errors 'did not appear to be wilful', reversing the disqualification of many candidates.[68] The bottom line, Sukumar Sen reported, was that, 'election accounts do not appear to have been kept properly by most candidates'.[69]

There were reports of wealthy candidates spending huge sums. It was alleged that the Raja of Challapalli spent Rs.5 lakh in his pursuit of a seat in what is today Andhra Pradesh. During his campaign, he was said to have purchased 'a thousand cycles', as well as cars and other vehicles.[70] For both Union and state ministers, their tours were often not included in election returns, for they combined official business and electioneering. Nehru flew in a small plane to tour much of the country, with landing strips constructed for his visits. Special trains were put on where airports were not available.[71] It was not just Congress candidates whose expenses ran beyond their willingness to account for them. Hiren Mukerjee, the Communist Party leader from West Bengal, boasted that for his campaign in the first elections, in 'lane after lane in Calcutta there were festoons, placards, posters, done by God knows who'. He disavowed responsibility for accounting for these expenditures, telling the Lok Sabha, 'I cannot possibly get to know what has been spent by my friends in one part or another of my constituency. That kind of election accounts should not be demanded of me by the law.'[72] Indeed, it was widely agreed that not only were the requirements for keeping track of expenses 'tedious' and 'torturous',[73] but that the accounts eventually filed were ultimately 'fictitious'.[74]

As India geared up for the second general election, therefore, the government proposed changes to the Representation of the People Act. Introducing the bill to the Lok Sabha, the minister for legal affairs, H. V. Pataskar, acknowledged that the system of accounting for expenses had been 'difficult to comply with, with a clear and honest conscience'.[75] Pataskar explained that parties had complained because they spent money 'not for the purpose of the election of a particular candidate but of all the candidates' in their party. It was 'impossible', they claimed, to determine which part of this general expenditure went to individual candidates. The result was that expenses tended to be allocated 'arbitrarily' to individual candidates.[76] Therefore, the amendments the government proposed included a provision that would exclude the expenditure of recognised political parties from returns filed by individual candidates.

This provision caused widespread dismay as the bill made its way through the legislative process. Among the opposition MPs, the unease was connected to speculation about how much Congress was raising for the forthcoming elections. Hari Vishnu Kamath, a Praja Socialist Party leader, suggested Congress was raising Rs.5 crore.[77] Renu Chakravartty worried about the consequences of such huge expenditure for smaller parties, 'with the result that the smaller man, the poorer man, and the poorer parties will be put at a disadvantage'.[78] From great statesmen of the opposition like Hiren Mukerjee to more humble members of Congress who delivered their speeches in Hindi, such as Seth Achal Singh, many argued that elections ought to be fought 'without expenses'. Singh was sure that, '[i]f expenses should be increased, then corruption will spread [karapshan phelega]'.[79] The award for parliamentary oratory in this case ought to go to H. V. Kamath, who warned that 'the flood-gates of corruption, of unfairness, and of unfreeness, etc., will be opened and we shall have to say good-bye to fair and free elections in our country'.[80] In the end, Pataskar was forced to withdraw the proposal. For the remaining elections in the Nehru era, it was widely acknowledged that 'candidates invariably spent much more on elections than was permitted, but none could admit this in the returns filed under the law'.[81] The Congress Party, meanwhile, spent Rs.5 crore on the second general election, and similar amounts on the third.[82]

Having failed to change the rules on the way candidates accounted for their expenses, the Congress-led government seemed to pursue every other avenue to open up spending in the elections. As we saw in chapter 4, the Union government raised taxes across the board in the latter half of the 1950s, but expenditure on elections was exempted.[83] When the government passed the Companies Act of 1956, it permitted corporate donations to political parties, so long as the enterprise was not government owned and the company's memorandum of association permitted it. Two major industrial outfits, Indian Iron and Steel Co. and Tata Iron and Steel Co. (TISCO), promptly obtained permission from the courts to alter their memoranda of association to allow them to donate to political parties. TISCO argued in the Bombay High Court that 'the stability, security, profits and future expansion of the company were linked up with the continuance of the Congress Government' and therefore contributions to the Congress Party were an integral part of running its operations. The judges agreed that the argument was 'lawfully tenable', even as they warned there were 'great dangers' in the move.[84] Given that over the next few years several senior Tata men, including A. D. Shroff and M. R. Masani, would go on to form the Swatantra Party, which opposed Congress policies on the regulation of big business, one is left to wonder whether support for Congress was really what the directors had in mind. Either way, the case underscored the connection between business donations and elected politicians.

After the experience of the second general election, several MPs put forward proposals to ban donations to political parties as the Companies Act was amended in 1960. In the discussion, a clearer picture of political donations in the second election emerged. Introducing the bill as minister for commerce and industry, Lal Bahadur Shastri noted that once again people had found 'subterfuge methods' to work around the provisions of the law to make donations. Banning donations altogether, he argued, would only move them further underground. He also defended the integrity of party policy-making, arguing that donations did not affect the ideology of the parties.[85]

From across the political spectrum, MPs rose to support a ban on corporate donations. Some derided these donations for the way they seemed to erode Indian socialism. Acharya Kripalani, erstwhile Congressman but by 1960 a stalwart of the opposition, mocked the Congress government for taking donations from big business, alleging that 'they talk of socialism but they do not believe in socialism'.[86] Hiren Mukerjee concurred, telling the Lok Sabha that it hardly seemed India was building a socialist society at all: it had 'become almost a pathetic fallacy, the attempt to build socialism in the way that the Congress Party is proceeding'.[87]

Many drew an explicit connection between donations and corruption. Kripalani alleged that the party bosses collected funds, and 'some of them pocket the money they get'.[88] Several MPs mentioned the fact that in Uttar Pradesh, sugar factories were told to donate one rupee to Congress for every maund of sugar produced. Mahavir Tyagi, a Congressman from Dehra Dun, concluded simply, 'I say this is corruption[.]'[89] But it was Minoo Masani, leader of the Swatantra Party, who put his finger on the issue. He accepted that donations did not influence the ideology of political parties, but told the House that they did have an effect on quotidian decisions of government: 'Who shall produce a car and who shall produce a tank? Where shall it be produced? Who will have a permit or licence? Who will export the raw materials? This is the quid pro quo for the donations given.'[90] Indeed he, like others in the Lok Sabha, alleged that ministers used their power over licences and permits to reward those who donated, and punish those who did not. Contributions to the ruling Congress Party, Masani concluded, were ultimately not truly voluntary.[91] In the end, the government accepted that there ought to be a ceiling on donations, and that all contributions to political parties ought to be declared on company balance sheets; but corporate donations would be a feature of Indian elections until Indira Gandhi tried to ban them in 1969.[92]

Although large-scale corruption tied to permit-and-licence raj is often dated to the late 1960s or early 1970s, it can be traced at least to the second general election. The slow exposure of the problem is clear when one notes that one of the big scandals of the era—the Serajuddin affair, mentioned above—did not break until 1963. Muhammed Serajuddin and his two nephews, M. L. Rahaman and M. K. Rahaman, owners of Serajuddin and Co., were Calcutta-based merchants, involved in mining and exporting manganese and chromite. Serajuddin, his nephews and several others initially came under suspicion for under-valuing their exports, thereby evading export duty, as well as for bribing tax inspectors in the 1950s.[93] Serajuddin and Co. was also a big political donor to the Congress Party in the 1950s. When the Serajuddin scandal first broke, it took down Keshav Dev Malaviya, Union minister for mines and fuel. Malaviya had received a donation of Rs.10,000 from Serajuddin before the second general election. Afterwards, Serajuddin was awarded prospecting licences for manganese, even though the firm was not eligible for such a licence. A 'private' enquiry ordered by Nehru and conducted by Supreme Court Justice S. K. Das found that the donation and the grant of the licence 'smacked of a favour granted in lieu of benefits received'.[94] Malaviya resigned his post, claiming that he was 'innocent of these scandalous accusations'.[95] The prime minister, with his health visibly deteriorating, but still at the helm, seemed reluctant to countenance the possibility of corruption in his cabinet. Nehru told the Lok Sabha that he was 'not personally convinced that Shri Malaviya has done anything which casts a reflection on his impartiality and integrity'.[96]

Serajuddin and Co. had also made big donations in Orissa in the 1950s, where Chief Minister Harekrushna Mahtab and his deputy Biren Mitra collected Rs.1.5 lakh from the company. Banamali Patnaik, Orissa's new Congress chief minister in 1963, called on the Congress Party to investigate whether Mahtab had 'actually spent the money for party purposes'.[97] It took nearly a decade for the inquiry committee, chaired by Sarjoo Prasad, to report. So it was not until 1973 that the public came to know that Mahtab was 'guilty of gross favouritism, improprieties and abuse of power as chief minister in granting lease of chromite mines to Mr Serajuddin to the great detriment and loss to the state'.[98] By the time this became known, a broader narrative of corruption in the Congress Party had taken hold, but the blame was pinned on Indira Gandhi.

It is a little acknowledged fact, however, that in the final years of Nehru's tenure, the scandals fed into concerns that India's democratic system was not being operated as intended by its leaders. These affairs seemed to give the lie to the hope that political and economic democracy would reinforce one another. When it came to electioneering, Nehru was rather out of step with the times when, in September 1961, he went to Kanpur and collected more than Rs.1 lakh in donations, but with deep discomfort. He told meetings of business leaders that he 'felt a little ashamed' in taking their money, and urged them not to donate to Congress if they were also donating to other parties.[99] He returned a cheque drawn on one of the businesses involved in the Mundhra affair (see chapter 5).[100] Nehru's personal integrity stands in contrast to behaviour revealed by the findings of the Committee on the Prevention of Corruption, which was appointed in 1962. Chaired by K. Santhanam, the committee documented the 'widespread impression' that existed in the country that since independence some ministers had 'enriched themselves illegitimately', obtaining advantages for themselves and their relatives 'inconsistent with any notion of purity in public life'. Crucially, the report continued that '[t]he general belief about failure of integrity amongst Ministers is as damaging as actual failure'. The committee went on to recommend that a code of conduct for ministers be drawn up.[101] Such a code was drafted as part of the reset of Indian democracy to be discussed at the end of this chapter. But first, we turn to an additional element of the crisis: the fear that elected officials were interfering with the administration in ways that were contrary to the basic tenets of political democracy.

Democratising the Administration, the Peaceful Transfer of Power and the Crisis in Kerala

While Ambedkar was the plaintiff at an election tribunal after the first elections, the aftermath of the second elections saw Nehru a defendant. He had stood for and won election in the double-member constituency of Phulpur in Uttar Pradesh. Shortly after his victory, one of his opponents, Sita Ram Khemka, general secretary of the All-India Cow Protection Committee, filed a petition against the premier's election on the grounds of 'corrupt practice' and 'undue official influence'.[102] Khemka alleged that Nehru had 'fought the elections as Prime Minister of India taking unique advantage of all the privilege and advantages of that office and that this had materially affected the results of the elections'.[103] Nehru did not accord the tribunal much attention, even though the petition made its way to the Supreme Court before it was finally put to rest.[104] Still, Khemka had touched upon something that had been causing disquiet since the first general election: there was a sense that Congress was working the administration in ways that tilted it towards the ruling party. This would make it harder to have what Radhakrishnan had termed 'changes of governments without breaking heads'.

Not only Nehru, but other ministers too used the pretext of official tours to travel during elections. Representing Ganjam South, B. C. Das told the Lok Sabha that in one by-election he had witnessed the 'entire Cabinet' of his state, some ten or twelve ministers, going from village to village on an official tour, promising to open schools, repair roads and so on during the day. When night came, they would swap the national flag for the Congress flag, and tour the same villages canvassing for votes.[105] H. V. Kamath articulated a complaint commonly heard among the opposition that during elections, All India Radio was 'nothing less than the ruling party's megaphone'. He claimed that opposition party speeches were ignored, while 'a petty speech of a Congress Minister [. . .] opening a restaurant or some tea shop or pan shop—that was reported on the All India Radio'.[106] One must control for the hyperbole that was a common way of eliciting laughs and scoring points while speechifying in the Lok Sabha, but Kamath had hit on a point that was repeated by other members of the opposition benches.[107]

Interventions related to elections that tilted matters in favour of the Congress Party seem to have been most egregious in the most contested territories. In Hyderabad, after the invasion of 1948, the unelected government had promised elections, but the inexperienced Congress Party could not corral its factions into a cohesive machine, despite the assistance of Sardar Patel. Elections were postponed, and members of the Congress were brought into an unelected cabinet when it appeared that a popular vote would be unlikely to produce an outcome favourable to the Party.[108] When a revived Majlis-i Ittehadul Muslimeen won a majority in the Hyderabad municipality in 1960 (see chapter 3), the municipal corporation was promptly merged with that of Secunderabad to eliminate the possibility of a major metropolis being run by a Muslim party.[109] At the other end of the country, Jammu and Kashmir did not elect members to the Lok Sabha in the first three general elections, sending representatives nominated by the president instead.[110] Meanwhile, Sheikh Abdullah and then Bakshi Ghulam Muhammad imprisoned their electoral rivals or rejected their nomination papers, producing elected legislatures that secured their power locally and kept relations with New Delhi as stable as possible.[111]

Quotidian acts also bent the system in favour of Congress. Recall, from chapter 5, that Congress leaders were critical of the administrative apparatus that they had inherited, and that they tried to develop a new type of civil servant. These new administrators would ditch the old adherence to 'neutrality' and would instead put their 'heart and soul' into their work.[112] While the language was politically neutral, in practice this entailed a drive to recruit and promote administrators who were favourably disposed to the Congress programme. All this seemed not to trouble Congress-controlled governments until an opposition party took power and tried to make similar changes. This happened first in Kerala.

The Communist Party ascended to form a government in Kerala after the second general election gave them sixty out of 127 seats in the state assembly. The background to this victory was a short and not distinguished history of rule by Congress and Congress-backed governments which had been characterised by in-fighting and misrule. At the all-India level, the Communist Party had committed itself to democracy and the peaceful pursuit of socialism in 1951, after the uprising in Telangana had been defeated. In Kerala, they made excellent political capital out of Congress's missteps.[113] The formation of the first non-Congress government in independent India prompted some soul-searching in the Congress, eliciting calls for its 'revitalising', and manifestos, from several senior figures outside Nehru's inner circle, on the meaning of socialism.[114]

Relations between the centre and the state, or between Congress and the Communist Party seem to have developed on two parallel planes. On one, almost as soon as the Communists assumed power in April 1957, allegations and counter-allegations were thrown about. Communist leader S. A. Dange told a meeting in Bombay that U. N. Dhebar, the Congress president, was contemplating engaging in 'tricks and constitutionalism' to deprive the party of power in the state.[115] B. T. Ranadive warned of 'a conspiracy on the part of the Congress and vested interests in Kerala to create difficulties for the Communist Government'.[116] In some quarters of the Congress Party, alarmist interpretations of Communist Party rule quickly took hold. Shriman Narayan, the Congress general secretary, visited the state during the summer of 1957, and submitted a report to Dhebar 'conveying a dark and disquieting picture of the law and order situation' in Kerala. Citing a litany of complaints, Narayan claimed the services were 'demoralised and feel helpless'.[117] Some of the more intemperate anti-communists interpreted the Communist Ministry's activities strictly through classic communist texts, and insisted that every move was but a step towards violent revolution.[118] On this plane, the crisis was at hand almost as soon as the Communist Party came to power in Kerala, and all sides claimed that democracy itself was at stake.

And yet on another plane, relations were relatively cordial, and took on a formal air of normality. Nehru seems to have accepted the arrival of a non-Congress government with equanimity. He and Kerala's new Communist chief minister, E.M.S. Namboodiripad (known as EMS), exchanged letters and then held meetings in New Delhi in which their disagreements were aired, but they promised to cooperate with one another.[119] Rajendra Prasad told a crowd at Trivandrum he was 'happy that this experiment' was being conducted in Kerala.[120] One Kerala Pradesh Congress Committee publication patronisingly noted that the hope among the opposition was that governing would be an 'ennobling experience' for the communists, who might be 'mellowed by their responsibilities'.[121]

Meanwhile, communists in Kerala began to adjust to the idea of governing. Their threefold programme began with a commitment to mobilise all resources for the 'development of a modern Industrial-cum-Agricultural economy', and a promise to 'recast' the distribution of wealth so that the 'masses producing the wealth do get a greater share than they are getting today'. These two aims were premised on a third: the transformation of the administration, which on account of being created during colonial rule, was 'inefficient[, . . .] unjust and oppressive'.[122] The Ministry moved to reassure businesses that, in spite of what had been promised in its election manifesto, it had no plans for large-scale nationalisation in the state.[123] If all of this sounds familiar it is because it was crafted to copy the Congress programme. As EMS explained, the Ministry's aims were 'natural concomitants of the national goal which has been accepted by all sections of our people—the goal of building a Socialist Society.' Indeed, the Communists began to proclaim that '[w]e are, if you want to put it that way, the true Congressmen'.[124]

It was not radical redistribution or a remarkably different path to development that set the stage for conflict over Kerala. Although the opposition mobilised over education, land reform and other policy issues, it was reform of the administrative services that was at the centre of the crisis for India's democracy. The language of the Communist Ministry's reform programme is virtually indistinguishable from that promoted by Congress at the centre and discussed above, in chapter 5. EMS had appointed and chaired an administrative reforms committee, which declared that the existing system was 'over-centralised' with rules that were 'unduly rigid', and 'destroyed initiative at lower levels'. The committee recommended 'a thorough re-orientation in [the] attitudes, outlook, skill and training' of the services, towards the introduction of more 'democratic' methods of rule.[125] If the rhetoric was indistinguishable from that which underpinned the reforms undertaken by Congress governments since independence, the result was different. For while the language was politically neutral, the effect of the reforms initiated across India since independence had been to align administrators more closely with the political programme of the Congress Party. When the Communists sought to replicate these reforms in Kerala, it meant either favouring those state servants who were most amenable to the Communist Party leadership, or finding ways to circumvent those who were reluctant to implement its programme. The Ministry did both. On the one hand there were dozens of transfers, suspensions, promotions and demotions. On the other, the Ministry introduced non-official committees to shadow administrators and 'democratise' their work. Some ten thousand non-officials, mostly Communists, joined committees to oversee work at the division and subdivision level on every aspect of administration, from food distribution to public works.[126]

To the Communist Ministry, these 'people's committees' were essential to democracy and development, which required both 'flexibility' and cooperation with the people. According to the chief minister, these were traits that were lacking in permanent officials, but which non-official political workers had in abundance.[127] Echoing the likes of Durgabai Deshmukh and S. K. Dey, Namboodiripad argued that 'leaving all questions of implementation to the permanent official would make a mockery of democracy'.[128] To the opposition, however, the transfers and the people's committees constituted 'organised partisan interference' in the administration. They alleged that the reforms had led to the 'demoralisation' and 'paralysation' in the services.[129]

Analogous changes concerning the police and criminal justice set up a wider conflict over the services. At the end of July 1957, the Ministry announced a new policy for the police, who were instructed not to interfere in peaceful mass movements. Namboodiripad laid out what he called the 'Communist conception of the normal role of the police' in simple terms: 'The Police should not be used in an anti-people way.' He explained that there were 'well-defined' limits to people's movements, which included no resort to violence, and not encircling the houses of employers and owners, but within these limits, employers 'could not expect the police to help' when workers resorted to strike action.[130] The Ministry ordered police to end the 'evil practice of shadowing of political workers', and all restrictions on meetings were withdrawn.[131] Congress seized on the changes to claim that lawlessness was taking hold in Kerala, and the administration was breaking down. Shriman Narayan alleged that 'the services, especially the police, are demoralised and feel helpless'.[132]

As early as 1958, Namboodiripad counter-charged that the Congress Party was involved in a 'deliberately organised' campaign to tell civil servants in Kerala 'they need not obey' his government. Alleging that Congress regimes, too, bent the administration to their will, he accused Congress of double standards, and offered to meet all-India leaders to lay out the 'norms and standards' that ought to apply to all governments and political parties in India.[133] Congress did not take him up on his offer at the time. The stage was set for a conflict over political interference in the services.

The crisis would burst open when the opposition parties managed to unite in protest, in 1959. The proximate cause was the Ministry's Education Bill. The bill proposed more state control over Kerala's successful but largely private educational sector, providing more job security for teachers and limiting the role of school management. The Ministry also redrafted textbooks to include a more communist-friendly reading of history. Minoo Masani's Democratic Research Service, an anti-communist body, summed up its complaints regarding the new textbooks thus: while India's freedom struggle was allocated a mere seven lines in the new books, 'Red China' was allocated eight pages.[134] The bill galvanised the opposition, which embarked upon protests in the middle months of 1959. The movement was characterised by arson and violence as well as police firing and lathi charges.[135]

The nature of the anti-communist coalition was such that each part of it—Congress, the Praja Socialist Party, Christians, the Nair Service Society, the Muslim League—joined for its own reasons. But all united in calling for the removal of the Communists and framing their struggle as a battle for India's democracy. Lal Bahadur Shastri, Union minister for commerce and industry, told a meeting of Congress workers that 'democracy was being openly violated' in Kerala, and as proof he cited the Communist Party's 'partisan' interference in the administration.[136] A group of ten Christian leaders, ranging from the Reverend Dr C. E. Abraham, principal of Serampore College, to C. P. Mathen, former MP and ambassador in the Sudan, warned that the continuation of the Communist Party regime 'will be the death-knell of democracy'. Their primary grievance was with the education bill, but they also alleged that 'democratic conventions and proprieties [had been] thrown to the winds' by the Communist Ministry.[137]

Urged on by Indira Gandhi, who had recently taken over the presidency of Congress, the centre dismissed the Communist Ministry and declared presidential rule in Kerala at the end of July 1959.[138] The opposition declared a victory for democracy; the Communists insisted that the opposition's aims had been 'totally undemocratic and unconstitutional'.[139] Rather than resulting in a resort to arms, as the more hyperbolic critics of the Communists had feared it might, this episode called into question India's ability to abide by one of the fundamental tenets of democracy—the peaceful transfer of power—and was pulled into the larger conversation about how to reform Indian democracy in the late 1950s and early 1960s.

Democratic Doubt

By the end of the first decade of the Republic, doubts about the way the system of parliamentary democracy was being operated in India were being expressed from several quarters. In the larger context of Asian politics, there seemed to be a sharp turn away from parliamentary democracy at the end of the 1950s. Sukarno had shifted Indonesia to what he called 'guided democracy' in 1957. In Pakistan Muhammad Ayub Khan staged the country's first coup in October 1958. In the same month, U Nu had requested the military to step in to govern Burma. The following year, S.W.R.D. Bandaranaike was assassinated in Ceylon. In the midst of these events, India's leading political science journal could run an article with the title, 'Is Parliamentary Government Suitable to India?', without eliciting outrage. The author, Devavrat N. Pathak, who was a reader in politics at Gujarat University, answered in the affirmative, but that the question was asked in earnest is evidence of the mood in some circles of India's elite.

The most prominent critic of parliamentary democracy was Jayaprakash Narayan. A devoted Gandhian and a friend of the prime minister whom Nehru addressed as 'bhai', JP, as he was known, had been one of the founding members of the Congress Socialist Party before independence. After 1947, he initially joined the socialist opposition, declaring that parliamentary democracy required a strong opposition. Shortly thereafter, however, he disavowed politics to pursue Bhoodan and Sarvodaya. But this did not stop him thinking about politics. Soon after the first general election, he began to wonder out loud whether there might be 'some other way' for India to pursue democracy, beyond the system established by the

Constitution.[140] Fundamentally concerned with social inequality, JP worried that the pressures of development would lead towards totalitarianism. 'If democracy is to survive in Asia', he told the nation via All India Radio in 1953, 'it must prove its superiority in solving the problems of economic inequality and exploitation as well as those of economic development.' He lamented that, while India had 'copied the form of Western democracy, we have not shown yet that Indian democracy is capable of handling these problems with speed and efficiency'.[141]

During the course of the first two general elections, JP grew deeply cynical about parliamentary democracy. As the second election drew to a close, he wrote to Nehru to tell him that 'whatever their outcome, the verdict is inescapable that the present political system has proved a failure'.[142] First, he regretted that India's first-past-the-post system produced governments that did not represent a majority of voters. He noted that in the first general election, Congress had secured only 45 per cent of votes for the Lok Sabha: 'The majority had voted against Congress. Yet the Congress secured an overwhelming majority of seats in the legislatures.'[143] Second, he worried that people did not vote on the issues, which were 'in the shadow', but that 'the most persuasive platform [...] is proving to be caste'. Caste was, in his view, 'the greatest single impediment to India's progress', for it was the cause of the country's 'social injustice and inequality'.[144] And yet, its influence in India's democracy was growing.

Even if Nehru was publicly circumspect about parliamentary democracy, he was not keen to upend India's existing institutions. Replying to JP's critique, the prime minister bluntly wrote, 'I do not think the present system has failed[.]' He conceded that '[o]f course, the party system [...] has many faults. The parliamentary democracy that we have adopted is also full of faults.' Nevertheless, he insisted, '[W]e adopted it because [...] it was better than the other possible courses.' Writing to his friend, Nehru worried about 'disruptive and reactionary' forces, but he identified them as religious, caste and linguistic chauvinism, rather than anything to do with the democratic system India had chosen. Pointing to political instability in Western Asia and in South-East Asia, he determined that, although Congress had 'many' failings, the primary service it had done for the country was in 'checking these tendencies to disruption and instability and trying to bring about cohesion in the country'. If parliamentary democracy should fail in India, Nehru concluded, 'it will not fail because the system in theory is bad, but because we could not live up to it'.[145]

Still, a discourse about India's democratic inadequacies was gaining currency as the country entered its second decade of freedom. This included a critique from within government that was not directed at parliamentary democracy per se, but which aimed to improve development by deepening democracy. As discussed in chapter 4, as Community Development reached every corner of the country, and the initial zeal for collective self-help waned, the Government of India appointed Balwantray Mehta to look into the programme and recommend new ways of rousing the enthusiasm of the people. Mehta's committee concluded in 1957 that '[r]ural development and rural welfare are possible only with local initiative and local discretion'.[146] The mechanism they recommended to induce and produce local initiative was village self-government, with the village panchayat at its heart. Panchayats offered the promise of the 'progressive dispersal of authority' which, it was hoped, would be accompanied by 'progressive increase of competence both in officials and non-officials', easing the monopolistic grip of experts and government officials.[147] Among senior officials in government, panchayats were regarded as central to the 'political education' of rural India. Participation in them would nudge people to think, 'not only of tomorrow but also next year and five years time'. They would realise resources are scarce and 'objectives frequently compete with one another' and they would understand that difficult choices often have to be made.[148] While Panchayati Raj certainly had its own antecedents, the proposals found fertile ground in an India that was growing cynical about its democracy.

A cascade of violent crises eventually spurred attempts at reform, not of the parliamentary system, but of the manners and conventions of the people using it. Indeed, caste, communal and linguistic passions seemed to rise as India racked up more elections, causing much consternation among Delhi's elite. In Bombay, the campaign for partition of the state into Maharashtra and Gujarat witnessed anti-Gujarati violence in the winter of 1955–56.[149] After Kerala's political unrest in 1959, there was Assam, where anti-Bengali legislation provoked protests in which fifteen Bengali speakers were killed by police in May 1961. The cities of Jabalpur in Madhya Pradesh and then Aligarh and Meerut in Uttar Pradesh saw Hindu–Muslim riots in 1961.[150] In Punjab, the language issue took on new urgency as Master Tara Singh began a 'fast unto death' to demand the creation of a Punjabi-speaking state.

During this period, India's political elites began a conversation about making some renovations to their democracy. One mode of reform was the drafting of voluntary codes of conduct, mutually agreed by all sides, to set out the boundaries of acceptable political behaviour. For example, between 1957 and 1958 Gulzarilal Nanda, then Union minister for labour, employment and planning, alarmed that 'violence and strikes and lockouts

[. . .] had become a feature of industrial relations in the country', took up the idea. In early 1958, three central organisations of employers, and India's four main trade unions agreed a code which enjoined 'parties to settle all disputes and grievances through negotiation, conciliation and arbitration' and they agreed to forego 'coercion, intimidation, victimisation, go-slow, strikes or lockouts without notice'.[151] The following year in Madras, where the Dravida Munnetra Kazhagam was gaining traction, and also causing consternation with its call for a separate Dravidinad, an all-party agreement was drawn up in which political parties vowed not to 'exploit' students for political purposes.[152]

The Communist government in Kerala had appointed a Police Reorganisation Committee, which in turn recommended a code be drawn up to guide political parties' conduct and maintain 'a decent public life'. At the height of the agitation to remove the government of Kerala in 1959, Nehru, responding to a question at a press conference, told those assembled that he thought 'it would be a very good thing' if political parties could agree a 'code of conduct' for themselves.[153] P. T. Chacko, home minister in the Congress-led coalition which replaced the Communist Ministry, secured an agreement among all political parties for a code in December 1960. In Kerala, this first code called for parties to inform the police in advance of their meetings and processions, to eschew insulting 'the private life, personal habits or physical peculiarities of opponents' and to avoid defamatory remarks or derogatory posters concerning any religion, community or 'political thought'.[154]

Before the third general election, similar codes were drafted in several states. Though the parties in each state agreed their own terms, they all had shared features, including a call to abstain from 'exploiting caste and communal feelings' for electoral purposes, to avoid personal attacks on their rivals and to eschew interference in rival meetings and processions.[155] This was all part of the prehistory of the Model Code of Conduct, which by the twenty-first century has become an elaborate set of rules around elections.[156] While other scholars have noted that the Model Code of Conduct had its origins in Kerala at this time, they have misunderstood it as a product of the 'broad consensus' of the period, neglecting the extent to which it arose from the democratic doubts of the era.[157]

In the early 1960s, these codes become part of a conversation about what a symposium organised by the Gokhale Institute of Politics called the 'traditions of democracy'.[158] This shifted the focus from institutions and processes, where India had reasonable cause to laud its own success, to the everyday lived experience of democracy, concerning which India's elites were more fretful. This conversation took place in newspapers, periodicals and conferences, as well as in a proliferation of books about Indian democracy, administration, socialism and other prominent topics of the day.

In the summer of 1961, the great and the good convened in several fora to consider how to dampen what was called 'communalism and separatism' in the country. A Committee on Emotional Integration was appointed in May. Chief ministers and central leaders met the following month and considered but rejected proposals to ban what were called 'communal parties' from participating in India's democracy. However, as noted above, they did agree that the Indian Penal Code and the Representation of the People Act ought both to be amended to provide for greater penalties for those who promoted 'enmity' between different groups on grounds of 'religion, caste, race, community or language'.[159]

At the end of September 1961, a National Integration Conference was held. Inaugurating the conference, Vice President Radhakrishnan observed that caste had changed, saying that while it was diminishing as a social evil, it was becoming 'a political evil, an administrative evil', for caste loyalties were being exploited for 'winning our elections or getting more people into jobs'. Zakir Husain, governor of Bihar, and himself a future vice president, 'drew the loudest applause' when he declared that 'we have let loose forces which are creating disintegration because we want to win elections'. Husain also deplored corruption, saying that people were coming to the conclusion that it 'pays to be dishonest' and that this 'must be stopped'.[160] Notwithstanding the fiery self-reflection of the opening speeches, the conference avoided descending into a row by concentrating on 'broad approaches and principles',[161] and working through unanimity. Inevitably, its final statement was rather platitudinous.[162]

What was not inevitable, however, was the way the conversation was steered from introspection among India's politicians to discussion of the failings of the Indian people. National integration, the conference attendees agreed, 'has to grow silently in the minds of hearts and men', through education.[163] Slipping into nationalist pedagogical mode, the conference agreed to a suggestion of JP and the Sarva Seva Sangh to launch a mass campaign to persuade every adult to take the following pledge:

> I, as a citizen of India, affirm my faith in the universal principle of civilised society, namely that every dispute between citizens, or groups,

institutions or organisations of citizens, should be settled by peaceful means; and, in view of the growing danger to the integrity and unity of the country, I hereby pledge myself never to resort to physical violence in case of any dispute, whether in my neighbourhood or in any other part of India.[164]

The following year it was decided that 'National Integration Week' would be held from 2 to 9 October, during which time universities, colleges and panchayats were all marshalled in the effort to secure pledges from citizens.[165] India had travelled from its first elections, after which ordinary Indians were lauded for their 'practical common sense', to a place where, after a decade of experience, their leaders declared the people were in need of education. This was a settling into familiar postcolonial nationalist routines among leaders who, though engaged in some introspection, were unsure how to change the way elected politicians worked the system, and so deflected their efforts towards the people.

Conclusion

Was India's democracy a failure in the Nehru years? Certainly not—provided that its success is interpreted in rather narrow terms. India's Constitution, its Election Commission, its legislatures were all established within reasonably successful parameters. To deploy a metaphor from our time, they were the essential hardware necessary for the democratic system. However, this hardware required software and users, and this is where the myth of the successful democracy begins to become apparent. The codes that would run on this complex system were not written by the designers of the hardware. The idealists of the Constituent Assembly were aware of how democracy had functioned in India prior to 1947, but they were convinced that a free India would operate differently. They were sure that supposedly defunct customs like casteism could be discarded, and that they could provide safeguards against unwelcome new ones, such as the corrupting influence of money and the manipulation of the administration in favour of the ruling party.

Self-confidence is also a measure of success: by the end of the first decade of democratic rule, India's democratically elected leaders were expressing doubt in their own system. To be sure, even the communists had come onto the side of democracy. And yet, casteism, corruption and the crisis in Kerala, combined with an increase in political violence, fed into a narrative of doubt and demands for reform. Free India's first generation of leaders did not write the Constitution and then sit on their laurels. They remained alert to the way the system changed as it was put into practice. Their attention to the need for constant renewal is something that was shared with India's modernists, who are the subject of the next chapter.

FIGURE 7.1. Saraswati Temple, Birla Institute of Technology and Science, Pilani.
Image credit: Sarthi92/Shutterstock.com.

CHAPTER SEVEN

The Myth of High Modernism in India

NO OBJECT IS called upon more often to represent postcolonial India's approach to modernism than the enormous dam. The large multi-purpose dam has come to stand as a metaphor for the approach to innovation, and, indirectly for the attitude to the past during the Nehru years. With the exception of art historians, when scholars think of modernism in India, they almost invariably link it with gigantism, elitism and inauthenticity.[1] The term brings to mind the monumental buildings of Chandigarh and the complex array of dams and power stations of the Damodar Valley Corporation. Moreover, modernist approaches to social problems are often derided as authoritarian. Modernist projects, it is assumed, were imposed upon ordinary people without any conversation or negotiation.[2] In addition, India's modernism was internationalist, and for this reason, it has been dismissed as derivative, inauthentic.[3] Overwhelmingly, this interpretation of Indian modernism is associated with Nehru, who, it is true, once told a visiting dignitary as they toured a new dam, 'These are the new temples of India where I worship[.]'[4] The only alternative to this high modernism in the Indian context, we are told, was Gandhism, which, so the myth goes, was concerned with a parochial conception of the village community and with an impractical desire for economic self-sufficiency at the village level.[5] It was authentic, certainly, but atavistic. Thus, Indians had a choice between a static, antediluvian vision of India rooted in village life, and a project of Modernism-with-a-capital-M for the country, which was nothing more than a destructive, and ultimately doomed, westernisation.

The image that opens this chapter (Fig. 7.1) is not of a dam. It is a picture of the Birla temple at Pilani, which was constructed in the grounds of the Birla Institute of Technology and Science (BITS) and opened in 1959. The temple is dedicated to Saraswati. The goddess of learning is an unusual choice for a central deity in a Hindu temple, but not so unusual here, given the temple's location on the BITS campus. Structurally, it draws on the classical design of the Kandariya Mahadeva temple in Khajuraho in Madhya Pradesh. On this mandir, however, the erotic sculptures of the medieval temple are absent. Around the facade of the Saraswati temple are instead three rows of sculptures. They not only present scenes from Hindu myths, as well as Vaishnava and Shaiva motifs, but also depict eminent people from the history of the world, from Christ to Kabir, Madan Mohan Malaviya to Marx, Tagore to Marie Curie. This is not a metaphor. This is a modern temple. Deploying new materials and classic designs, it both references and moves beyond the constraints of past forms. It celebrates Indian brilliance, and recognises that Indian achievements sit within a global field of experience. It takes an ecumenical approach to iconography, bringing in people of all faiths and none to sit on the facade of a Hindu temple. As this chapter will show, this kind of production is just as much a statement of Indian modernism as any dam.

The myth of inauthentic, western modernism in India is partly a product of how we have understood the key concepts of modernity and modernism until recently. Modernity comprises a set of processes set in train somewhere around the fifteenth century and gaining pace by the nineteenth century. These concerned economic connectivity and technical innovation, as well as state-making practices, changing understandings of the self and new experiences of time. When nineteenth-century thinkers began to recognise these processes, they grouped them together to tell a story about historical change which they named modernity. Initially, European and American theorists of modernity assumed that it developed first in the west, and spread from there, via emulation or empire, to the rest of the world.

This west-to-rest model of modernity, however, has been thoroughly discredited over the past two decades. Historians have uncovered the ways in which European and American wealth was built on the backs of enslaved Africans and indentured labourers from Asia. The wealth of those parts of the world that came to regard themselves as 'white' was powered by extraction of everything from silver to sugar from the colonised world. Asian and African 'backwardness', then, was not the result of local inadequacies, as nineteenth-century imperialists claimed, but the product of the methods by which advancing countries brought about their own development. Modernity generated not just scientific and economic progress, in other words, but also poverty, inequality and what came to be understood as tradition and backwardness. Not only did modernity manifest itself in multifarious ways, but it produced highly uneven results.[6]

Modernism, in turn, is the term that covers one set of responses to the recognition of the phenomenon of modernity in the late nineteenth and twentieth centuries. These responses took place across most fields, from architecture to economics. Because modernity was seen at that time as originating in the west, modernism was conflated with westernisation. But as modernity comes to be seen as a dynamic set of processes encompassing the whole globe, definitions of modernism must keep up. Indeed, just as we now recognise multiple modernities, it is best to speak of multiple modernisms, as the art historian Partha Mitter has argued. These shared modernisms were plural, heterogeneous and, in his words, 'messy'.[7]

If this is the case, how did India's modernism come to be understood as authoritarian, inauthentic and indifferent to the Indian people and their past? The notion that India's version of modernism was imposed from above by western experts seems to be affirmed by the documents available to historians. India recruited western experts for its big modernist projects. These individuals and institutions tended to keep detailed records of their work at the time, and these archives have since been thrown open to scholars. As we have seen, Indian archival materials do not exist to the same extent. This one-sided source base tends to provide a lopsided portrayal of these international collaborations: India and Indians often come across as passive recipients of western expertise. Since 1998, when James C. Scott argued, without reference to India per se, that large dams and the architecture of Le Corbusier constituted what he called 'authoritarian high modernism', this perspective has remained fairly dominant, even as related fields have moved on.[8]

India, in this story, had a simple choice: conform or resist. In turn, this choice has been projected onto India's great men: Nehru the moderniser, Gandhi the resister. Why has this binary wherein Nehru represents modernism and Gandhi stands for authenticity come to frame the way we understand India's options after independence? On the Nehru side, it is easy to imagine a singular, authoritarian modernism coming from a prime minister who wielded enormous power by pulling the levers of a centralising, homogenising state. Equally, because the Soviet Union had state-sanctioned art and architecture, those who assume Indian socialism was modelled on the Soviet version find it easy to make analogous assumptions about Indian modernism. Some scholars have read the art and architecture of the time as expressions of non-alignment, secularism and other tenets of Nehruvianism.[9] In other words, our understanding of India's modernism occupies its place within a constellation comprised of the myths explored in earlier chapters.

Nehru was associated with many of these projects, to be sure, but primarily as patron or in a symbolic role. His diary was chock-full of ceremonies that saw him cutting ribbons and laying foundation-stones. He was the honorary president of innumerable organisations. He lent prestige to institutions and programmes just by associating himself with them, and he understood that this was his main function. To give but one example of his approach: just after independence, Nehru accepted the chair of the Council on Scientific and Industrial Research. But he did so promising that he would not have time to work on the details. The actual work would be the responsibility of Shanti Swarup Bhatnagar.[10] Acting as patron allowed Nehru 'to show what importance the new Government attaches to scientific development in India'.[11] One should not discount the significance of this figurehead role, but Nehru did not draw up the blueprint for a programme of Indian modernism, let alone personally oversee the details of its implementation. As for the Gandhi–Nehru split, there were, to be fair, people who identified as Gandhians in India, and many of them raised loud if nuanced objections to some of the government's policies. It is a mistake, however, to regard them as a discrete rival camp,[12] for many Gandhians were either in government or cooperated with modernists on their projects.[13]

The people of the decolonising world did not merely resist or conform to modernism as it was presented to them: they also shaped, channelled and colonised the processes of modernity in infinite ways, and they initiated and inspired modernist ideas as well. Undoubtedly, there were some in India who thought that the only way to be authentic was to follow what they imagined to be Indian tradition. But the people who were modernists—those that are the subject of this chapter—did not accept that there was any contradiction between being authentically Indian and being modern. Instead, many believed the experiments they were undertaking in India both drew on existing universal truths and would reveal new ones which could be spread to the wider world. It is as if these Indian modernists had already reached the place of multiple modernities and plural modernism at which today's scholars have only recently arrived. With its eclectic sources of inspiration and its untroubled pluralism, the Saraswati temple at BITS is just one example of this Indian modernism.

Modernists, for all their different methods, approaches, materials and agendas, did have certain features in common. Most of India's modernists tended to be members of the country's small, English-educated elite. This tiny circle overlapped partially with India's nationalist elite and its establishment figures in development, architecture, politics and science, and many knew one another as friends. As a group, they shared an experimental attitude to their various projects. As they pushed at intellectual frontiers, they did not embark on their work in the certainty of success, but expected to advance by trial and error. At the same time, they held out the promise of emancipation through innovation. Just as modernity was not an exclusively western phenomenon, modernism did not necessarily entail a repudiation of India's past or what had come to be understood as Indian tradition. There were multiple approaches to the past among India's modernists. Ordinary Indians were often the object of their interventions, and modernists tended to approach those outside their own circle in didactic mode. Seeking to enlighten and improve these people's lives with their productions, many modernists preferred to work from a clean slate. This could make them indifferent to existing communities, even as they laid claim to elements of what they called Indian tradition.

Large dams are not the sole or even the most representative examples of India's modernism, but this chapter begins with these gigantic irrigation and electricity projects precisely because of what they have come to represent in the myth-making about Nehru's India. It then discusses the international collaboration to build the city of Chandigarh, before exploring the way Indians developed modernism for the masses in the form of affordable housing. The chapter concludes with a discussion of government patronage of Indian modern art in the 1950s and 1960s.

The Rural Panacea: The Multi-Purpose Irrigation Project

There is good reason for large dams to have come to stand as signifiers of India's modernism. For one, India built quite a number of them after 1947. At independence, the country had 118 dams of all heights, but during the first and second five-year plans, more than five hundred river valley schemes of all kinds, including seventy-four dams over one hundred feet (thirty metres) in height were introduced.[14] Secondly, advocates of these projects presented themselves as agents of modernity. Building a dam and its associated irrigation and electricity facilities was a complex project. It required mobilising labour and capital, moving earth, redirecting water, pouring huge volumes of concrete and removing and rehabilitating (at least in theory) communities displaced by the new structure. Given the number and scale of the challenges involved, dams, unsurprisingly, were interpreted as a test of the capacity of the state to harness nature to direct economic development and improve social life. Multi-purpose projects in particular were imagined as comprehensive technical solutions to problems of flooding, famine, power generation and improvement more broadly. The fantasies they aroused and the damage they have wrought are by now well known.[15]

In repeating the claim that large dams were the modern temples of independent India, scholars make a number of further assumptions. First, there is the implication that a single dogma lay behind these constructions. A look at the modernist visions that were elaborated by the various experts working on these dams reveals that this was not the case. Instead, one finds a surprising variety of approaches and working methods. These differences coexisted even among people working on the same project. To draw out this point, let us turn to the Damodar Valley Corporation (DVC). After the Bengal famine, the DVC was conceived as an answer to many of the problems of the region. Although not unanimously accepted, the idea of a river valley development scheme had widespread support in the aftermath of the catastrophic famine of 1943, in which three million people perished. Advocates of the project included the eminent physicist Meghnad Saha, the development economist Sudhir Sen and two of the future chairmen of the Central Water and Power Commission, A. N. Khosla and Kanwar Sain. The DVC was modelled on what its advocates wanted to believe the Tennessee Valley Authority (TVA) had achieved, and it called upon American experts from that project to help them replicate the perceived successes of the TVA. The DVC was conceived just before independence. With dams large and small, irrigation canals and power stations, it was designed to provide power generation, navigation, irrigation, flood control, malaria control, drinking water and improved living conditions for those displaced in West Bengal and Bihar. The DVC did build four dams, plus irrigation canals, and it also constructed a thermal power station and laid power lines. However, the project did not end up irrigating as many acres as projected, it did not provide the flood protection promised, and the Corporation was never profitable.[16]

Within this one project, however, different understandings of the agency of the dam versus humans coexisted. Focusing on just two of these contrasting visions helps bring some of these differences into relief. One confident of human ability to mitigate natural calamities like droughts and floods'.[28]

When it came to assessing the DVC, Sain's approach was again more narrowly technical than Sudhir Sen's. Though he acknowledged that the DVC had to satisfy more than one master in terms of administration, his appraisal of the Corporation was primarily quantitative: measuring the acres of irrigation promised against what was delivered.[29] He made no mention of farmers, cropping patterns or the cess collected from users.[30] When he considered the fact that the area was still subject to floods, his only answer was that the proposed scheme of eight dams had not been not fully implemented.[31] In other words, there was only the technology and its inevitable repercussions, with no room in the picture for negotiation with local communities. For Sain, the answer to development lay in ever more refined technological solutions.

For all their differences, both men were keen to identify universal principles that could be derived from India's experiences, and then disseminate their knowledge to the world. Indeed, both Sudhir Sen and Kanwar Sain went on to advise other developing countries. Sen became the UN resident advisor to the Volta River Project in Ghana in the early 1960s.[32] Sain became what he described as a 'technical ambassador' overseeing UN work on the Mekong River Basin Development in Laos, Thailand, Cambodia and Vietnam in the same period.[33]

By introducing Sudhir Sen and Kanwar Sain, I do not intend to replace the Gandhi-Nehru dichotomy with another one. Rather, the aim is to underscore the variety of approaches to modernism, even amongst those who, because they were associated with dam-building, some might call the high priests of developmental modernism. The artificial division of Indians, whether policymakers, economists, geographers or engineers, into camps aligned with Gandhi or Nehru fails to give credit to their individual creativity, let alone to their collective habit of maintaining an independence of mind. The metaphor of the dam as a modern temple implies that a single dogma motivated all of those who worked on these projects, but India's modernists shared a broad field of ideas, not a singular ideology.

By comparing dams to temples, scholars also presume the Indians involved in these projects maintained a blind faith in them. This, too, mischaracterises India's modernists. Their prevailing attitude becomes evident if we examine what happened when it became apparent that the DVC was failing to live up to expectations. From its early days, worries arose about whether it would deliver on the promises of its designers. According to Daniel Klingensmith, the DVC was unable to build constituencies among beneficiaries to gain credit for its work and create the impetus for further development of the valley. Beneficiaries of the scheme refused to give credit to the DVC for improvements, and declined to use the facilities as intended. Agriculture downstream remained untransformed: cultivators continued to produce only *kharif* (autumn) crops for which the main source of water was the monsoon; they did not take up the opportunity to produce a second season of crops using water from the new sources of irrigation. Moreover, peasants refused to pay for water, and politicians roused public ire against the DVC for the rates it charged. In terms of power production, in its early days, the DVC produced an excess of power, for which West Bengal and Bihar did not wish to pay. When demand for electricity rose, the two states began to produce their own, rather than relying on the production capacities of the DVC.[34]

Rehabilitation schemes for the displaced failed. As the DVC bill was debated in the Constituent Assembly in the late 1940s, N. V. Gadgil, then minister for works, mines and power, had assured the assembly that Adivasi inhabitants of areas to be flooded 'will get cottages for hovels, honest means for doubtful living and faith for fanaticisms', and he went on to pledge that 'whatever is good in their culture [...] attempts will be made to preserve'.[35] Instead of becoming part of model villages, however, many of the new houses were abandoned or torn down. When officials moved to offering cash instead of residential rehabilitation, many accepted the cash and ended up on the streets of Calcutta.

When it came to flood prevention, the DVC's failures were brought into sharp relief in October 1959. After a season of heavy monsoon rains and then a cyclone, the reservoirs of the dams at Maithon and Panchet were set to exceed the maximum safety level. To protect the dams from giving way completely, the DVC released some five hundred thousand cusecs of water. Thousands of residents of Burdwan were forced to flee as the water engulfed the lower Damodar valley.[36] Worse, silting had curtailed the capacity of existing channels to provide drainage, meaning that flood waters failed to recede, and hundreds of square miles remained under water for more than three weeks.[37]

Within a decade of its inauguration, the DVC fell under attack from all sides. Nehru, writing to his minister for irrigation and power, Hafiz Mohammad Ibrahim, noted that after the immediate problems of flood relief had been addressed, experts should be appointed to answer his questions, 'What has been the effect of the Damodar dams? Have they increased the liability to floods?'[38] In the Bihar Vidhan Sabha, one MA from Jharkhand demanded the resignation of the irrigation minister for his failure to rehabilitate Adivasis displaced by the dams.[39] West Bengal was locked in a dispute with the DVC over its failure to pay dues amounting to Rs.1 crore to the Corporation.[40] The Public Accounts Committee of the Lok Sabha criticised the DVC for the 'uncoordinated manner' in which it handled one of its canal projects, and its 'general lackadaisical approach in handling disciplinary cases'.[41] *The Times of India* called the DVC a 'sad story of avoidable waste and frustrated hopes'.[42]

Even in this story of failure, however, we can begin to discern something about modernism. These first projects were recognised as providing important experience which could lay the groundwork for what was hoped to be better work in future. As early as the summer of 1949, doubts had been raised about the path the DVC was taking. The TVA chairman Arthur E. Morgan was in India at the time, serving on the University Education Commission, and Sudhir Sen turned to him to review the situation. Morgan reported that '[t]he DVC was a highly worthwhile experiment, and it would be wise to allow it to continue undisturbed'.[43] It is the spirit of learning through experimentation, rather than rigid conformity to dogma, which animated these modernisers. This determination did not dim, even after a decade of disappointments. Even as it criticised the DVC, *The Times of India* called for the experience of the Corporation to be used for 'prescribing minimum standards for development elsewhere'.[44] None of this internal critique came close to fathoming the real costs of building multi-purpose irrigation projects.

By the end of the twentieth century, it had become generally accepted that large dams had not proven to be the panacea that had been promised.[45] In the late 1950s and early 1960s, at least one of India's modernists was beginning to have his doubts. A year before the catastrophic floods in the Damodar valley, Nehru had commended small irrigation projects to the Central Board of Irrigation and Power, saying that 'this idea of having big projects for the sake of bigness is not good at all'. The prime minister reasoned that smaller works would have the benefit of not displacing people, and that it was easier for people to both understand the value of small projects and to make use of them.[46] This was, of course, part of the larger trend of thinking small in the latter part of the 1950s, which included Community Development and Panchayati Raj, discussed in chapter 4. To underscore the fact that Nehru's preferences did not become government diktats, however, it should be noted that Hafiz Mohammad Ibrahim announced in 1961 that future plans for large dams would require 'special provision be made for storing a larger volume of water against the possibility of floods'.[47] In other words, even after Nehru began singing the praises of small irrigation, others planned to make large dams even bigger.

The environmental destruction and the social dislocation large dams cause are reason enough to be wary of such projects. Even judged on a cost–benefit basis, the benefits have been neither overwhelming nor fairly distributed.[48] If we look at process rather than conclusions, however, we can understand the modus operandi of India's modernists. Far from blindly adhering to some imported dogma, experimentation and innovation remained their prevailing methods. As evidence and experience accumulated, some adjusted in small ways, while others advocated a larger shift altogether. Belief in the possibility of improvement through experimentation remained the dominant perspective, even if the field of view was narrow, and as we now know, ultimately flawed.

Town Planning and Architecture

As we move through the different areas of Indian modernism, we find the relaxed pluralism of Sudhir Sen, or the Saraswati temple at Pilani, was not exceptional. When it comes to town planning and architecture, instances of modernist forms that did not engage at all with local preferences, materials or motifs were in fact rather rare. Let us turn to Chandigarh, which was built as the capital of the new province of Punjab after Lahore, the capital of undivided Punjab, had landed on the Pakistani side of the Radcliffe Line at partition. Chandigarh, as a city planned with foreign expertise, has become a symbol of independent India's alien, elitist modernism.[49] When we approach it to take a closer look, however, this image quickly dissolves like a mirage on the hot Punjabi plains.

At the heart of the myth of Chandigarh is the renowned Swiss architect Charles-Édouard Jeanneret, more commonly known by the sobriquet Le Corbusier. His fame derived from his position as one who helped define modernism in architecture. Le Corbusier had been a founding member of the Congrès Internationaux d'Architecture Moderne (CIAM). The organisation, established in 1928, promoted standardisation in architecture and rationalisation in town planning with the aim of increasing order and efficiency in cities. The CIAM style rested on the idea that function ought to come before form: simplified structures were preferred over ornamental buildings.

Like a cartoon villain with an oversize shadow, however, Le Corbusier's influence over the Chandigarh project has been overstated. Firstly, the many different planners, architects and engineers on the project all had their own modernisms which they brought to their work.[50] Secondly,

Le Corbusier was not the first man hired for the job. Nehru had initially approached the American town planner Albert Mayer to help him build the new capital of Punjab. Mayer was part of the Anglo-American garden city movement, which was a precursor to the CIAM in many ways. By the 1940s, social thinkers like Radhakamal Mukherjee and town planners like Patrick Geddes were arguing that the urban and rural, far from being part of different temporalities, were linked. Like the garden cities of Britain, India's new townships built from the 1940s to the 1960s incorporated these insights. In this vein, they were designed to accommodate the 'villager in the city'. This approach entailed breaking these urban centres into smaller, more inward-looking units. These blocks, as they were called in Chandigarh's case, were built around schools, temples and community halls. They were designed to foster face-to-face interaction and retain the sense of a small village-like community.[51] The CIAM shared concerns with the garden city movement: in the middle decades of the twentieth century, urban planners of all stripes were preoccupied with creating order in urbanisation, being attentive to hygiene by prescribing minimum standards of space, air and light for dwellings and dividing cities into zones where different activities would take place.[52] One of the few areas where CIAM diverged from the garden city movement was in the former's preference for high-density, high-rise living spaces. When Mayer's preferred architect, Mathew Nowicki, perished in a plane crash and Mayer stepped away from the Chandigarh project, Le Corbusier inherited Mayer's plan. He was able to take over without a great deal of disruption because he and Mayer came from similar intellectual environments.

After taking over, Corbu, as he was known in the world of mid-century progressive architecture, had a relatively modest impact on the overall character of the new city. To be sure, the Swiss architect designed the Capital Complex. These buildings were important not only in terms of their form, but for their function, for they are the Palace of Justice (High Court), the Palace of Assembly (Vidhan Sabha) and the Secretariat. These structures stand out for their monumental size, curved lines and bold colours, all held together by that most modernist of materials, reinforced concrete. Beyond the Capital Complex, however, Corbu's influence was more limited. He changed only a few things in the plan bequeathed to him: he moved the Capital Complex from the middle of the city to its northern end; whereas Mayer's grid system had included curved roads, Le Corbusier included only straight ones in a more rigid grid; Mayer's superblocks were planned for mixed incomes, but the new boss introduced separate blocks for different income groups.[53]

Not only did he take over an existing design, but Le Corbusier stepped into a project about which the Indians concerned had definite ideas. When he first met with the members of the Planning Commission in April of 1952 to discuss the project, the opening assertion from India's planners was that while the Government of India was 'anxious' to get assistance from outside, the 'solution' for the new city would 'have to be evolved in India'. Le Corbusier responded by quoting with approval the words of P. N. Thapar, the director of public works and head of the Chandigarh Capital Project, who had told him when the two had met earlier, 'I do not want any foreigner—except what is absolutely essential and [that] too for as little time as possible.'[54] Corbu reciprocated by visiting the project only briefly, roughly twice each year.

Far from being concerned only with the monumental, when they first met Le Corbusier, members of India's Planning Commission assailed him with a barrage of questions about affordable housing. They asked what he knew about minimum space requirements, and improved methods for building with inexpensive materials like mud walls and bamboo. They informed their foreign expert that high-rise housing was unlikely to be suitable for Indian conditions. One member, N. S. Manikar, informed the Swiss, 'The experience of Bombay and other big towns showed that apartment houses are not suitable for Indian conditions, particularly for poor people.' Housing in the new city would have to be limited to one- or at the most two-storey structures, because courtyards were essential to family life and accommodation often had to be provided for animals.[55]

Indeed, the overall character of the city owes much to a committee known as the Chandigarh Capital Project, which included the chief engineer of Chandigarh, P. L. Verma, and P. N. Thapar, the head of the committee. Thapar's idea was to use Chandigarh as a 'school for architects where Indians themselves discover their needs and devise methods to meet them'. As he was brought on board, Corbu commended this proposal, describing it as a 'great opportunity' for India's young architects.[56]

As Le Corbusier visited the site only fleetingly, the training was left to three of his associates: his cousin and long-time collaborator Pierre Jeanneret, plus the British husband and wife team Jane Drew and Maxwell Fry. Fry and Drew were paid-up members of the Modern Architectural Research Group, the British offshoot of the CIAM.[57] It was the CIAM approach, Fry would argue, that enabled them to accommodate the local climate and incorporate social customs into the design of Chandigarh's more mundane buildings. While the pair had begun to develop this method in West Africa, the new capital of Punjab was particularly challenging because of the large variations between the cold of the winter, the heat of the summer and the wet of the monsoon. In deciding which climate to prioritise, Fry and Drew looked to 'Mughal architecture and traditional village building', and decided it was best to favour structures suitable for the hot season.[58]

Jane Drew's working methods incorporated Indian materials, ideas and preferences. She turned to the new city's doctors to help her design hospitals and consulted workers to help her understand their housing needs. She used local materials, especially local brick, not least because it was far less expensive than concrete, stone or wood. And she incorporated popular forms such as jallis (screens) and canopies in residential architecture.[59] Existing or even 'ancient' Indian practices were not excluded from Drew's designs: materials or devices with a functional use were readily incorporated into her structures. Thus, her counsel for the design of a hospital in the city included the advice that 'you must adapt not adopt western technology. Understand the principles that make for comfort and medical care. Know how materials behave in tropical climates.'[60] Fry made the case that all of this was in line with the CIAM principle of 'functional analysis as preceding the act of creation'.[61]

This adaptive and consultative approach meant that the first houses designed for Chandigarh tended to incorporate not only local designs and materials, but also local prejudices. Early blueprints for middle-class houses for Sector 22, for example, 'strictly followed the established customs and taboos' according to Drew, to the point that they included special passageways to allow Dalit sweepers into the residence without crossing the main living areas. However, Drew reported that 'very early' in the course of the project, it became clear that, to her Indian clients, 'tradition was not important except where it followed the climate and habits of living'. Later houses in Sector 22, therefore, included kitchens with stoves at waist height rather than on the floor, and rooms that opened onto one another while providing no hidden passages for the help.[62] Meanwhile, it was decided that shopkeepers would build their own shops on the back of designs provided by the architects. This self-build style of architecture was popular in international circles at the time and dovetailed perfectly with India's self-help socialism and its postcolonial nationalism. Rather than an oppressive, homogenising standard, we have unnamed Indians designing and weaving the fabric of their own city, changing it as they got to grips with the possibilities on offer, with all the mixed consequences one might expect from such a collective endeavour.

The grand buildings and the middle-class feel of Chandigarh have given rise to the erroneous assumption that Punjab's new capital deliberately excluded the poor, but in fact low-cost housing constituted over 80 per cent of the houses built in the new city. The most affordable homes, designed for 'sweepers, tonga drivers, cobblers and the peons of the Government', were built at the cost of around Rs.2,000–2,500 each, or around £150–190 at the time.[63]

Indians were central to thinking about how their compatriots would live in the city. Urmila Eulie Chowdhury, who filled the role of senior architect for Chandigarh between 1951 and 1963, was another whose thinking was built into the city. After studying in Kobe, Japan, she had received her BArch from the University of Sydney, and lived in the US for a short time before joining the Chandigarh project. Eulie, as she was known, had a reputation as an 'imposing personality' and reportedly lived a 'bohemian and unconventional lifestyle'.[64] Describing the city's housing, she also articulated the group's approach to the past. Housing design for Chandigarh, she explained, 'seeks to interpret contemporary Indian life, which is a blend of traditional habits and Westernized ideas and which is changing rapidly in this fast-moving world'. She continued, '[A] compromise must be made between existing living habits, and the habits which, of necessity, will be coming to the fore as a result of a changing economic pattern.'[65]

One of Eulie's contemporaries in Chandigarh was Jeet Malhotra, who decades later would go on to become the chief architect of Punjab as well as president of the Indian Council of Architecture. Summarising the principles that guided him and the other architects working on these dwellings, Malhotra declared, 'The main criterion of a good house, whether meant for a rich or a poor man, is its ability to provide its inhabitant a proper environment for their healthy growth, both from the spiritual as well as the physical points of view.'[66] At the same time, they had to work within a strict budget at a time when the cost of both land and materials was rising. To reduce the use of land, and curtail the cost of services such as electricity and water, low-cost housing tended to be built in terraces.

Parsimony was imperative, but the pursuit of beauty would not be neglected. In accord with modernist aesthetics, this was to be achieved not through elaborate decoration, but by artfully organising space and objects. 'Cup-boards, shelves and niches' were 'built in the walls at useful places' to provide for more orderly living. Malhotra observed that 'niches also make the interiors of the houses more beautiful and easy to decorate without spending much money'. As the visual impact of the large number of low-cost houses became apparent, it dawned on Drew and Malhotra that the external appearance of these houses had to be given attention. As

Malhotra noted, 'A single house in this category may only be of importance to the persons living in it; but when they are constructed in terrace formation they tend to look impressive structures of greater public interest.'[67]

Far from imposing western models on a naïve India, we find the foreign expert altered by the time she spent with these Indian men and women on these projects. Reflecting on her experience with the construction of low-cost housing in Chandigarh, Drew remarked, 'I have had to conclude that the time is past when the Architect believed he had to consecrate his talents only to houses for the rich or to public and commercial buildings.'[68] From her work in Chandigarh, Drew sought to derive principles upon which such low-cost houses ought to be designed and constructed elsewhere. She argued, for example, that these one- and two-room dwellings ought to be built of 'materials common to or similar to those of the houses of the rich', so as to avoid breaking up the visual harmony of a block 'in a brutal way'. She, like Malhotra, made the case that, aesthetically, 'the houses of the poor are as important in a city as the houses of the rich'.[69]

The key to forging what Eulie Chowdhury called the compromise between existing living patterns and newly emerging ones, however, was that it had to be forged in new productions. Motifs, ideas and patterns could be old, but structures, and ideally the cities in which they were sited, had to be built from scratch. In his role as inaugurator-in-chief, Nehru voiced this idea as visited Chandigarh to open the new Punjab High Court building in 1955. He commended the 'people of Punjab' for not making the 'mistake of putting some old city as the capital'. For, he explained, if they had moved the capital to an old city, the state would have become 'mentally stagnant' and 'could not have taken a grand step forward'.[70] Deploying elements of 'tradition' coded these new productions not only as Indian, but as legitimate. As they staked a claim to Indian tradition, however, these modernists made it abstract and divisible.

Whatever components were useful or aesthetically pleasing would be redeployed; everything else could be discarded, including existing communities. Thus, Chandigarh, in spite of using local materials and motifs, and for all its deference to the preferences of its new Indian residents, was built on land acquired at a pittance from the inhabitants of fifty villages. Decades later these former villagers felt they had neither been properly compensated nor rehabilitated.[71] Sudhir Sen exhibited an inclination similar to that of the planners of Chandighar when he recommended that the DVC acquire all land around the Damodar and redistribute it into economically viable blocks as part of a comprehensive reimagining of the working of the economy in the valley. The desire to start fresh, even when the design incorporated some recognisable elements of what was called tradition, was a powerful impulse among India's modernists.

MODERNISM FOR THE MASSES

While eclecticism without anxiety was the predominant disposition of the educated elite who constituted India's modernists, planning, design and engineering were not focused exclusively on the middle classes, or those in cities, nor were they primarily concerned with monumentalism, as some have claimed.[72] Modernist design and engineering could also be aimed at the masses.[73] Three features of this modernism are worth stressing. First, it was intended to improve the lives of ordinary people using modernist techniques. It was not so much authoritarian as pedagogic in style, urging people to learn to improve their own lives. Second, and as such, it was not egalitarian; it tended to reinforce existing social hierarchies, especially those of caste. Finally, Indians attempted to derive universal principles from the Indian experience which could be applied to the wider 'tropics'. Just as in other fields, experimentation and innovation were the call of the hour.

This modernism for the masses was an example of how India's elites integrated themselves into the country's postcolonial nationalism: they redirected their energies towards everyday nation-building, while their approach remained fundamentally pedagogical. In Hyderabad, Dr S. P. Raju, director of the Engineering Research Laboratories (ERL) developed a programme of 'research for the masses' in his laboratories. With the goal of 'improving the living conditions of the common people', Raju and his team focused on designs which were 'simple, efficient and economical', to make them accessible to India's villagers.[74] To this end, the Labs' designs used 'only village materials, village labour and village knowledge'.[75] In the early years after independence, the ERL conducted research on bricks for the living quarters of road-gangs, on rammed earth for homes and on small earth dams.[76] One of the primary aims of the research was to 'design a village home, where the family, with father, mother and children, can have not only healthful but also joyful living'.[77] The house, which measured just 180 square feet (16.7 square metres), was composed of one ten-by-twelve-foot (3×3.6 metres) room, plus a kitchen, toilet and veranda. Another of ERL's star inventions was the 'smokeless chulha', a hearth for cooking in the ordinary village home that would not only improve air quality in the kitchen, but would reduce consumption of firewood.[78] The ERL also designed what they called a 'poor man's frigidaire' for food storage, and a dry pit latrine with improved ventilation. As in the case of many of the modernist one-room houses designed in the 1950s, Raju focused on storage as the key to providing order in a small home. His kitchen included 'arrangements for drying wet wood, a sink, a masala grinding stone or hole and arrangements for storage of shelves and pots hanging from the roof for protection from ants'. His design included a loft above the door for storage, niches and shelves built into the walls as well as a 'puja, worship or prayer corner'. For Raju, 'local aesthetics' were reserved for the construction, colouring and finishing of niches and shelves, while pegs and bamboo poles could also be 'of the village pattern'.[79]

In 1952, Raju presented his design for a model rural house at a symposium, Scientific Principles and their Application in Tropical Building Design and Construction, at which he and 150 other experts from India, Burma, Ceylon and Indonesia convened along with a handful of observers from various UN organs and agencies. Two years later, New Delhi hosted the United Nations Seminar on Housing & Community Improvement. The British town planner Jacqueline Tyrwhitt presided over the conference, travelling across India and South-East Asia over nearly a year meeting politicians, architects and engineers to draw up a list of invitees.[80] Raju worked alongside her as a consultant.[81] Accompanying the 1954 UN seminar was a low-cost housing exhibition, for which seventy-four model houses had been commissioned for visitors to view. Each was a tiny experiment, a new approach to living to be examined and tested by visitors. Inaugurating the exhibition, Rajendra Prasad expressed the hope that it would inspire Indians to plan their own houses.[82] In fact, it was municipalities who constructed the majority of this type of accommodation, and they tended to build these new structures in separate colonies, especially for Dalits. This practice reinforced the latters' social exclusion, even as they were brought into the pedagogy of modernism.[83]

In yet another expression of India's internationalism, these dwellings were aimed at using the Indian experience, alongside those of other recently decolonised countries, to elaborate principles applicable to the wider world. Thus, at the 1954 UN seminar it was noted that cities in Asia were experiencing 'phenomenal' growth, and that a 'bold and imaginative approach' was required to meet their housing needs. Rather than 'adapting western techniques' Asian countries would have to 'invent rational approaches which depart from the policies and practices of the industrialized countries' to meet the need of the hour.[84]

Raju and others like him, therefore, set out to develop the principles upon which these new approaches might be based. Proposing guidelines for the design of improved village homes 'in the tropics', he set out the rules of engineering design. He argued that designs must be 'immediately applicable'; they must be 'within the range of local conditions', meaning they had to take into account 'local materials, labour, intelligence, economics and even local prejudices'; designs had to be 'expandable' and must incorporate solutions to problems of environmental hygiene, such as water supply and drainage; and finally, they had to be suitable for 'aided self-help schemes', whereby a family or group of families would build their own houses, 'with its own labour in the ancient tradition'.[85]

Like other modernisers, Raju and those who worked in his field maintained faith in the possibility that improved living spaces would improve the lives of those who occupied them. Orderly homes, the modernists believed, would produce not just orderly people, but happy and healthy ones too. The introduction of order did not require modernists to jettison India's history or dispense with its social hierarchies. Instead, they regarded the past as divisible, and borrowed from it what was useful, beautiful or demanded by their clients, adapting and updating to suit what Eulie Chowdhury called their 'fast-moving world'. Modernism for the masses was derived from Indian experience, but was not limited to India. Raju confidently asserted that in this realm, India would not take advice from Europeans and Americans. Just as Sudhir Sen and Kanwar Sain took their dam-building knowledge to West Africa and South-East Asia, Raju hoped to take what had been learned from India's own experiments and bring this knowledge to the wider decolonising world. Western experts did not have a monopoly on the ambition to universalise their discoveries; India's modernists shared this disposition as well.

Modernist Visual Art

Beyond these two most iconic modernist projects—large dams and the construction of Chandigarh—there were innumerable areas of life that were touched by modernism, including dance, drama, literature and science. India's modernists were a tiny elite, but they had seemingly boundless energy. There is not space here to explore all of these subjects, unfortunately, but an exploration of modernist visual arts reveals the role of the government in India's modernism beyond development projects, as well as some further characteristics of India's modernists.

We have seen that even though the DVC and Chandigarh were initiated and funded by the central government, the participants in these projects articulated multiple modernisms through their work. It should not be surprising, therefore, that although there was government involvement in the arts in the 1950s and 1960s, this did not amount to state-directed artistic production.[86] Abul Kalam Azad, as Union education minister, established three national academies between 1953 and 1954: the Sangeet Natak Akademi for music, dance and drama; the Sahitya Akademi for literature; and the Lalit Kala Akademi for the fine arts. In 1961, the three Akademis would move to Rabindra Bhavan in New Delhi, a modernist building designed by Habib Rahman. Like the experimental enterprises discussed in chapter 5, these entities were initially set up by executive order and were intended to be run as 'autonomous' bodies. Indeed, as he inaugurated the National Lalit Kala Akademi in August 1954, Azad recalled that in establishing these institutions, his intention had always been that 'the role of the Government must be secondary' in the life of the arts.[87] While Azad hoped to provide support from the rear, the states also established their own academies in the same fields, ensuring that official sponsorship of the arts was far from unified.

The Lalit Kala Akademi had an expansive agenda covering the past and the future of Indian art, for artists and for the Indian public. Firstly, it aimed to identify and catalogue India's historic artworks, from archaeological finds to twentieth-century productions. As Azad put it to the crowd attending the inauguration of the new institution, the Akademi 'must work to preserve the glorious traditions of the past and enrich them by the work of modern artists'. This project was central to the Akademi's second aim: in the words of the Union education minister, the Akademi had to work 'to refine public tastes'.[88] Many of India's English-speaking elites did not have high opinions of popular aesthetics. In an editorial on the establishment of the Lalit Kala Akademi, *The Times of India* observed scornfully, 'Judged by [...] the ugly things that fill the average Indian home, the deterioration in public taste has been incredible.'[89] With this pedagogical aim in mind, the Government of India set about producing a 'comprehensive history of Indian art' in a series of illustrated albums. The Akademi also published an eponymous journal to maintain 'sound traditions of scholarship and research' in the field.[90]

Modern art, or contemporary art as some preferred to call it, was part of this endeavour. So while the first of the Lalit Kala's publications was a Mughal album, the second was a survey of contemporary art. Although in its first incarnation the *Lalit Kala Journal* tended to be dominated by discussions of archaeological finds, manuscripts and other orientalist concerns, its first issues did include pieces on the modernist paintings of Nandalal Bose and the sculpture of Ramkinkar Baij. In 1962, a separate journal, *Lalit Kala Contemporary*, both opened more space for the appreciation of modern art and reified disciplinary boundaries between it and India's 'traditional' arts.

A further function of the Lalit Kala Akademi was patronage. Official commissions and government pensions for artists had virtually evaporated with the demise of the princely states. The Government of India recognised that it would be called upon to fill the void. Even so, the first director of the Akademi, Dr D. P. Roy Chowdhury, warned that it was 'not possible for any Government or a few lovers of art [. . .] to relieve each and every individual artist of his or her struggle by a regular supply of commissions'. Echoing the approach to socialism, which called on postcolonial nationalism to fill the gap, he and Azad both appealed to India's 'common people' to support the arts.[91]

As part of its overall mission, the Akademi soon began planning India's first National Exhibition of Art. Hosted in the newly inaugurated National Gallery of Modern Art in New Delhi's Jaipur House, the Exhibition opened in the spring of 1955. In response to the call for submissions, 335 artists sent in 1,025 entries. The judging committee, which included no practising artists, chose 254 exhibits from 132 artists for display. Assessing the selection in the Lalit Kala Akademi's journal, the modern art critic S. A. Krishnan noted that it was obvious that the Akademi was 'not committed to encouraging or upholding any particular school or style of art'. Instead, it was the 'avowed intention and policy of the Akadami to present in its National Exhibitions works belonging to every style and school of thought provided they merit selection'.[92] As it is now, India's art world was then, too, characterised by a huge diversity of methods, subjects and dispositions. One set of artists tended to mimic the traditional decorative arts of the medieval period, especially miniature painting. Others tended to follow closely the academic technique and subjects of European naturalist painters. A further grouping tended to adopt the materials, methods and styles commonly associated with 'western' modernist art. Within each camp, there were further divisions, each with its own unique combination of subject, materials and style. All were included in the Exhibition. Summoning as much generosity as he could muster, Krishnan called the selection 'truly national in character'.[93]

Other critics were not so charitable. Indeed, Krishnan admitted that '[n]o recent Exhibition of Art has occasioned so much of controversy, dissension and disappointment'.[94] While *The Times of India* could bring itself to commend the Exhibition for providing cash prizes, it declared the selection 'erratic' and 'depressingly amorphous'. Its critic, A. S. Raman, despaired that 'many paintings and drawings which would not have found a place in a school exhibition received the approval of the judges'. In selecting entries covering every corner of India and including every style, the newspaper declared, the Exhibition was 'devoid of any sense of direction'.[95] At least some members of the public seem to have agreed, for two works were vandalised: someone took a razor blade to K. S. Kulkarni's *Girls with Pitchers*, as well as to an abstract work by Amina Lodhie.[96]

In turn, the committee of judges deflected this scorn onto India's artists. In a public statement, the committee chided them that 'the foremost Exhibition in the country deserves [a] better response from artists', and admonished them to make more of an effort in future years.[97] The judges declined to award the highest prize, a gold plaque and Rs.2,000.[98] The first prize of Rs.1,000 went to the modernist painter M. F. Husain, for his mural *Zameen*. This large canvas has multiple compartments, in which two-dimensional human and animal figures and pictographs were painted in earth tones to evoke Indian rural life, both timeless and contemporary. A series of smaller prizes were each split in two. In all, eleven winners pocketed a total of Rs.4,000.[99]

The second National Exhibition of Art, which was opened to coincide with the Buddha Jayanti festival in May 1956, treated its audience to the same spectacle, though the number of submissions declined from over one thousand to only 650 entries. *The Times of India* again derided the display, calling it 'national in the merely geographical sense of the term'.[100] As if to emphasise the judges' refusal to choose a style to promote, the winner of the gold plaque was Jyoti Manshankar Bhatt, for his *Krishna-Lila*. Although Bhatt would later become famous for his photographic work, *Krishna-Lila* was a miniature painting in the traditional style, a work that could not have been more different from M. F. Husain's *Zameen*.

The sheer ecumenicalism of the Akademi's approach to selection, which continued for yet another year in 1957, put S. A. Krishnan in a contemplative mood. Writing a retrospective on the first three years of one of the Lalit Kala Akademi's premier events, the critic was left asking, 'What is national? [...] And is the National Exhibition of Art really National?' He wondered if 'national' referred only to art produced by nationals of India, or if 'there is a spirit in our art which might be described as essentially Indian and, therefore, national'. Apparently defeated by what he called the 'catholicity' of the Akademi's selection, he concluded, 'There cannot be any definite answers to these questions.' The policy of including works from every corner of India, not favouring any one school or style, was perfectly 'safe and reasonable'. However, it left Krishnan with the sense that the whole thing suffered from an 'absence of a sense of direction'. He concluded that 'collective exhibitions organised on the basis of piecemeal representation are pointless', and he declared that the National Exhibition of Art did 'not serve any significant purpose'. He urged the Akademi to find an 'alternative' means of showing the nation the contemporary art scene.[101] And with that, the Lalit Kala Akademi's own journal stopped reviewing its annual National Exhibition of Art.

Far from directing a singular and homogeneous 'Nehruvian national-modern aesthetic',[102] the Lalit Kala Akademi focused on inclusive representation of all of India's artistic communities. This could be understood as a method of postcolonial nationalism, designed to conjure common feelings—even if in this case the sentiment evoked was if anything one of collective distaste. The different 'schools' in the Indian art world, which agreed on almost nothing else, 'joined hands though only for the negative purpose of denouncing the Lalit Kala Akadami'.[103]

While the Lalit Kala Akademi was not insignificant, not least because of the funding it could provide, it was not the driving force behind Indian art in the period. Instead, a proliferation of new art collectives arose after independence, each of which had distinct ideas about the meaning and purpose of modernism in art. Members of the Delhi Silpi Chakra, which was formed in late 1949 largely of artists who had moved with partition to the capital, explicitly connected their work with ordinary Indians, writing in their manifesto that 'the art of a nation must express the soul of its people and ally with the process of progress'.[104] At the end of the period, the Society of Contemporary Artists, formed in Calcutta in 1960, also set out to create an artistic voice to represent the times.[105] Still other groups were not so connected to the political. Although when F. N. Souza founded the Progressive Artists' Group he had aimed to bring art closer to the people, by July 1948 the collective was declaring that 'the gulf between the so-called people and the artist cannot be bridged'.[106] More forcefully, Group 1890, founded in August 1962 in Bhavnagar, disavowed any attempt to speak for a wider public. Its manifesto announced, 'Art for us is not born out of a preoccupation with the human condition. We do not sing of man, nor are we his messiahs.'[107] Beyond the collectives, there were innumerable artists working on their own, with or without manifestos. Clearly with such a diverse range of ideas and opinions at play, there was no sustained or coherent connection between visual art and the politics of the day. There was no state-sanctioned modernism in Indian art.

If they did not agree on an approach to politics or the life of the nation, what did these artists share? For one, there was a comfortable internationalism in many of these circles at the time.[108] As Jaya Appasamy, one of the founding members of the Delhi Silpi Chakra, and editor of the journal *Lalit Kala Contemporary*, put it in 1964, since independence, 'India has renewed her contact with the world. Our artists are able to travel abroad and to be stirred and challenged by art activity elsewhere.'[109] Although some of these exchanges involved European and American countries, they also included China, Japan and Latin America. At the same time, there was a seemingly endless set of exchanges of artistic exhibitions with other countries, from Germany to Indonesia and Japan. This comfortable internationalism meant that the modernist artists of the day drew inspiration from and inspired artists all over the world.

However, the most successful artists, in terms of recognition, critical acclaim and sales, maintained some connection to India's past, even if this 'tradition' was often 'not easily recognisable because of its complete transformation in their hands'.[110] Inevitably, each of India's modernists had his or her own approach to the question of how the past should inform their work. Meera Mukherjee, for example, employed methods from India's traditional craftsmen to sculpt modernist forms of Indian subjects. Born in Calcutta, Mukherjee studied first under Abanindranath Tagore and then at the Akademie der Bildenden Künste, Munich. There, she was encouraged to go home and familiarise herself with India's own great traditions. Mukherjee studied the techniques of village craftsmen from across India and adopted their different bronze-casting methods for her sculptures. As subjects, she chose ordinary people, such as earth carriers, or children on a handcart, as well as heroic historical figures such as Ashoka.[111]

The painter K. G. Subramanyan had a related, but not identical approach. Reflecting in 1964 on the connection between his work and India's past, Subramanyan observed that the world had undergone a radical 'change of face' in the previous one hundred years, and artists were still grappling for language 'to hold our new ideas'. 'We are in a sense, the primitives of a new age,' he observed. The new visual experiences of the age 'excite us, bother us, overwhelm us, put us to the most excruciating tortures of pleasure and pain'. Talk of the simple resuscitation of artistic tradition demonstrated only 'a total ignorance of this situation'. Thoughtless revivalism, he declared, was 'absurd'. At the same time, the idea of a totally novel 'international idiom' was 'equally meaningless', an invention of 'salesmen-critics' only interested in creating a world-wide market for art. Instead, 'What makes a work of art irresistible is, I believe, this welling up of sensibilities from a specific environment, carrying the salt of the soil as it were.'[112] This sentiment was echoed by artists and aficionados.[113]

Early independent India's modernist artists had a dynamic understanding of Indianness, one that located Indian authenticity in the act of creation, as much in the present as in the past.

Jaya Appasamy, upon taking up her post as editor of *Lalit Kala Contemporary* in 1964, attempted to summarise the developments in India's modern art scene since 1947. 'Contemporary art is characterised by an immense freedom,' she noted, and any rules that artists followed were of their own creation.[114] In many ways, this captures the nature of modernism in India in the Nehru years. There was an intense energy, and enormous freedom to experiment with ideas, forms and institutions that would do justice to the feeling of newness that hung in the air.

Conclusion

Is there a shadow of truth in the claim that Indian modernism was centrally directed, inauthentic and authoritarian? Perhaps. A shadow, though, reduces an object to two dimensions, flattening its textures and dimming its colours into a uniform black. It fails to convey the complexity of the original object, opening up the possibility for it to be misrecognised. Modernism in India was internationalist, true, but that did not mean its adherents blindly followed scripts laid out by foreigners ignorant of India. It is fair to say that modernists did not have a strong allegiance to the past, but they did not jettison it altogether. Most viewed India's past as divisible, and they sought to extract what was either aesthetically pleasing or useful from the country's historical practices, separating what they liked from what could be discarded. Many modernists had a keen desire to change the lives of Indians, but for the most part they operated in pedagogic mode, rather than in an authoritarian manner. Their mistakes were viewed as part of the essential experimentation at the heart of modernist thought. Given all its variety, and the often fierce independence of those who took part in these modernist projects, it should be clear that there was no state-sanctioned style of art or architecture in Nehru's India.

There is a tendency in a great deal of historical scholarship to try to locate the work of individuals within the ideology of the day. This approach simply does not work, not least because 'ideological' is not a word that appropriately characterises the norms, ideas or people of independent India, least of all Nehru. Nor does it the capture the frequency or alacrity with which those in these modernist circles pushed those norms in new directions, or tried to break with them altogether. It is perhaps worth repeating, more than forty years on, T. J. Clark's insight, that artists have a complex relation to ideology and to the 'totality of a historical situation', and for this reason we ought to distrust 'the analogy between artistic form and social ideology'.[115] The myth that India had to choose between a homogenising, authoritarian modernism espoused by Nehru, and an authentic but stagnant future rooted in Gandhian communitarianism wilfully ignores the irrepressible and multitudinous creativity in evidence in the country after independence.

Coda

TO HAVE ANY merit a portrait must present something instantly recognisable on the canvas, even if the presentation is somewhat unexpected. Over the past seven chapters, I have tried to paint a new picture of independent India while arguing that the set of abstract nouns which people use as shorthand when referring to different aspects of the 'Nehruvian' era are myths. Of course, the best research avoids the most egregious myth-making tendencies, and the most recent, detailed studies of each of these themes sometimes come close to calling out the myths associated with them. It is when they remain unexamined, or when they are marshalled to form part of an argument about something else, especially about the present, that the myths are produced and amplified most powerfully. Below, I lay out the simplistic assumptions that lie behind each term addressed in the preceding chapters when it is dropped into conversation or text with the notion that everyone knows what it means. Alongside this summary, the Coda recapitulates the arguments of the chapters, explaining why the casual use of these terms fails to do them justice. In some cases, the ideal was present, but not in the way it has generally been understood, or not to the extent that has been assumed. At other times, the ambition or intention implied in the concept was never there at all. In other words, they are all myths, but they are not all myths in the same way.

The myth of Nehru the architect relies on a powerful metaphor. This epithet imbues Nehru with extraordinarily precise vision as the man who drew up the blueprint for the shape that he wanted independent India to take. This assertion relies on the idea that Nehru had the desire to draw up such a detailed plan. It also invests him with exceptional powers, for it assumes that he was able to marshal the people and resources necessary to bring his vision to fruition. This myth places Nehru at the heart of nearly every project of the day, as it is claimed that he took a 'personal interest' in them. And it also expands his influence to that of a near-autocrat. Indeed, in some cases, the myth goes as far as to claim that Nehru was virtually that, because, it is alleged, he allowed a cult of personality to develop around himself, either out of arrogance or as a means to realise his vision.

This is a myth for a number of reasons. Firstly, Nehru never had the intention to be the architect of independent India. Certainly, he was its first prime minister and he served in this role for seventeen years. And yes, he had significant influence, and he worked according to his principles and was guided by goals for the near and distant future. But the idea that he had a blueprint kept either in his head or articulated in five-year plans, and that most projects of the age can be understood as part of that plan is simply inaccurate. Nehru was India's lay historian and he understood the contingent nature of world history. He was aware that he could try to set the nation out on a path, but that the route would have many unexpected twists and turns, not least because he was on this journey with humanity in all its complexity. Nehru wanted to persuade people to join him on the voyage he wished to take, but he had no desire to compel anyone to come along. Indeed, he cavilled at the more obvious trappings of autocracy: he was uncomfortable with blind devotion and consistently resisted the iconisation that is central to a cult of personality.

Rather than seeing him as The Architect, it is better to understand Nehru as fulfilling a number of roles as prime minister: patron, mediator, educator and symbol. As prime minister, he spent an inordinate amount of time cutting ribbons and opening conferences. He seems to have always been on site when a new institute was inaugurated or ground broken for a new infrastructure project. These schemes were invariably directed by others, many of whom had approached Nehru with an idea and had been given permission and encouragement to run with it. Perhaps the most influential position Nehru set out for himself was to sponsor other intelligent and energetic individuals to work on projects aligned with his own principles and aims for the country. As patron, Nehru could lend the weight of his stature and his office to a venture. And as mediator, he could use his influence to clear out blockages in India's bureaucracy, or salve wounded egos to help people work together.

Perhaps the role he relished most was that of educator. Nehru thought deeply about India and its problems, about the world and its future. His thoughtfulness rarely produced a coherent programme of action; indeed, his feel for nuance militated against any such thing. But he had principles, and he had goals, and he liked to explain them to others. His aim as an educator was to bring others on board, not to browbeat them into obedience. In persuading others to join him, he could bring their energies and creativity to bear in the nation-building and world-making projects in which he was taking part. His role as symbol was part of this pedagogical project: he allowed his image and his name to be associated with the ideals and the projects he sponsored. He understood the nature of democracy, especially in a young country like India, and had an instinct for the importance of the embodiment of ideals in individuals. In these four roles, Nehru did influence the country he served. But we must avoid posthumously investing him with superhuman powers.

The myth of non-alignment is a different case, for the intention was certainly there. Officials in India's foreign policy circles vocally made the case for India to remain aloof from the two competing power blocs of the Cold War. In the early years after independence, India argued against superpower rivalry at every possible occasion, and sought to position itself as a mediator to resolve the conflicts arising out of the Cold War. Later, it was a founding member of the Non-Aligned Movement.

Non-alignment is a myth, nevertheless, firstly because it was not an accurate reflection of India's own material entanglement with the world of the superpowers. India was born out of the British Empire, and that empire had been at the centre of global capitalism since at least the nineteenth century. Even as British power waned, the US stepped into Britain's shoes, propagating much the same message and deepening the economic ties of British imperial capitalism. In 1947, India's relationship with Britain, the US and other western, capitalist powers like the Federal Republic of Germany was complex and deep. It encompassed all the things the Cold Warriors fretted about, especially economic aid and military procurement, and it went beyond them, extending to educational ties and even film distribution. The Soviets and their small band of allies were late to the game, and could never really match the depth or breadth of what the western Europeans and Americans could offer. Apart from earnest pleas to avoid another world war, India's proclamations of and manoeuvres towards genuine independence from both power blocs were ambitious ideals the country was aiming for. The myth of non-alignment is a case of mistaking an aspiration for reality.

Non-alignment is also a myth because it is a matter of substituting a part for the whole. Non-alignment was one element of Indian foreign policy, but it cannot explain all of India's actions on the international plane. It defines the country's foreign policy in terms of other actors, slotting India between the conflicting agendas of the superpowers, without taking cognisance of the fact that it articulated its own vision of international order that was more expansive. India's vision had very little to do with the Cold War, except insofar as it could only be realised if the rivalry between the two blocs were to be overcome. What linked most of India's foreign policy positions was that they were post-imperial. On the one hand, many of the problems India faced, from ill-defined borders to responsibilities dispersed across the world, derived from the fact that it was no longer in the British Empire; it was in a post-imperial condition. On the other, India wished to bring about the end of imperialism for others, and to remake the international order as it created a post-imperial world. Non-alignment can be understood as just a part of India's post-imperial foreign policy, because it was centred on preventing newly independent nations from being resubordinated in new relationships with the superpowers which would be similar to old imperial ones. Panning out from non-alignment, then, one can see that India's international vision was expressed in a set of working methods: cooperation, friendship and institution-building. It also brought to the international arena a heightened attention to people and their wishes. These guided India in its goals of ending imperialism and rectifying the racial, political and economic inequalities it had produced. Even though these aims and working methods can be discerned as patterns in Indian foreign policy, this did not mean they produced a coherent whole. Indeed, because foreign policy operated on several levels and was complicated by attention to people, even following its own working principles could sometimes land India in tangled and intractable conflicts.

The myth of hegemonic secularism has a number of aspects. Firstly, it is assumed that secularism had a stable and agreed meaning that was widely shared among officials in early independent India. An agreed definition of the term, the story goes, produced consensus on what was required of government servants and politicians to ensure a secular state. Secondly, the myth presents this secularism as something that not only emanated from Nehru, like all of the myths, but pervaded the different echelons of government across the subcontinent. Not only did the rank and file of government servants agree on what secular government entailed, but their everyday actions reflected this understanding. Thirdly, it is assumed that the place of Muslims and Dalits was secured through this secularism, that they were content with the way it worked. All of this together ensured communal conflict was not a significant feature of the era.

As with non-alignment, the term secularism was certainly in circulation during the Nehru years. A careful reading of the different specific contexts in which secularism was evoked, however, reveals that the sphere within which a shared meaning of the term existed was circumscribed. It seemed to have been widely agreed that secularism required the celebration of India's diversity. This was achieved most easily when it came to marking holidays and preserving archaeological sites. Celebrating in this way enabled India to claim the world's religions as its own, and demonstrate their long history on Indian soil, without showing favour to one set of followers or another. For Dalits, this sphere was defined by the law: the Constitution and the Untouchability (Offences) Act were celebrations of the country's intent to end the discrimination that defined Dalits' existence. As part of this programme, India lauded members of its most famous minorities. These extraordinary individuals represented both their own communities and the nation, always leaning ever so slightly towards the latter. In the tiny but well-publicised realm of the iconic, India had developed a formula for its secularism, and the formula seemed to work.

In the much larger sphere of everyday life, however, the abstract noun secularism did not provide a blueprint for government servants or politicians making decisions on citizenship, property disputes or access to public life. Indeed, quotidian decisions about who belonged in India showed a marked tendency to exclude Muslims from citizenship. In disputes over property and sacred sites, public servants seemed almost invariably to choose the path of least resistance, capitulating to demands that sacrificed Muslim interests. We see the same pattern in everyday decisions concerning Dalits. India's legislators passed laws to improve the lives of Dalits *expecting* that they would not be enforced, and accepting that ending everyday discrimination would be an almost miraculous achievement. In this sphere, the definition of secularism was disputed. It did not provide a ready formula for resolving conflicts. And, like non-alignment, it was an aspiration, which must not be mistaken for reality.

To be fair, the iconic sphere attempted to set the public tenor of the era, and tone matters. Celebrating India's many communities and making efforts to help them feel a sense of belonging did not bring Muslims or Dalits full equality. In this atmosphere, however, policy, legislation or large-scale actions that might have reversed small gains were rendered more difficult. At the same time, criticism of Hinduism, which had been central to both Hindu reform and Indian secularism, remained part of the national conversation. It is this position which has eroded in the past four decades.

The myth of socialism in the Nehru years relies on linking Indian socialism with the Soviet variety. Because India had five-year plans, like the Soviets, Indian socialism is understood to have been centred on planning. In turn, planning is said to have embodied the state's desire to control as much of the economy as possible. It follows that this version of socialism assumes a central role for the state in the economy, especially in industry. The natural concomitant of this is a distaste for private enterprise. It follows, too, that the flip side of this focus on industrialisation was a neglect of the countryside. At the heart of this misunderstanding of Indian socialism is the idea that the state monopolised all socialist initiative, and there was no room for popular or private participation.

With regard to socialism, then, it is a case of the myth propagating an erroneous understanding of socialism itself. There was no single global definition of socialism, even in the heyday of the ideology. Many different political parties and governments across the globe developed socialisms with their own local flavours to suit local needs. To claim that the Soviets had a monopoly on this political ideology is nothing more than a debating strategy of Cold Warriors and neo-liberal ideologues. India had five-year plans, yes, but these plans had neither the ambition nor the machinery to create a command economy. Because of this, the plans were more like Christmas wish-lists than predictions of output. The role of the state was surprisingly circumscribed. There was no large-scale nationalisation, and even in areas where it was undertaken, private companies tended to remain in the most profitable markets. State-owned manufacturing mostly took the form of new enterprises. In some cases, such as steel and pharmaceuticals, they shared space with private corporations. Government regulated, taxed and licensed private enterprises, but it also supported them with loans, training and access to resources. Companies were invited to find their own part to play in India's socialist programme. In the countryside, socialism was conceived in terms of mass participation, especially in foodgrain production, but also in the promise (never fulfilled) of full land ownership, and contribution to public works. The era was defined by scarcity, and India's was a self-help socialism.

The central shortcoming of Indian socialism was that, far from producing a more equal society, it tended to exacerbate India's multiple inequalities. Corporate welfare benefited the top tiers of workers, while relegating others to a more precarious existence. Middling farmers prospered from the land reforms and production incentives of the 1950s, while the ranks of landless labourers increased. Dalits and Other Backward Classes tended to find it harder to improve their position than the higher castes. This observation should not, however, lead one to conclude that socialism was worse for equality than the free market. Like secularism, Indian socialism held back the forces that, since the 1980s, have produced more drastic inequalities. In the last four decades, while the role of the state in industry has changed, perhaps the greater transformation is in sentiment. The pedagogical and patronising approach to development, with responsibility for the uplift of the poor invested in the higher castes, has quite rightly been removed, but it has been replaced not by any new sense of collective endeavour, but by individualism.

The myth of the strong state, meanwhile, relies on the idea that the imperial power had built up the police and services in the country in a manner that can be characterised as strong. This word could mean any number of things, but in India's case it is often paired with the term centralised. The strong, centralised state, was also assumed to be effective: when governments or officials set out to do something, they could use the levers of state power to make it happen. There is an implication within this assumption that the state was efficient and that officials had integrity: in other words, that government waste and corruption were not the problems they would later come to be in India. Moving from this erroneous characterisation of the colonial state, the myth then asserts that independent India's leaders readily 'took the reins' and began driving the administration as it already was, even as they wished to use it for their own ends. This implies in turn that India's nationalists, who had been so critical of the colonial state, suddenly came to accept it. They did so, so the story goes, precisely because of its strength, which they regarded as essential in the face of the problems of partition, the integration of the princely states and the pursuit of development after 1947.

Of all the subjects in this book, this one comes closest to pure myth. The imperial power could call upon significant force when it had to—for example, to put down nationalist campaigns, or to bring about a tenuous peace after communal violence. Force ought to be differentiated from strength, however. One does not have to look further than the Bengal famine, or the widespread use of emergency provisions to circumvent the ordinary criminal justice system during the Second World War, to understand that an effective and responsive state was not a hallmark of the late colonial period. India's governing elites were aware of this, and they were highly critical of the police and administration they had inherited, regarding them as overly centralised, unnecessarily rigid and undemocratic. This had two consequences. First, the Constitution was invested with powers to compensate for the known weaknesses of the administration and the police. Second, the new machinery designed for the project of reconstructing the Indian nation was often built at a distance from the existing administrative apparatus. This often involved, even if somewhat contradictorily, attempts designed in New Delhi to decentralise and democratise the administration. The bureaucracy grew more complex, but also more varied during the Nehru years, developing a baffling array of forms to deal with the wider responsibilities of the nation-building project. Unfortunately, even the newly imagined state, in all its variety, was not a paragon of efficiency or responsiveness.

India's successful democracy is a legend that cannot be dismantled in the same way. The myth here relies on the very real success that India had in conducting elections over the years. This accomplishment was secured by an intricate constitutional framework and institutions like the Election Commission. It was achieved in spite of the scale of the task of enumerating and empowering an electorate in a population that was large and growing. Compared to the electorate in other democracies, India's voters did not have a great deal of education; the majority indeed were illiterate. And yet, the Election Commission and India's leaders designed a voting system, and then adjusted it, to work for the voters. Elections were carried off without violence, and apparently with limited misunderstanding.

The myth of the successful democracy is a case, firstly, of mistaking a part for the whole. India successfully conducted elections, true, but India's politicians understood democracy to be about much more than just the technical feat of ensuring smooth-running election machinery. India's democracy was not just for counting votes. It was intended to transform Indian society. Democracy was supposed to convert ordinary Indians into people who saw themselves as individuals invested with changeable political and economic interests. This process of individuation was meant to reduce the importance of caste, in Indian politics as well as in the lives of ordinary people. This is why reservations for SCs and STs were only put in place for ten years: they were supposed to be rendered redundant by the combination of development and the working of India's democracy. Instead, over the course of the first two elections, caste itself was transformed and became an integral part of the way Indians worked their democratic system.

Equally, it was expected that participation in India's democracy would be an ennobling experience for voters and politicians alike. Having a say in their own future was meant to instil in everyone an increased sense of responsibility and a greater will to undertake public service. As the system was operated, however, the insidious influence of money crept into the nooks and crannies of India's democracy, and seemed to spread. A sense grew that politicians were on the make, and that they collaborated with the wealthy. Finally, to truly be successful, a democratic structure must enable power to be transferred from one party to another. And yet, the system had been bent to smooth the way to continued Congress rule in most parts of the country. When the Communist Party took power in Kerala, and began to mould the administration in similar ways, this prompted a crisis of democracy in the country.

It follows that the second reason the successful democracy is a myth is because it ignores the very real concerns India's elites had about the workings of their democratic system in these three areas. By the 1960s, India's elected leaders were engaged in a series of conversations about how to improve and secure their democracy. It was widely agreed that the existing machinery was not being wielded as expected, and that further mechanisms were required. In the final years of Nehru's premiership, therefore, he found himself involved in discussions aimed at setting out more detailed rules of the road for political parties, for elected officials and for the voters themselves. All of this was part of a larger conversation about how to deepen the habits of democracy that operated alongside, but also beyond, the formal machinery required to run elections.

Finally, we come to the myth of high modernism in India. This refers to the idea that Nehru pursued a modernist vision of the future which was alien to Indian soil because it was imported by western experts. These European and American men and women, the story goes, thrust their designs upon Indians, without regard to local tastes, habits, conditions or traditions. It is assumed, too, that modernism was a sort of blind faith, the proponents of which were indifferent to the lived experience of their designs and were impervious to change. The only competing ideology available at the time, it is said, was Gandhism, which propagated an outmoded understanding of India's needs.

In this instance, the myth has been raised upon on a one-dimensional understanding of the term modernism. Modernists had a shared vision: they believed in the power of human creations to transform lives and livelihoods. They were not, however, all of one mind, for even two men with similar backgrounds working on the same project could disagree on how a multi-purpose dam interacted with the bureaucracy that operated it and the people it served. Modernists preferred to work from a clean slate, and the upheavals this caused should not be underestimated. Yet this did not mean that they were utterly indifferent to Indian conditions or traditions. Modernists tended effortlessly to combine whatever they regarded as useful or aesthetically pleasing, no matter the origins of the ingredients. For western modernists, their experience in India could prompt them to think of their own work differently. Above all, the Government of India did not dictate any of this. The official approach to contemporary art and design was ecumenical in the extreme. Everyone was invited, and the result was not a single Nehruvian aesthetic, but a huge and eclectic mix that attempted to encompass the country's and the world's multifarious styles in their full variety.

The seven abstract ideas summarised once more above are inadequate descriptors of the Nehru era. They do not do full justice to it. In addition to nuancing the accepted understanding of what the Nehruvian era entailed, the preceding chapters have gone further, and provided a few additional characterisations of the period. First, it is time to move beyond the idea that India had a 'founding moment', lasting either until the inauguration of the Constitution, or through the first five-year plan and the first general election. These first years were crucial, but they did not set up all that would follow. Indian politicians and governments at the state and national levels continued to think in new ways and draft new initiatives, all the way through the Nehru years.

Second, this was an experimental age, characterised not by rigid dogmas, but by a heuristic approach to everything, from reducing superpower conflict to designing a new city. Indeed, scholars will find that Nehru himself and the energetic elites that he patronised often invoked the word 'experiment' to describe the work they were undertaking. What did experimentation entail? First, it was a way of approaching problems. The experimental mindset involved a sense that new routes forward for India must be cut, but that the full course of these paths could not be known in advance. India's future could not be forged according to a plan drawn up in Moscow or a blueprint designed in Switzerland. The way forward had to be carved through the hard work of Indians themselves. Second, experimentation often entailed a social-science approach to problems. This was the heyday of the pilot project, the small-scale experiment that could be evaluated and assessed before being rolled out on a larger scale. Third, it was understood that the experiment could and ought to be adjusted in light of experience. Course corrections were not only possible, but also expected. Examining these experiments has revealed a picture of the postcolonial state that is neither as centralising and homogenising, nor as ambitious or effective, as many scholars have assumed.

Experimentation was part of a learning experience, which was central to postcolonial nationalism, the third distinctive attribute of the age. India's new leaders had achieved independence on the back of a mass movement and they were not keen to demobilise Indians after 1947. Instead, they wished to channel nationalist sentiment and energy in new directions. This included fostering feelings of kinship among Indians that were central to the social transformations of secularism and socialism. Nationalism is first and foremost an emotion. That the conjuring of certain emotional connections and their use to inspire action among the population was central to the political programmes of independent India has not been fully appreciated by earlier generations of scholarship.

Just as anti-colonial nationalism had been concerned with disciplining as well as with mobilising the population, this postcolonial nationalism was pedagogical. Though they had challenged the racial and civilisational hierarchies of imperialism during the national movement, India's elites had internalised the idea that their country was young and had much growing up to do. Nehru took on the role of India's premier educator, and openly relished the opportunity to explain to the people what he was doing and what he hoped they would do as the nation marched forward together. Projects emanating from New Delhi, therefore, tended to resemble a complicated dance: they called upon ordinary Indians to articulate their own needs and to act to transform their own lives, but also informed them of the terms on which they could do so. This pedagogical inclination extended outward beyond India, too. India's leaders were learning from their experience, and part of their mission was to teach the decolonising world.

This impulse is part of the fourth characteristic of India in the Nehru years: internationalism. This had a number of dimensions. Firstly, Nehru and the other elites of the foreign policy apparatus understood that the world was changing fast and they articulated a vision for the international sphere as it emerged from empire. India did not produce a clear blueprint, but rather a plea to work through institutions and according to certain principles, including friendship, anti-imperialism and racial equality. In other words, India did not see itself as a marginal player in the great dramas of the age. It tried to hold itself up as a guiding light. This leadership role was directed primarily at the decolonising world, where India saw itself as an exemplar in everything from democracy to affordable housing. Additionally, this internationalism was reciprocal. Indians hoped to influence the world, and they invited the world to influence India. This entailed an openness to ideas that may have been associated with the west, but were often understood as universal.

Finally, the Nehru era was the zenith of the power of India's nationalist elites. By and large, they used their power not to stabilise but to transform India—peacefully. Although there were plenty of disagreements, these debates rarely revolved around starkly divided visions for the direction

India ought to take. Within these relatively small elite circles, there was not complete agreement, but they shared some ideas on how to move their country forward. These included a commitment to peaceful change, an openness to experimentation, an understanding of the role of elites in educating the people, a dedication to fostering certain feelings among the population as a means of spurring them to contribute to the projects of the age and a comfortable internationalism. The experiments, the lessons and the developments of the era eventually brought forth enormous changes in India's politics, economics and society. The first leaders of independent India wanted to transform their country. Many of them had a nuanced understanding of historical change and they grasped that the peaceful revolutions they called for would bring forth consequences that they could neither foresee nor fully control. These transformations would eventually challenge the paramountcy of the very elites who had dominated the Nehru era.

ACKNOWLEDGEMENTS

THE LONDON SCHOOL of Economics is the site of origins in more ways than one, for I did my undergraduate degree there, and many of the people who populate the pages of this book also passed through this institution. Above all I would like to thank my students on the final-year undergraduate course, 'Independent India: Myths of Freedom and Development'. Through our conversations they helped me ask new questions about Indian history. Marc Baer, Tanya Harmer and Piers Ludlow—colleagues at the LSE—read and commented on chapters at various points in the writing process. Though not directly related to this project, the sustained support and good humour of colleagues, especially Tanya (again), Dina Gusejnova, Nigel Ashton, Matthew Jones, Piers (again) and Demetra Frini helped to keep me going over the past decade. At the LSE Library and Archive my thanks go in particular to Paul Horsler, Daniel Payne and the staff in the Women's Library Reading Room, who have been immensely helpful during my research there.

This work draws on research conducted over the years at the National Archives of India, the Nehru Memorial Museum and Library, the Andhra Pradesh State Archives (now the Telangana State Archives) and the Delhi State Archives, and I am grateful to the staff for their assistance and advice. Thanks are due, too, to the wonderful staff at the British Library, the UK National Archives, the RIBA Archives at the Victoria & Albert Museum, the Senate House Library and the SOAS Library in London, as well as the Centre for South Asian Studies, Cambridge.

I owe a special debt of gratitude to Mirak Raheem, who read a first draft of every chapter, and improved the project from the outset. Thanks also go to Arathi Sriprakash and Dann Naseemullah, who read some very early drafts of chapters. My PhD students, Tom Wilkinson and Medha Bhattacharya, commented on a draft in the depths of the pandemic when we could meet, but no libraries were yet open. It's not a simple task to critique your supervisor's work! Thank you, I have gained tremendously from our conversations about this period. William Gould, Raphaëlle Khan, Nikhil Menon, Chris Moffat, Ornit Shani and Benjamin Siegel all read a chapter or sometimes more, providing invaluable constructive criticism. Any errors are, of course, my own.

For gems of advice often dropped off-hand, advanced copies of work, favours, friendship, criticism and support, large and small, thank you: Zaen Alkazi, Sunil Amrith, Sarah Ansari, Aditya Balasubramanian, Joya Chatterji, Rohit De, Diva Gujral, Raghav Kishore, Maanik Nath, Ian Patel, Ram Rawat, Bérénice Guyot-Réchard, Uditi Sen and Naoko Shimazu; and special thanks to Kay Peddle and Lucy Rhymer for early advice on the project. I drew inspiration from Matthew Restall's book *Seven Myths of the Spanish Conquest*, and Sebastian Major's podcast 'Our Fake History'. There was no obvious place for them in the citations, but exposure to these historians helped me grapple with how to write the history of myths.

The LSE's Research Support Fund's small awards allowed me to hire research assistants to get the project up and running and then to tie it up. For help wading through the vast materials at the LSE Library in the early months of the project, I was lucky to be able to tap into the enthusiasm of three amazing undergraduate students, Takshil Sachdev, Arundhati Suma-Ajith and Cerys Boulger. At the other end of the project, Ishika Srivastava helped with fact-checking and indexing. In the final months, Priya Sandhu scanned and uploaded documents, checked references, drafted a bibliography and did some copyediting with incredible efficiency and irrepressible good humour.

I presented work in progress at the SOAS History Seminar and at the Centre for South Asian Studies at the University of Cambridge. An early iteration of my thoughts on Indian socialism was presented at the 'South Asia Day' at Wolfson College, Oxford in 2017. David Washbrook was kind enough to comment with the incisiveness, good humour and generosity that he was famous for: South Asian history is poorer for his passing. A request from Mytheli Srinivas, Uditi Sen and Anjali Bhardwaj Datta to put something together for their workshop on 'Women, Nation-Building and Feminism' at Wolfson College, Cambridge in September 2018 was a welcome invitation to move in new directions. Thank you to Jon Wilson and Neilesh Bose for inviting Raphaëlle Khan and myself to present at the workshop 'Sovereignty and Power in South Asia and Beyond', at King's College London in June 2019.

A massive thank you goes to Ben Tate and the team at Princeton University Press. The anonymous peer reviewers of the manuscript provided exceptionally useful feedback, of which I am enormously appreciative. I should also like to pay tribute to the anonymous peer reviewers of the satellite articles that I have written while researching this period in India's history. Many offered constructive feedback, while a few more or less said,

'I do not believe you', or, 'What is the point of this?', and, in forcing me to respond, made my research as a whole stronger.

An army of childcare workers made this work possible, as did a handful of friends. The solidarity of Anouski and Matt Roberts and of Michelle Costic and Adam Lee during the pandemic simply cannot be put into words. Thank you too to my old friends Osob Dahir and Veda Poon, for walking chats about life, writing and everything in between. To my family in the US, India, Singapore and Australia, thank you for . . . well, just doing what families do, and being part of the beautiful messiness of our lives over the years. And finally, this work is for Ashwin, Sid and Imara, for giving everything outside of this book meaning.

ABBREVIATIONS

- AMU   Aligarh Muslim University
- BITS   Birla Institute of Technology and Science
- BJP   Bharatiya Janata Party
- CIAM   Congrès Internationaux d'Architecture Moderne
- CIC   Ceylon Indian Congress
- CSWB   Central Social Welfare Board
- DVC   Damodar Valley Corporation
- EC   Election Commission of India
- ERL   Engineering Research Laboratories
- FDI   Film Division of India
- ICS   Indian Civil Service
- IOR   India Office Records
- JNSW   Prasad, ed., *Jayaprakash Narayan: Selected Works*
- MIM   Majlis-i Ittehadul Muslimeen
- NAI   National Archives of India
- NEFA   North-East Frontier Agency
- NMML   Nehru Memorial Museum and Library
- PCC   Pradesh Congress Committee
- PEO   Programme Evaluation Organisation
- PRC   People's Republic of China
- RIBA   Royal Institute of British Architects
- RPI   Republican Party of India
- SCS   Scheduled Castes
- STS   Scheduled Tribes
- SWJN2   Gopal, ed., *Selected Works of Jawaharlal Nehru*, Second Series
- TISCO   Tata Iron and Steel Company
- TVA   Tennessee Valley Authority

NOTES

Chapter 1

1. Part 1: https://www.youtube.com/watch?v=x2O6lMn2LtQ&t=38s; Part 2: https://www.youtube.com/watch?v=-Me9ifMn-1A&t=8s; Part 3: https://www.youtube.com/watch?v=umPoU70oUEc; Part 4: https://www.youtube.com/watch?v=-jkrbbhWnN0&t=156s.

2. Khilnani, *Idea of India*; Nanda, *Jawaharlal Nehru*, 302; Brown, *Political Life*, 185.

3. Brecher, *Nehru*, 595; Nanda, *Jawaharlal Nehru*; Brown, *Nehru*, 93-135; Zachariah, *Nehru*, 214-53; Anderson, *Indian Ideology*, 131.

4. Gopal, *Jawaharlal Nehru*, 312; Brown, *Political Life*, 275-82.

5. Gopal, *Jawaharlal Nehru*, 311.

6. 'Throwing Out Nehru', BBC Radio 4, 20 August 2017. The claim also creeps into serious scholarship: Nayudu, 'Soviet Peace Offensive', 38.

7. Guha, 'Verdicts on Nehru'.

8. Dikötter, *Dictator*, ix-xvi.

9. Plamper, *Stalin Cult*, 34.

10. Leese, *Mao Cult*, 89.

11. Waterlow, *Only a Joke*.

12. Khan, 'Performing Peace'; Amin, 'Gandhi as Mahatma'.

13. Ansari and Gould, *Boundaries of Belonging*, 28-36.

14. Gopal, *Jawaharlal Nehru*; Brown, *Nehru*, 94-95.

15. 11 November 1957, in Gopal, gen. ed., *Selected Works of Jawaharlal Nehru, Second Series* (hereafter *SWJN2*), vol. 40, 741.

16. 24-25 September 1961, *SWJN2*, vol. 71, 341-43.

17. Shankar, *Don't Spare Me*, 389.

18. 'Index of Popularity of Party Leaders', 74.

19. See chapter 5.

20. Statement at the Annual General Meeting of the Congress Party in Parliament, 29 April 1958, *SWJN2*, vol. 42, 501-2.

21. Nehru, *Bunch of Old Letters*, v.

22. *Times of India*, 30 April 1958, 1, 7.

23. *Bombay Chronicle*, 2 May 1958, 1.

24. *Times of India*, 30 April 1958, 1.

25. *Times of India*, 2 May 1958, 7.

26. Speech at the Congress Parliamentary Party meeting, 3 May 1958, 29 April 1958, *SWJN2*, vol. 42, 508-13.

27. Only JP (Jayaprakash Narayan) and Indira felt otherwise. JP called on him to step down temporarily. And Indira worried that the threat should be followed up, lest he not be taken seriously.

28. *Times of India*, 2 May 1958, 7.
29. Brown, *Nehru*, 137; Gopal, *Jawaharlal Nehru*, 158.
30. *New York Times*, 28 May 1964, 17.
31. Jayaprakash Narayan, Tribute to Nehru after his passing away, 27 May 1964. Prasad, ed., *Jayaprakash Narayan: Selected Works* (hereafter *JNSW*), vol. 8, 405.
32. Unattributed author, 'Jawaharlal Nehru', 907.
33. *New York Times*, 28 May 1964, 17.
34. *Times of India*, 29 May 1964, 8.
35. Radhakrishnan, 27 May 1964, *On Nehru*, 7.
36. *Times of India*, 1 June 1964, 7.
37. *Times of India*, 2 June 1964, 11.
38. *Times of India*, 13 June 1964, 5.
39. Chalapathi Rau, *Nehru for Children*, 5; On the Children's Book Trust, *Times of India*, 10 December 1965, 8.
40. *Times of India*, 27 June 1964, 1.
41. Radhakrishnan, 14 November 1964, *On Nehru*, 42.
42. Dikshit, Natwar-Singh and Parthasarathi, eds, *Jawaharlal Nehru*, xi.
43. I.e., https://nehruselectedworks.com.
44. 'Index of Popularity of Party Leaders', 91; 'After Nehru—Who?', 25.
45. Radhakrishnan, 26 May 1965, *On Nehru*, 67.
46. E.g., https://www.siasat.com/political-leaders-pay-tributes-nehru-birth-anniversary-1727364/.
47. This is particularly the case on issues related to secularism, especially partition and Kashmir. See https://www.siasat.com/partition-basis-religion-was-historical-mistake-amit-shah-1529314/; https://www.siasat.com/khattar-blames-jawaharlal-nehru-kashmir-issue-1489068/. Each topic seems to furnish a new way to criticise Nehru; e.g., on policy towards China: https://www.news18.com/news/opinion/opinion-nehru-let-go-of-opportunities-that-would-have-given-india-clear-edge-over-china-2699361.html.
48. Ramesh, *To the Brink*, 92–100.
49. Chandavarkar, 'Customs of Governance'.
50. Mialet, *Hawking Incorporated*.
51. Khilnani, *Idea of India*, 30; Brecher, *Nehru*, 599–602; Gopal, *Jawaharlal Nehru*, 316.
52. Nehru, 'Basic Approach', 71.
53. Nehru to Shyam K. Pandit, 2 March 1957, *SWJN2*, vol. 37, 579.
54. Brecher, *Nehru*, 622; Brown, *Political Life*, 202–6.
55. Nanda, *Jawaharlal Nehru*, 296.
56. Brecher, *Nehru*, 627.
57. Gopal, *Jawaharlal Nehru*, 164.
58. Ibid., 65.
59. Ibid., 304.
60. Ibid., 220.
61. Ibid., 152.
62. Brown, *Political Life*, 192.
63. Khosla, ed., *Letters for a Nation*, 24–25.
64. Gopal, *Jawaharlal Nehru*, 161.

65. Brown, *Political Life*, 198–99.
66. Roy, 'Nehruvian', 192.
67. Nehru, '"Socialist Goal"', 185.
68. *New York Times*, 28 May 1964, 17.
69. Karnik, 'Jawaharlal Nehru: Foreign Policy', 92–108.
70. *New York Times*, 29 May 1964, 6.
71. Radhakrishnan, 26 May 1965, *On Nehru*, 61.
72. Ibid., 9.
73. Natarajan, 'Mind and Face'.
74. Bhargava, ed., *Secularism*.
75. *Wall Street Journal*, 28 May 1964, 1, 18.
76. Radhakrishnan, 27 May 1964, *On Nehru*, 8.
77. Ganguli, 'Nehru and Socialism', 1217.
78. Unattributed author, 'Socialist Legacy', 1225.
79. Raj, 'Nehru, the Congress', 1233.
80. Radhakrishnan, 27 May 1964, *On Nehru*, 8.
81. Mukerjee, *Gentle Colossus*, 135.
82. Kothari, 'Meaning of Jawaharlal Nehru', 1203.
83. Unattributed author, 'Nehru and the Administration', 1243.
84. Jayaprakash Narayan to Indira Gandhi, 27 July 1964, *JNSW*, vol. 8, 431.
85. Bose, 'Gandhi and Jawaharlal'; A. M., 'We, the People'.
86. Radhakrishnan, 29 May 1964, *On Nehru*, 12–13.
87. Zachariah, *Developing India*.
88. Kothari, 'Meaning of Jawaharlal Nehru'.
89. Kothari, 'Political Consensus'.
90. Kothari, 'Crisis of the Moderate State'.

Chapter 2

1. *Times of India*, 23 September 1950, 10.
2. *Times of India*, 13 January 1957, 5.
3. *Times of India*, 16 January 1957, 4.
4. *Times of India*, 21 January 1957, 9.
5. *Times of India*, 17 January 1957, 5.
6. Segrave, *American Films Abroad*, 216–17.
7. Jain, *Economic Aspects*, 13.
8. Segrave, *American Films Abroad*, 216–17.
9. Nanda, *Jawaharlal Nehru*, ch. 12; Brown, *Nehru*, 127–32; Brown, *Political Life*, ch. 13; On ambassadors and envoys, Das Gupta, *Indian Civil Service*; Raghavan, *War and Peace*, 21–22; Chaudhuri, *Forged in Crisis*, ch. 2; Bhagavan, *Peacemakers*; Khilnani, *Idea of India*, 39.
10. 4 December 1947, *SWJN2*, vol. 4, 597.
11. McGarr, *Cold War in South Asia*; Engerman, *Price of Aid*.
12. Westad, *Global Cold War*.
13. Khilnani et al., *Nonalignment 2.0*, xii; Chaudhuri, *Forged in Crisis*, 21.
14. Mišković, 'Introduction', 7.

15. Das Gupta, *Indian Civil Service*; Nayudu, '"India Looks at the World"'; Rajgotra, *Life in Diplomacy*; McGarr, '"India's Rasputin"', 256; Ramesh, *Chequered Brilliance*.

16. This is distinguished from Chacko's 'postcoloniality', as the argument here does not stress identity-building: Chacko, *Indian Foreign Policy*, 3; and differentiated from Chatterjee Miller's in that he stressed the goal of victimhood: Chatterjee Miller, 'Recollecting Empire', 221.

17. Abraham, 'Prolegomena', 82.

18. Khan, 'India's Search'.

19. Chaudhuri, *Forged in Crisis*, ch. 2; Ankit, 'Between Vanity'; British envoys did the same in India: McGarr, *Cold War in South Asia*, 27.

20. Madsen, 'Long Goodbye'.

21. Chari, 'Indo-Soviet Military Cooperation', 231.

22. Balasubramanian and Raghavan, 'Present at the Creation'.

23. Venkataramani, 'Manganese as a Factor'; Sarkar, '"Wean Them Away"'.

24. Natarajan, *American Shadow*, 38.

25. Central Statistical Organisation, *Monthly Abstract*, 36.

26. Hunck, *India's Silent Revolution*, 118.

27. Ibid., 49.

28. Misra, *Business, Race and Politics*, 188.

29. Hunck, *India's Silent Revolution*, 82.

30. Federation of British Industry, *British Industry*, 13.

31. Hunck, *India's Silent Revolution*, 82.

32. Federation of British Industry, *British Industry*, 13.

33. Hunck, *India's Silent Revolution*, 100, 123.

34. Natarajan, *American Shadow*, 82–86; *Times of India*, 22 October 1950, 8 and 22 March 1951, 9.

35. Agreement between the Government of India and the Government of the USSR, 27 January 1949, NAI, Ministry of Food, Policy Branch, PY(V)-1557(1)C/49.

36. Sharma, *Indo-Soviet Trade*, 187–88.

37. Ibid., 228–31.

38. Sanchez-Sibony, *Red Globalization*.

39. Frankel, *When Nehru Looked East*.

40. Engerman, *Price of Aid*, 13–14.

41. Kirk, *India and the World Bank*, 8. The Aid India Group included Austria, Belgium, Britain, Canada, Denmark, The Federal Republic of Germany, France, Italy, Japan, Netherlands, Norway, Sweden and the US.

42. Sanchez-Sibony, *Red Globalization*, 140; Tansky, *US and USSR Aid*, 97.

43. Tansky, *US and USSR Aid*, 103.

44. Ibid., 15.

45. TISCO's operations at Jamshedpur employed British and German crews for the rolling mills and steel works, as well as Austrians, Italians and Chinese workers across the company's operations. Harris, *Jamsetji Nusserwanji Tata*, 202.

46. Nayudu, 'Soviet Peace Offensive', 43.

47. *Times of India*, 7 March 1955, 10.

48. *Times of India*, 25 August 1955, 10.
49. Ministry of Food and Agriculture, *Indian Agricultural Team*; Ministry of Education, *Education in the Soviet Union*; National Productivity Council of India, *Textile Industry*.
50. Aunesluoma, *Britain, Sweden and the Cold War*.
51. Frankel, *When Nehru Looked East*.
52. Sanchez-Sibony, *Red Globalization*, 166.
53. Ankit, 'Mountbatten and India'; Engerman, *Price of Aid*, ch. 6.
54. *Times of India*, 22 June 1955, 11.
55. Khilnani et al., *Non-alignment 2.0*, ii.
56. This is a wider understanding of internationalism than Bhagavan's, as it is not limited to international organisations: Bhagavan, *Peacemakers*.
57. Gautam, 'India's Foreign Policy II', 107.
58. Bhagavan, *Peacemakers*, ch. 6.
59. Nayudu, 'Nehru Years'; Bhagavan, *Peacemakers*, xi.
60. Setalvad, 'India and the United Nations', 107.
61. Rajan, 'Indian Foreign Policy', 205.
62. Ibid., 217.
63. Ibid., 210–11.
64. Devere, Mark and Verbitsky, 'Language of Friendship'.
65. Skaria, 'Gandhi's Politics', 956–57.
66. Chacko, *Indian Foreign Policy*, ch. 3.
67. Quoted in Setalvad, 'India and the United Nations', 110.
68. Ali, 'India's Role', 22.
69. Bhagavan, *Peacemakers*, chs 4, 6.
70. Raghavan, *War and Peace*, 16.
71. Amrith, *Decolonizing International Health*, ch. 1.
72. Balasubramanian and Raghavan, 'Present at the Creation'.
73. Bhagavan, *Peacemakers*.
74. Kirk, *India and the World Bank*, ch. 1; Balasubramanian and Raghavan, 'Present at the Creation'.
75. *Times of India*, 2 March 1954, 8.
76. Sidhu, 'Accidental Global Peacekeeper', 79, 87.
77. Abraham, 'From Bandung to NAM', 204–8.
78. Acharya and Tan, 'Introduction'; Lawrence, 'Rise and Fall'.
79. *Times of India*, 20 February 1954, 9.
80. Press Note, Press Information Bureau, Government of India, 15 August 1949, British Library, India Office Records (IOR) L/P&J/7/15292.
81. E.g., Abraham, *How India Became Territorial*, ch. 3.
82. Khan and Sherman, 'India and Overseas Indians'.
83. Kelly and Kaplan, 'Diaspora and Swaraj'.
84. Press note, 15 August 1949, IOR/L/P&J/7/15292.
85. Quoted in Vahed, '"Nehru is just another coolie"', 60.
86. Quoted in Bhagavan, *Peacemakers*, 74.
87. *Times of India*, 19 June 1947, 5.

88. Note, Indo-Ceylon negotiations. Internal MEA & CR correspondence. Resumption of Indo-Ceylon Negotiations, 1947–48, NAI, Ministry of External Affairs, Overseas II, Nos. 69(1)-OSII, 1947.

89. *Times of India*, 12 March 1955, 7.

90. Letter to the editor by F.S.N., *Times of India*, 9 September 1953, 6.

91. *Times of India*, 15 May 1948, 9.

92. *Times of India*, 22 June 1959, 1.

93. *Times of India*, 19 June 1947, 5.

94. In Ceylon they were ousted from clerical jobs on plantations, *Times of India*, 2 September 1950, 10; in Burma they were replaced by Burmese as dockworkers and agricultural labourers, *Times of India*, 14 July 1948, 4; they were later barred from working as teachers, doctors and engineers in Burma, *Times of India*, 11 May 1964, 7.

95. *Times of India*, 17 July 1954, 1 and 28 May 1964, 3.

96. *Times of India*, 12 March 1955, 7.

97. *Times of India*, 14 November 1959, 10.

98. *Times of India*, 20 April 1952, 10.

99. *Times of India*, 4 May 1952, 1.

100. E.g., *Times of India*, 20 April 1954, 5.

101. *Times of India*, 21 May 1964, 7.

102. *Times of India*, 21 July 1949, 7.

103. *Times of India*, 17 July 1954, 1.

104. *Rajya Sabha Debates*, vol. 60, no. 9, 2 June 1967, 1899–1901.

105. Khan and Sherman, 'India and Overseas Indians'.

106. Khan, *Muslim, Trader, Nomad, Spy*, 3.

107. Geary, 'Rebuilding the Navel'.

108. Harder, 'Defining Independence'.

109. Harder, 'Not at the Cost of China'.

110. Acharya and Tan, 'Introduction', 5.

111. Thakur, 'India's Diplomatic Entrepreneurism', 285, 289–95.

112. Ramesh, *Chequered Brilliance*, 398–402.

113. Lok Sabha, *Panchsheel*; Percival Wood, 'Alternative Regional Identity'.

114. Harder, 'Defining Independence', 115–16.

115. Raghavan, 'Missed Opportunity?', 105–9; Das Gupta, *Indian Civil Service*, 281.

116. Kennedy, *International Ambitions*, 218–22.

117. Knaus, *Beyond Shangri-La*, 69.

118. McGranahan, *Arrested Histories*, 92.

119. Goldstein, *History*, 180, 187.

120. Ibid., 193.

121. Ibid., 360–64.

122. *Times of India*, 22 April 1959, 1.

123. Jayaprakash Narayan, Presidential Address at the All-India Tibet Convention, 30–31 May 1959, *JNSW*, vol. 7, 421, emphasis in original.

124. Resolution adopted by the National Council of the CPI, Meerut, 11–15 November 1959, in Communist Party of India, *India–China Border Dispute*, 15.

125. Resolution adopted by the Central Executive Committee of the CPI, New Delhi, 9–12 May 1959, in Communist Party of India, *India–China Border Dispute*, 3–7.

126. *Lok Sabha Debates*, Second Series, vol. 27, no. 27, 16 March 1959, 6460.
127. Bentz, 'Being a Tibetan Refugee', 92.
128. Guyot-Réchard, 'Fear of Being Compared'.
129. Guyot-Réchard, *Shadow States*, chs 4–5.
130. Guyot-Réchard, 'Fear of Being Compared', 7–9.
131. *Lok Sabha Debates*, Second Series, vol. 27, no. 27, 16 March 1959, 6458.
132. *Lok Sabha Debates*, Second Series, vol. 49, no. 25, 13 December 1960, 5198–99.
133. *Lok Sabha Debates*, Second Series, vol. 44, no. 1, 1 August 1960, 147.
134. *Times of India*, 31 March 1959, 1.
135. Keith, *Diplomacy of Zhou Enlai*, 130–31.
136. Raghavan, 'Missed Opportunity?', 100–125; Guha, 'Nehru and China', 27; Shankar, 'Showing Character', 107.
137. Das Gupta, *Indian Civil Service*, 284.
138. Guyot-Réchard, 'Fear of Being Compared', 10.
139. Guyot-Réchard, *Shadow States*, 246–50.
140. *Times of India*, 24 November 1962, 7.
141. Khan, *Great Partition*; Zamindar, *Long Partition*.
142. Tan, 'Sir Cyril Goes to India'; Chatterji, *Spoils of Partition*, ch. 1.
143. Raghavan, 'Finality of Partition', 159.
144. Chester, *Borders and Conflict*, 167.
145. Gould, Sherman and Ansari, 'Flux of the Matter'; Roy, *Partitioned Lives*, ch. 5.
146. Ansari and Gould, *Boundaries of Belonging*.
147. Raghavan, *Animosity at Bay*, 8; Chatterji, 'Secularisation'.
148. Marston, 'Indian Army'.
149. Menon and Bhasin, *Borders and Boundaries*.
150. Raghavan, 'Making of South Asia's Minorities', 48.
151. Zamindar, *Long Partition*, ch. 3; Chatterji, 'Secularisation'.
152. On the others, see Raghavan, *War and Peace*, chs 2–3.
153. UNCIP had discovered Pakistani troops in August 1948, Shankar, 'Nehru's Legacy', 5; Mullik, *Years with Nehru*, 3–4.
154. Shankar, 'Nehru's Legacy', 4.
155. Ibid., 14.
156. Mullik, *Years with Nehru*, 22.
157. Election Commission, *Report on the Third General Elections*, 111–12; Ayyangar, *Report of the Commission*.
158. For a full list of Presidential Orders under Article 370, see Noorani, *Article 370*, ch. 11.
159. Kanjwal, 'Building a New Kashmir', 32.
160. *Times of India*, 22 April 1959, 6.
161. Quoted in Noorani, *Article 370*, 312.
162. Noorani, *Article 370*, 8–9.
163. Chadha Behera, *Demystifying Kashmir*, 110.
164. Mullik, *Years with Nehru*, 32.
165. Gagné, *Caring for Glaciers*, ch. 3.
166. Kanjwal, 'Building a New Kashmir', ch. 4.

167. Quoted in *The Times of India*, 15 September 1957, 5; also *Times of India*, 23 December 1956, 1.

168. *Times of India*, 22 April 1959, 6.

Chapter 3

1. Works were undertaken at Sarnath, Kushinagar, Sravasti, Sankissa, Sanchi, Rajgir and Nalanda. Ministry of Education, *Annual Report 1955-56*, 94. Ober, 'From Buddha Bones', 1314.

2. *Times of India*, 24 May 1956, 3.

3. *Times of India*, 25 May 1956, 3.

4. *Times of India*, 26 May 1956, 8.

5. *Times of India*, 25 May 1956, 3.

6. Nehru, Speech at Public Meeting, 24 May 1956, *SWJN*2, vol. 33, 21.

7. *Times of India*, 24 May 1956, 21.

8. Ibid., 7.

9. *Times of India*, 25 May 1956, 3.

10. *Times of India*, 24 May 1956, 1.

11. *Times of India*, 26 May 1956, 8.

12. Tejani, *Indian Secularism*.

13. Pandey, *Construction of Communalism*.

14. Brass, 'Partition of India', 75.

15. Bhargava, 'What is Secularism For?'; Baxi, 'Constitutional Discourse'; Chatterjee, 'Religious Minorities'.

16. Historians of Christianity have done a lot of thinking about secularism: Chatterjee, *Making of Indian Secularism*; Thomas, *Privileged Minorities*. On Muslims as central to secularism: Hasan, *Legacy*, ch. 5; Bhargava, *Promise*, ch. 7.

17. Newbigin, 'Codification of Personal Law'; Tejani, *Indian Secularism*; Rao, *Caste Question*.

18. Nehru, *Autobiography*, 374.

19. Gopal, *Jawaharlal Nehru*, 14-15.

20. *Siasat Daily*, 16 December 1951, inside pages (translations from Urdu by the author).

21. *Siasat Daily*, 1 November 1956, inside pages; Brown, *Political Life*, 224-25.

22. Khilnani, *Idea of India*, 178; Kesavan, 'India's Embattled Secularism'.

23. Madan, 'Secularism in Its Place'; Bilgrami, 'Secularism, Nationalism'; Brown, *Nehru*, 109-17.

24. Nandy, 'Closing the Debate'; Ganguly, 'Crisis of Indian Secularism'; Nigam, *Insurrection*; Needham and Sunder Rajan, 'Introduction'; Jaffrelot, 'Fate of Secularism'.

25. Bhargava, ed., *Secularism*; Needham and Sunder Rajan, eds, *Crisis of Secularism*; Srinivasan, ed., *Future of Secularism*.

26. Chatterji, *Bengal Divided*; Nair, *Changing Homelands*.

27. Sen, *Decline of the Caste Question*, ch. 4; Rook-Koepsel, *Democracy and Unity*, ch. 3.

28. Gooptu, *Politics of the Urban Poor*; Gould, *Hindu Nationalism*; Newbigin, *Hindu Family*.

29. Tejani, *Indian Secularism*, 250–54; Needham and Sunder Rajan, 'Introduction', 24.
30. Sherman, *Muslim Belonging*; Bhargava, 'What is Secularism For?'; Tejani, 'Defining Secularism', 720.
31. Gould, 'Contesting "Secularism"'.
32. Huber, *Holy Land Reborn*, 294–95.
33. *Times of India*, 24 May 1956, 1.
34. Ministry of Information and Broadcasting, *India's Minorities*, 19.
35. *Times of India*, 3 October 1958, 8.
36. *Times of India*, 9 March 1958, 3.
37. *Times of India*, 2 February 1958, 4.
38. Zamindar, *Long Partition*, 8.
39. Ibid., 102–6.
40. Ibid., 105–6; Robinson, *Jamal Mian*.
41. Jayal, *Citizenship*, 56–58; when the Citizenship Act came into force in 1955, however, it closed down this route to citizenship altogether: Sutton, 'Divided and Uncertain Loyalties', 286–87.
42. Jayal, *Citizenship*, 62.
43. Roy, *Mapping Citizenship*.
44. Sutton, 'Divided and Uncertain Loyalties', 279.
45. Sherman, 'Migration, Citizenship'.
46. Gould, Sherman and Ansari, 'Flux of the Matter', 250–52.
47. Sherman, *Muslim Belonging*, 117.
48. Gould, Sherman and Ansari, 'Flux of the Matter', 248–49.
49. Ministry of Information and Broadcasting, *India's Minorities*, 24.
50. Ibid., 26.
51. Ministry of Education, *Annual Report 1954–55*, 88–90.
52. Sherman, *Muslim Belonging*, 78–79.
53. Gautier, 'Role of Muslim Universities', ch. 1.
54. Ibid., 105–7.
55. Chatterji, *Partition's Legacies*, ch. 9.
56. Lahiri, *Marshalling the Past*, ch. 5.
57. Sherman, *Muslim Belonging*, 37–39.
58. Noorani, 'Babri Masjid-Ram Janmabhoomi'.
59. Geva, 'Scramble for Houses', 776.
60. Chatterji, 'South Asian Histories', 1064.
61. *Siasat Daily*, 18 December 1951, editorial (translations from Urdu by the author).
62. *Siasat Daily*, 14 November 1952, editorial.
63. *Siasat Daily*, 20 January 1953, 'Deccan Desh'.
64. Sherman, *Muslim Belonging*, ch. 2.
65. Bajpai, *Debating Difference*, 50–52.
66. Brass, *Language, Religion*, 182; Hasan, *Islam in the Subcontinent*, 367.
67. Ahmad, *Islamism and Democracy*, ch. 7.
68. Sherman, *Muslim Belonging*, 145.
69. *Times of India*. 19 December 1956, 11.
70. Hasan, *Legacy*; Sherman, *Muslim Belonging*, 44.

71. All India Congress Committee Circular from J. Nehru to all Pradesh Congress Committees, 19 September 1951, Andhra Pradesh State Archives, Burgula Ramakrishna Rao Papers, vol. 5.
72. Sherman, *Muslim Belonging*, 144.
73. Fakhri, *Dravidian Sahibs*, 163.
74. Jha, 'Democracy on a Minor Note', 230–33.
75. Jawaharlal Nehru to Meer Noor Hussain, 15 July 1962, *SWJN2*, vol.77, 337.
76. *Times of India*, 9 August 1962, 7.
77. Hasan, 'Muslims since Independence', 823–24.
78. *Times of India*, 9 August 1962, 7.
79. Tejani, *Indian Secularism*; Rao, *Caste Question*, ch. 4.
80. Sarkar, 'Enfranchised Selves'.
81. Newbigin, *Hindu Family*, 99.
82. On Ambedkar's political thought, see, e.g., Kumar, *Radical Equality*; Skaria, 'Ambedkar, Marx'; Cháirez-Garza, 'B. R. Ambedkar, Franz Boas'; Berg, *Dynamics*.
83. Ambedkar, *What Congress*; Jaffrelot, *Silent Revolution*, part 1; Zelliot, 'Congress and the Untouchables'.
84. Quotation from All India Scheduled Castes Students' Federation, Report of the Second Session held at Nagpur on 25, 26 and 27 December 1946 (Nagpur: Scheduled Castes Federation, 1947), 5, cited in Sen, *Decline of the Caste Question*, 150.
85. Guha, ed., *Makers of Modern India*, 313.
86. *Times of India*, 23 November 1951, 1.
87. Sen, *Decline of the Caste Question*; Rook-Koepsel, *Democracy and Unity*, ch. 3.
88. Jaffrelot, *Ambedkar and Untouchability*, ch. 8; Estimates of numbers of converts on the day range from 380,000 to 500,000. The number of Buddhists in Maharashtra rose from 2,500 in 1951 to 2.5 million a decade later: Gokhale, *From Concessions*, ch. 5.
89. Jawaharlal Nehru, Statement in the Lok Sabha, 6 December 1956, *SWJN2*, vol. 36, 695–96.
90. *Times of India*, 8 December 1956, 6.
91. *Times of India*, 7 December 1956, 9.
92. Zelliot, 'Understanding Dr B. R. Ambedkar', 809.
93. Extract from *The Free Press Journal*, 8 September 1961, in 'Disposal and removal of pictures and statues of the British era in India', UK National Archives Dominions Office, f.133/150. On the replacement (or lack thereof) of British era statues, see Ansari and Gould, *Boundaries of Belonging*, 62–63.
94. *Times of India*, 15 April 1962, 5.
95. Rawat, 'Making Claims', 596–600.
96. Rawat, *Reconsidering Untouchability*, ch. 5; Sen, *Decline of the Caste Question*, chs 1–2.
97. Gandee, '(Re-)Defining Disadvantage'.
98. Bajpai, *Debating Difference*, 23.
99. Jaffrelot, *Silent Revolution*, ch. 7.
100. *Constituent Assembly Debates*, 29 November 1948, vol. 7, 62.168.
101. Ibid., 62.112.
102. *Constituent Assembly Debates*, 23 November 1949, vol. 11, 1163.95.

103. Kaur, 'Narrative Absence', 298.
104. Bandyopadhyay, 'Partition and the Ruptures'.
105. Kaur, 'Narrative Absence', 284.
106. Central Advisory Board for Harijan Welfare, *Scavenging Conditions Enquiry*, 99.
107. Pandey, '"Nobody's People"'.
108. Sen, 'Myths Refugees Live By'.
109. Sen, *Decline of the Caste Question*, ch. 6.
110. Shrikant, *Report ... for the Period Ending December 1951*, 60.
111. Ibid., 18–19.
112. Ibid., 26.
113. Ibid., 61.
114. Ibid., 18, 21.
115. *Lok Sabha Debates, Part II—Proceedings other than Questions and Answers* (hereafter *Lok Sabha Debates, Part II*), vol. 3, no. 14, 17 April 1953, 4461 (translations from Hindi in this section by the author).
116. Ibid., 4462–63.
117. Ibid., 4461.
118. Ibid., 4498.
119. Ibid., 4473–501.
120. *Times of India*, 18 April 1953, 1.
121. *Lok Sabha Debates, Part II*, vol. 6, no. 4, 26 August 1954, 410.
122. Ibid., 405.
123. *Lok Sabha Debates, Part II*, vol. 6, no. 6, 30 August 1954, 544 (translation from Hindi by the author)
124. Sherman, '"A New Type of Revolution"', 496.
125. Galanter, 'Abolition of Disabilities', 256.
126. Ibid., 273; Shrikant, *Report ... for the Year 1960–61*, 30–31.
127. *Lok Sabha Debates*, Second Series, vol. 10, no. 30, 19 December 1957, 6482.
128. Ibid.
129. *Madras Legislative Council Debates*, vol. 21, no. 5, 1 November 1957, 162.
130. *Hindustan Times*, 11 September 2016, https://www.hindustantimes.com/india-news/freedom-fighter-dalit-icon-remembering-tamil-nadu-s-immanuel-sekaran/story-EzBsVdnsQj9gQzuuNKdDiI.html.
131. *Madras Legislative Assembly Debates*, vol. 5, no. 2, 26 October 1957, 28.
132. *Lok Sabha Debates*, Second Series, vol. 10, no. 29, 18 December 1957, 6284–85.
133. *Lok Sabha Debates*, Second Series, vol. 10, no. 30, 19 December 1957, 6494 (translation from Hindi by the author).
134. *Times of India*, 2 November 1957, 6.
135. *Times of India*, 8 January 1959, 5; for a forensic history of these events, see Manikumar, *Murder in Mudukulathur*.
136. Galanter, 'Abolition of Disabilities', 274.
137. *Madras Legislative Assembly Debates*, vol. 5, no. 2, 26 October 1957, 33.
138. *Lok Sabha Debates*, Second Series, vol. 10, no. 29, 18 December 1957, 6253–54.

139. Lynch, *Politics of Untouchability*, 96–110; Gokhale, *From Concessions*, ch. 6; Rawat, *Reconsidering Untouchability*, 177–82; Jaffrelot, *Silent Revolution*, 109–12.
140. Rawat, *Reconsidering Untouchability*, 182.
141. Jaoul, 'Learning the Use', 179–80.
142. *Times of India*, 3 April 1967, 6; Madan dismisses secularism for being merely an 'attitude': see Madan, 'Secularism in Its Place', 750. Other scholars have found more substance in structures of feeling: Subramanian, *Shorelines*.
143. *Times of India*, 2 October 1961, 7.
144. *Times of India*, 1 October 1961, 9.
145. Ibid.

Chapter 4

1. Westad, *Cold War*, 423; Roy, *India in the World Economy*, 224. This claim dates from the polemics of the 1950s: Sackley, 'Road from Serfdo"', 405.
2. E.g., Chatterjee, 'Development Planning'; Kaviraj, *Trajectories*, 115; Brown, *Nehru*, 123–24.
3. *Times of India*, 4 February 1959, 1.
4. *Times of India*, 12 November 1957 (supplement), vi.
5. Nehru, *Discovery of India*, 29.
6. Cf. Frankel, *India's Political Economy*, 16–17; Khilnani, *Idea of India*, 86.
7. Sackley, 'Road from Serfdom'.
8. Balasubramanian, 'Contesting "Permit-and-Licence Raj"'.
9. Sitapari, *Half Lion*.
10. Engerman, 'Learning from the East', 229.
11. Niclas-Tolle, *Socialist Opposition*; Sharma, '"Yeh Azaadi Jhooti Hai"'.
12. Bayly, 'Ends of Liberalism'.
13. The following paragraphs are based on Sherman '"New Type of Revolution"'.
14. Chandra, *Rise and Growth*.
15. Kaviraj, *Trajectories*, 115; Chakrabarty, 'In the Name of Politics'.
16. Sampurnanand, *Indian Socialism*, 9–10.
17. Nehru, 'Basic Approach', 73.
18. Kaur, *Concept of Social Service*, 17.
19. Frankel, *India's Political Economy*; Chatterjee, 'Development Planning'; Kudaisya, '"Mighty Adventure"'; Menon, '"Help the Plan"'.
20. Sanchez-Sibony, *Red Globalization*, 130.
21. Chibber, *Locked in Place*, 24, Ekbladh, *Great American Mission*.
22. Zachariah, *Developing India*, 31.
23. Engerman, 'Learning from the East', 232.
24. Ministry of Food and Agriculture, *Indian Agricultural Team*, 159–60.
25. Waterbury, 'Long Gestation', 353.
26. Newbigin, 'Accounting for the Nation'.
27. *Times of India*, 27 August 1949, 3.
28. Chibber, *Locked in Place*, 150.
29. Menon, *Planning Democracy*, chs 1–2.
30. Chibber, *Locked in Place*, 173–78.

31. Krishnaswami, *Indian Union*, 44.
32. Mahalanobis, 8 January 1958, 'Address'.
33. Banerjee, 'Unorganized Sector', 75.
34. Jain, *City of Hope*, 6.
35. Ghosh, *Gandhi's Emissary*, 232.
36. Ibid..
37. Rao, *Economic Review*, 14-15.
38. Ghosh, *Gandhi's Emissary*, 236-38.
39. *Times of India*, 14 February 1952, 6.
40. Ghosh, *Gandhi's Emissary*, 242.
41. Ibid., 243-44.
42. *Times of India*, 29 February 1952, 4.
43. Sackley, 'Village Models'; Loveridge, 'Between Hunger and Growth'.
44. Dey, *Nilokheri*.
45. Rao, *Economic Review*, 51.
46. Ibid., 50.
47. Ghosh, *Gandhi's Emissary*, 260.
48. *Times of India*, 25 July 1953, 7.
49. *Times of India*, 3 May 1954, 3.
50. *Times of India*, 7 July 1955, 1. Nearly identical plans were made for Nilokheri.
51. *Times of India*, 12 February 1954, 5; 5 July 1954, 1.
52. Ghosh, *Gandhi's Emissary*, 241.
53. Jain, *City of Hope*, 27.
54. Ghosh, *Gandhi's Emissary*, 232.
55. Jain, *City of Hope*, 6.
56. Tyabji, *Forging Capitalism*, ch. 2.
57. *Times of India*, 3 February 1948, 1.
58. Chibber, *Locked in Place*, 133-35.
59. Tomlinson, *Economy of Modern India*, 177.
60. Das Gupta, *State and Capital*, 96.
61. Prasad, 'Nationalisation of Road Transport', 331.
62. McCartney, *India—the Political Economy*, 95.
63. Kale, *Electrifying India*.
64. Mukherji, 'State, Economic Growth', 85; Kaviraj, *Trajectories*, 115.
65. McCartney, *India—the Political Economy*, 96-97.
66. *Times of India*, 15 February 1955, 4.
67. *Times of India*, 28 February 1955, 5.
68. 5 March 1955, *SWJN*2, vol. 28, 6.
69. Ibid., 8.
70. Ibid., 13.
71. E.g. *Times of India*, 26 January 1951, A11.
72. *Times of India*, 10 May 1947, 1.
73. *Times of India*, 25 October 1950, 5.
74. Shankar, 'Handling the Tax Dodger'.
75. Ministry of Finance and Department of Economic Affairs, *Report*, 208.
76. *Times of India*, 26 January 1951, A11.

77. Ibid.

78. Ministry of Finance and Department of Economic Affairs, *Report*, 207. (One crore = 10 million.)

79. Unattributed author, 'Income Tax Arrears', 1177.

80. Planning Commission, *Second Five Year Plan*, 55.

81. *Times of India*, 26 January 1951, A11; Tyabji, *Forging Capitalism*, ch. 5.

82. The following section is drawn from Taraporevala, *Principles of Taxation*.

83. Unattributed author, 'Extra-Fiscal Measures', 699; Taraporevala, *Principles of Taxation*, 5.

84. Taraporevala, *Principles of Taxation*, 7.

85. *Lok Sabha Debates*, Second Series, vol. 55, no.56, 28 April 1961, 14455 (translation from Hindi by the author); Bardhan, 'Tax Payer Psychosis', 447.

86. Ministry of Labour and Employment, *Employers' Obligations*, Appendix 1, List of Labour Acts.

87. On the origins of Jamshedpur, see Raianu, *Tata*, ch. 2.

88. Kling, 'Paternalism', 74.

89. Ahuja, 'Beveridge Plan?'.

90. Labour Investigation Committee, *Report on Labour Conditions*, 84–85.

91. Labour Bureau, *Labour Conditions in Tanning and Leather*, 1.

92. Industries, Labour and Co-operation Department, *Leather Industry and Trade*, 30.

93. Bhattacharya, 'Transforming Skin', 335.

94. Verma, *Leather Footwear Industry*, 7.

95. *Times of India*, 11 January 1950, 5.

96. Labour Bureau, *Labour Conditions in Bicycle Factories*, 1.

97. *Times of India*, 27 September 1955, 5.

98. Ibid.

99. *Times of India*, 23 November 1955, 14.

100. *Times of India*, 23 June 1952, 8.

101. Ibid.

102. *Times of India*, 23 November 1955, 14.

103. *Times of India*, 23 June 1952, 8.

104. *Times of India*, 9 October 1965, 8.

105. *Times of India*, 24 February 1968, 8.

106. *Times of India*, 31 March 1969, 5; on gender and bicycles, see Arnold and DeWald, 'Cycles of Empowerment?', 987.

107. United Nations Industrial Development Organization, *Bicycles*, 87.

108. *Times of India*, 20 March 1965, 4.

109. Hazari, *Structure of the Corporate Private Sector*, 304–5.

110. Banerjee, 'Unorganized Sector', 86.

111. Frankel, *India's Political Economy*, ch. 4; Varshney, *Democracy, Development*, ch. 2; Gupta, *Postcolonial Developments*, ch. 1; Anderson, *Indian Ideology*, 110; Khilnani, *Idea of India*, 78–79.

112. Siegel, 'Kibbutz and the Ashram'; Saha, 'Food for Soil'.

113. Jawaharlal Nehru, All India Radio Address, 29 June 1949, *SWJN2*, vol. 12, 47.

114. *Tribune*, 15 June 1950, NMML, Munshi papers, reel 124, f.406.

115. *Indian Nation*, 28 June 1950, NMML, Munshi papers, reel 124, f.406.
116. Sherman, 'From "Grow More Food"'; also Siegel, *Hungry Nation*.
117. Ministry of Food and Agriculture, *Grow More Food Enquiry Committee*, 42.
118. Siegel, '"World Has Changed"'; Kaviraj, *Trajectories*, 114.
119. *Times of India*, 16 May 1961, 1.
120. Planning Commission, *Progress of Land Reform*.
121. Fuller accounts include Herring, *Land to the Tiller*; Chakravorty, *Price of Land*.
122. *Times of India*, 11 January 1958, 6.
123. Appu, 'Tenancy Reform'.
124. *Times of India*, 4 January 1958, 6.
125. *Times of India*, 8 January 1958, 6.
126. Besley et al., 'Long-Run Impacts', 74.
127. Labour Bureau, *Agricultural Labour: Compendium*, 252.
128. Omvedt, 'Women and Rural Revolt', 13.
129. Labour Bureau, *Agricultural Labour: Report*; *Times of India*, 22 December 1960, 7; Kurien, *Dynamics*, 99-101.
130. *Times of India*, 11 January 1959, 1.
131. Swatantra Party: *Times of India*, 27 November 1961, 5.
132. Ministry of Information and Broadcasting, *Acharya Vinoba Bhave*, 39-42.
133. Department of Information and Public Relations, *Bhoodan*, 6.
134. Ministry of Information and Broadcasting, *Acharya Vinoba Bhave*, 10-12.
135. Trumbull, 'Vinoba's Loot', 8.
136. Robert Trumbull, *New York Times*, 10 February 1952, 28.
137. Department of Information and Public Relations, *Bhoodan*, 7.
138. Bhave, *Sarvodaya and Communism*, 27.
139. E.g. Narayan, 'Socialism and Sarvodaya'.
140. Nehru to M. K. Vellodi, chief minister, Hyderabad, 15 May 1951, NAI, Ministry of States, f.16(8)-H/51.
141. Nehru to chief ministers, 17 May 1951, *SWJN*2, vol. 16:1, 564.
142. Sherman, 'Gandhian Answer'.
143. Planning Commission, *Progress of Land Reform*, 20-22.
144. *Times of India*, 15 September 1962, 8.
145. Programme Evaluation Organisation, *Resettlement Programme*, 76-81.
146. Das Gupta, 'Tagore's Ideas'; Guha, *Gandhi*, ch. 4.
147. Immerwahr, *Thinking Small*, 218n.
148. Sherman, 'Not Part of the Plan?'.
149. Wilkinson, 'Youth Movements and Mobilisations'.
150. Immerwahr, *Thinking Small*, 75; Sackley, 'Village Models'.
151. Dey, *Nilokheri*, 40.
152. Ministry of Community Development, *Road to Welfare State*, 8.
153. Dey, *Nilokheri*, xiii; also 98.
154. Ministry of Community Development, *Road to Welfare State*, 11.
155. Ibid., 8.
156. Ibid., 11, 13.
157. E.g., ibid., 33.

158. Ibid., 43.
159. Ibid., 30.
160. Ibid., 45.
161. Ibid., 16.
162. Ibid., 3.
163. Ibid., 16.
164. Committee on Plan Projects, *Report of the Team*, 5–8.
165. Dey, 'Some Issues', 12.
166. Ministry of Community Development and Cooperation, *Panchayati Raj Elections*.
167. Immerwahr, *Thinking Small*, 88.
168. Dey 'Some Issues', 15–16.
169. Dey, *Community Development*, 18, 21.
170. Nath, 'Institutional Transplants'.
171. Programme Evaluation Organisation, *Resettlement Programme*, 22–32.
172. Ministry of Community Development, *Three Basic Institutions*.
173. This section is based on Sherman, 'Education in Early Postcolonial India'.
174. Ellis, 'Children and Childhood', chs 1–4.
175. Lal Shrimali, *Education*, 36.
176. Ministry of Education, *National Seminar*, 37–38.
177. Ibid., 12.
178. Ibid., 37–38.
179. Government of India, *Three Basic Institutions*, 14.
180. On the channelling of Community Development resources to areas with political connections, see Subramanian, *Shorelines*, 149.
181. *Times of India*, 4 August 1967, 11.
182. *Times of India*, 5 October 1964, 6; on similar treatment in urban areas, see, Paik, *Dalit Women's Education*, ch. 5.
183. Dey, 'Some Issues', 15–16.
184. *Times of India*, 22 October 1959, 12.
185. Kurien, *Dynamics*, 122.
186. Siegel, 'Modernizing Peasants', 74.
187. Lal, *African Socialism*; Crawford, 'Political Thought of Tan Malaka'.

Chapter 5

1. Mitchell, 'Society, Economy'.
2. Brown, *Political Life*, 206; Nanda, *Jawaharlal Nehru*; Parekh, 'Nehru and the Crisis'; Anderson, *Indian Ideology*, 105–6; Khilnani, *Idea of India*, esp. 33–41.
3. Kaviraj, *Imaginary Institution*, 222–24; Prakash, 'Anxious Constitution-Making'; Mehta, 'Indian Constitutionalism', 26–27; Austin, 'Expected and the Unintended'; Khosla, *Founding Moment*, ch. 2.
4. Chatterjee, *Nationalist Thought*, 160; Parekh, 'Nehru and the Crisis'; Nanda, *Jawaharlal Nehru*, 301; Brown, *Nehru*, 139–40; Kaviraj, *Trajectories*, 68–69.
5. Roy, *Beyond Belief*.
6. Nandy, 'Federalism', 32–33.

7. Seal, 'Imperialism and Nationalism'.
8. Sherman, *State Violence*; Chandavarkar, *Imperial Power*.
9. 29 March 1954, *SWJN2*, vol. 25, 253.
10. *Times of India*, 29 March 1954, 5.
11. Azad, *Azadi e Hind*, 273.
12. E.g., Jalal, *Sole Spokesman*, 243.
13. These were outlined in the Cabinet Mission Plan. See Jalal, *Sole Spokesman*.
14. Jaffrelot, *Ambedkar and Untouchability*, ch. 7.
15. Khosla, *Founding Moment*, 105.
16. For a recent summary of this view, see Chhibber and Verma, *Ideology and Identity*, chs 1, 3.
17. Khosla, *Founding Moment*.
18. Austin, *Working a Democratic Constitution*; De, *People's Constitution*.
19. Kohli, *Democracy and Discontent*, 3, 303.
20. Harriss-White, *India Working*, 101; Hansen, 'Sovereigns'.
21. Gupta, *Red Tape*; Ansari and Gould, *Boundaries of Belonging*.
22. Brown notes this, but claims 'little practical was done' to enact change: Brown, *Political Life*, 208.
23. Husain, 'Administrator and the People', 267.
24. Patil, 'Democratisation', 213.
25. Pillai, 'New Civil Servant', 2.
26. Attlee, 'Civil Servants, Ministers', 96.
27. Gadgil, 'Accountability', 195.
28. Pant, 'Public Servant', 182.
29. Gould, Sherman and Ansari, 'Flux of the Matter'; Gould, *Bureaucracy, Community*.
30. Gould, *Bureaucracy, Community*, 145–52.
31. Santhanam, *Union-State Relations*, 44; *Times of India*, 8 April 1958, 9.
32. *Times of India*, 28 December 1952, 8.
33. Kulkarni, *Central Social Welfare Board*, 68.
34. Kulkarni, 'Social Welfare', 470.
35. Apart from Durgabai, the other women on the first Board included Indira Gandhi, Krishnabai Nimbkar and Sujati Das, though membership did evolve. *Times of India*, 26 July 1953, 11.
36. Sen, 'Social Work, Refugees'.
37. Jadhav, 'Story of a Welfare Centre', 79.
38. Senapatty, 'Orissa Chairman', 13.
39. Sherman, 'Not Part of the Plan?'.
40. Rajendra Prasad, *Times of India*, 12 November 1954, 8.
41. *Times of India*, 8 April 1958, 9. Also, Kulkarni, *Central Social Welfare Board*, 3.
42. Planning Commission, *First Five Year Plan*, 633.
43. On Durgabai's scepticism, see *The Times of India*, 25 January 1953.
44. Prasad speaking at the first conference of the chairmen of state social welfare advisory boards, *Times of India*, 12 November 1954, 8.
45. Klingensmith, 'One Valley', 180; Sen, *Wanderings*, 46, 55.
46. Programme Evaluation Organisation, *Evaluation Report*, 7.

47. Ibid., 8.
48. Ibid., 9.
49. Ibid., 13–14.
50. Ibid., 29.
51. *Times of India*, 1 January 1958, 8.
52. Ghosh, *Gandhi's Emissary*, 259.
53. Deshmukh, *Social Welfare*, 6, 15.
54. Gorwala, *Report*, 15.
55. Mehta, 'Public Enterprises', 144.
56. *Times of India*, 6 August 1951, 4.
57. Saraiya, 'Administration', 114–15.
58. Gorwala, *Report*, 30.
59. Menon, *Parliamentary Supervision*, Appendix A; Narain, 'Management of Public Enterprises', 307–12.
60. Appleby, *Re-Examination*.
61. One lakh = one hundred thousand.
62. Tyabji, *Forging Capitalism*, ch. 6.
63. *Lok Sabha Debates*, Second Series, vol. 49, no. 22, 13 December 1960, 5387.
64. *Times of India*, 21 January 1955, 7; 13 September 1955, 3.
65. *Times of India*, 15 April 1959, 9.
66. *Times of India*, 4 October 1960, 9; 8 January 1961, 8.
67. *Times of India*, 28 February 1958 (supplement), xvi.
68. *Times of India*, 3 December 1959, 8.
69. *Times of India*, 23 December 1959, 7.
70. *Times of India*, 9 February 1960, 7.
71. *Lok Sabha Debates*, Second Series, vol. 49, no. 22, 13 December 1960, 5388.
72. Ibid., 13 December 1960, 5390.
73. Ibid., 5391.
74. Franda, *West Bengal*, 96–194.
75. Kale, *Electrifying India*, ch. 3; Attwood, *Raising Cane*, 192–94.
76. Department of Industries, Government of Bombay, *Brochure Indicating Possibilities*, 1.
77. Tyabji, *Forging Capitalism*, 28–32.
78. Panjabrao Deshmukh, *Lok Sabha Debates, Part II*, vol. 14, nos 12–13, 11 October 1951, 4701.
79. See Tyabji, *Forging Capitalism*.
80. Gulzarilal Nanda, *Lok Sabha Debates, Part II*, vol. 14, no. 12, 11 October 1951, 4741.
81. Chibber, *Locked in Place*, 136–42, 155–57.
82. Panjabrao Deshmukh, *Lok Sabha Debates, Part II*, vol. 14, no.12, 11 October 1951, 4687.
83. Banarsi Prasad Jhunjhunwala, ibid., 4711; Gould, *Bureaucracy, Community*, 155.
84. Balasubramanian, 'Contesting "Permit-and-Licence Raj"'.
85. Mehra, 'Planning Delhi', 361.
86. De, *People's Constitution*, 289.
87. Das Gupta, *State and Capital*, 88.

88. Banerjee and Ghosh, 'Indian Planning', 124–25.
89. Planning Commission, *Industrial Planning*, 18.
90. Ibid., 20.
91. Ibid., 18, emphasis in original.
92. Ibid., 17.
93. Ibid., 18.
94. Unattributed author, 'Industrial Planning', 746.
95. Gould, *Bureaucracy, Community*; Ansari and Gould, *Boundaries of Belonging*, ch. 3.
96. Arthagnani [pseudonym], 'Growth of the House of Birlas', 749.
97. Unattributed author, 'Industrial Planning', 746.
98. Haynes, 'Making of the Hyper-Industrial City', 346.
99. Ibid., note 44.
100. Menon, 'Battling the Bottle'; Hardiman, 'From Custom to Crime'.
101. De, *People's Constitution*, 45–46.
102. Government of Bombay, *People's Raj*, 57.
103. *Times of India*, 29 March 1950, 1.
104. Government of Bombay, *People's Raj*, 58.
105. Ibid.
106. *Times of India*, 8 April 1951, 8.
107. *Times of India*, 1 October 1953, 1.
108. *Times of India*, 2 April 1952, 4.
109. *Times of India*, 29 July 1952, 3.
110. Planning Commission, *Study Team on Prohibition*, vol. 1, 162.
111. *Times of India*, 16 September 1952, 10.
112. De, *People's Constitution*, 58–59.
113. Planning Commission, *Study Team on Prohibition*, vol. 2, 11.
114. *Times of India*, 13 July 1952, 3.
115. Peter Alvares, *Bombay Legislative Assembly Debates, Official Report*, vol. 17, part 12, 9 October 1950, 853.
116. R. A. Khedgikar, ibid., part 15, 12 October 1950, 1071.
117. Morarji Desai, ibid., part 17, 14 October 1950, 1171.
118. *Times of India*, 1 July 1954, 3.
119. *Times of India*, 9 September 1952, 5.
120. *Times of India*, 5 June 1952, 1.
121. *Bombay Legislative Assembly Debates, Official Report*, vol. 18, part 12, 24 February 1951, 641; *Times of India*, 28 February 1951, 1.
122. *Times of India*, 4 January 1958, 9.
123. *Times of India*, 24 June 1951, 1.
124. *Times of India*, 25 August 1951, 5.
125. Planning Commission, *Study Team on Prohibition*, vol 1, 162.
126. *Times of India*, 1 January 1964, 1.
127. Ibid.
128. *Times of India*, 1 January 1964, 7.
129. Sherman, *State Violence*.
130. *Times of India*, 9 October 1954, 6; 20 April 1955, 11.

131. *Times of India*, 1 June 1952, 10; 21 October 1955, 9.
132. *Times of India*, 1 June 1952, 10; 7 March 1955, 6.
133. *Times of India*, 24 September 1952, 7; 22 December 1960, 7.
134. Sherman, *State Violence*.
135. *Times of India*, 27 February 1950, 9.
136. Bombwall, 'Impact of Emergency Provisions', 191–94.
137. Ibid., 200.
138. Pant, 'Public Servant', 182–83.

Chapter 6

1. Election Commission, *Report on the First General Elections*, 127–28.
2. Ibid., 123–24.
3. Ibid., 10.
4. Shani, *How India Became Democratic*; Singh and Rao, *Election Commission*; Vittorini, 'Two Bullocks'.
5. Khosla, *Founding Moment*; De, *People's Constitution*; Sarkar, 'Indian Democracy'; Varshney, 'India Defies the Odds'; Khilnani, 'India's Democratic Career'.
6. Khilnani, *Idea of India*, 45–48; Kothari, 'Crisis of the Moderate State'.
7. Jaffrelot, *Religion, Caste and Politics*; Kohli, *Democracy and Discontent*; Chatterjee and Katznelson, *Anxieties of Democracy*.
8. Ganguly, 'Illiberal India?'; Komireddi, *Malevolent Republic*.
9. Chowdhury and Keane, *To Kill a Democracy*.
10. Kaviraj, *Enchantment*, 196; Khilnani, *Idea of India*, 40.
11. Jayal, 'State and Democracy'.
12. For a recent summary of political science literature, see Naseemullah, 'Patronage vs. Ideology'.
13. Radhakrishnan, *Occasional Speeches*, 67, 73 ('Address to the Commonwealth Parliamentary Conference, 2 December 1957'; 'Speech at Luncheon Given by Both the Houses of Parliament of Ceylon, 3 February 1958').
14. Ibid., 68 ('Address').
15. Cited in Shani, *How India Became Democratic*, 52.
16. Cited in Rook-Koepsel, *Democracy and Unity*, 56.
17. Khosla, *Founding Moment*, 10–13.
18. Godsmark, *Citizenship, Community and Democracy*, ch. 2; Jalal, *Sole Spokesman*.
19. Radhakrishnan, 'Democracy', 16.
20. Ambedkar, 4 November 1948–25 November 1949, 'Draft Constitution Discussion' 179.
21. B. R. Ambedkar, 29 July 1947, cited in Khosla, *Founding Moment*, 36; Gilmartin, 'One Day's Sultan'.
22. Shani, *How India Became Democratic*, 4.
23. Guha, *India after Gandhi*, 134.
24. *Manchester Guardian*, 2 February 1952, 4.
25. Election Commission, *Report on the First General Elections*, 11.
26. *Times of India*, 22 December 1953, 9.
27. *Times of India*, 6 November 1953, 1.

28. *Times of India*, 3 December 1957, 8.
29. 6 December 1957, *SWJN2*, vol. 40, 453.
30. Ibid., 454.
31. Ibid., 461.
32. Ambedkar, 10 October 1951, 'Statement.'
33. *Times of India*, 24 November 1951, 1, 7.
34. *Times of India*, 23 November 1951, 1.
35. Ambedkar, 4 November 1948–25 November 1949, 'Draft Constitution Discussion', 180.
36. Bajpai, *Debating Difference*, 124–28; Khosla, *Founding Moment*, 147–51.
37. Representation of the People Act, 1951, Part 7, Chapter 1, 'Corrupt Practice', §123 (3).
38. *Constituent Assembly Debates*, 24 August 1949, vol. 9, 123.178.
39. *Times of India*, 7 October 1952, 7; 2 October 1952, 5; 4 October 1952, 3.
40. *Times of India*, 18 October 1952, 4.
41. Election Commission, *Report on the First General Elections*, 53.
42. Shri Ranga, *Lok Sabha Debates*, Second Series, vol. 7, no. 43, 9 September 1957, 12876.
43. *Lok Sabha Debates*, Second Series, vol. 7, no. 44, 10 September 1957, 13016.
44. *Times of India*, 6 January 1958, 3.
45. *Times of India*, 16 January 1958, 5.
46. Two-Member Constituencies (Abolition) Act, 1961.
47. Srinivas, *Religion and Society*; Srinivas, 'Note on Sanskritisation'.
48. Mustafi, 'Issues in the General Elections'.
49. Venkata Rao, 'Selection of Candidates', ii.
50. Kothari and Maru, 'Caste and Secularism', 33.
51. Patel, *Democracy at Work*, 6.
52. Jayaprakash Narayan, 'Foundations of Democracy in India', speech under the auspices of Congress for Cultural Freedom, 17 December 1957, *JNSW*, vol. 7, 269.
53. *Times of India*, 24 August 1955, 5.
54. *Times of India*, 5 October 1957, 5.
55. Jaffrelot and Kumar, eds, *Ambedkar and Democracy*, 'Introduction'.
56. *Lok Sabha Debates*, Second Series, vol. 36, no. 11, 30 November 1959, 2446–48.
57. Ibid., 2461–69.
58. Ibid., 2550.
59. *Lok Sabha Debates*, Second Series, vol. 56, no. 6, 14 August 1961, 2174.
60. Kothari and Maru, 'Caste and Secularism', 40–43.
61. Speech on the National Integration Resolution, 5 October 1961, *SWJN2*, vol. 71, 336.
62. *Lok Sabha Debates*, Second Series, vol. 58, no. 20, 1 September 1961, 6500–6501.
63. Ibid., 6506–8.
64. Kothari and Maru, 'Caste and Secularism', 45.
65. Election Commission, *Report of the Third General Elections*, ch. 17.
66. Jaffrelot, *Silent Revolution*.
67. *Times of India*, 27 August 1973, 6.
68. Election Commission, *Report on the First General Elections*, ch. 20 and p. 172.

69. Ibid., 170.
70. *Lok Sabha Debates, Part II*, vol. 7, no. 44, 20 September 1955, 14628.
71. Ibid., 14635-36.
72. *Lok Sabha Debates, Part II*, vol. 5, no. 65, 15 May 1956, 8430.
73. *Lok Sabha Debates, Part II*, vol.7, no. 44, 20 September 1955, 14686-87.
74. *Lok Sabha Debates, Part II*, vol. 7, no. 45, 21 September 1955, 14722.
75. *Lok Sabha Debates, Part II*, vol. 7, no. 44, 20 September 1955, 14596.
76. Ibid., 14597.
77. *Lok Sabha Debates, Part II*, vol. 5, no. 65, 15 May 1956, 8410 and 8705.
78. *Lok Sabha Debates, Part II*, vVol. 7, no. 44, 20 September 1955, 14627.
79. *Lok Sabha Debates, Part II*, vol. 5, no. 65, 15 May 1956, 8460 (translation from the Hindi by the author).
80. Ibid., 8440-41.
81. *Times of India*, 14 December 1963, 8.
82. *Times of India*, 17 August 1960, 8.
83. Exempted under the Expenditure Tax Bill, *Times of India*, 27 August 1957, 9.
84. *Times of India*, 3 July 1957, 6.
85. *Lok Sabha Debates*, Second Series, vol. 48, no. 12, 29 November 1960, 2866-69.
86. Ibid., 2881.
87. Ibid., 2896.
88. Ibid., 2884.
89. *Lok Sabha Debates*, Second Series, vol. 48, no. 13, 30 November 1960, 3098.
90. Ibid., 3107.
91. Ibid., 3108-10.
92. Sridharan and Vaishnav, 'Political Finance', 20.
93. *Times of India*, 2 April 1963, 6; 7 May 1966, 4.
94. *Times of India*, 15 June 1963, 1.
95. *Lok Sabha Debates*, Third Series, vol. 19, no. 4, 17 August 1963, 955.
96. Ibid., 956.
97. *Times of India*, 5 July 1963, 9.
98. *Times of India*, 28 February 1973, 6.
99. Reports of Speeches, 24 and 25 September 1961, *SWJN2*, vol. 71, 341.
100. Nehru to A. P. Jain, 25 September 1951, *SWJN2*, vol. 71, 344.
101. Ministry of Home Affairs, *Report of the Committee*, 101.
102. *Times of India*, 31 July 1957, 3.
103. *Times of India*, 23 July 1957, 8.
104. *Times of India*, 25 February 1958, 11.
105. *Lok Sabha Debates, Part II*, vol. 7, no. 45, 21 September 1955, 14702-3.
106. *Lok Sabha Debates, Part II*, vol. 7, no. 44, 20 September 1955, 14646-47.
107. E.g., Renu Chakravartty, ibid., 14369.
108. Sherman, *Muslim Belonging*, 123-27.
109. Jha, 'Democracy on a Minor Note', 242.
110. Shani, *How India Became Democratic*, 159, 223.
111. Mullick, *My Years with Nehru*, 22; Bose, *Kashmir*, 77-78.
112. Pant, 'Public Servant', 182.
113. Nair, *How Communists*, 30-31.

114. *Times of India*, 16 April 1957, 7; one of the more prominent pamphlets was Sampurnanand, 'Congress Ideology'.
115. *Times of India*, 6 April 1957, 5.
116. *Times of India*, 9 April 1957, 3.
117. *Times of India*, 19 July 1957, 1.
118. Unattributed author, *Sixteen Months*; Masani, *Lok Sabha Debates*, Second Series, vol. 33, Number 11, 17 August 1959, 2901–3.
119. Nehru to E.M.S. Namboodiripad, 17 April 1957, *SWJN2*, vol. 37, 335–38; *Times of India*, 20 May 1957, 3.
120. Rajendra Prasad, 14 August 1957, quoted in Pillai, *Red Interlude*, 6.
121. Pillai, *Red Interlude*, 5.
122. Namboodiripad, 'Introduction'.
123. *Times of India*, 3 October 1957, 4.
124. *The Statesman*, 4 June 1957, quoted in Democratic Research Service, *Kerala under Communism*, 27.
125. Namboodiripad, *Report*, 21.
126. Democratic Research Service, *Kerala under Communism*, 31.
127. Namboodiripad, *Twenty-Eight Months*, 34–35.
128. Ibid., 31.
129. Democratic Research Service, *Kerala under Communism*, 36.
130. *Times of India*, 24 July 1957, 7.
131. Statement by the Central Executive Committee, 11 August 1958: Communist Party of India, *Truth about Kerala*, 2.
132. *Times of India*, 19 July 1957, 1.
133. *Times of India*, 9 September 1958, 9.
134. Democratic Research Service, *Kerala under Communism*, 47.
135. Indian Commission of Jurists, *Report*, ch. 3.
136. *Times of India*, 21 June 1959, 3.
137. *Times of India*, 4 July 1959, 9.
138. Jeffrey, 'Smoking Gun'.
139. Ghosh, *Forward to the Defence*, 9.
140. Jayaprakash Narayan, 24 June 1953, *JNSW*, vol. 6, 356.
141. Jayaprakash Narayan, 'The Challenge to Democracy', talk broadcast on All India Radio, Delhi, 22 July 1953, *JNSW*, vol. 6, 362–63.
142. Narayan to Nehru, 1 March 1957, *JNSW*, vol. 7, 173.
143. Jayaprakash Narayan 'A Plea for Electoral Adjustment with Opposition Parties', before 16 September 1956, *JNSW*, vol. 7, 136.
144. Jayaprakash Narayan, 'An Appeal to the Voters, Press Statement', 15 February 1957, *JNSW*, vol. 7., 166.
145. Nehru to Narayan, 3 April 1957, *JNSW*, vol. 7, 577–81.
146. Committee on Plan Projects, *Report of the Team*, 8.
147. Ministry of Community Development and Cooperation, *Ten Point Test*, 5–6.
148. Ministry of of Community Development and Cooperation, *Seminar on Public Administration*, 2.
149. Godsmark, *Citizenship, Community and Democracy*.
150. Jaffrelot, *Hindu Nationalist Movement*, 165–66.

151. *Times of India*, 16 March 1958, 10.
152. *Times of India*, 10 July 1959, 8.
153. Press conference, 7 July 1959, *SWJN2*, vol. 50, 29.
154. *Times of India*, 21 December 1960, 1.
155. *Times of India*, 3 January 1962, 6.
156. Available at https://eci.gov.in/mcc/.
157. Singh and Rao, *Election Commission*, 185–86; Gilmartin, 'One Day's Sultan', 251.
158. *Times of India*, 25 May 1961, 1.
159. *Times of India*, 2 June 1961, 1.
160. *Times of India*, 29 September 1961, 1.
161. Letter to Asoka Mehta, 20 September 1961, *SWJN2*, vol. 71, 353.
162. Statement of the National Integration Conference, 1 October 1961, *SWJN2*, vol. 71, 356–64.
163. Ibid., 358.
164. Jayaprakash Narayan, 'An Essential Requisite of National Integration', *JNSW*, vol. 8, 217.
165. *Times of India*, 17 August 1962, 1.

Chapter 7

1. Roy, *Beyond Belief*, chs 2 and 4; Wakeman, *Practicing Utopia*.
2. Scott, *Seeing Like a State*, ch. 3; Khagram, *Dams and Development*, 33–41.
3. Kalia, *Chandigarh*; Kalia, 'Modernism, Modernization'; Khilnani, *Idea of India*, 130–33.
4. Quoted in Amrith, *Unruly Waters*, 179.
5. Chatterjee, *Nationalist Thought*; Zachariah, *Developing India*, ch. 4.
6. Within the vast literature on this subject, two seminal works are Pomeranz, *Great Divergence*, and Chakrabarty, *Provincializing Europe*.
7. Mitter, 'Decentering Modernism', 540.
8. Scott, *Seeing Like a State*.
9. Brown, 'Reviving the Past', 311; Brown, *Art for a Modern India*; Khullar, *Worldly Affiliations*.
10. Anderson, *Nucleus and Nation*, ch. 9.
11. Speech at the meeting of the governing body of the Council of Scientific and Industrial Research, 25 August 1947, *SWJN2*, vol. 4, 548.
12. E.g., Chatterjee, *Nationalist Thought*; Zachariah, *Developing India*.
13. Sherman, 'Gandhian Answer'; Frankel, *India's Political Economy*, 15.
14. Sain, *Modern Trends*, 7.
15. Khagram, *Dams and Development*.
16. Klingensmith, *'One Valley'*.
17. Sain, *Reminiscences*, 2–6.
18. Sen, *Wanderings*, 3.
19. Ibid., 5.
20. Ibid., 37.
21. Sain, *Reminiscences*, 78–79.

22. Sain, *Modern Trends*, 1.
23. Sen, *Wanderings*, 104.
24. Ibid.
25. Klingensmith, 'One Valley', 176.
26. Sen, *Wanderings*, 46.
27. Ibid., 57.
28. Sain, 'Social Repercussions', 189.
29. Sain, *Reminiscences*, 53.
30. Ibid., 54–55.
31. Ibid., 56.
32. Sen, *Wanderings*, 67–68.
33. Sain, *Reminiscences*, 379.
34. Franda, *West Bengal*.
35. Quoted in Klingensmith, 'One Valley', 136.
36. *Times of India*, 3 October 1959, 1.
37. *Times of India*, 21 October 1959, 6.
38. Nehru to Hafiz Mohammad Ibrahim, 16 October 1959, SWJN2, vol. 53, 373.
39. *Times of India*, 24 December 1959, 6.
40. *Times of India*, 23 October 1961, 6.
41. *Times of India*, 7 December 1961, 14.
42. *Times of India*, 1 May 1959, 6.
43. Sen, *Wanderings*, 48.
44. *Times of India*, 23 October 1961, 6.
45. *Times of India*, 25 September 2000, 14.
46. Speech at the Annual Meeting of the Central Board of Irrigation and Power, 18 November 1958, SWJN2, vol. 45, 493–94.
47. *Times of India*, 8 August 1961, 9.
48. Duflo and Pande, 'Dams'.
49. Khilnani, *Idea of India*, 130–33; Brown, 'Reviving the Past', 131–32; Wakeman, *Practicing Utopia*, 127.
50. Prakash, *Chandigarh's Le Corbusier*, ch. 2.
51. Glover, 'Troubled Passage'; Chowdhury, 'Recent Work', 148.
52. Domhardt, 'Garden City Idea'; Wakeman, *Practicing Utopia*, ch. 1.
53. Banerjee, 'US Planning Expeditions', 198.
54. Minutes of the meeting of the Planning Commission to meet M Le Corbusier, 17 April 1952, Fry & Drew Papers, Royal Institute of British Architects Collections, Victoria & Albert Museum, London (hereafter RIBA Collections), F&D/1/1.
55. Ibid.
56. Ibid.
57. Maxwell Fry and Jane Drew Interview Transcript, 1986, Fry & Drew Papers, RIBA Collections, F&D/1/5.
58. Fry, 'Problems', 20.
59. Jackson, 'Fry and Drew's Early Housing', 10–11.
60. Note by Jane Drew, [undated], Fry & Drew Papers, RIBA Collections, F&D/4/5.
61. Fry, 'Problems', 20.

62. Drew, 'Sector 22', 25.
63. Ibid., 22; see also Shaw, 'Town Planning', 870–71.
64. Desai, *Women Architects*, 55–56.
65. Chowdhury, 'Recent Work', 152.
66. Malhotra, 'Low-Cost Housing', 36.
67. Ibid.
68. Jane Drew, Senior Architect to the Government of Punjab, Chandigarh Project, Note on Low-Cost Housing, [undated], Fry & Drew Papers, RIBA Collections, F&D/1/1.
69. Ibid.
70. 19 March 1955, *SWJN*2, vol. 28, 26.
71. *Times of India*, 14 May 2012, available at https://timesofindia.indiatimes.com/city/chandigarh/Displaced-for-making-Chandigarh-their-marginalization-is-still-on/articleshow/13136226.cms.
72. Roy, 'Moving Pictures'.
73. Karim, *Of Greater Dignity*.
74. *Times of India*, 13 July 1950, 8.
75. Raju, 'Improving Village Homes', 19.
76. *Times of India*, 13 July 1950, 8.
77. Raju, 'Improving Village Homes', 19.
78. *Times of India*, 13 July 1950, 8.
79. Raju, 'Improving Village Homes', 23.
80. 'United Nations Seminar on Housing & Community Improvement, New Delhi 21 January–17 February 1954' RIBA Collections, J. Tyrwhitt Papers TyJ/31.
81. United Nations, *Seminar on Housing*, 51.
82. *Times of India*, 21 January 1954, 1.
83. Thatra, 'Dalit Chembur'; Shaikh, *Outcaste Bombay*, ch. 3.
84. United Nations, *Seminar on Housing*, ix.
85. Raju, 'Improving Village Homes', 21–22.
86. For contrary arguments, see Ghosh, 'In Defiance'; Bhattacharjya, 'Productive Distance'.
87. *Times of India*, 6 August 1954, 1.
88. Ibid.
89. *Times of India*, 7 August 1954, 6.
90. Unattributed author, 'Editorial', *Lalit Kala*, 9.
91. *Times of India*, 6 August 1954, 1.
92. Krishnan, 'First National Exhibition', 147.
93. Ibid.
94. Krishnan, 'First National Exhibition', 145.
95. *Times of India*, 24 April 1955, 7.
96. Ibid.
97. Quoted in Krishnan, 'First National Exhibition', 145.
98. Ibid., 147.
99. Ibid.
100. *Times of India*, 25 May 1956, 5.
101. Krishnan, 'Contemporary Scene', 113–14.

102. Sunderason, *Partisan Aesthetics*, 187–89.
103. *Times of India*, 24 April 1955, 7.
104. Quoted by Pran Nath Mago, in Mago, 'Delhi Silpi Chakra'.
105. Kumari, 'Society', citing Kapur, *Modern Painting*.
106. Statement by F. N. Souza in the Progressive Artists' Group Bombay exhibition catalogue, July 1948, quoted in Kapur, *Contemporary Indian Artists*, 9.
107. Swaminathan, 'Manifesto'.
108. Khullar, *Worldly Affiliations*.
109. Appasamy, 'Editorial', 4.
110. Krishnan, 'Brief Survey'.
111. *Times of India*, 4 April 1983, 4; 5 December 1982, 8.
112. Subramanyan, 'Artist on Art'.
113. Raj Anand, 'Editorial'; Paniker, 'Artist on Art', 19–20.
114. Appasamy, 'Editorial', 4–5.
115. Clark, 'On the Social History', 12.

BIBLIOGRAPHY

Archive and Manuscript Sources

Andhra Pradesh State Archives (now Telangana State Archives), Hyderabad
Centre for South Asian Studies, Cambridge
India Office Records, British Library, London
National Archives of India, New Delhi
Nehru Memorial Museum and Library, New Delhi
Royal Institute of British Architects Collections, Victoria & Albert Museum, London
UK National Archives

Online Archive and Manuscript Sources

Critical Collective—criticalcollective.in

Assembly Debates

Bombay Legislative Assembly Debates
Constituent Assembly Debates
Lok Sabha Debates
Madras Legislative Assembly Debates
Madras Legislative Council Debates
Rajya Sabha Debates

Newspapers

The Times of India (ProQuest Historical Newspapers)
The Bombay Chronicle
The New York Times (ProQuest Historical Newspapers)
The Wall Street Journal (ProQuest Historical Newspapers)
The Siasat Daily
The Hindustan Times
The Tribune
Indian Nation
The Manchester Guardian (ProQuest Historical Newspapers)

Published Primary Sources

A. M. 'We, the People'. *The Economic Weekly* 16, nos 29-31 (special number, July 1964): 1195-98.
'After Nehru—Who?' *Monthly Public Opinion Surveys* 7, nos 2-4 (1961-62): 23-28.

Ali, Asaf. 'India's Role in One World'. *The Annals of the American Academy of Political and Social Science* 258, no. 1 (1948): 22–26.

Ambedkar, B. R. 'Draft Constitution Discussion, 4 November 1948–25 November 1949'. In Jaffrelot and Kumar, eds, *Ambedkar and Democracy*, 174–99.

Ambedkar, B. R. 'Statement by Dr. B. R. Ambedkar in Parliament in Explanation of His Resignation from the Cabinet' (10 October 1951). In B. R. Ambedkar, *Writings and Speeches*, ed. Vasant Moon, vol. 14:2 (Annexure 1). New Delhi: Dr. Ambedar Foundation, Ministry of Social Justice and Empowerment, Government of India (2nd edn) 2019, 1315–27; available at http://drambedkarwritings.gov.in/upload/uploadfiles/files/Volume_14_02.pdf.

Ambedkar, B. R. *What Congress and M. K. Gandhi Have Done to the Untouchables*. Bombay: Thacker, 1945.

Anand, Mulk Raj. 'Editorial'. *Lalit Kala Contemporary* 1 (1962): 3–7.

Appasamy, Jaya. 'Editorial: An Introduction to Contemporary Indian Art'. *Lalit Kala Contemporary* 3 (1964): 3–5.

Appleby, Paul. *Re-Examination of India's Administrative System, with Special Reference to Administration of Government's Industrial and Commercial Enterprises*. New Delhi: Government of India, Cabinet Secretariat Organisation & Methods Division, 1956.

Arthagnani [pseudonym]. 'Growth of the House of Birlas: Lessons for Licensing Policy'. *Economic and Political Weekly* 2, no. 16 (1967): 748–50.

Attlee, Clement. 'Civil Servants, Ministers, Parliament and the Public'. *Indian Journal of Public Administration* 1, no. 2 (1955): 95–103.

Ayyangar, N. Rajagopala. *Report of the Commission of Inquiry into Certain Charges of Misconduct against Shri Bakhshi Gulam Mohammad*. Srinagar: Home Department, Jammu & Kashmir Government, 1967.

Bardhan, Pranab Kumar. 'Tax Payer Psychosis in India'. *The Economic Weekly* 14, no.10 (1962): 447–49.

Bhave, Vinoba. *Sarvodaya and Communism*. Tanjore: Sarvodaya Prachuralaya, 1957.

Bombwall, K. R. 'The Impact of Emergency Provisions on Federalism and Democracy in India'. In *Essays on Indian Federalism: Presented to Professor M Venkatarangaiya*, ed. S. P. Aiyar and Usha Mehta. Bombay: Allied Publishers Pvt Ltd, 1965, 187–209.

Bose, Nirmal Kumar. 'Gandhi and Jawaharlal'. *The Economic Weekly* 16, nos 29–31 (special number, July 1964): 1189.

Central Advisory Board for Harijan Welfare, Ministry of Home Affairs. *Report of the Scavenging Conditions Enquiry Committee*. New Delhi: Government of India, 1960.

Central Statistical Organisation, Department of Statistics, Government of India. *Monthly Abstract of Statistics* 17, no. 8 (1964).

Chalapathi Rau, M. *Nehru for Children*. New Delhi: Children's Book Trust, 1967.

Chowdhury, U .E. 'Recent Work of Pierre Jeanneret'. *Progressive Architecture*, no. 2 (February 1964):148–53, available at https://www.usmodernist.org/PA/PA-1964-02.pdf.

Committee on Plan Projects. *Report of the Team for the Study of Community Projects and National Extension Service*. New Delhi: Government of India, 1957.

Communist Party of India. *The India–China Border Dispute and the Communist Party of India: Resolutions, Statements and Speeches.* New Delhi: New Age Printing Press, 1963.

Communist Party of India. *The Truth about Kerala.* Trivandrum: Central Executive Committee, Communist Party of India, 1958.

Democratic Research Service. *Kerala under Communism.* Bombay: Democratic Research Service, 1959.

Department of Industries, Government of Bombay. *Brochure Indicating Possibilities for Establishing Large and Medium Scale Industries for Private Enterprise in the State of Bombay during the Second Five Year Plan Period.* Bombay: Government of Bombay, 1956.

Department of Information and Public Relations. *Bhoodan—Concept of Land through Love.* Hyderabad: Government of Hyderabad, 1954.

Deshmukh, Durgabai. *Social Welfare and Economic Development: Two Lectures Delivered at the Asian Institute for Economic Development and Planning.* Bangkok: Asian Institute for Economic Development and Planning, 1964.

Dey, S. K. *Community Development through Sahakari Samaj.* New Delhi: Government of India, Ministry of Community Development and Cooperation, 1962.

Dey, S. K. *Nilokheri.* London: Asia Publishing House, 1962.

Dey, S. K. 'Some Issues'. In *Panchayati Raj, Planning and Democracy*, ed. M. V. Mathur and Iqbal Narain. Bombay: Asia Publishing House, 1969.

Drew, Jane. 'Sector 22'. *MARG* 15, no. 1 (December 1961): 22–25.

Election Commission of India. *Report on the First General Elections in India 1951–52*, vol. 1 (General). New Delhi: Government of India, 1955.

Election Commission of India. *Report on the Third General Elections in India*, vol. 1 (General). New Delhi: Election Commission, 1963–66.

Federation of British Industry. *British Industry and the Development of India.* London: Federation of British Industry, 1961.

Fry, E. Maxwell. 'Problems of Chandigarh Architecture'. *MARG* 15, no. 1 (1961): 20–25.

Gadgil, N. V. 'Accountability of Administration'. *Indian Journal of Public Administration* 1, no. 3 (1955): 193–203.

Ganguli, B. N. 'Nehru and Socialism'. *The Economic Weekly* 16, nos 29–31 (special number, July 1964): 1213–18.

Gautam, Mohanlal. 'India's Foreign Policy II—The Congress View'. *India Quarterly* 7, no. 2 (1951): 105–12.

Ghosh, Ajoy. *Forward to the Defence of Kerala and Indian Democracy!* New Delhi: New Age Printing Press, 1959.

Gopal, Sarvepalli, general editor. *Selected Works of Jawaharlal Nehru*, Second Series [*SWJN2*], 85 vols. New Delhi: Orient Longman, 1984–2020.

Gorwala, A. D. *Report on the Efficient Conduct of State Enterprises.* New Delhi: Government of India, Planning Committee: 1951.

Government of Bombay. *The People's Raj, Republic Day Number.* Bombay: Government of Bombay, 1956.

Harris, F. R. *Jamsetji Nusserwanji Tata: A Chronicle of His Life.* Bombay: Blackie & Son Ltd, 1958.

Hazari, R. K. *The Structure of the Corporate Private Sector: A Study of Concentration, Ownership and Control*. London: Asia Publishing House, 1966.

Hunck, J. M. *India's Silent Revolution: A Survey of Indo-German Cooperation*. Dusseldorf: Verlag Handelsblatt, 1958.

Husain, Zakir. 'The Administrator and the People'. *Indian Journal of Public Administration* 3, no. 3 (1962): 265-69.

'Index of Popularity of Party Leaders'. *Monthly Public Opinion Surveys* 2, nos 4-7 (1957): 74-94.

Indian Commission of Jurists. *Report of the Kerala Enquiry Committee*. Bombay: The Service, 1959.

Industries, Labour and Co-operation Department. *Report of the Committee for Leather Industry and Trade*. Madras: Government of Madras, 1954.

Jadhav, Tara B. 'The Story of a Welfare Centre in Saurashtra'. *Social Welfare* 2, no. 1 (1955): 78-79.

Jain, Rikhab Dass. *The Economic Aspects of the Film Industry in India*. Delhi: Atma Ram & Sons, 1960.

Karnik, V. B. 'Jawaharlal Nehru: Foreign Policy'. In *Jawaharlal Nehru: A Critical Tribute*, ed. A. B. Shah. Bombay: Manaktalas, 1965.

Kaur, Rajkumari Amrit. *The Concept of Social Service: Its Relation to World Needs and Problems*. London: The National Council of Social Service, 1951.

Khosla, Madhav, ed. *Letters for a Nation from Jawaharlal Nehru to his Chief Ministers, 1947-1963*. Gurgaon: Penguin Books, 2015.

Kothari, Rajni. 'The Meaning of Jawaharlal Nehru'. *The Economic Weekly* 16, nos 29-31 (special number, July 1964): 1203-7.

Kothari, Rajni. 'Political Consensus in India: Decline and Reconstruction'. *Economic and Political Weekly* 4, no. 42 (1969): 1635-44.

Kothari, Rajni and Rushikesh Maru. 'Caste and Secularism in India: Case Study of a Caste Federation'. *The Journal of Asian Studies* 25, no. 1 (1965): 33-50.

Krishnan, S. A. 'A Brief Survey of the Post-Independent Era'. *Pushpanjali* 2, no. 1 (1965), available at https://criticalcollective.in/CC_ArchiveInner2.aspx?Aid=345&Eid=552#Essay_Title345.

Krishnan, S. A. ('S. A. K'). 'The Contemporary Scene: A Retrospective View of the National Exhibition of Art'. *Lalit Kala: A Journal of Oriental Art Chiefly Indian* 3, no. 4 (1956-57): 113-18.

Krishnan, S. A. ('S. A. K'). 'First National Exhibition of Art'. *Lalit Kala: A Journal of Oriental Art Chiefly Indian*, nos 1-2 (1955-56): 145-47.

Krishnaswami, A. *The Indian Union and the States*. Oxford: Pergamon Press, 1965.

Kulkarni, P. D. *The Central Social Welfare Board: A New Experiment in Welfare Administration*. London: Asia Publishing House, 1961.

Kulkarni, P. D. 'Social Welfare in Five Year Plans'. In *History and Philosophy of Social Work in India: A Souvenir Volume of the Silver Jubilee Celebrations of the Tata Institute of Social Sciences*, ed. A. R. Wadia. Bombay: Allied Publishers Pvt Ltd., 1961, 469-80.

Labour Bureau. *Agricultural Labour in India: A Compendium of Basic Facts*. New Delhi: Government of India, 1969.

Labour Bureau, *Agricultural Labour in India: Report on the Second Agricultural Labour Enquiry, 1956-57*. New Delhi: Government of India, 1960.

Labour Bureau. *Report on Survey of Labour Conditions in Bicycle Factories in India.* New Delhi: Government of India, 1965.

Labour Bureau. *Report on Survey of Labour Conditions in Tanning and Leather Finish Factories in India, 1965-66.* New Delhi: Government of India, 1969.

Labour Investigation Committee. *Report on Labour Conditions in Tanneries and the Leather Industry.* New Delhi: Government of India, 1946.

Lal Shrimali, Kalu. *Education in Changing India.* London: Asia Publishing House, 1965.

Lok Sabha, *Panchsheel: Its Meaning and History.* New Delhi: Lok Sabha Secretariat, 1958.

Mahalanobis, P. C. 'Address Delivered as President of the National Institute of Sciences of India, 8 January 1958'. In Mahalanobis, *Talks on Planning.* London: Asia Publishing House, 1962, 70.

Malhotra, Jeet. 'Low-Cost Housing'. *MARG* 15, no. 1 (1961): 32-38.

Mehta, Balwantray. 'Public Enterprises and Parliamentary Control'. *Indian Journal of Public Administration* 4, no. 2 (1958): 143-53.

Menon, V. K. Krishna (chairman). *Parliamentary Supervision over State Undertakings: Being a Report of the Sub-Committee of the Congress Party in Parliament.* New Delhi: Congress Party in Parliament, 1959.

Ministry of Community Development. *Road to Welfare State.* New Delhi: Government of India, 1957.

Ministry of Community Development. *Three Basic Institutions.* Faridabad: Government of India, 1959.

Ministry of Community Development and Cooperation, *Panchayati Raj: The Ten Point Test.* New Delhi: Government of India, 1961.

Ministry of Community Development and Cooperation. *Report on the Committee on Panchayati Raj Elections.* New Delhi: Government of India, 1965.

Ministry of Community Development and Cooperation. *Seminar on Public Administration in Panchayati Raj at Savoy Hotel, Mussoorie, 9 to 13 April 1962: Agenda Papers.* Mussoorie: Central Institute of Community Development, 1962.

Ministry of Education. *Annual Report 1954-55.* New Delhi: Government of India. 1955, available at https://dspace.gipe.ac.in/xmlui/handle/10973/29317.

Ministry of Education. *Annual Report 1955-56.* New Delhi: Government of India, 1956, available at https://dspace.gipe.ac.in/xmlui/handle/10973/29318.

Ministry of Education. *Education in the Soviet Union: A Report on the Visit of the Indian Delegation to the USSR, 1961.* New Delhi: Government of India, 1962.

Ministry of Education. *National Seminar on Compulsory Education.* New Delhi: Government of India Press, 1961.

Ministry of Finance and Department of Economic Affairs. *Report of the Taxation Enquiry Commission, 1953-54,* vol. 2. New Delhi: Government of India, 1954.

Ministry of Food and Agriculture. *Report on the Grow More Food Enquiry Committee.* New Delhi: Government of India, 1952.

Ministry of Food and Agriculture. *Report of the Indian Agricultural Team to USSR, Poland and Czechoslovakia, September-October 1954.* New Delhi: Government of India, 1956.

Ministry of Home Affairs. *Report of the Committee on the Prevention of Corruption.* New Delhi: Government of India, 1964.

Ministry of Information and Broadcasting. *Acharya Vinoba Bhave*. New Delhi: Government of India, 1955.

Ministry of Information and Broadcasting. *India's Minorities*. New Delhi: Government of India, 1948.

Ministry of Labour and Employment. *Employers' Obligations under Labour Laws*. New Delhi: Government of India, 1961.

Mullik, B. N. *My Years with Nehru: Kashmir*. Bombay: Allied Publishers, 1971.

Mustafi, A. K. 'Issues in the General Elections'. *The Indian Journal of Political Science* 13, no. 3/4 (1952): i.

Nair, R. Ramakrishnan. *How Communists Came to Power in Kerala*. Trivandrum: The Kerala Academy of Political Science, 1965.

Namboodiripad, E.M.S. 'Introduction'. In *Kerala on the March*. Trivandrum: Government of Kerala, Department of Public Relations, 1957, i–ii.

Namboodiripad, E.M.S. *Report of the Administrative Reforms Committee*. Trivandrum: Government of Kerala, 1958.

Namboodiripad, E.M.S. *Twenty-Eight Months in Kerala: A Retrospect*. New Delhi: People's Publishing House, 1959.

Narain, Iqbal. 'The Management of Public Enterprises: A Study of Some Aspects in the Context of the "Socialistic Pattern"'. *Indian Journal of Public Administration* 4, no. 3 (1958): 302–18.

Narayan, Jayaprakash. 'Socialism and Sarvodaya' [1951]. In *Socialism, Sarvodaya and Democracy: Selected Works of Jayaprakash Narayan*, ed. Bimla Prasad. London: Asia Publishing House, 1964, 91–96.

Natarajan, L. *American Shadow over India*. Bombay: People's Publishing House, 1952.

Natarajan, S. 'The Mind and Face of Secularism'. *The Economic Weekly* 16, nos 29–31 (special number, July 1964): 1253–60.

National Productivity Council of India. *Textile Industry in USSR and Czechoslovakia*. New Delhi: Government of India, 1962.

Nehru, Jawaharlal. *An Autobiography, with Musings on Recent Events in India*. London: John Lane The Bodley Head, 1936.

Nehru, Jawaharlal. 'The Basic Approach'. In Sampurnanand, *Indian Socialism*, 67–79.

Nehru, Jawaharlal. *A Bunch of Old Letters: Written Mostly to Jawaharlal Nehru and Some Written by Him*. London, Asia Publishing House, 1958.

Nehru, Jawaharlal. *The Discovery of India*. Calcutta: The Signet Press, 1946.

Nehru, Jawaharlal. '"The Socialist Goal": Extract from Maulana Azad Memorial Lectures (1959)', in Nehru, *Congressmen's Primer for Socialism (A Compilation)*, ed. H. D. Malaviya. New Delhi: All India Congress Committee, 1964, 185–89.

Paniker, K.C.S. 'The Artist on Art: Some Thoughts'. *Lalit Kala Contemporary* 5 (1966): 19–20.

Pant, Govind Ballabh. 'Public Servant in a Democracy'. *Indian Journal of Public Administration* 1, no. 3 (1955): 181–83.

Patel, H. M. *Democracy at Work in India*. Ahmedabad: Harold Laski Institute of Political Science, 1961.

Pathak, Devavrat N. 'Is Parliamentary Government Suitable to India?' *The Indian Journal of Political Science* 19, no. 4 (1958): 335–42.

Patil, Ramrao Krishnarao. 'Democratisation of Administration'. *Indian Journal of Public Administration* 1, no. 3 (1955): 212–16.

Pillai, Kainikkara Padmanabha. *The Red Interlude in Kerala: A Kerala Congress Pradesh Publication*. Trivandrum: The Kerala Pradesh Congress Committee, 1959.

Pillai, N. R. 'The New Civil Servant'. *Indian Journal of Public Administration* 1, no. 1 (1955): 1–2.

Planning Commission. *The First Five-Year Plan*. New Delhi: Government of India, 1952.

Planning Commission. *Industrial Planning and Licensing Policy: Final Report*. New Delhi, Government of India: 1967.

Planning Commission. *Progress of Land Reform*. New Delhi: Government of India, 1963.

Planning Commission. *Report of the Study Team on Prohibition*, vols 1 and 2. New Delhi: Government of India, 1964.

Planning Commission. *Second Five-Year Plan*. New Delhi: Government of India, 1956.

Prasad, Bimal, ed. *Jayaprakash Narayan: Selected Works [JNSW]*. 8 vols. New Delhi: Nehru Memorial Museum and Library, 2005.

Prasad, Jagdish. 'Nationalisation of Road Transport in Uttar Pradesh'. *Indian Journal of Public Administration* 2, no. 4 (1956): 329–38.

Programme Evaluation Organisation. *Evaluation Report on the Working of the Welfare Extension Projects of the Central Social Welfare Board*. New Delhi: Government of India, 1959.

Programme Evaluation Organisation. *Resettlement Programme for Landless Agricultural Labourers: Case Studies of Selected Colonies*. New Delhi: Government of India, 1968.

Radhakrishnan, Sarvepalli. 'Democracy: A Habit of Mind' (presidential address delivered at the Annual Session of Andhra, Mahasabha, Madras, September 1938). In S. Radhakrishnan, *Education, Politics and War*. Poona: V. N. Dixit for the International Book Service, 1944, 10–25.

Radhakrishnan, Sarvepalli. *Occasional Speeches and Writings, October 1952–February 1959*. New Delhi: Publications Division, Ministry of Information and Broadcasting, Government of India, 1960.

Radhakrishnan, Sarvepalli. *On Nehru*. New Delhi: Ministry of Information and Broadcasting, 1965.

Raj, K. N. 'Nehru, the Congress, and Class Conflict'. *The Economic Weekly* 16, nos 29–31 (special number, July 1964): 1231–34.

Rajan, M. S. 'Indian Foreign Policy in Action'. *India Quarterly* 16, no. 3 (1960): 203–36.

Raju, S. P. 'Improving Village Homes in the Tropics'. In *Proceedings of the Symposium on Scientific Principles and their Application in Tropical Building Design and Construction, Held at New Delhi, December 21-24, 1952* (= *Bulletin of the National Institute of Sciences of India*, no. 6). New Delhi: National Institute of Sciences of India), 19–24.

Rao, V.K.R.V. *An Economic Review of Refugee Rehabilitation in Faridabad Township*. New Delhi: Delhi School of Economics, 1954.

Rao, V. Venkata. 'Selections of Candidates by Political Parties'. *The Indian Journal of Political Science* 13, no. 3/4 (1952): i–ii.

Representation of the People Act, 1951, available at https://legislative.gov.in/sites/default/files/O4_representation%20of%20the%20people%20act,%201951.pdf.

Sain, Kanwar. *Modern Trends in the Design & Construction of Dams & Power-Houses*. Delhi: Atma Ram and Sons, 1962.

Sain, Kanwar. 'The Social Repercussions of Hydraulic Projects in India'. *Civilisations* 5, no. 2 (1955): 183–91.

Sain, Kanwar. *Reminiscences of an Engineer*. New Delhi: Young Asia Publications, 1978.

Sampurnanand. 'Congress Ideology and Programme'. In Sampurnanand, *Indian Socialism*, 57–66.

Sampurnanand. *Indian Socialism*. London: Asia Publishing House, 1958.

Santhanam, K. *Union-State Relations in India*. London, Asia Publishing House, 1960.

Saraiya, R. G. 'Administration of Nationalised Undertakings'. *Indian Journal of Public Administration* 2, no. 2 (1956): 111–20.

Sen, Sudhir. *Wanderings: In Search of Solutions of the Problem of Poverty*. Madras: Macmillan India Ltd, 1989.

Senapatty, Dolly. 'Orissa Chairman Talks about Day-to-Day WEP Work'. *Social Welfare* 3, no. 9 (1956): 13.

Setalvad, M. C. 'India and the United Nations'. *India Quarterly* 6, no. 2 (1950): 107–29.

Shankar, Keshav Pillai. *Don't Spare Me, Shankar*. New Delhi: Children's Book Trust, 1983.

Shankar, T. R. 'Handling the Tax Dodger—The Tughlakian Way'. *The Economic Weekly* 1, no. 25 (1949): 9–10.

Shrikant, L. M. *Report of the Commissioner for Scheduled Castes and Scheduled Tribes for the Period Ending December 1951*. New Delhi: Government of India Press, 1951.

Shrikant, L. M. *Report of Commissioner for Scheduled Castes and Scheduled Tribes for the Year 1960–61*. New Delhi: Government of India Press, 1962.

Shrimali, Kalu Lal. *Education in Changing India*. London: Asia Publishing House, 1965.

Srinivas, M. N. 'A Note on Sanskritisation and Westernisation'. *The Far Eastern Quarterly* 15, no. 4 (1956): 481–96.

Srinivas, M. N. *Religion and Society among the Coorgs of South India*. Oxford: Clarendon Press, 1952.

Subramanyan, K. G. 'The Artist on Art'. *Lalit Kala Contemporary* 3 (1964): 13–15.

Swaminathan, Jagdish. 'Manifesto' (from Group 1890 Exhibition catalogue, 1963), available at https://criticalcollective.in/ArtistGInner2.aspx?Aid=197&Eid=163#Essay_Title197.

Taraporevala, Russi Jal. *Principles of Taxation for Underdeveloped Countries: Indian Tax Surveyed: Proposals for Improvement Suggested*. Bombay: n.p., 1959.

Trumbull, Robert. 'Vinoba's Loot with Love'. In *Bhoodan as Seen by the West: An Appraisal of the Land-Gift Mission by Some Western Seekers*. Tanjore: Sarvodaya Prachuralayam (Akhil Bharat Sarva Seva Sangh Prakashan), 1958, 1–12.

Unattributed author. 'Editorial'. *Lalit Kala: A Journal of Oriental Art Chiefly Indian*, vols 1–2 (1955–56): 9–10.

Unattributed author. 'Extra-Fiscal Measures to Widen Tax Base'. *The Economic Weekly* 11, no. 25 (1959): 699–700.

Unattributed author. 'Industrial Planning and Licensing Policy: A Summary of the Hazari Report'. *Economic and Political Weekly* 2, no. 16 (1967): 746–48.

Unattributed author, 'Jawaharlal Nehru', *The Economic Weekly* 16, no. 22 (1964): 907–8.

Unattributed author. 'Nehru and the Administration'. *The Economic Weekly* 16, nos 29–31 (special number, July 1964): 1243–46.

Unattributed author. *Sixteen Months of Communist Rule in Kerala: A General Review*. Calicut: Amala Printing Works, 1958.

Unattributed author. 'The Socialist Legacy'. *The Economic Weekly* 16, nos 29-31 (special number, July 1964): 1219-25.

United Nations. *Report on the United Nations Seminar on Housing & Community Improvement*. New Delhi: United Nations, 1954.

United Nations Industrial Development Organization. *Bicycles: A Case Study of Indian Experience*. New York: United Nations, 1969.

Venkataramani, M. S., 'Manganese as a Factor in Indo-American Relations'. *Indian Quarterly* 14, no. 2 (1958): 131-54.

Verma, R. I. *Leather Footwear Industry in Uttar Pradesh with Special Study at Kanpur* (Census of India 1961, vol. 15: Uttar Pradesh, Part 7A, Handicrafts Survey Monograph 2). New Delhi: Government of India, 1964.

Works Cited

Abraham, Itty. 'From Bandung to NAM: Non-Alignment and Indian Foreign Policy, 1947-65'. *Commonwealth and Comparative Politics* 46, no. 2 (2008): 195-219.

Abraham, Itty. *How India Became Territorial: Foreign Policy, Diaspora, Geopolitics*. Palo Alto, CA: Stanford University Press, 2014.

Abraham, Itty. 'Prolegomena to Non-Alignment: Race and the International System'. In *The Non-Aligned Movement and the Cold War: Delhi—Bandung—Belgrade*, ed. Nataša Mišković, Harald Fischer-Tiné and Nada Boškovska. Abingdon: Routledge, 2014, 78-94.

Acharya, Amitav and See Seng Tan, 'Introduction: The Normative Relevance of the Bandung Conference for Contemporary Asian and International Order'. In *Bandung Revisited: The Legacy of the 1955 Asian-African Conference for International Order*, ed. See Seng Tan and Amitav Acharya. Singapore: NUS Press, 2008, 1-16.

Ahmad, Irfan. *Islamism and Democracy in India: The Transformation of Jamaat-e-Islami*. Princeton, NJ: Princeton University Press, 2009.

Ahuja, Ravi. 'A Beveridge Plan for India? Social Insurance and the Making of the Formal Sector'. *International Review of Social History* 64, no. 2 (2019): 207-48.

Amin, Shahid. 'Gandhi as Mahatma: Gorakhpur District, Eastern UP, 1921-22'. In *Subaltern Studies III: Writings on South Asian History and Society*, ed. Ranajit Guha. Delhi: Oxford University Press, 1984.

Amrith, Sunil. *Decolonizing International Health: India and Southeast Asia, 1930-65*. Houndmills: Palgrave Macmillan, 2006.

Amrith, Sunil. *Unruly Waters: How Mountain Rivers and Monsoons Have Shaped South Asia's History*. London: Penguin Books, 2018.

Anderson, Perry. *The Indian Ideology*. London: Verso, 2013.

Anderson, Robert S. *Nucleus and Nation: Scientists, International Networks, and Power in India*. Chicago: The University of Chicago Press, 2010.

Ankit, Rakesh. 'Between Vanity and Sensitiveness: Indo-British Relations during Vijayalakshmi Pandit's High-Commissionership (1954-61)'. *Contemporary British History* 30, no. 1 (2015): 20-39.

Ankit, Rakesh. 'Mountbatten and India 1948–64.' *International History Review* 37, no. 5 (2015): 241–61.

Ansari, Sarah and William Gould. *Boundaries of Belonging: Localities, Citizenship and Rights in India and Pakistan*. Cambridge: Cambridge University Press, 2020.

Appu, P. S. 'Tenancy Reform in India'. *Economic and Political Weekly* 10, nos 33–35 (special number, August 1975): 1339–75.

Arnold, David and Erich DeWald. 'Cycles of Empowerment? The Bicycle and Everyday Technology in Colonial India and Vietnam'. *Comparative Studies in Society and History* 53, no .4 (2011): 971–96.

Attwood, Donald W. *Raising Cane: The Political Economy of Sugar in Western India*. Boulder, CO: Westview Press, 1992.

Aunesluoma, Juhana. *Britain, Sweden and the Cold War, 1945–54: Understanding Neutrality*. Basingstoke: Palgrave Macmillan, 2003.

Austin, Granville. 'The Expected and the Unintended in Working a Democratic Constitution'. In *India's Living Constitution: Ideas, Practices and Controversies*, ed. Zoya Hasan, E. Sridharan and R. Sudarshan. London: Anthem Press, 2002, 319–43.

Austin, Granville. *Working a Democratic Constitution: A History of the Indian Experience*. New Delhi: Oxford University Press, 1999.

Azad, Abul Kalam. *Azadi e Hind*. Lahore: Maktaba Jamal, 2003.

Bajpai, Rochana. *Debating Difference: Group Rights and Liberal Democracy in India*. New Delhi: Oxford University Press, 2011.

Balasubramanian, Aditya. 'Contesting "Permit-and-Licence Raj": Economic Conservatism and the Idea of Democracy in 1950s India'. *Past & Present* 251, no. 1 (2021): 189–227.

Balasubramanian, Aditya and Srinath Raghavan. 'Present at the Creation: India, the Global Economy and the Bretton Woods Conference'. *Journal of World History* 29, no. 1 (2018): 65–94.

Bandyopadhyay, Sekhar. 'Partition and the Ruptures in Dalit Identity Politics in Bengal'. *Asian Studies Review* 33, no. 4 (2009): 455–67.

Banerjee, Debdas and Anjan Ghosh. 'Indian Planning and Regional Disparity in Growth'. In *Economy, Society and Polity: Essays in the Political Economy of Indian Planning in Honour of Professor Bhabatosh Datta*, ed. Amiya Kumar Bagchi. New Delhi: Oxford University Press, 1988, 104–65.

Banerjee, Nirmala. 'The Unorganized Sector and the Planner'. In *Economy, Society and Polity: Essays in the Political Economy of Indian Planning in the Honour of Professor Bhabatosh Datta*, ed. Amiya Kumar Bagchi. New Delhi: Oxford University Press, 1988, 71–103.

Bannerjee, Tridib. 'US Planning Expeditions to Postcolonial India: From Ideology to Innovation in Technical Assistance'. *Journal of the American Planning Association* 75, no. 2 (2009): 193–208.

Baxi, Upendra. 'The Constitutional Discourse on Secularism'. In *Reconstructing the Republic*, ed. Upendra Baxi, Alice Jacob and Tarlok Singh. New Delhi: Har-Anand Publications, 1999, 211–33.

Bayly, C. A. 'The Ends of Liberalism and the Political Thought of Nehru's India'. *Modern Intellectual History* 12, no. 3 (2015): 605–26.

Behera, Navnita Chadha. *Demystifying Kashmir*. Washington, DC: Brookings Institution Press, 2006.

Bentz, Anne-Sophie. 'Being a Tibetan Refugee in India'. *Refugee Survey Quarterly* 31, no. 2 (2012): 80–107.

Berg, Dag-Erik. *Dynamics of Caste and Law: Dalits, Oppression and Constitutional Democracy in India*. Cambridge: Cambridge University Press, 2020.

Besley, Timothy, Jessica Leight, Rohini Pande and Vijayendra Rao. 'Long-Run Impacts of Land Regulation: Evidence from Tenancy Reform in India'. *Journal of Development Economics* 118 (2015): 72–87.

Bhagavan, Manu. *The Peacemakers: India and the Quest for One World*. New Delhi: Harper Collins Publishers India, 2012.

Bhargava, Rajeev. *The Promise of India's Secular Democracy*. New Delhi: Oxford University Press, 2010.

Bhargava, Rajeev, ed. *Secularism and its Critics*. New Delhi: Oxford University Press, 1998.

Bhargava, Rajeev. 'What is Secularism For?'. In Bhargava, ed., *Secularism*, 486–542.

Bhattacharjya, Nilanjana. 'A Productive Distance from the Nation: Uday Shankar and the Defining of Indian Modern Dance'. *South Asian History and Culture* 2, no. 4 (2011): 482–501.

Bhattacharya, Shahan. 'Transforming Skin, Changing Caste: Technical Education in Leather Production in India, 1900–1950'. *The Indian Economic & Social History Review* 55, no. 3 (2018): 307–43.

Bilgrami, Akeel. 'Secularism, Nationalism, and Modernity', in Bhargava, ed., *Secularism*, 380–417.

Bose, Sumantra. *Kashmir: Roots of Conflict: Paths to Peace*. Cambridge, MA: Harvard University Press, 2003.

Brass, Paul. *Language, Religion and Politics in North India*. Cambridge: Cambridge University Press, 1974.

Brass, Paul. 'The Partition of India and Retributive Genocide in the Punjab, 1946–47: Means, Methods and Purposes'. *Journal of Genocide Research* 5, no. 1 (2003): 71–101.

Brecher, Michael. *Nehru: A Political Biography*. London: Oxford University Press, 1959.

Brown, Judith. *Nehru*. London: Longman, 1999.

Brown, Judith. *Nehru: A Political Life*. London: Yale University Press, 2003.

Brown, Rebecca M. *Art for a Modern India, 1947–1980*. Durham, NC: Duke University Press, 2009.

Brown, Rebecca. 'Reviving the Past: Post-Independence Architecture and Politics in India's Long 1950s'. *Interventions* 11, no. 3 (2009): 293–315.

Chacko, Priya. *Indian Foreign Policy: The Politics of Postcolonial Identity from 1947 to 2004*. London: Routledge, 2012.

Cháirez-Garza, Jesús Francisco. 'B. R. Ambedkar, Franz Boas and the Rejection of Racial Theories of Untouchability'. *South Asia: Journal of South Asian Studies* 41, no. 2 (2018): 281–96.

Chakrabarty, Dipesh. '"In the Name of Politics": Democracy and the Power of the Multitude of India'. *Public Culture* 19, no. 1 (2007), 35–57.

Chakrabarty, Dipesh. *Provincializing Europe*. Princeton, NJ: Princeton University Press, 2000.

Chakravorty, Sanjoy. *The Price of Land: Acquisition, Conflict, Consequence*. New Delhi: Oxford University Press, 2013.

Chandavarkar, Rajnarayan. 'Customs of Governance: Colonialism and Democracy in Twentieth Century India'. *Modern Asian Studies* 41, no. 3 (2007): 441–70.

Chandavarkar, Rajnarayan. *Imperial Power and Popular Politics: Class, Resistance and the State in India c.1850–1950*. Cambridge: Cambridge University Press, 1998.

Chandra, Bipin. *The Rise and Growth of Economic Nationalism in India*. New Delhi: Anamika Publishers, 2004.

Chari, P. R. 'Indo-Soviet Military Cooperation: A Review'. *Asian Survey* 19, no. 1 (1979): 230–44.

Chatterjee, Nandini. *The Making of Indian Secularism: Empire, Law and Christianity*. Cambridge: Cambridge University Press, 2011.

Chatterjee, Partha. 'Development Planning and the Indian State'. In *State and Politics in India*, ed. Partha Chatterjee. New Delhi: Oxford University Press, 1997, 271–98.

Chatterjee, Partha. *Nationalist Thought and the Colonial World: A Derivative Discourse*. Minneapolis: University of Minnesota Press, 1993.

Chatterjee, Partha. 'Religious Minorities and the Secular State: Reflections on an Indian Impasse'. *Public Culture* 8 (1995): 11–39.

Chatterjee, Partha and Ira Katznelson. *Anxieties of Democracy: Tocquevillean Reflections on India and the United States*. New Delhi: Oxford University Press, 2012.

Chatterjee Miller, Manjari. 'Recollecting Empire: "Victimhood" and the 1962 Sino-Indian War'. *Asian Security* 5, no. 3 (2009): 216–41.

Chatterji, Joya. *Bengal Divided: Hindu Communalism and Partition*. Cambridge: Cambridge University Press, 1994.

Chatterji, Joya. *Partition's Legacies*. Albany, NY: State University of New York Press, 2019.

Chatterji, Joya. 'Secularisation and Partition Emergencies: Deep Diplomacy in South Asia'. *Economic and Political Weekly* 48, no. 50 (2013): 42–50.

Chatterji, Joya. 'South Asian Histories of Citizenship, 1946–1970'. *The Historical Journal* 55, no. 4 (2012): 1049–71.

Chatterji, Joya. *The Spoils of Partition: Bengal and India, 1947–1967*. Cambridge: Cambridge University Press, 2007.

Chaudhuri, Rudra. *Forged in Crisis: India and the United States Since 1947*. New Delhi: Oxford University Press, 2014.

Chester, Lucy P. *Borders and Conflict in South Asia: The Radcliffe Boundary Commission and the Partition of Punjab*. Manchester: Manchester University Press, 2009.

Chhibber, Pradeep K. and Rahul Verma. *Ideology and Identity: The Changing Party Systems of India*. New Delhi: Oxford University Press, 2018.

Chibber, Vivek. *Locked in Place: State-Building and Late Industrialisation in India*. Princeton, NJ: Princeton University Press, 2003.

Chowdhury, Debasish Roy and John Keane. *To Kill a Democracy: India's Passage to Despotism*. Oxford: Oxford University Press, 2021.

Clark, T. J. *Image of the People: Gustave Courbet and the 1848 Revolution*. London/New York: Thames and Hudson, 1973.

Crawford, Oliver. 'The Political Thought of Tan Malaka'. PhD dissertation, University of Cambridge, 2019.

Das Gupta, Amit. *The Indian Civil Service and Indian Foreign Policy, 1923–1961*. London: Routledge, 2021.

Das Gupta, Chirashree. *State and Capital in Independent India: Institutions and Accumulations*. New Delhi: Cambridge University Press India, 2016.

Das Gupta, Uma. 'Tagore's Ideas of Social Action and the Sriniketan Experiment of Rural Reconstruction, 1922–41'. *University of Toronto Quarterly* 77, no. 4 (2008): 992–1004.

De, Rohit. *A People's Constitution: The Everyday Life of Law in the Indian Republic*. Princeton, NJ: Princeton University Press, 2018.

Desai, Madhavi. *Women Architects and Modernism in India: Narratives and Contemporary Practices*. Abingdon: Routledge, 2017.

Devere, Heather, Simon Mark and Jane Verbitsky. 'A History of the Language of Friendship in International Treaties'. *International Politics* 48, no. 1 (2011): 46–70.

Dikötter, Frank. *How to Be a Dictator: The Cult of Personality in the Twentieth Century*. London: Bloomsbury, 2019.

Dikshit, Sheila, K. Natwar-Singh and G. Parthasarathi, eds. *Jawaharlal Nehru: Centenary Volume*. New Delhi: Oxford University Press, 1989.

Domhardt, Konstanze Sylva. 'The Garden City Idea in the CIAM Discourse on Urbanism: A Path to Comprehensive Planning'. *Planning Perspectives* 27, no. 2 (2012): 173–97.

Duflo, Esther and Rohini Pande. 'Dams'. *The Quarterly Journal of Economics* 122, no. 2 (2007): 601–46.

Ekbladh, David. *The Great American Mission: Modernization and the Construction of an American World Order*. Princeton, NJ: Princeton University Press, 2010.

Ellis, Catriona. 'Children and Childhood in the Madras Presidency, 1919–1943', PhD dissertation, University of Edinburgh, 2016.

Engerman, David C. 'Learning from the East: Soviet Experts and India in the Era of Competitive Coexistence'. *Comparative Studies of South Asia, Africa and the Middle East* 33, no. 2 (2013): 227–38.

Engerman, David C. *The Price of Aid: The Economic Cold War in India*. Cambridge, MA: Harvard University Press, 2018.

Fakhri, S. M. Abul Khader. *Dravidian Sahibs and Brahmin Maulanas: The Politics of the Muslims of Tamil Nadu, 1930–1967*. New Delhi: Manohar Publishers, 2008.

Franda, Marcus F. *West Bengal and the Federalizing Process in India*. Princeton, NJ: Princeton University Press, 1968.

Frankel, Francine R. *India's Political Economy: The Gradual Revolution, 1947–2004*. New Delhi: Oxford University Press, 2006.

Frankel, Francine R. *When Nehru Looked East: Origins of India–US Suspicion and India–China Rivalry*. New York: Oxford University Press, 2020.

Gagné, Karine. *Caring for Glaciers: Land, Animals and Humanity in the Himalayas*. Seattle: University of Washington Press, 2018.

Galanter, Marc. 'The Abolition of Disabilities: Untouchability and the Law'. In *The Untouchables in Contemporary India*, ed. J. Michael Mahar. Tucson, AZ: University of Arizona Press, 1972, 227–314.

Gandee, Sarah. '(Re-)Defining Disadvantage: Untouchability, Criminality and "Tribe" in India, c. 1910–1950s'. *Studies in History* 36, no. 1 (2010): 71–97.
Ganguly, Sumit. 'The Crisis of Indian Secularism'. *Journal of Democracy* 14, no. 4 (2003): 11–25.
Ganguly, Sumit. 'An Illiberal India?'. *Journal of Democracy* 31, no. 1 (2020): 193–202.
Gautier, Laurence. 'The Role of Muslim Universities in the Redefinition of Indian Muslim Identities after Partition (1947–1990s)', PhD dissertation, University of Cambridge, 2017.
Geary, David. 'Rebuilding the Navel of the Earth: Buddhist Pilgrimage and Transnational Religious Networks'. *Modern Asian Studies* 48, no. 3 (2014): 645–92.
Geva, Rotem. 'The Scramble for Houses: Violence, a Factionalized State, and Informal Economy in Post-Partition Delhi'. *Modern Asian Studies* 51, no. 3 (2017): 769–824.
Ghosh, Sudhir. *Gandhi's Emissary*. London: Cresset Press, 1967.
Ghosh, Suman. 'In Defiance of the State: The Nehru Era and Satyajit Ray's Films'. *South Asian Studies* 32, no. 2 (2016): 144–54.
Gilmartin, David. 'One Day's Sultan: T. N. Seshan and Indian Democracy'. *Contribution to Indian Sociology* 43, no. 2 (2009): 247–84.
Glover, William J. 'The Troubled Passage from "Village Communities" to Planned New Town Developments in Mid-Twentieth-Century South Asia'. *Urban History* 39, no. 1 (2012):108–27.
Godsmark, Oliver. *Citizenship, Community and Democracy in India: From Bombay to Maharashtra, c. 1930–1950*. London: Routledge, 2018.
Gokhale, Jayashree. *From Concessions to Confrontation: The Politics of an Indian Untouchable Community*. Bombay: Popular Prakashan, 1993.
Goldstein, Melvyn C. *A History of Modern Tibet*, vol. 3: *The Storm Clouds Descend, 1955–1957*. Berkeley, CA: University of California Press, 2014.
Gooptu, Nandini. *The Politics of the Urban Poor in Early Twentieth-Century India*. Cambridge: Cambridge University Press, 2001.
Gopal, Sarvepalli. *Jawaharlal Nehru: A Biography*, vol. 2: *1947–1956*. London: Jonathan Cape, 1979.
Gould, William. *Bureaucracy, Community and Influence in India: Society and the State, 1930s–1960s*. Abingdon: Routledge, 2011.
Gould, William. 'Contesting "Secularism" in Colonial and Postcolonial North India: Nationalism Ideology and Bureaucratic Practice, 1930–1950s'. *Contemporary South Asia* 14, no. 4 (2003): 481–94.
Gould, William. *Hindu Nationalism and the Language of Politics in Late Colonial India*. Cambridge: Cambridge University Press, 2004.
Gould, William, Taylor C. Sherman and Sarah Ansari. 'The Flux of the Matter: Loyalty, Corruption and the Everyday State in the Post-Partition Government Services of India and Pakistan'. *Past & Present* 219, no.1 (2013): 237–79.
Guha, Ramachandra. *Gandhi: The Years That Changed the World*. London: Penguin Books, 2018.
Guha, Ramachandra. *India after Gandhi*. London: Macmillan, 2007.
Guha, Ramachandra. 'Jawaharlal Nehru and China: A Study in Failure?' *Harvard-Yenching Institute Working Papers* (2011): 11–12.

Guha, Ramachandra, ed. *Makers of Modern India*. New Delhi: Penguin India, 2010.

Guha, Ramachandra. 'Verdicts on Nehru: Rise and Fall of a Reputation'. *Economic and Political Weekly* 40, no. 19 (2005): 1958–62.

Gupta, Akhil. *Postcolonial Developments: Agriculture in the Making of Modern India*. Durham, NC: Duke University Press, 1998.

Gupta, Akhil. *Red Tape: Bureaucracy, Structural Violence and Poverty in India*. Durham, NC: Duke University Press, 2012.

Guyot-Réchard, Bérénice. 'The Fear of Being Compared: State-Shadowing in the Himalayas, 1910–1962'. *Political Geography* 75 (2019): 1–13.

Guyot-Réchard, Bérénice. *Shadow States: India, China and the Himalayas, 1910–1962*. Cambridge: Cambridge University Press, 2017.

Hansen, Thomas Blom. 'Sovereigns beyond the State'. In *Sovereign Bodies: Citizens, Migrants and States in the Postcolonial World*, ed. Thomas Blom Hansen and Finn Stepputat. Princeton, NJ: Princeton University, Press, 2005, 141–59.

Harder, Anton. 'Defining Independence in Cold War Asia: Sino-Indian Relations, 1949–1962'. PhD dissertation, London School of Economics, 2016.

Harder, Anton. 'Not at the Cost of China: New Evidence regarding US Proposals to Nehru for Joining the United Nations Security Council'. Cold War International History Project (CWIHP) *Working Paper* Series, no. 76 (2015).

Hardiman, David. 'From Custom to Crime: The Politics of Drinking in Colonial South Gujarat'. In *Subaltern Studies IV: Writings on South Asian History and Society*, ed. Ranajit Guha. New Delhi: Oxford University Press, 1985, 165–228.

Harriss-White, Barbara. *India Working: Essays on Society and Economy*. Cambridge: Cambridge University Press, 2003.

Hasan, Mushirul. 'Indian Muslims since Independence: In Search of Integration and Identity'. *Third World Quarterly* 10, no. 2 (1988): 818–42.

Hasan, Mushirul. *Islam in the Subcontinent: Muslims in a Plural Society*. New Delhi: Manohar Publishers, 2002.

Hasan, Mushirul. *Legacy of a Divided Nation: India's Muslims from Independence to Ayodhya*. Boulder, CO: Westview Press, 1997.

Haynes, Douglas. 'The Making of the Hyper-Industrial City in Western India: The Transformation of Artisanal Towns into Middle-Sized Urban Centres, 1930–1970'. *South Asia: Journal of South Asian Studies* 36, no. 3 (2013): 336–53.

Herring, Ronald J. *Land to the Tiller: The Political Economy of Agrarian Reform in South Asia*. New Haven, CT: Yale University Press, 1983.

Huber, Toni. *The Holy Land Reborn: Pilgrimage and The Tibetan Reinvention of Buddhist India*. Chicago: University of Chicago Press, 2008.

Immerwahr, Daniel. *Thinking Small: The United States and the Lure of Community Development*. Cambridge, MA: Harvard University Press, 2015.

Jackson, Iain. 'Maxwell Fry and Jane Drew's Early Housing and Neighbourhood Planning in Sector-22 Chandigarh'. *Planning Perspectives* 28, no. 1 (2013): 1–28.

Jaffrelot, Christophe. *Dr Ambedkar and Untouchability: Analysing and Fighting Caste*. London: Hurst & Co., 2005.

Jaffrelot, Christophe. 'The Fate of Secularism in India'. In *The BJP in Power: Indian Democracy and Religious Nationalism*, ed. Milan Vaishnav. Washington, DC: Carnegie

Endowment of International Peace, 2019, available at https://carnegieendowment.org/2019/04/04/files/fate-of-secularism-in-india-pub-78689.

Jaffrelot, Christophe. *The Hindu Nationalist Movement in Indian Politics*. London: Hurst & Co., 1996.

Jaffrelot, Christophe. *India's Silent Revolution: The Rise of the Lower Castes in North India*. London: Hurst & Co, 2003.

Jaffrelot, Christophe. *Religion, Caste and Politics in India*. Delhi: Primus Books, 2010.

Jaffrelot, Christophe and Narender Kumar, eds. *Dr Ambedkar and Democracy: An Anthology*. New Delhi: Oxford University Press, 2018.

Jain, L. C. *The City of Hope: The Faridabad Story*. New Delhi: Concept Publishing Company, 1998.

Jalal, Ayesha. *The Sole Spokesman: Jinnah, the Muslim League and the Demand for Pakistan*. Cambridge: Cambridge University Press, 1985.

Jaoul, Nicolas. 'Learning the Use of Symbolic Means: Dalits, Ambedkar Statues and the State in Uttar Pradesh'. *Contributions to Indian Sociology* 40, no. 2 (2006): 175–207.

Jayal, Niraja Gopal. *Citizenship and its Discontents: An Indian History*. Cambridge, MA: Harvard University Press, 2013.

Jayal, Niraja Gopal. 'The State and Democracy in India or What Happened to Welfare, Secularism and Development'. In *Postcolonial India: History, Politics and Culture*, ed. Vinita Damodaran and Maya Unnithan-Kumar. New Delhi: Manohar Books, 2002, 95–124.

Jeffrey, Robin. 'Jawaharlal Nehru and the Smoking Gun: Who Pulled the Trigger on Kerala's Communist Government in 1959?'. *Journal of Commonwealth and Comparative Politics* 29, no. 1 (1991): 72–85.

Jha, Shefali. 'Democracy on a Minor Note: The All-India Majlis-e-Ittehād ul Muslimān and Its Hyderabadi Muslim Publics'. PhD dissertation, University of Chicago, 2017.

Kale, Sunila S. *Electrifying India: Regional Political Economies of Development*. Palo Alto, CA: Stanford University Press, 2014.

Kalia, Ravi. *Chandigarh: In Search of an Identity*. Carbondale, IL: Southern Illinois University Press, 1987.

Kalia, Ravi. 'Modernism, Modernization and Post-Colonial India: A Reflective Essay'. *Planning Perspectives* 21, no. 2 (2006): 133–56.

Kanjwal, Hafsa. 'Building a New Kashmir: Bakshi Ghulam Muhammad and the Politics of State-Formation in a Disputed Territory (1953–1963)'. PhD dissertation, University of Michigan, 2018.

Kapur, Geeta, *Contemporary Indian Artists*. New Delhi: Vikas, 1978.

Kapur, Geeta. *Modern Painting since 1935*. Oxford: Phaidon, 1981.

Karim, Farhan. *Of Greater Dignity than Riches: Austerity & Housing Design in India*. Pittsburgh: University of Pittsburgh Press, 2019.

Kaur, Ravinder. 'Narrative Absence: An "Untouchable" Account of Partition Migration'. *Contributions to Indian Sociology* 42, no. 2 (2008): 281–306.

Kaviraj, Sudipta. *The Enchantment of Democracy and India*. New Delhi: Permanent Black, 2011.

Kaviraj, Sudipta. *The Imaginary Institution of India: Politics and Ideas*. New York: Columbia University Press, 2010.

Kaviraj, Sudipta. *The Trajectories of the Indian State*. New Delhi: Permanent Black, 2010.

Keith, Ronald C. *The Diplomacy of Zhou Enlai*. New York: Palgrave Macmillan, 1989.

Kelly, John and Martha Kaplan. 'Diaspora and Swaraj, Swaraj and Diaspora'. In *From the Colonial to the Postcolonial: India and Pakistan in Transition*, ed. Dipesh Chakrabarty, Rochona Majumdar and Andrew Sartori. New Delhi: Oxford University Press India, 2007, 311–31.

Kennedy, Andrew Bingham. *The International Ambitions of Mao and Nehru: National Efficacy Beliefs and the Making of Foreign Policy*. Cambridge: Cambridge University Press, 2015.

Kesavan, Mukul. 'India's Embattled Secularism'. *The Wilson Quarterly* 27, no. 1 (2003): 61–67.

Khagram, Sanjeev. *Dams and Development: Transnational Struggles for Water and Power*. Ithaca, NY: Cornell University Press, 2004.

Khan, Raphaëlle. 'India's Search for Sovereignty: Independence and the International Order, 1919–1961'. PhD dissertation, Kings College London, 2017.

Khan, Raphaëlle and Taylor C. Sherman. 'India and Overseas Indians in Ceylon and Burma, 1946–1965: Experiments in Post-Imperial Sovereignty'. *Modern Asian Studies* (forthcoming).

Khan, Sulmaan Wasif. *Muslim, Trader, Nomad, Spy: China's Cold War and the People of the Tibetan Borderlands*. Chapel Hill, NC: University of North Carolina Press, 2015.

Khan, Yasmin. *The Great Partition: The Making of India and Pakistan*. New Haven, CT: Yale University Press, 2007.

Khan, Yasmin. 'Performing Peace: Gandhi's Assassination as a Critical Moment in the Consolidation of the Nehruvian Secular State'. *Modern Asian Studies* 45, no. 1 (2011): 57–80.

Khilnani, Sunil. *The Idea of India*. New York: Farrar, Strauss and Giroux, 2017.

Khilnani, Sunil. 'India's Democratic Career'. In *Democracy: The Unfinished Journey 508 BC to AD 1993*, ed. John Dunn. Oxford: Oxford University Press, 1992, 189–206.

Khilnani, Sunil, Rajiv Kumar, Pratap Bhanu Mehta, Prakash Menon, Nandan Nilekani, Srinath Raghavan, Shayam Saran and Siddarth Varadarajan. *Nonalignment 2.0: A Foreign & Strategic Policy for India in the 21st Century*. London: Penguin, 2013.

Khosla, Madhav. *India's Founding Moment: The Constitution of a Most Surprising Democracy*. Cambridge, MA: Harvard University Press, 2020.

Khullar, Sonal. *Worldly Affiliations: Artistic Practice, National Identity, and Modernism in India, 1930–1990*. Berkeley, CA: University of California Press, 2015.

Kirk, Jason A. *India and the World Bank: The Politics of Aid and Influence*. London: Anthem Press, 2010.

Kling, Blair B. 'Paternalism in Indian Labour: The Tata Iron and Steel Company of Jamshedpur'. *International Labour and Working Class History* 53 (1998): 69–87.

Klingensmith, Daniel. *'One Valley and a Thousand': Dams, Nationalism, and Development*. New Delhi: Oxford University Press, 2007.

Knaus, John Kenneth. *Beyond Shangri-La: America and Tibet's Move into the Twenty-First Century*. Durham, NC: Duke University Press, 2012.

Kohli, Atul, ed. *The Success of Indian Democracy*. Cambridge: Cambridge University Press, 2001.

Kohli, Atul. *Democracy and Discontent: India's Growing Crisis of Governability*. Cambridge: Cambridge University Press, 1990.

Komireddi, K. S. *Malevolent Republic*. London: C. Hurst & Co., 2019.

Kothari, Rajni. 'The Crisis of the Modern State and the Decline of Democracy'. In *Democracy in India*, ed. Niraja Gopal Jayal. New Delhi: Oxford University Press, 2001, 101–27.

Kudaisya, Medha. '"A Mighty Adventure": Institutionalising the Idea of Planning in Post-Colonial India, 1947–60'. *Modern Asian Studies* 43, no. 4 (2009): 939–78.

Kumar, Aishwary. *Radical Equality: Ambedkar, Gandhi and the Risk of Democracy*. Palo Alto, CA: Stanford University Press, 2015.

Kumari, Krittika. 'Society of Contemporary Artists, Kolkata, 1960', available at https://criticalcollective.in/ArtistGInner2.aspx?Aid=301&Eid=303.

Kurien, C. T. *Dynamics of Rural Transformation: A Study of Tamil Nadu, 1950–1975*. New Delhi: Orient Longman, 1981.

Lahiri, Nayanjot. *Marshalling the Past: Ancient India and its Modern Histories*. New Delhi: Permanent Black, 2012.

Lal, Priya. *African Socialism in Postcolonial Tanzania: Between the Village and the World*. Cambridge: Cambridge University Press, 2015.

Lawrence, Mark. 'The Rise and Fall of Nonalignment'. In *The Cold War in the Third World*, ed. Robert J. McMahon. Oxford: Oxford University Press, 2013, 139–55.

Laxman, R. K. *Brushing up the Years: A Cartoonist's History of India, 1947–2004*. New Delhi: Penguin Viking, 2005.

Leese, David. *Mao Cult: Rhetoric and Ritual in China's Cultural Revolution*. Cambridge: Cambridge University Press, 2011.

Loveridge, Jack. 'Between Hunger and Growth: Pursuing Rural Development in Partition's Aftermath, 1947–1957'. *Contemporary South Asia* 25, no. 1 (2017): 56–59.

Lynch, Owen M. *The Politics of Untouchability: Social Mobility and Social Change in a City of India*. New York: Columbia University Press, 1969.

Madan, T. D. 'Secularism in Its Place'. *The Journal of Asian Studies* 46, no. 4 (1987): 747–59.

Madsen, Chris. 'The Long Goodbye: British Agency in the Creation of Navies for India and Pakistan'. *Journal of Imperial and Commonwealth Studies* 54, no. 3 (2014): 463–48.

Mago, Pran Nath. 'Delhi Silpi Chakra', excerpted from Pran Nath Mago, *Contemporary Art in India: A Perspective*. New Delhi: National Book Trust, 2001, 71–73; available at https://criticalcollective.in/ArtistGInner2.aspx?Aid=224&Eid=199#Essay_Title224.

Manikumar, K. A. *Murder in Mudukulathur: Caste and Electoral Politics in Tamil Nadu*. New Delhi: LeftWord Books, 2017.

Marston, Daniel P. 'The Indian Army, Partition and the Punjab Boundary Force, 1945–47'. *War in History* 16, no. 4 (2009): 469–505.

McCartney, Matthew. *India: The Political Economy of Growth, Stagnation and the State, 1951–2007*. Abingdon: Routledge, 2009.

McGarr, Paul. *The Cold War in South Asia: Britain, the United States and the Indian Subcontinent, 1945–65*. Cambridge: Cambridge University Press, 2013.

McGarr, Paul. '"India's Rasputin"?: V. K. Krishna Menon and Anglo-American Misperceptions of Indian Foreign Policymaking, 1947–1964'. *Diplomacy & Statecraft* 22, no. 2 (2011): 239–60.

McGranahan, Carole. *Arrested Histories: Tibet, the CIA, and Memories of a Forgotten War*. Durham, NC: Duke University Press, 2010.

Mehra, Diya. 'Planning Delhi ca. 1936-1959'. *South Asia: Journal of South Asian Studies* 36, no. 3 (2013), 354-74.

Mehta, Uday Singh. 'Indian Constitutionalism: The Articulation of a Political Vision'. In *From the Colonial to the Postcolonial: India and Pakistan in Transition*, ed. Dipesh Chakrabarty, Rochona Majumdar and Andrew Sartori. New Delhi: Oxford University Press India, 2007, 13-30.

Menon, Nikhil. 'Battling the Bottle: Experiments in Regulating Drink in Late Colonial Madras'. *Indian Economic and Social History Review* 52, no. 1 (2015): 29-51.

Menon, Nikhil. '"Help the Plan—Help Yourself": Making Indians Plan-Conscious'. In *The Postcolonial Moment in South and Southeast Asia*, ed. Gyan Prakash, Michael Laffan and Nikhil Menon. London: Bloomsbury, 2018, 221-42.

Menon, Nikhil, *Planning Democracy: Modern India's Quest for Development*. Cambridge: Cambridge University Press, 2022.

Menon, Ritu and Kamla Bhasin. *Borders and Boundaries: Women in India's Partition*. Delhi: Kali for Women, 1998.

Mialet, Hélène. *Hawking Incorporated: Stephen Hawking and the Anthropology of the Knowing Subject*. Chicago: University of Chicago Press, 2012.

Mišković, Nataša. 'Introduction'. In *The Non-Aligned Movement and the Cold War: Delhi—Bandung—Belgrade*, ed. Nataša Mišković, Harald Fischer-Tiné and Nada Boškovska. Abingdon: Routledge, 2014, 1-18.

Misra, Maria. *Business, Race and Politics in British India, c. 1850-1960*. Oxford: Oxford University Press, 1999.

Mitchell, Timothy. 'Society, Economy and the State Effect'. In *State/Culture: State-formation after the Cultural Turn*, ed. George Steinmetz. Ithaca, NY: Cornell University Press, 1999, 76-97.

Mitter, Partha. 'Decentering Modernism: Art History and Avant-Garde Art from the Periphery'. *The Art Bulletin* 90, no. 4 (2008): 531-48.

Mukerjee, Hiren. *The Gentle Colossus: A Study of Jawaharlal Nehru*. New Delhi: Oxford University Press, 1988.

Mukherji, Rahul. 'The State, Economic Growth and Development in India'. *India Review* 8, no. 1 (2009): 81-106.

Nair, Neeti. *Changing Homelands: Hindu Politics and the Partition of India*. Cambridge, MA: Harvard University Press, 2011.

Nanda, B. R. *Jawaharlal Nehru: Rebel and Statesman*. New Delhi: Oxford University Press, 1995.

Nandy, Ashis. 'Closing the Debate on Secularism: A Personal Statement'. In Needham and Sunder Rajan, eds, *Crisis in Secularism*, 107-17.

Nandy, Ashis. 'Federalism, the Ideology of the State and Cultural Pluralism'. In *Federalism in India: Origins and Development*, ed. N. Mukarji and Balveer Arora. New Delhi: Vikas Publishing House, 1992, 33-56.

Naseemullah, Adnan. 'Patronage vs. Ideology in Indian politics'. *Commonwealth & Comparative Politics* 59, no. 2 (2021): 193-214.

Nath, Maanik. 'Do Institutional Transplants Succeed? Regulating Raiffeisen Cooperatives in South India, 1930-1960'. *Business History Review* 95, no. 1 (2021): 59-85.

Nayudu, Swapna Kona. 'The Nehru Years: Indian Non-Alignment as the Critique, Discourse and Practice of Security, 1947–1964'. PhD dissertation, Kings College London, 2015.

Nayudu, Swapna Kona. '"India Looks at the World": Nehru, the Indian Foreign Service and World Diplomacy'. *Diplomatica* 2 (2020): 100–117.

Nayudu, Swapna Kona. 'The Soviet Peace Offensive and Nehru's India, 1953–1956'. In *India and the Cold War*, ed. Manu Bhagavan. Chapel Hill, NC: University of North Carolina Press, 2019, 36–56.

Needham, Anuradha Dingwaney and Rajeswari Sundar Rajan, eds, *The Crisis of Secularism in India*. New Delhi: Permanent Black, 2007.

Needham, Anuradha Dingwaney and Rajeswari Sundar Rajan. 'Introduction'. In Needham and Sunder Rajan, eds, *Crisis in Secularism*, 1–42.

Newbigin, Eleanor. 'Accounting for the Nation, Marginalizing the Empire: Taxable Capacity and Colonial Rule in the Early Twentieth Century'. *History of Political Economy* 52, no. 3 (2020): 455–72.

Newbigin, Eleanor. 'The Codification of Personal Law and Secular Citizenship: Revisiting the History of Law Reform in Late Colonial India'. *Indian Economic and Social History Review* 46, no. 1 (2009): 84–104.

Newbigin, Eleanor. *The Hindu Family and the Emergence of Modern India: Law, Citizenship and Community*. Cambridge: Cambridge University Press, 2013.

Niclas-Tolle, Boris. *The Socialist Opposition in Nehruvian India, 1947–64*. Frankfurt: Peter Lang, 2015.

Nigam, Aditya. *The Insurrection of the Little Selves: The Crisis of Secular-Nationalism in India*. New Delhi, Oxford University Press, 2006.

Noorani, A .G. *Article 370: A Constitutional History of Jammu and Kashmir*. New Delhi: Oxford University Press, 2011.

Noorani, A. G. 'The Babri Masjid–Ram Janmabhoomi Question'. *Economic and Political Weekly* 24, nos 44–45 (1989): 2461–66.

Ober, Douglas. 'From Buddha Bones to Bo Trees: Nehruvian India, Buddhism and the Poetics of Power'. *Modern Asian Studies* 53, no. 4 (2019): 1312–50.

Omvedt, Gail. 'Women and Rural Revolt in India'. *Social Scientist* 6, no. 1 (1977): 1–18.

Paik, Shailaja. *Dalit Women's Education in Modern India: Double Discrimination*. London, Routledge, 2014.

Pandey, Gyanendra. *The Construction of Communalism in Colonial North India*. New Delhi: Oxford University Press, 1990.

Pandey, Gyanendra. '"Nobody's People": The Dalits of Punjab in the Forced Removal of 1947'. In *Removing Peoples: Forced Removal in the Modern World*, ed. Richard Bessel and Claudia B. Haake. Oxford: Oxford University Press, 2009, 297–319.

Parekh, Bhikhu. 'Jawaharlal Nehru and the Crisis of Modernisation'. In *Crisis and Change in Contemporary India*, ed. Upendra Baxi and Bhikhu Parekh. London: Sage, 1995, 21–56.

Plamper, Jan. *The Stalin Cult: A Study in the Alchemy of Power*. New Haven, CT: Yale University Press, 2012.

Pomeranz, Kenneth. *The Great Divergence: China, Europe and the Making of the Modern World Economy*. Princeton, NJ: Princeton University Press, 2000.

Prakash, Gyan. 'Anxious Constitution-Making'. In *The Postcolonial Moment in South and Southeast Asia*, ed. Gyan Prakash, Michael Laffan and Nikhil Menon. London: Bloomsbury, 2018, 145-55.

Prakash, Vikramadiyta. *Chandigarh's Le Corbusier: The Struggle for Modernity in Postcolonial India*. Seattle: University of Washington Press, 2002.

Raghavan, Pallavi. *Animosity at Bay: An Alternative History of the India-Pakistan Relationship*. New Delhi: Oxford University Press, 2020.

Raghavan, Pallavi. 'The Finality of Partition: Bilateral Relations between India and Pakistan, 1947-57.' PhD dissertation, University of Cambridge, 2012.

Raghavan, Pallavi. 'The Making of South Asia's Minorities: A Diplomatic History, 1947-52'. *Economic and Political Weekly* 51, no. 21 (2016): 45-52.

Raghavan, Srinath. 'A Missed Opportunity?: The Nehru-Zhou Enlai Summit of 1960'. In *India and the Cold War*, ed. Manu Bhagavan. Chapel Hill, NC: University of North Carolina Press, 2019, 100-125.

Raghavan, Srinath. *War and Peace in Modern India*. Basingstoke: Palgrave Macmillan, 2010.

Raianu, Mircea. *Tata: The Global Corporation that Built Indian Capitalism*. Cambridge, MA: Harvard University Press, 2021.

Rajgotra, Maharajahkrishna. *A Life in Diplomacy*. New Delhi: Penguin India, 2016.

Ramesh, Jairam. *A Chequered Brilliance: The Many Lives of V. K. Krishna Menon*. New Delhi: Penguin Random House India, 2019.

Ramesh, Jairam. *To the Brink and Back: India's 1991 Story*. New Delhi: Rupa Publications, 2015.

Rao, Anupama. *The Caste Question: Dalits and the Politics of Modern India*. Berkeley, CA: University of California Press, 2009.

Rawat, Ramnarayan. 'Making Claims for Power: A New Agenda in Dalit Politics of Uttar Pradesh, 1946-48'. *Modern Asian Studies* 37, no. 3 (2003): 585-612.

Rawat, Ramnarayan. *Reconsidering Untouchability: Chamars and Dalit History in North India*. Bloomington, IN: University of Indiana Press, 2011.

Robinson, Francis. *Jamal Mian: The Life of Maulana Jamaluddin Abdul Wahab of Farangi Mahall, 1919-2012*. Karachi: Oxford University Press, 2018.

Rook-Koepsel, Emily. *Democracy and Unity in India: Understanding the All-India Phenomenon*. Abingdon: Routledge, 2019.

Roy, Anupama. *Mapping Citizenship in India*. New Delhi: Oxford University Press, 2010.

Roy, Haimanti. *Partitioned Lives: Migrants, Refugees, Citizens in India and Pakistan, 1947-1965*. New Delhi: Oxford University Press, 2012.

Roy, Srirupa. *Beyond Belief: India and the Politics of Postcolonial Nationalism*. New Delhi: Permament Black, 2007.

Roy, Srirupa. 'Moving Pictures: The Postcolonial State and Visual Representations of India'. *Contributions to Indian Sociology* 36, nos 1-2 (2002): 234-63.

Roy, Srirupa. 'Nehruvian'. In *Key Concepts in Modern Indian Studies*, ed. Gita Dharampal-Frick, Monika Kirloskar-Steinbach, Rachel Dwyer and Jahnavi Phalkey. New Delhi: Oxford University Press, 2015, 190-93.

Roy, Tirthankar. *India in the World Economy: From Antiquity to the Present*. Cambridge: Cambridge University Press, 2012.

Sackley, Nicole. 'The Road from Serfdom: Economic Storytelling and Narratives of India in the Rise of Neoliberalism'. *History and Technology* 31, no. 4 (2015): 397–419.

Sackley, Nicole. 'Village Models: Etawah, India, and the Making and Remaking of Development in the Early Cold War'. *Diplomatic History* 37, no. 4 (2013): 749–78.

Saha, Madhumita. 'Food for Soil, Food for People: Research on Food Crops, Fertilizers, and the Making of "Modern" Indian Agriculture'. *Technology and Culture* 54, no. 2 (2013): 289–316.

Sanchez-Sibony, Oscar. *Red Globalization: The Political Economy of the Soviet Cold War from Stalin to Khrushchev*. Cambridge: Cambridge University Press, 2014.

Sarkar, Jayita. '"Wean Them Away from French Tutelage": Franco-Indian Nuclear Relations and Anglo-American Anxieties during the Early Cold War, 1948–1952'. *Cold War History* 15, no. 3 (2015): 375–94.

Sarkar, Sumit. 'Indian Democracy: The Historical Inheritance'. In *The Success of Indian Democracy*, ed. Atul Kohli. Cambridge: Cambridge University Press, 2001, 23–46.

Sarkar, Tanika. 'Enfranchised Selves: Women, Culture and Rights in Nineteenth-Century Bengal'. *Gender & History* 13, no. 3 (2001): 546–65.

Scott, James C. *Seeing Like a State: How Certain Schemes to Improve the Human Condition Have Failed*. New Haven, CT: Yale University Press, 1998.

Seal, Anil. 'Imperialism and Nationalism in India'. In *Locality, Province and Nation: Essays on Indian Politics 1870–1940*, ed. John Gallagher, Gordon Johnson and Anil Seal. Cambridge: Cambridge University Press, 1973, 1–27.

Segrave, Kerry. *American Films Abroad: Hollywood's Domination of the World's Movie Screens from the 1890s to the Present*. Jefferson, NC: McFarland & Company, 1997.

Sen, Dwaipayan. *The Decline of the Caste Question: Jogendranath Mandal and the Defeat of Dalit Politics in Bengal*. Cambridge: Cambridge University Press, 2018.

Sen, Uditi. 'The Myths Refugees Live By: Memory and History in the Making of Bengali Refugee Identity'. *Modern Asian Studies* 48, no. 1 (2014): 37–76.

Sen, Uditi. 'Social Work, Refugees and National Belonging: Evaluating the "Lady Social Workers" of West Bengal'. *South Asia: Journal of South Asian Studies* 44, no. 2 (2021): 344–61.

Shaikh, Juned. *Outcaste Bombay: City Making and the Politics of the Poor*. Seattle: University of Washington Press, 2021.

Shani, Ornit. *How India Became Democratic*. Cambridge: Cambridge University Press, 2018.

Shankar, Mahesh. 'Nehru's Legacy: Why a Plebiscite Never Happened.' *India Review* 15, no. 1 (2016): 1–21.

Shankar, Mahesh. 'Showing Character: Nehru, Reputation, and the Sino-Indian Dispute, 1957–1962'. *Asian Security* 11, no. 2 (2015): 99–115.

Sharma, Shalini. '"Yeh Azaadi Jhooti Hai": The Shaping of the Opposition in the First Year of the Congress Raj'. *Modern Asian Studies* 48, no. 5 (2014): 1358–88.

Sharma, Subhash Chandra. *Indo-Soviet Trade since Independence*. New Delhi: Radha Publications, 1992.

Shaw, Annapurna. 'Town Planning in Postcolonial India, 1947–65: Chandigarh Re-Examined.' *Urban Geography* 30, no. 8 (2013): 857–78.

Sherman, Taylor C. 'Education in Early Postcolonial India: Expansion, Experimentation and Planned Self-Help'. *History of Education* 47, no. 4 (2018): 504–20.

Sherman, Taylor C. 'From "Grow More Food" to "Miss a Meal": Hunger, Development and the Limits of Postcolonial Nationalism in India, 1947-1957'. *South Asia: Journal of South Asian Studies* 36, no. 4 (2013): 571-88.
Sherman, Taylor C. 'A Gandhian Answer to the Threat of Communism? Sarvodaya and Postcolonial Nationalism in India'. *Indian Economic and Social History Review* 53, no. 2 (2016): 249-70.
Sherman, Taylor C. 'Migration, Citizenship and Belonging in Hyderabad (Deccan), 1948-56.' *Modern Asian Studies* 45, no. 1 (2011): 81-107.
Sherman, Taylor C. *Muslim Belonging in Secular India: Negotiating Citizenship in Postcolonial Hyderabad*. Cambridge: Cambridge University Press, 2015.
Sherman, Taylor C. '"A New Type of Revolution": Socialist Thought in India, c. 1930s-1960s'. *Postcolonial Studies* 21, no. 4 (2018): 485-504.
Sherman, Taylor C. 'Not Part of the Plan? Women, State Feminism and Indian Socialism in the Nehru Years'. *South Asia: Journal of South Asian Studies* 44, no. 2 (2021): 298-312.
Sherman, Taylor C. *State Violence and Punishment in India*. London: Routledge, 2010.
Sidhu, Waheguru Pal Singh. 'The Accidental Global Peacekeeper'. In *India and the Cold War*, ed. Manu Bhagavan. Chapel Hill, NC: University of North Carolina Press, 2019, 79-99.
Siegel, Benjamin. *Hungry Nation: Food, Famine and the Making of Modern India*. Cambridge; Cambridge University Press, 2018.
Siegel, Benjamin. 'The Kibbutz and the Ashram: Sarvodaya Agriculture, Israeli Aid, and the Global Imaginaries of Indian Development'. *American Historical Review* 125, no. 4 (2020): 1175-204.
Siegel, Benjamin. 'Modernizing Peasants and "Master Farmers": Progressive Agriculture in Early Independent India'. *Comparative Studies of South Asia, Africa and the Middle East* 37, no. 1 (2017): 64-85.
Siegel, Benjamin. '"The World Has Changed": Development, Land Reform, and the Ethical Work of India's Independence'. In *The Postcolonial Moment in South and Southeast Asia*, ed. Gyan Prakash, Michael Laffan and Nikhil Menon. London: Bloomsbury, 2018, 201-19.
Singh, Ujjwal Kumar and Anupama Rao. *Election Commission of India: Institutionalising Democratic Uncertainties*. New Delhi: Oxford University Press, 2019.
Sisson, Richard, and Stanley Wolpert, eds. *Congress and Indian Nationalism: The Pre-Independence Phase*. Berkeley: University of California Press, 1988.
Sitapari, Vinay. *Half Lion: How P. V. Nirasimha Rao Transformed India*. New Delhi: Penguin Random House India, 2016.
Skaria, Ajay. 'Ambedkar, Marx and the Buddhist Question'. *South Asia: Journal of South Asian Studies* 38, no. 3 (2015): 450-65.
Skaria, Ajay. 'Gandhi's Politics: Liberalism and the Question of the Ashram'. *South Asia Quarterly* 101, no. 4 (2002): 955-86.
Sridharan, Eswaran and Milan Vaishnav. 'Political Finance in a Developing Democracy: The Case of India'. In *Costs of Democracy: Political Finance in India*, ed. Devesh Kapur and Milan Vaishnav. New Delhi: Oxford University Press, 2018, 15-35.
Srinivasan, T. N., ed. *The Future of Secularism*. New Delhi: Oxford University Press, 2006.

Subramanian, Ajantha. *Shorelines: Space and Rights in South India*. Palo Alto, CA: Stanford University Press, 2009.
Sunderason, Sanjukta. *Partisan Aesthetics: Modern Art & India's Long Decolonization*. Palo Alto, CA: Stanford University Press, 2020.
Sutton, Deborah. 'Divided and Uncertain Loyalties: Partition, Indian Sovereignty and Contested Citizenship in East Africa, 1948-1955'. *Interventions* 9, no. 2 (2007): 276-88.
Tan, Tai Yong. 'Sir Cyril Goes to India: Partition, Boundary-Making and Disruptions in the Punjab'. *International Journal of Punjab Studies* 4, no. 1 (1997): 1-20.
Tansky, Leo. *US and USSR Aid to Developing Countries: A Comparative Study of India, Turkey and the UAR*. New York: Frederick A Praeger Publishers, 1967.
Tejani, Shabnum. 'Defining Secularism in the Particular: Caste and Citizenship in India, 1909-1950'. *Politics and Religion* 6 (2013): 703-29.
Tejani, Shabnum. *Indian Secularism: A Social and Intellectual History*. New Delhi: Permanent Black, 2007.
Thakur, Vineet. 'India's Diplomatic Entrepreneurism: Revisiting India's Role in the Korean Crisis, 1950-52'. *China Report* 29, no. 3 (2013): 273-98.
Thatra, Geeta. 'Dalit Chembur: Spatializing the Caste Question in Bombay, c. 1920s-1970s'. *Journal of Urban History* 28 (2020): 1-35.
Thomas, Sonja. *Privileged Minorities: Syrian Christianity, Gender and Minority Rights in Postcolonial India*. Seattle: University of Washington Press, 2018.
'Throwing Out Nehru'. BBC Radio 4, 20 August 2017. Available in the UK to account holders at https://learningonscreen.ac.uk/ondemand/index.php/prog/0F68C48A?bcast=124849888.
Tomlinson, B. R. *The Economy of Modern India, 1860-1970* (The New Cambridge History of India, vol 3.3). Cambridge: Cambridge University Press, 1993.
Tyabji, Nasir. *Forging Capitalism in Nehru's India: Neocolonialism and the State, c. 1940-1970*. New Delhi: Oxford University Press, 2015.
Vahed, Goolam. '"Nehru is just another coolie": India and South Africa at the United Nations, 1946-55'. *Alternation* 15 (2015): 54-84.
Varshney, Ashutosh. *Democracy, Development and the Countryside: Urban-Rural Struggles in India*. Cambridge: Cambridge University Press, 1995.
Varshney, Ashutosh. 'India Defies the Odds: Why Democracy Survives'. *Journal of Democracy* 9, no. 3 (1998): 36-50.
Vittorini, Simona. 'Two Bullocks, a Ladder and a Lamp: Electoral Symbols in Nehruvian India'. *Nations and Nationalism* 20, no. 2 (2014): 297-316.
Wakeman, Rosemary. *Practicing Utopia: An Intellectual History of the New Town Movement*. Chicago: University of Chicago Press, 2016.
Waterbury, John. 'The Long Gestation and Brief Triumph of Import-Substituting Industrialization'. *World Development* 27, no. 2, (1999) 323-41.
Waterlow, Jonathan. *It's Only a Joke, Comrade!: Humour, Trust and Everyday Life under Stalin*. Oxford: CreateSpace Independent Publishing Platform, 2018.
Westad, Odd Arne. *The Cold War: A World History*. London: Allen Lane, 2017.
Westad, Odd Arne. *The Global Cold War: Third World Interventions and the Making of Our Times*. Cambridge: Cambridge University Press, 2005.
Wilkinson, Tom. 'Youth Movements and Mobilisations in India, c. 1930-1970', PhD dissertation, London School of Economics, forthcoming.

Wood, Sally Percival. 'Constructing an Alternative Regional Identity: *Panchsheel* and India-China Diplomacy at the Asian-African Conference 1955'. In *Alterities in Asia, Reflections on Identity and Regionalism*, ed. Leong Yew. Abingdon: Routledge, 2011, 46–64.

Zachariah, Benjamin. *Developing India: An Intellectual and Social History, c. 1930–50*. New Delhi: Oxford University Press, 2005.

Zacharia, Benjamin. *Nehru*. London: Routledge, 2004.

Zamindar, Vazira Fazila-Yacoobali. *The Long Partition and the Making of Modern South Asia: Refugees, Boundaries, Histories*. New York: Columbia University Press, 2007.

Zelliot, Eleanor. 'Congress and the Untouchables, 1917–1950'. In *Congress and Indian Nationalism: The Pre-Independence Phase*, ed. Richard Sisson and Stanley Wolpert. Berkeley, CA: University of California Press, 1988, 182–97.

Zelliot, Eleanor. 'Understanding Dr B. R. Ambedkar'. *Religion Compass* 2, no. 5 (2008): 808–18.

INDEX

Abdullah, Sheikh, 14, 48–50, 106, 165
Abraham, C. E., 168
Adivasis, 152, 186, 187
administrative reforms committee, Kerala, 167
Afghans, 63
Ahmedabad, 132
Ajanta, 53, 65
Akademie de Bildenden Künste, 201
Aksai Chin plateau, 40, 45
Ali, Asaf, 33, 59
Aligarh, 171
Aligarh Muslim University, 67
Allahabad, 1
All India Cooperative Union, 94, 129
All-India Cow Protection Committee, 163
All-India Jamaat-e-Islami, 70
All India Radio, 11, 17, 164, 170
All-India Scheduled Castes Federation, 155
Alva, Violet, 80
Alvares, Peter, 139
Alwar, 63
Amaravati, 58
Ambedkar, Bhimrao Ramji, 3, 55, 73–74, 81, 121, 147–148, 150–156, 163
Amritsar, 65, 80
Andhra Mahila Sabha, 125
Andhra Pradesh, 159
Anglo-Indians, 124
Appasamy, Jaya, 201–202
Appleby, Paul, 130
Arabs, 63, 183
Archaeological Survey of India, 53
Arumugam, R. S., 79–80
Arunachal Pradesh, 25, 40–41
Aryanayakam, Asha Devi, 94
Asansol, 101
Ashoka (emperor), 53, 73, 201
Asian Institute for Economic Development and Planning, 128
Assam, 44, 71, 106, 107, 145, 171
Assam Rifles, 44
Attlee, Clement, 123
Aundh, 35

Ayodhya, 56, 68
Azad, Abul Kalam, 6, 59, 60, 67, 69, 71, 120, 197–198

Babri Masjid, 56, 68
Bahujan Samaj Party, 158
Baij, Ramkinkar, 197
Bandaranaike, S.W.R.D., 169
Bandung Conference, 35, 40
Bangalore, 27
Bangkok, 128
Banihal, 50–51
basic education, 67, 94
Benares, 107
Benegal, Shyam, 1–3
Bengal famine, 104, 126, 182, 210
Bengali, 171
Bhabha, Homi J., 34
Bhagalpur, 99, 104
Bhagavad Gita, 108
Bhaktavatsalam, M., 80
Bharatiya Janata Party, 12, 56, 146
Bhatnagar, Shanti Swarup, 180
Bhatt, Jyoti Manshankar, 199
Bhattacharjea, Ajit, 158
Bhave, Vinoba, 107–109
Bhilai, 30, 85
Bhoodan, 89, 107–109, 169
Bhopal, 53, 58
Bhupnagar, 109
Bhutan, 41
bicycles, 94, 101–103
Big Landed Estates Abolition Act, Jammu and Kashmir, 106
Bihar, 53, 58, 99, 104, 109, 128, 132, 135, 173, 182, 186–187
Biharis, 38
Bijapur, 65
Bilaspur, 77
Birla Institute of Technology and Science, 176, 178
Bodh Gaya, 53–54
Bombay (city), 7, 21, 28, 61, 74, 95, 135, 150, 153–154, 165, 190

Bombay (state), 81, 91, 110, 128, 129, 132–133, 136–141, 158, 171
Bombay Plan, 95
Bombay Prohibition Act, 137–141
Bombay State Prohibition Board, 137, 138
Bosch, 27
Bose, Nandalal, 197
Boundary Disputes Tribunal, 46
Bretton Woods, 34
Britain, 1, 17, 25–27, 47, 183, 189, 206
British Empire, 22, 25, 33, 35, 51, 206
Buddha Jayanti, 53–54, 58, 73, 74, 77, 199
Buddhism, 40, 53–54, 56, 58, 65, 73, 74, 155
Burdwan, 186
Burma, 36–39, 44, 53, 54, 62, 169, 195

Cabinet Mission, 120
Calcutta, 43, 54, 68, 80, 100, 101, 132, 162, 186, 200, 201
Cambodia, 54, 185
Capital Complex, Chandigarh, 189
Cariappa, K. M., 25–26
Central Social Welfare Board, 14, 124–129
Central Water and Power Commission, 182, 183
Centre of Developing Studies, 19
Ceylon, 36–39, 54, 61, 62, 169, 195
Ceylon Indian Congress, 37–38
Chacko, P. T., 172
Chakravartty, Renu, 157, 160
Chandigarh, 177, 181, 188–194
Chattopadhyay, Kamaladevi, 34, 93, 94
Chavan, Y. B., 74
Chhattisgarh, 85
China, People's Republic of, 5, 31, 33, 39–45, 51, 168, 201
Chinese Communist Party, 40, 42, 43
Chingleput, 157
Chittaranjan Locomotives, 131
Chittorgarh, 65
Chola Temple, 65
Chowdhury, D. P. Roy, 198
Chowdhury, Urmila Eulie, 192, 193, 196
Christianity, 56, 65
Christians, 59, 81, 168
citizenship, 36–38, 47, 62–63, 208
Citizenship Act (1955), 63
Clark, T. J., 202–203
Coca-Cola, 28
Cold War, 17, 22, 23, 25–30, 31, 32, 35, 40, 51, 87, 206, 207, 209

collective fines, 139–140, 142
Colombo Plan, 28
Commonwealth, 26, 28, 149
communal riots, 71, 171
communism, 22, 88, 97
Communist Party of India, 6, 44, 165–169, 174
communists, 6, 29, 44, 108, 165–169, 174
Community Development, 50, 89, 91, 110–116, 117, 124, 128, 171, 187
Companies Act (1956), 160
Congrès Internationaux d'Architecture Moderne, 188
Congress Party, 1, 3, 6, 7–9, 11–12, 13, 15, 16, 31, 34, 37, 44, 46, 48, 54–55, 56–57, 59, 61, 67, 70–71, 72, 73, 77, 86, 87, 95, 96, 107, 120, 124, 135, 137, 141, 145, 146, 148, 150, 151, 152, 155, 156, 157, 158, 159–162, 163–165, 166, 167, 168, 169, 170, 172, 183, 212
Congress Socialist Party, 86, 169
Constituent Assembly (Jammu and Kashmir), 48–49
Constituent Assembly of India, 41, 70, 73, 75, 121, 148, 151, 152, 174, 186
Constitution of India, 2, 45, 49–50, 55, 58, 62–63, 64, 65, 70, 71, 72–73, 74–75, 76, 77, 81, 82, 112, 114, 121, 122, 125, 137, 141–143, 146, 147, 148, 149, 150, 151–152, 153, 155, 165, 170, 174, 175, 208, 210, 211, 213
cooperatives, 34, 93, 94, 105, 108, 112, 113–114, 116, 126, 130, 133
corruption, 14, 18, 49, 64, 136, 158–163
Council on Scientific and Industrial Research, 180
Curie, Marie, 178

Dalai Lama, 42–43
Dalits, 55, 56, 57, 59, 70, 72–81, 82, 100–101, 107, 115, 121, 146, 150–158, 191, 195, 207–208, 209, 211. *See also* Scheduled Castes
Damodar Valley Corporation, 124, 127, 130, 177, 182–188
Dange, S. A., 165
Dangleput District, 115
Darivala, J. C., 138
Das, B. C., 164
Das, Mono Mohan, 75
Das, Ram, 78

Das, S. K., 162
Datar, B. N., 77
Dayal, Harishwal, 42
Delhi School of Economics, 93
Delhi Silpi Chakra, 200, 201
Democratic Research Service, 168
Deo, Shankarrao, 90
Desai, Morarji, 139
Deshmukh, Chintaman Dwarkanath, 125
Deshmukh, Durgabai, 14, 125, 167
Devi, Nalini, 35
Dewey, John, 147
Dey, S. K., 14, 110–113, 115–116, 167
Dhebar, U. N., 7, 165–166
Dravida Munnetra Kazhagam, 172
Drew, Jane, 190–193
Durbin, E.F.M., 129

East Africa, 35, 42, 63
Economic and Political Weekly, 136
Economic and Social Commission for Asia and the Far East, 34
Economic and Social Council, 34
Economic Weekly, 9, 18, 19
education, 29, 35, 65, 67, 72, 74, 77, 78, 81, 82, 88–89, 98, 99, 100, 114–115, 137, 139, 141, 149, 150, 155, 156, 166, 168–169, 171, 173–174, 206, 211
Election Commission, 49, 145–147, 154, 159, 174, 211
Engineering Research Laboratories, 194–195
English language, 21, 103, 142, 181, 197
Etawah, 92

Faridabad, 89, 92–95, 101, 111
Federal Republic of Germany, 27, 28, 93, 201, 206
Federation of Indian Chambers of Commerce and Industry, 97
Festival of Soviet Films, 21–22
Fiji, 36
Filmfare Awards, 61
Films Division of India, 1–4
First World War, 26
floods, 182, 186
Ford Foundation, 91, 110, 116, 130
France, 26, 54
Friedman, Milton, 86
Fry, Maxwell, 190–191

Gadgil, Narhar Vishnu, 123, 186
Gaikwad, Bhaurao Krishnaji (Dadasaheb), 81
Gandhi, Indira, 1, 3, 11–12, 146, 158, 162, 163, 169
Gandhi, Mohandas Karamchand (Mahatma), 1, 3, 5, 7, 19, 73, 74, 78, 95, 108, 109, 120–121, 124, 137, 152, 179–180, 183, 185
Ganjam South, 164
Gardner, Ava, 21
Gaya, 109, 132
Geddes, Patrick, 189
General Post Office, 10
Ghana, 185
Ghosh, Sudhir, 92–94, 111, 128
Giri, V. V., 37
Goa, 54
Gokhale Institute of Politics, 172
Golden Temple, 65
Gol Gumbaz, 65
Gopal, Sarvepalli, 4
Gorwala, A. D., 129–130
Government of India Act (1935), 148
Granger, Stewart, 21
Grow More Food, 104–105
Gujarat, 56, 65, 81, 110, 112, 132, 141, 142, 171
Gujarat University, 169
Guomindang, 40, 41
Gupta, B. M., 75

Hanumanthaiya, Kengal, 96
Harijans. *See* Dalits
Hayek, Friedrich von, 86
Hazari, R. K., 135–136
Himachal Pradesh, 145
Himalayas, 43
Hindi, 77, 99, 160
Hindu Code Bill, 151
Hindu Mahasabha, 6, 55
Hindu nationalism, 55–56, 68, 146
Hindus, 17, 47, 48, 59, 67, 72–81, 153–154, 178, 208
Hindustan Antibiotics, 131
Hindustan Steel, 103
Hoshiyarpur-Rachit, 78
Husain, M. F., 61, 199
Husain, Zakir, 59, 67, 123, 173
Hussain, Syud, 59
Hydari, Akbar, 59, 61
Hyderabad, 16, 48, 63–64, 65, 67–68, 69, 70, 71, 107–108, 164, 194

INDEX

Ibrahim, Hafiz Mohammad, 186
Income Tax Investigation Commission, 97–98
India House, London, 9
Indian Administrative Service, 49, 122–124
Indian Air Force, 26
Indian Army, 25–26, 44
Indian Civil Service, 63–64
Indian Committee for Cultural Freedom, 17
Indian Council of Architecture, 192
Indian Foreign Service, 24
Indian Institute for Public Administration, 120, 123
Indian Institute of Public Opinion, 6
Indian Journal of Political Science, 154
Indian Journal of Public Administration, 123
Indian Merchants Chamber, 96
Indian National Congress. *See* Congress Party
Indian Navy, 26
Indian Penal Code, 156, 173
Indian Police Service, 49
Industrial Development (Regulation) Bill, 134–136
Industrial Finance Corporation, 124
industrialisation, 16, 90, 91, 95–96, 104, 129–130, 134–136, 166
Intelligence Bureau, 42, 50
Intensive Agricultural Area Programme, 116
International Bank of Reconstruction and Development, 28
International Labour Organization, 34
Islam, 56
Italy, 28

Jabalpur, 71, 171
Jaffrey, Saeed, 1
Jainism, 65
Jaipur House, 198
Jallianwala Bagh, 80
Jamia Millia Islamia, 67
Jamiatul Ulama, 68, 70
Jammu and Kashmir, 14, 16, 45–51, 63, 104, 106, 164
Jamshedpur, 27, 29, 99
Jana Sangh, 6, 43
Japan, 28, 192, 201
Jawaharlal Nehru Memorial Fund, 4, 10
Jawahar Tunnel, 16, 50

Jeanneret, Charles-Edouard. *See* Le Corbusier
Jeanneret, Pierre, 190
Jesus Christ, 178
Jharkhand, 99, 186
Jhunjhunwala, Banarsi Prasad, 99, 135
Jinnah, Muhammad Ali, 1–2
Junagarh, 48

Kabir, 178
Kadambathur, 115
Kaldor, Nicholas, 98–99
Kalimpong, 42
Kalyan, 138
Kamath, Hari Vishnu, 160, 164
Kamatipura, 138
Kandariya Mahadeva temple, 178
Kanpur, 6, 100, 163
Kanyapur, 101
Karl, Marx, 86, 108, 178
Karnik, V. B., 17
Karol Bagh, 76
Karve, D. G., 91
Kashmir. *See* Jammu and Kashmir
Katari, Ram Dass, 26
Katju, K. N., 53, 54, 77–78
Katti, D. A., 155–156
Kaur, Rajkumari Amrit, 34, 59, 60, 88
Kaushal, Kamini, 21
Kelly, Grace, 21
Kenya, 35, 42
Kerala, 6, 71, 107, 149, 163–172, 174, 212
Khajuraho, 178
Khan, Ali Akbar, 61
Khan, Mehboob, 61
Khan, Muhammad Ayub, 169
Khandekar, H. J., 152–153
Khedgikar, R. A., 139
Khemka, Sita Ram, 163–164
Khosla, A. N., 182
Khote, Durga, 21
Khrushchev, Nikita, 29
Killick Nixon, 132
Kishtwar, 104
Kohistan, 145
Kolaba District, 107
Konarak Temple, 65
Korea, 2, 32
Kosi river, 104
Kotelawala, John, 37–39
Kothari, Rajni, 18, 19, 155

INDEX [281]

Kripalani, J. B., 59, 161
Krishnamachari, T. T., 7, 98, 131
Krishnan, S. A., 198–199
Kunzru, Hriday Nath, 94

labour: agricultural, 76, 88–89, 105–107, 109–110, 111, 194, 196, 209; cooperatives, 93; indentured, 35–36, 178; industrial, 99, 100–101, 134, 171–172
Labour Party (UK), 17, 129
Lad, P. M., 21
Ladakh, 40, 50
Lalit Kala Akademi, 196–202
Lalit Kala Contemporary, 198, 201–202
Lalit Kala Journal, 197
land reform, 39, 89, 105–106, 166, 209
Laos, 185
Latin America, 201
Laxman, R. K., 8
League of Nations, 34, 40
Lebanon, 34
Le Corbusier, 179, 188–190
Lenin, Vladimir, 86
Liberalism, 18
Life Insurance Corporation of India, 96, 130–131
Lodhie, Amina, 199
Lokanathan, Palamadai S., 34
Lok Sabha, 9, 14, 18, 27, 43, 44, 45, 56, 61, 73–74, 77–78, 79, 80, 99, 125, 131, 134–135, 142, 150, 151, 154, 155–157, 159, 161–162, 164–165, 170, 187
London, 9, 53, 183
London School of Economics, 19, 90, 98, 183
Ludhiana, 101

Madhya Pradesh, 65, 77, 85, 107, 171, 178
Madras (city), 43, 54, 100
Madras (state), 65, 71, 75, 78–80, 100, 104, 107, 114–115, 116, 124, 137, 157, 172
Maha Bodhi Society, 53, 58, 74
Mahalanobis, P. C., 90–91, 92, 117
Maharashtra, 65, 81, 107, 123, 132, 141, 171
Mahmud, Syed, 71–72
Mahtab, Harekrushna, 158, 162–163
Maithon, 186
Majlis-i Ittehadul Muslimeen, 70, 71
Malaviya, Keshav Dev, 158, 162
Malaya, 62
Malhotra, Jeet, 192–193

Manchester Guardian, 149
Manikar, N. S., 190
Maravar, 78–80
Maru, Rushikesh, 155
Marxism, 183
Masani, M. R., 59, 60, 161–162
Mathai, A. O., 3
Mathen, C. P., 168–169
Mayer, Albert, 189
McMahon line, 40, 43
Meerut, 171
Mehrotra, Lalji, 38
Mehta, Asoka, 43
Mehta, Balwantray, 112, 131, 171
Mehta, Hansa, 34
Mekong River Basin, 185
Menon, V. K. Krishna, 41, 45
Mercedes-Benz, 27
Milland, Ray, 21
Minimum Wages Act, 81
Ministry of External Affairs, 23
Mirajkar, S. S., 7
Mitra, Biren, 162
Modern Architectural Research Group, 190
Mohammad, Bakshi Ghulam, 14, 49–51, 165
Mohindergarh, 145
Morgan, Arthur E., 187
Motor Industries Co. Ltd., 27
Mountbatten, Louis, 48, 120
Mudaliar, Ramaswami, 32, 34
Mudukulathur, 78–80
Mughals, 191, 197
Mukerjee, Hiren, 18, 159, 160, 161
Mukherjee, Meera, 201
Mukherjee, Radhakamal, 189
Mukherjee, S. N., 121
Mullik, B. N., 42, 45, 50
Mundhra scandal, 130–131, 163
Murthy, B. S., 80
Muslim League, 1, 46, 54–55, 63, 70, 71, 120, 124, 168
Muslims, 16, 47, 49, 50, 55, 56, 57, 59–72, 81, 82, 124, 207, 208
Mysore, 75, 96

Nagaland, 25, 41, 44–45, 142
Nagarjunakonda, 58
Naidu, Sarojini, 3, 7, 61
Naik, Vasantrao, 141
Nair Service Society, 168
Nalanda, 58

Namboodiripad, E.M.S., 166–169
Nanda, B. R., 4
Nanda, Gulzarilal, 49, 90, 105, 134, 171
Narayan, Jayaprakash, 9, 14, 43, 155, 169–170, 173
Narayan, Shriman, 165, 168
Nargis, 21, 61
Nasser, Gamal Abdel, 23
National Conference, Kashmir, 48–49
National Exhibition of Art, 198–200
National Extension Scheme, 50, 80
National Gallery of Modern Art, 198
National Integration, 71, 82–83, 156, 173–174
nationalisation, 27, 89, 95–96, 166, 209
Nehru, Jawaharlal, 1–20, 23, 29, 32, 36, 37, 39, 40, 41, 42, 44–45, 50, 54, 61, 70–71, 73–74, 88, 94, 117, 120–121, 145, 151, 152, 156, 158, 159, 162, 163–164, 166, 169, 170, 172, 185, 186, 187–188, 203; as architect, 22, 55–56, 86, 119, 177, 179, 204–205, 212; as educator, 15–16, 97, 104, 150, 193, 214; as mediator, 14–15, 67, 68–69, 183; as patron, 14, 23, 44, 49, 90, 92–93, 108, 111, 189; as symbol, 16, 69, 163–164, 180, 212
Nehru, Kamala, 1
Nehru, Motilal, 2
Nehru, Rameshwari, 76
Nehru-Kotelawala Pact, 38–39
Nehruvian Consensus, 16, 17, 19
Nepal, 41, 44, 53, 54
New York Times, 10, 17
Nilokheri, 92, 93, 111
Non-Aligned Movement, 23, 35, 206
North East Frontier Agency (NEFA), 43–45
Nowicki, Mathew, 189

Orissa (Odisha), 65, 85, 104, 158, 162–163
Other Backward Classes, 81, 114, 121, 146, 209
overseas Indians, 25, 31, 33, 35–39, 61, 62, 63, 100
Owaisi, Abdul Wahid, 71

Pakistan, 2, 28, 31, 33, 44, 45–48, 54, 55, 61–65, 67, 69–70, 104, 169
Panchayati Raj, 112–113, 115, 171, 187
Panchet, 186
Panchsheel, 41
Pandit, Vijaya Lakshmi, 34, 36, 38
Pant, Apa, 35, 42

Pant, G. B., 68, 74, 155
Panthic Party, 61
Parliament House, 81
Parsis, 59, 139
Pataskar, H. V., 159–160
Patel, H. M., 155
Patel, Vallabhbhai, 3, 64, 90
Pathak, Devavrat N., 169
Patnaik, Banamali, 162
permit-and-licence raj, 135–136, 162
Philippines, 34
Phizo, Angami Zapu, 44
Phulpur, 163
Pilani, 176, 178, 184, 188
Pilibhit, 114
Pillai, K. Shankar, 6, 10
Pillai, Narayanan Raghavan, 123, 124
Pimpri, 131
Planning Commission, 7, 86, 87, 89–91, 95, 105, 108, 124, 125, 128, 129, 130, 135, 140, 190
Pochampalli, 107
Police Action, Hyderabad, 63, 64, 68, 69, 70
Police Reorganisation Committee, Kerala, 172
Poonch, 47
Portuguese territories in India, 54
Praja Parishad, 50
Praja Socialist Party, 43, 160, 168
Prasad, Rajendra, 37, 49–50, 54, 58, 74, 76, 94, 127, 148, 149–150, 166, 195
Prasad, Sarjoo, 162
Programme Evaluation Organization, 91, 109, 128
Progressive Artists' Group, 200
Prohibition, 136–141
Pune, 35, 131
Punjab, 46–47, 56, 64, 65, 76, 78, 92–95, 101, 106, 107, 142, 171, 188–194
Purdue University, 111

Qing Empire, 39
Quit India Movement, 79

Rabindra Bhavan, 197
Rachuk, Igor, 21
Radcliffe, Cyril, 46, 188
Radhakrishnan, Sarvepalli, 10, 11, 17, 18, 19, 51, 81, 147, 148, 164, 173
Rahaman, M. K., 162

Rahaman, M. L., 162
Rahman, Habib, 197
Raipur, 77
Rajagopalachari, C., 3
Rajahmundry, 125
Rajasthan, 65, 107, 142
Rajpura, 92
Raju, S. P., 194–196
Ram, Jagjivan, 74
Ramanathapuram, 78–80
Ranadive, B. T., 165
Rangoon, 39
Rao, V.K.R.V., 82–83, 93
Rashtriya Swayamsevak Sangh, 55, 124
Rau, B. N., 41, 121
Reddy, Ramachandra, 107
refugees, 42–43, 44, 59, 62, 67, 68, 76, 92–94, 101, 110–111
Rehman, A. R., 35
Representation of the People Act, 152–153, 156–157, 159, 173
Republican Party of India, 81, 155–156
Reserve Bank of India, 96
Rikhye, Indar Jit, 34
Roorkee University, 183
Roosevelt, Franklin Delano, 129
Rourkela, 30, 85
Roy, B. C., 15
Russia. *See* Soviet Union

Saha, Meghnad, 182
Sahitya Akademi, 197
Sain, Kanwar, 182–185, 196
Sampurnanand, 13, 88
Sanchi, 53, 54, 58, 65, 77
San Francisco, 34
Sangeet Natak Akademi, 197
Santhanam, K., 163
Saraiya, R. G., 129
Sarva Seva Sangh, 173
Sarvodaya, 108, 111, 169
Saxena, Shibban Lal, 75
Scheduled Castes, 73–77, 109, 113, 114, 142, 144, 151–152, 155–156
Scheduled Tribes, 74–76, 142, 151–152
Second World War, 22, 26, 27, 29, 33, 34, 36, 89, 97, 103, 107, 111, 134, 210
Secunderabad, 164
Sekaran, Immanuel, 79
Sen, Sudhir Kumar, 101
Sen, Sukumar, 145, 149, 154, 159

Sen-Raleigh Bicycles, 101–102
Serajuddin, Mohammed, 158, 162–163
Setalvad, M. C., 31
Shah, K. T., 90
Shah, M. S., 96
Shastri, Lal Bahadur, 11, 39, 161, 168
Shatrunjaya Temple, 65
Shia Muslims, 59
Shorapur, 68–69
Shrikant, L. M., 76
Shroff, A. D., 161
Sikhism, 56, 65
Sikhs, 47, 59, 81, 124
Sikkim, 35, 41, 42
Simla, 94
Sindh, 129
Singh, Maharaja Hari, 47, 48
Singh, Sardar Baldev, 59–61
Singh, Seth Achal, 160
Sino-Indian War, 26, 45
Society of Contemporary Artists, 200
South Africa, 9, 36, 61, 62, 100, 110
Souza, F.N., 200
Soviet Union, 15, 21–22, 23, 25–30, 40, 85, 86, 88, 89–90, 179–180, 183, 206, 208–209
Srinagar, 16, 49
Sriniketan, 110
Srinivas, M. N., 154
Stalin, Joseph, 5, 29
Stalinism, 88, 92
stamps (postal), 5, 10, 11, 53, 65, 66
sterling balances, 26
Subramanyan, K. G., 201
Sudan, 149, 168
Sukarno, 169
Sunni Muslims, 59
Supreme Court of India, 45, 49, 139, 164
Surat, 132, 140
Swatantra Party, 86, 107, 135, 157, 161
Sylhet, 110

Tagore, Abanindranath, 201
Tagore, Rabindranath, 110, 178
Taiwan, 40
Taj Mahal, 66
Tamil Nadu, 71, 79, 157
Tata Iron and Steel Company, 28–29, 85–86, 97, 99, 103, 160–161
Taungoo District, 38
Teen Murti Bhavan, 3, 10, 119

temple, Hindu, 65, 67–68, 75, 138, 176, 178, 180, 182, 184, 188, 189
Tennessee Valley Authority, 94, 129, 182
textiles, 136
Thailand, 54, 185
Thapar, P. N., 190
Theosophy, 55
Thevar, U. Muthuramalinga, 79–80
Thiruvalangadu, 65
Tibet, 40–44, 52, 54
Times of India, 7, 8, 10, 80, 84, 85, 93, 97, 102, 158, 187, 197, 198, 199
Tipu Sultan, 66
Tito, Josip Broz, 23
Trinidad, 36
Tripathi, Vishwambhar Dayalu, 131
Tripuri, 92
Trivandrum, 166
Tyagi, Mahavir, 161
Tyrwhitt, Jacqueline, 195

Union of Soviet Socialist Republics. *See* Soviet Union
United Kingdom. *See* Britain
United Nations, 33, 34, 41, 47, 48, 103, 195; General Assembly, 32, 34, 36; Security Council, 40–41
United States of America, 22, 23, 25–30, 41, 48, 110, 183
Universal Declaration on Human Rights, 34, 52
University of Bombay, 35
University of Calcutta, 101
University of Cambridge, 1, 90, 92, 98
University of Michigan, 111
University of Oxford, 35
University of Sydney, 192
Untouchability (Offences) Act, 77–78, 156, 208
U Nu, 169
Urdu, 69, 71
Usman, Brigadier, 64
Uttar Pradesh, 13, 53, 64, 68, 81, 88, 95–96, 100, 104, 107, 114, 123, 124, 135, 142, 154, 161, 163, 171, 183

Vande Mataram, 37
Veerambal, 80
Verma, P. L., 190
Victoria and Albert Museum, 53
Vietnam, 185
Vijaya Stambha, 65
Volta River Project, 185

Wagh, B. V., 74, 81
Wall Street Journal, 18
Warsaw Pact, 22
welfare state, 111–112, 123, 125, 129
West Bengal, 42, 67, 75, 76, 101, 132, 142, 157, 159, 182, 186–187
West Germany. *See* Federal Republic of Germany
Wilson, Harold, 17
World Health Organization, 34, 131

Xingjiang, 40

Zabotkina, Olga, 21
Zeyawaddy, 38
Zhou Enlai, 40–41, 44–45

GPSR Authorized Representative: Easy Access System Europe - Mustamäe tee 50, 10621 Tallinn, Estonia, gpsr.requests@easproject.com

www.ingramcontent.com/pod-product-compliance
Lightning Source LLC
Chambersburg PA
CBHW011955150426
43199CB00020B/2867